Living La... ...SENTIALS

GE...

GERMAN

PHRASEBOOK • DICTIONARY

Richard Pettit, Ph.D.
Area Chief, Western Europe,
Council for International Exchange of Scholars,
Washington, D.C.

Crown Publishers, Inc., New York

ACKNOWLEDGMENTS

For their help with this book, I would like to thank Kathryn Mintz, Living Language Director; Jacqueline Natter, Editorial Associate; and especially my wife, Elzbieta Sikorska.

The editors wish to thank the following people for their contributions to this project: Jacques Chazaud, Peter Davis, Lauren Dong, Linda Kocur, and Mark McCauslin.

ABOUT THE AUTHOR

Richard Pettit is an American Germanist who has lived for ten years in Germany and Austria. He is the author of the book *Rainer Maria Rilke in und nach Worpswede*.

Published by Crown Publishers, Inc., 201 East 50th Street, New York, New York, 10022. Member of the Crown Publishing Group. LIVING LANGUAGE, LIVING LANGUAGE TRAVELTALK, and colophon are trademarks of Crown Publishers, Inc.

Manufactured in the United States of America

Library of Congress Cataloging in Publication Data
Pettit, Richard
    Living language traveltalk. German : phrasebook, dictionary / by Richard Pettit.—1st ed.
    1. German language—Conversation and phrase books—English.
2. German language—Textbooks for foreign speakers—English.
I. Title.   PF3121.P46   1991
438.3′421—dc20   90-23144

ISBN 0-517-57786-0

10 9 8 7 6 5 4 3 2

First Edition

CONTENTS

PREFACE ix

PRONUNCIATION GUIDE 2

German-English
  Pronunciation Chart 2

Pronouncing the German
  Alphabet 6

1 USEFUL EXPRESSIONS 8

Courtesy 8
Greetings 8
Approaching Someone for
  Help 9
Question Words 10
Numbers 11
Other Numbers and
  Quantities 12

Currency and Banking 13
Dialogue 14
Changing Money 15
Tipping 17
Paying the Bill 17
Telling Time 18
The 24-Hour Clock 19

2 AT THE AIRPORT 21

Dialogue 21
Clearing Customs 22
Luggage and Porters 23
Airport Transportation and
  Services 24

Flight Arrangements 25
Common Airport Signs and
  Terms 27

3 FINDING YOUR WAY 28

Dialogue 28
Finding Your Way on
  Foot 29
Public Transportation 31
Taking a Cab 33
Traveling by Train 34

At the Station 35
Tickets, Reservations, and
  Inquiries 36
On Board 38
Traveling by Boat 38

4 ACCOMMODATIONS 39

Dialogue 40
Checking In 41
Requests for Hotel
  Services 43

Problems 45
Checking Out 45
Camping 46

5 SOCIALIZING 48

Dialogue 48
Introductions 49
First Contact 50
Jobs and Professions 51
Making Friends 52

The Family 54
At Home 55
Talking About
  Language 57

6 DINING OUT 59

Dialogue 59
Types of Eating and
  Drinking Places 60
Mealtimes and Eating
  Habits 63
Finding a Restaurant/Making
  Reservations 63
At the Restaurant/
  Ordering 64
Table Accessories and
  Condiments 65
Special Requests 66
Phrases You'll Hear 67
Complaints 68
The Bill 69

Deciphering the Menu 69
Typical Menu
  Categories 70
Methods of Cooking and
  Preparation 71
Typical Dishes 72
Appetizers, Soups, Salads,
  Vegetables, and Main
  Dishes 72
Sausages 76
Cheeses 77
Desserts 78
Wines 80
Beer 82
Other Beverages 83

7 PERSONAL SERVICES 85

Dialogue 85
At the Barbershop 86
At the Beauty Parlor 86

Laundry and
  Dry-Cleaning 87

8 HEALTH CARE 89

Dialogue 89
Consulting the
  Pharmacist 90
Finding a Doctor 92

Talking to the Doctor 93
Parts of the Body 95
What You'll Hear from the
  Doctor 96

Patients' Questions   98
At the Hospital/
  Accidents   99

At the Dentist's   100
At the Optician's   102

9 ON THE ROAD 103

Car Rentals   103
Dialogue   103
Driving/Parking   105
Distances and Liquid
  Measures   107

At the Service Station   108
Breakdown/Repairs   109
Road Signs   111

10 COMMUNICATIONS 114

Telephones   114
Dialogue   114
Phrases You'll Hear Over the
  Phone   117

The Post Office   118
Telegrams   120
The Media   120

11 SIGHTSEEING 122

Dialogue   122
Sightseeing in Town   123
At the Museum   127

In the Country   129
Country Sights   129
Religious Services   130

12 SHOPPING 131

Dialogue   131
General Shopping
  Expressions   135
Deciding and Paying   136
Women's and Men's Clothing
  and Accessories   137
Materials and Fabrics   139
Colors and Patterns   140
Sizes and Fitting   141
Shoes   141
Women's Clothing
  Sizes   142

Men's Clothing Sizes   142
At the Jeweler's   143
The Photo Shop   144
The Bookstore   146
The Stationery Shop   146
Electrical Appliances   148
Records/Cassettes   149
Toiletries   150
Shopping for Groceries   152
Weights and Measures   154

13 ENTERTAINMENT AND SPORTS   155

Dialogue 155
Participatory Sports 156
Swimming 156
Other Active Sports 158
Winter Sports 159
Spectator Sports 160

Cultural Diversions 160
Cinema 160
Theater, Opera, Ballet, and
    Concert Halls 161
Nightclubs and Discos 162

14 GENERAL INFORMATION   164

Days, Months, and
    Seasons 164
The Date 164
Age 165
Time Expressions 165
Public Holidays 167
Temperature
    Conversions 169
The Weather 170
Continents and
    Countries 170

Languages 172
Professions and
    Occupations 172
Emergency
    Expressions 173
Emergency Telephone
    Numbers 174
Signs and
    Announcements 174
Common Abbreviations 176

15 GRAMMAR IN BRIEF   178

Nouns and Articles 178
Adjectives and
    Declensions 179
Adverbs 182

Personal Pronouns 182
Verbs 183
Word Order 186

ENGLISH/GERMAN DICTIONARY   187
GERMAN/ENGLISH DICTIONARY   235

PREFACE

Are you planning a trip to Germany, Austria, or Switzerland? If so, this book will help you make the most of your trip. The *Traveltalk* ™ phrasebook/dictionary features more than 2,200 German expressions to use in the various situations you may encounter as a tourist. Each word has a phonetic transcription to help you with pronunciation.

No prior knowledge of German is necessary. All you have to do to make yourself understood is read the phonetics as you would any English sentence. We also recommend using the *Traveltalk* ™ German cassette so you can hear German spoken by native speakers and practice pronunciation. However this book is useful on its own, as it offers the following features:

Pronunciation Guide   The transcription system for this book is presented in this section through the use of simple English examples and explanations. Reading through it first will help you learn how to pronounce the phrases in subsequent chapters.

Chapter 1: Useful Expressions   Many common phrases are used repeatedly in a variety of contexts. For your convenience, these phrases have been grouped together in Chapter 1.

Chapters 2–13   reflect the full range of the visitor's experience. From arrival at the airport to saying farewell to new friends, *Traveltalk* ™ provides a comprehensive resource for every important context of your visit.

Sample Dialogues   give you a sense of how the language sounds in conversation.

Travel Tips and Cultural Highlights   Interspersed throughout the chapters are brief narratives highlighting cultural attractions and offering insider's tips for getting the most out of your visit.

General Information   is given throughout. Essential facts are presented to ease your transition into a new setting:

- legal holidays
- metric conversion tables
- important signs
- common abbreviations
- clothing/shoe size conversion charts

Grammar Guide   A concise and easy-to-follow grammar summary is included for those who would like to understand the structure of the language.

Two-Way 1,600-Word Dictionary   All of the key words presented in this book are listed in the German-English/English-German dictionary. They also provide a phonetic transcription of every German word and phrase.

The main focus of this Traveler's Companion is the Federal Republic of Germany (West Germany); however, most of the information will also apply and be useful in the German Democratic Republic (East Germany)*, Austria, and the German-speaking parts of Switzerland. You can of course use this book beforehand to prepare for your travels, but you will probably find it most useful "on the spot," so don't forget to include it when you pack for your trip. It's compact, handy, and will fit easily into a handbag or pocket.

Viel Glück und gute Reise! [feel glewk unt GOO-teh RYE-zeh] Good luck and have a good trip!

---

*As of October 3, 1990, West and East Germany were reunified politically and economically. In the text that follows, we have, nevertheless, retained some references to East Germany.

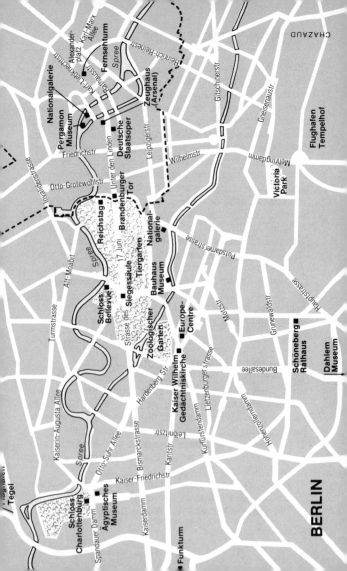

PRONUNCIATION GUIDE

Traveltalk ™ *German* follows standard High-German pronunciation, the accepted pronunciation among educated German speakers throughout Germany, Austria, Switzerland, and Luxembourg. There are a number of different variant dialects spoken in these countries, which may be difficult for you to understand at first, but you will be understood if you use the pronunciation given here. Each German word or phrase in this book is presented with its English equivalent and an easy-to-follow phonetic transcription (sound key) that indicates the correct pronunciation. Simply read and pronounce the transcription as you would read English, and you will be speaking comprehensible German. However, there are some German sounds that simply do not exist in English, so the transcriptions offered here are only an approximate guide. To improve your pronunciation use the accompanying audiocassette. It follows this text closely and gives you the opportunity to listen to and imitate native speakers of German. Try also to imitate the native speakers you encounter during your travels, and don't be afraid to practice your German with them. Some may want to practice their English, but most will be flattered by your attempts to learn their language and gladly help you.

GERMAN-ENGLISH PRONUNCIATION CHART

The chart below is your guide to the transcriptions used in this book. Study it to see how German sounds are properly pronounced. With practice you will be able to follow the transcriptions without having to consult this chart. Keep in mind these basic guidelines for correct German pronunciation:

1) German spelling is more consistent than English; once you learn the sounds, it will be easy to pronounce a word correctly just by reading it.

2) In general, German is spoken vigorously and crisply; words are not run together as often as they are in English.

3) Pay special attention to the vowels; they determine the over-

all pronunciation of a word and are crucial to making your-self understood.

4) There are no gliding vowel sounds in German, as in the English word *main*; German vowels are pronounced as single pure sounds, without moving the lips or tongue.

5) German vowels are generally long when doubled or followed by *h* or by a single consonant, and short when followed by two or more consonants.

6) The vowels *ö* and *ü* (modified with an umlaut), as well as the consonants *r* and *ch*, have no real sound equivalents in English and should be paid special attention (see explanations marked with * in chart below).

7) German words are generally stressed on the first syllable or, if they begin with an unaccented prefix, on the root syllable; stressed syllables are indicated in this text's transcriptions by capital letters as follows: *sagen* [ZAA-gen].

8) German sentence intonation, the variation of rising and fall-ing voice pitch, is similar to English.

Vowels

German Spelling	Approximate Sound in English	Phonetic Symbol	Example (Phonetic Transcription)
a (long)	father	[aa]	**Vater** [FAA-te(r)]
a (short)	cat (between cat and cut)	[ah]	**kann** [kahn]
e (long)	day	[ay]	**geben** [GAY-ben]
e (short)	best	[eh]	**fest** [fehst]
e (unstressed)	the (between eh and uh)	[eh]	**bitte** [BIT-teh]
-er (last syllable)	father (but barely pronounce the r)	[e(r)]	**Vater** [FAA-te(r)]
-en, -el, -et	(similar to English)	—	**leben** [LAY-ben]
i (long)	feet	[ee]	**ihm** [eem]
i (short)	bit	[i]	**bitte** [BIT-teh]

3

German Spelling	Approximate Sound in English	Phonetic Symbol	Example (Phonetic Transcription)
o (long)	note	[oh]	**oder** [OH-de(r)]
o (short)	lost (between lost and lust)	[o]	**Post** [post]
u (long)	moon, suit	[oo]	**gut** [goot]
u (short)	put	[u]	**Mutter** [MUT-te(r)]
y	like German ü, see below	[ew]	**typisch** [TEW-pish]

Vowels Modified with an Umlaut

ä (long)	day, like German long e	[ay]	**spät** [shpayt]
ä (short)	let, like German short e	[eh]	**hätte** [HEHT-teh]
ö (long or short)	*fur, but r is barely pronounced	[u(r)]	**schön** [shu(r)n]
ü (long or short)	*few, or as in French rue	[ew]	**Tür** [tewr]

Vowel Combinations (Diphthongs)

ai, ay, ei, ey	bite, ice, eye, rye	[i . . . e] or [eye] or [-ye]	**sein** [zine] **eitel** [EYE-tel] **drei** [drye]
au	now	[ow]	**braun** [brown]
eu, au	boy	[oy]	**Leute** [LOY-teh]
ie	feet	[ee]	**Dienst** [deenst]

Consonants

f, k, l, m, n, p, t, x	pronounced in most cases as in English	same English letters used as phonetic symbols

German Spelling	Approximate Sound in English	Phonetic Symbol	Example (Phonetic Transcription)
b (at end of word or between vowel and consonant)	u<u>p</u>, ta<u>p</u>	[p]	**gelb** [gehlp] **Obst** [opst]
b (elsewhere)	like English <u>b</u>, bad	[b]	**Buch** [bookh]
c (before ä, e, i, ö)	fi<u>ts</u> (rarely occurs in words of German origin)	[ts]	**circa** [TSEER-kah]
c (elsewhere)	<u>c</u>at	[k]	**Café** [kah-FAY]
ch (after a, o, u, au)	*hard <u>ch</u>, as in u<u>gh</u>, or Scottish lo<u>ch</u>, produced in back of mouth like clearing throat.	[kh]	**Loch** [lokh]
ch (after e, i, umlauts, consonants)	*soft <u>ch</u>, as exaggerated <u>h</u> in Hubert, produced in front of mouth	[kh]	**Licht** [likht]
chs	ba<u>cks</u>	[ks]	**sechs** [zehks]
d (at end of syllable or word)	ba<u>t</u>	[t]	**Bad** [baat]
d (elsewhere)	like English <u>d</u>, does	[d]	**dunkel** [DUN-kel]
g (at end of word)	pi<u>ck</u>	[k]	**weg** [vehk]
ig (at end of word)	soft <u>ch</u>, as exaggerated <u>h</u> in Hubert	[kh]	**billig** [BIL-likh]
g (elsewhere)	hard <u>g</u> (go)	[g]	**gehen** [GAY-en]
h (after a vowel)	silent, as in <u>h</u>onor	[ ]	**sehen** [ZAY-en]
h (elsewhere)	<u>h</u>old	[h]	**Haus** [hows]
j	<u>y</u>es	[y]	**jawohl** [yaa-VOHL]
qu	<u>k</u> + <u>v</u>, <u>k</u>it + <u>v</u>at	[kv]	**Quelle** [KVEHL-eh]

German Spelling	Approximate Sound in English	Phonetic Symbol	Example (Phonetic Transcription)
r	*rid, always rolled when stressed, may be either trilled with tongue tip or gargled; when unstressed, like the r in western	[r]	**Radio** [RAA-dee-oh] **gestern** [GEHS-tern]
s (before or between vowels)	zoo	[z]	**sind** [zint]
s (elsewhere)	see, best	[s]	**was** [vahs]
sch	shine	[sh]	**schon** [shohn]
sp, st (at start of syllable)	shine, sh + p/t	[sh]	**Stein** [shtine] **spät** [shpayt]
ß	cross	[s]	**muß** [mus]
eiß	ice	[ice]	**weiß** [vice]
th	tin, h is silent	[t]	**Thema** [TAY-mah]
tsch	church	[ch]	**deutsch** [doych]
tz	cats	[ts]	**Platz** [plahts]
v	four (in words of German origin)	[f]	**vier** [feer]
v	visa (in words of foreign origin)	[v]	**Visum** [VEE-zoom]
w	vest	[v]	**Wert** [vehrt]
z	cats	[ts]	**Zoo** [tsoh]

Pronouncing the German Alphabet

The German alphabet looks the same as the English one, except for the umlauted vowels, ä, ö, and ü and the letter β, the name of which combines the two letters s + z [EHS-tseht], but it is pronounced just like the double s [s]. The letters of the German alphabet are pronounced differently from their English counterparts, and there are also some differences in the way the German language is written, the main one being that all nouns are capitalized. The following table gives the correct pronunciation of the alphabet, using the phonetic symbols introduced above, as well as corresponding proper German names, which are often used to clarify the spelling of a word over the telephone. Germans would say, for instance: *A wie Anton* [ah vee AHN-tohn] to specify the letter A as in the name Anton.

A [ah]	as in	**Anton**	[AHN-tohn]
Ä [ay]		**Ärger**	[EHR-ge(r)]
B [bay]		**Berta**	[BEHR-tah]
C [tsay]		**Caesar**	[TSAY-zahr]
CH [sh]		**Charlotte**	[shahr-LOT-teh]
D [day]		**Dora**	[DOH-rah]
E [ay]		**Emil**	[AY-meel]
F [ehf]		**Friedrich**	[FREET-rikh]
G [gay]		**Gerda**	[GEHR-dah]
H [haa]		**Heinrich**	[HINE-rikh]
I [ee]		**Ida**	[EE-dah]
J [yot]		**Jutta**	[YOOT-tah]
K [kah]		**Konrad**	[KON-raat]
L [ehl]		**Ludwig**	[LOOD-vikh]
M [ehm]		**Martin**	[MAAR-tin]
N [ehn]		**Nordpol**	[NORT-pohl]
O [oh]		**Otto**	[OT-toh]
Ö [u(r)]		**Ökonom**	[u(r)-ko-NOHM]
P [pay]		**Paula**	[POW-lah]
Q [koo]		**Quelle**	[KVEHL-leh]
R [ehr]		**Richard**	[RIKH-ahrt]
S [ehs]		**Siegfried**	[ZEEK-freet]
T [TAY]		**Theodor**	[TAY-o-dohr]
U [oo]		**Ulrich**	[OOL-rikh]
Ü [ew]		**Übel**	[EW-bel]
V [fow]		**Viktor**	[VIK-tohr]
W [vay]		**Wilhelm**	[VIL-hehlm]
X [eeks]		**Xanten**	[KSAHN-ten]
Y [EWP-see-lawn]		**Ypsilon**	[EWP-see-lawn]
Z [tseht]		**Zeppelin**	[TSEH-peh-leen]

1/USEFUL EXPRESSIONS

COURTESY

Please.	**Bitte.**	BIT-teh.
Thank you.	**Danke.**	DAHN-keh.
You're welcome.	**Bitte.**	BIT-teh.
	(or) **Gern geschehen.**	gehrn geh-SHAY-en.
Excuse me/Sorry.	**Entschuldigung.**	ehnt-SHOOL-di-gung.
	(or) **Verzeihung.**	fehr-TSYE-ung.
It doesn't matter.	**Das macht nichts.**	dahs mahkht nikhts.

GREETINGS

Good morning.	**Guten Morgen.**	GOO-ten MOR-gen.
Good day/afternoon.	**Guten Tag.**	GOO-ten taak.
Good evening.	**Guten Abend.**	GOO-ten AA-behnt.
Good night.	**Gute Nacht.**	GOO-teh nahkht.
Hello. (telephone only)*	**Hallo.**	HAH-loh.
Good-bye.	**Auf Wiedersehen.**	owf VEE-de(r)-zay-en.
Good-bye. (telephone)	**Auf Wiederhören.**	owf VEE-de(r)-hu(r)-ren.
See you soon.	**Bis bald.**	bis bahlt.
See you later.	**Bis später.**	bis SHPAY-te(r).
See you tomorrow.	**Bis morgen.**	bis MOR-gen.
This is Mr./Mrs./Ms./Miss	**Das ist Herr/Frau/Fräulein . . .****	dahs ist hehr/frow/FROY-line . . .
How do you do?/Pleased to meet you.	**Sehr erfreut.**	zehr ehr-FROYT.
How are you?	**Wie geht es Ihnen?**	vee gayt ehs EE-nen?

*There is no German equivalent for the informal conversational "hello"; informally the shortened form of *Guten Tag*—*Tag*—is used, otherwise one of the other above greetings is used, depending on the time of day.
**Fräulein is used nowadays only to address waitresses and telephone operators. Unmarried women are addressed as *Frau*. There is no German equivalent for Ms.

8

Very well, thank you.	**Sehr gut, danke.**	zehr goot DAHN-keh.
And you?	**Und Ihnen?**	unt EE-nen?
Also well, thank you.	**Auch gut, danke.**	owkh goot DAHN-keh.

APPROACHING SOMEONE FOR HELP

Excuse me.	**Entschuldigung.***	ehnt-SHOOL-di-gung.
Could you help me?	**Könnten Sie mir helfen?**	KU(R)N-ten zee meer HEHL-fen?
Do you speak English?	**Sprechen Sie Englisch?**	SHPREKH-en zee EHN-glish?
Do you understand English?	**Verstehen Sie Englisch?**	fehr-SHTAY-en zee EHN-glish?
Yes./No.	**Ja./Nein.**	jaa/nine.
I'm sorry.	**Es tut mir leid.**	ehs toot meer lite.
I don't speak any/much German.	**Ich spreche kein/kaum Deutsch.**	ikh SHPREKH-eh kine/kowm doych.
What's your name?	**Wie heißen Sie?**	vee HICE-en zee?
My name is . . .	**Ich heiße . . .**	ikh HICE-eh . . .
I'm American/English.	**Ich bin Amerikaner(-in)/Engländer(-in).****	ikh bin ah-meh-ri-KAH-ne(r){-rin}/EHN-glehn-de(r){-rin}.
I'm a tourist.	**Ich bin Tourist(in).**	ikh bin too-RIST-(in).
I don't understand.	**Ich verstehe nicht.**	ikh fehr-STAY-eh nikht.
I understand a little.	**Ich verstehe ein wenig.**	ikh fehr-STAY-eh ine VEH-nikh.
Repeat, please.	**Wiederholen Sie, bitte.**	vee-de(r)-HOH-len zee BIT-teh.
Please speak more slowly.	**Bitte, sprechen Sie langsamer.**	BIT-teh SHPREKH-en zee LAHNG-zaam-me(r).

*There is no generally used German equivalent for "madam" or "sir." If you don't know the person's name, no form of address is used.
**The "in" ending indicates a female person (*Amerikanerin*). With nationalities and professions, no indefinite article is used, for instance: I am a student = *Ich bin Student.*

9

What do you call this/that in German?	**Wie heißt dies/das auf deutsch?**	vee heyst dees/dahs owf doych?
Could you write that down, please?	**Könnten Sie das bitte aufschreiben?**	KU(R)N-ten zee dahs BIT-teh OWF-SHRYE-ben?
Spell it, please.	**Buchstabieren Sie es, bitte.**	Bookh-shtah-BEE-ren zee ehs, BIT-teh.
Could you translate this for me/us?	**Könnten Sie mir/uns das übersetzen?**	KU(R)N-ten zee meer/uns dahs ew-be(r)-ZEHT-sen?
What does that mean?	**Was bedeutet das?**	vahs beh-DOY-tet dahs?
Okay./Agreed.	**In Ordnung.**	in ORT-nung.
Of course./That's right.	**Sicher./Das stimmt.**	ZIKH-e(r)/dahs shtimt.
Thank you very much.	**Vielen Dank.**	FEE-len dahnk.

QUESTION WORDS

Who?	**Wer?**	vehr?
Whom?	**Wem?/Wen?***	vaym/vayn?
What?	**Was?**	vahs?
Why?	**Warum?**	vah-ROOM?
When?	**Wann?**	vahn?
Where?	**Wo?**	voh?
Where to?	**Wohin?**	voh-HIN?
Where from?	**Woher?**	voh-HAYR?
Which?	**Welcher/Welche/Welches?**	VEHL-khe(r)/VEHL-kheh/VEHL-khes?
How?	**Wie?**	vee?
How far?	**Wie weit?**	vee vite?
How many?	**Wie viele?**	vee FEE-leh?
How much does it cost?	**Wieviel kostet das?**	VEE-feel KOS-tet dahs?

*German has four different grammatical cases (see Grammar in Brief); these forms for whom [wem (dative/indirect object) or wen (accusative/direct object)] depend on the function in the sentence.

NUMBERS*

Take time to learn how to count in German. You'll find that knowing the numbers will make everything easier during your trip.

zero	**null**	nul
one	**eins**	ines
two	**zwei**	tsvye
three	**drei**	drye
four	**vier**	feer
five	**fünf**	fewnf
six	**sechs**	zehks
seven	**sieben**	ZEE-ben
eight	**acht**	ahkht
nine	**neun**	noyn
ten	**zehn**	tsayn
eleven	**elf**	ehlf
twelve	**zwölf**	tsvu(r)lf
thirteen	**dreizehn**	DRYE-tsayn
fourteen	**vierzehn**	FEER-tsayn
fifteen	**fünfzehn**	FEWNF-tsayn
sixteen	**sechzehn**	ZEHKH-tsayn
seventeen	**siebzehn**	ZEEP-tsayn
eighteen	**achtzehn**	AHKH-tsayn
nineteen	**neunzehn**	NOYN-tsayn
twenty	**zwanzig**	TSVAHN-tsikh
twenty-one	**einundzwanzig**	INE-unt-tsvahn-tsikh
twenty-two	**zweiundzwanzig**	TSVYE-unt-tsvahn-tsikh
twenty-three	**dreiundzwanzig**	DRYE-unt-tsvahn-tsikh
thirty	**dreißig**	DRYE-sikh
forty	**vierzig**	FEER-tsikh
fifty	**fünfzig**	FEWNF-tsikh
sixty	**sechzig**	ZEHKH-tsikh
seventy	**siebzig**	ZEEP-tsikh
eighty	**achtzig**	AHKHT-tsikh
ninety	**neunzig**	NOYN-tsikh

*In Germany, as elsewhere in Europe, numerical punctuation is different than in English. The use of commas and decimal points is reversed, so that 1,000 English style becomes 1.000, and 6.5 is written 6,5 *(sechs Komma fünf)* in German and pronounced [ze(k)hs KOH-mah fewnf].

11

one hundred	**(ein)hundert**	(ine)HUN-dert
one hundred one	**hunderteins**	hun-dert-INES
one hundred two	**hundertzwei**	hun-dert-TSVYE
one hundred ten	**hundertzehn**	hun-dert-TSAYN
one hundred twenty	**hundertzwanzig**	hun-dert-TSVAHN-tsikh
two hundred	**zweihundert**	TSVYE-hun-dert
three hundred	**dreihundert**	DRYE-hun-dert
one thousand	**(ein)tausend**	(ine) TOW-zehnt
one thousand two hundred	**tausendzweihundert**	TOW-zehnt-tsvye-hun-dert
two thousand	**zweitausend**	TSVYE-tow-zehnt
one million	**eine Million**	INE-eh mil-YOHN
one billion	**eine Milliarde**	INE-eh mil-YAAR-deh

Ordinal Numbers*

first	**erste**	EHR-steh
second	**zweite**	TSVYE-teh
third	**dritte**	DRIT-teh
fourth	**vierte**	FEER-teh
fifth	**fünfte**	FEWNF-teh
sixth	**sechste**	ZEHKS-teh
seventh	**siebte**	ZEEP-teh
eighth	**achte**	AHKH-teh
ninth	**neunte**	NOYN-teh
tenth	**zehnte**	TSAYN-teh

*Ordinal numbers are treated like adjectives in German, agreeing in gender and number, and receive the appropriate adjective endings; for instance, "my first game" = mein erstes Spiel [mine EHR-stes shpeel].

OTHER NUMBERS AND QUANTITIES

half	**halb**	haalp
half a pound	**ein halbes Pfund**	ine HAAL-behs pfunt
half an hour	**eine halbe Stunde**	INE-eh HAAL-beh SHTUN-deh
half of .	**die Hälfte von**	dee HEHLF-teh fon
a quarter	**ein Viertel**	ine FEER-tel
a third	**ein Drittel**	ine DRIT-tel

a dozen	**ein Dutzend**	ine DU-tsehnt
ten percent	**zehn Prozent**	tsayn pro-TSEHNT
5.6%	**5,6 Prozent**	fewnf KO-mah zehks pro-TSEHNT
once	**einmal**	INE-maal
twice	**zweimal**	TSVAY-maal
the last time	**das letzte Mal**	das LET-steh maal
a lot of, many	**viele**	FEE-leh
few, a few	**wenig, ein paar**	VEH-nikh, ine paar
some	**einige**	INE-ni-geh
enough	**genug**	geh-NOOKH
a pair of	**ein Paar**	ine paar

CURRENCY AND BANKING

In Germany, the monetary unit is the *Deutsche Mark*, called *D-Mark* [DAY-mahrk] and abbreviated *DM*. It is divided into 100 *Pfennig* [PFEH-nikh], abbreviated *Pf*.

Coins: 1, 2, 5, 10, and 50 pfennigs; 1, 2, and 5 marks.
Banknotes: 5, 10, 20, 50, 100, 500, and 1,000 marks.

As with other European currencies, the *DM* banknotes are of varying colors and sizes, corresponding to their denominations, which makes it easier to distinguish them. Each note is a "work of art," featuring a portrait by the German Rennaissance artist Albrecht Dürer.

The Austrian monetary unit is the *Schilling* [SHIL-ling], abbreviated *S.* and divided into 100 *Groschen* [GRO-shen], abbreviated *g*.

Coins: 10 and 50 groschen; 1, 5, 10, and 20 schillings.
Banknotes: 20, 50, 100, 500, and 1,000 schillings.

The Swiss franc or *Franken* [FRAHN-ken], abbreviated *Fr.*, is the basic unit of currency in Switzerland and is divided into 100 *Rappen* [RAHP-pen], abbreviated *Rp*.

Coins: 5, 10, 20, and 50 rappen; 1, 2, and 5 francs.
Banknotes: 10, 20, 50, 100, 500, and 1,000 francs.

German banking hours are generally from 8:30 A.M. to 1 P.M. and 2:30 to 4 P.M., Monday through Friday, Thursday until 5:30 P.M. Swiss and Austrian banking hours may differ somewhat. Currency-exchange offices, called *Wechselstuben* [VEHK-sel-shtoo-behn] or *Geldwechsel* [GEHLT-vehks-el] (money exchange), are often open outside the regular banking hours. These, as well as branch offices of the major banks, are located at most airports and larger train stations. You can also change money or traveler's checks at most hotels, but banks invariably offer more favorable rates. Major credit cards and Eurocheques are now accepted at most hotels, restaurants, and shops. If you are exchanging large sums, you may want to compare bank rates. Three different rates are usually posted:

1) Ankauf [AHN-kowf]—the rate for buying a particular currency. This is the rate you will receive when you sell dollars, for instance, to obtain marks. This rate is higher, more favorable for you, at German banks than US banks, so you should wait until you arrive in Germany before exchanging most of the money you plan to spend on your trip.

2) Verkauf [fehr-KOWF]—the rate for selling a particular currency. This is always lower than the *Ankauf* rate, and generally it's to your advantage to wait until returning to the United States to buy back dollars with any marks or francs you may have left over from your trip.

3) Reiseschecks [RYE-zeh-shehks]—traveler's check rates, which are slightly lower than cash rates. Remember that you will need your passport in most places to exchange traveler's checks.

DIALOGUE: AT THE BANK (*IN DER BANK*)

Kundin:	**Könnten Sie mir bitte hundert Dollar wechseln?**	KU(R)N-ten zee meer BIT-teh HUN-dert DOL-lahr VEHK-seln?

Kassierer:	**Sicher. Der Wechselkurs heute ist zwei D-Mark pro Dollar. Das wären also zwei hundert D-Mark**	ZIKH-e(r). dehr VEHK-sel-koors HOY-teh ist tsvye DAY-mahrk pro DOL-lahr. dahs VAY-ren AHL-zoh tsvye HUN-dert DAY-mahrk.
Kundin:	**Schön. Hier haben Sie meine Reiseschecks.**	shu(r)n. heer HAA-ben zee MINE-eh RYE-zeh-shehks.
Kassierer:	**Würden Sie bitte die Schecks unterschreiben? Und ich brauche auch Ihren Reisepaß, bitte.**	VEWR-den zee BIT-teh dee shehks UN-te(r)-SHRYE-ben? unt ikh BROW-kheh owkh EE-ren RYE-zeh-pahs, BIT-teh.
Kundin:	**Natürlich. Hier ist er.**	nah-TEWR-likh. heer ist ehr.

. . . .

Customer:	Could you please change $100 for me?
Teller:	Certainly. The exchange rate today is two marks to the dollar. So that would be 200 marks.
Customer:	Fine. Here are my traveler's checks.
Teller:	Would you please sign the checks? And I need your passport, too.
Customer:	Of course. Here it is.

CHANGING MONEY

| Where's the nearest bank? | **Wo ist die nächste Bank?** | Vo ist dee NAYKH-steh bahnk? |
| Is there a currency exchange office nearby? | **Gibt es in der Nähe eine Wechselstube?** | Gipt ehs in dehr NAY-eh INE-eh VEHK-sel SHTOO-beh? |

15

I'd like to change . . .	Ich möchte —— wechseln.	Ikh MU(R)KH-teh —— VEHK-seln.
• dollars.	• Dollar	• DOL-lahr
• this check.	• diesen Scheck	• DEE-zen shehk
• some traveler's checks.	• einige Reiseschecks	• INE-ni-geh RYE-zeh-shehks
Do you accept personal checks?	Lösen Sie Barschecks ein?	LU(R)-zen zee BAAR-shehks ine?
Will you accept . . .	Nehmen Sie —— an?	NAY-men zee —— ahn?
• my credit card?	• meine Kreditkarte	• MINE-eh kray-DEET-KAHR-teh
• a bank draft/cashier's check?	• eine Bankanweisung	• INE-eh BAHNK-ahn-vye-zung
• a money order?	• eine Zahlungs-anweisung	• INE-eh TSAA-lungs-ahn-vye-zung
Do you need . . .	Brauchen Sie . . .	BROW-khen zee . . .
• my passport?	• den Reisepaβ?	• dehn RYE-zeh pahs?
• identification?	• den Personal-ausweis?	• dehn pehr-zoh-NAAL-OWS-vice?
• a letter of credit?	• einen Kreditbrief?	• INE-en kray-DEET-breef?
What's the exchange rate for . . . ?	Wie ist der Wechselkurs für . . . ?	Vee ist dehr VEHK-sel-koors fewr . . . ?
What commission do you charge?	Welche Gebühr erheben Sie?	VEHL-kheh geh-BEWR ehr-HAY-ben zee?
Where do I sign?	Wo unterschreibe ich?	Voh oon-te(r)-SHRYE-beh ikh?
I'd like to buy . . .	Ich möchte —— kaufen.	Ikh MU(R)KH-teh —— KOW-fen.
• West German marks	• D-Mark	• DAY-mahrk
• Swiss francs	• Schweizer Franken	• SHVYE-tse(r) FRAHN-ken
• Austrian schillings	• österreichische Schillinge	• U(R)-steh-rye-khish-e(r) SHIL-ling-eh
Please give me . . .	Geben Sie mir bitte . . .	GAY-ben zee meer BIT-teh. . . .
• small bills.	• kleine Scheine.	• KLINE-eh SHINE-eh.

16

• large bills.	• gro*ß*e Scheine.	• GROHS-seh eh.
• the rest in change.	• den Rest in Kleingeld.	• dehn rehst i gehlt.

TIPPING

In most European countries a 10–15% service charge is included in the bill. You will find this indicated at the bottom of restaurant menus in the German-speaking countries with the words: *Bedienung inbegriffen* (service included). Europeans either round off the bill, leaving small change, which is usually given directly to the waiter or service person when paying the bill, or leave nothing.

When in doubt, the following chart will serve as a rule of thumb.

Restaurant waitresses and waiters	small change by rounding off the bill
Checkroom/washroom/ restroom attendants	30–50 German pfennigs, 2–3 Austrian schillings, 30–50 Swiss rappen
Hotel porters/doormen/bellboys	1–5 German marks or Swiss francs, 5–10 Austrian schillings, depending on how often services are performed
Maids	10 German marks or Swiss francs, 50 Austrian schillings per week
Room service	1 German mark or Swiss franc, 5 Austrian schillings
Taxi drivers	10–15%, usually included in Switzerland
Hairdressers/barbers	10%, included in Switzerland
Tour guides	1 German mark or Swiss franc, 5 Austrian schillings

PAYING THE BILL

The bill, please.	Die Rechnung, bitte.	dee REHKH-nung, BIT-teh.

17

We'd like separate checks.	Wir möchten getrennt bezahlen.	veer MU(R)KH-ten geh-TREHNT beh-TSAA-len.
What is this charge for?	Wofür ist dieser Betrag?	vo-FEWR ist DEE-ze(r) beh-TRAHK?
Is service included?	Ist die Bedienung inbegriffen?	ist dee beh-DEE-nung IN-beh-grif-fen?
Can I pay with my credit card?	Kann ich mit meiner Kreditkarte bezahlen?	kahn ikh mit MINE-e(r) kray-DEET-KAHR-teh beh-TSAA-len?
That is for you.	Das ist für Sie.	dahs ist fewr zee.

TELLING TIME

What time is it?/How late is it?	Wieviel Uhr ist es?/Wie spät ist es?	VEE-feel oor ist ehs?/vee shpayt ist ehs?
At what time?	Um wieviel Uhr?	oom VEE-feel oor?
It's . . .	Es ist . . .	ehs ist . . .
• two o'clock.	• zwei Uhr.	• tsvye oor.
• 2:10.	• zwei Uhr zehn.	• tsvye oor tsayn.
• ten past two.	• zehn nach zwei.	• tsayn nahkh tsvye.
• 3:40.	• drei Uhr vierzig.	• drye oor FEER-tsikh.
• twenty to four.	• zwanzig vor vier.	• TSVAHN-tsikh for feer.
• 4:30.	• vier Uhr dreißig.	• feer oor DRYE-sikh.
• half past four.*	• halb fünf.*	• haalp fewnf.
• 6:15.	• sechs Uhr fünfzehn.	• zehks oor FEWNF-tsayn.
• quarter past six.*	• viertel nach sechs/viertel sieben.*	• VEER-tel nahkh zehks/VEER-tel ZEE-ben.

*It will be easier for you to tell time by simply stating the hour and minutes, as in the above examples, 2:10, 3:40, 4:30. When expressing quarter and especially half-hour intervals, however, German speakers usually stress the upcoming hour, so half past four becomes literally "halfway toward five," and 4:45 becomes *dreiviertel fünf,* "three quarters toward five," but you will also hear *viertel vor fünf,* "quarter to five," as one would say in English.

• twelve o'clock midnight/noon.	• zwölf Uhr Mitternacht/ Mittag	• tsvu(r)lf oor MIT-te(r)- nahkht/MIT-taak.
• one in the afternoon.	• ein Uhr nachmittags.	• ine oor NAHKH-mit- taaks.
• eleven at night.	• elf Uhr nachts.	• ehlf oor nahkhts.
five minutes ago.	vor fünf Minuten.	for fewnf mi-NOO-ten.
in half an/quarter of an hour.	in einer halben Stunde/ Viertelstunde.	in INE-e(r) haal-ben SHTUN-deh/VEER- tel-SHTOON-deh.
since 10:30 A.M.	seit halb elf morgens.	zite haalp ehlf MOR- gens.
after 8:00 P.M.	nach acht Uhr abends.	nahkh ahkht oor AA- behnts.
before 6:00 A.M.	vor sechs Uhr morgens.	for zehks oor MOR- gens.
more than 10 minutes	mehr als zehn Minuten.	mehr ahls tsayn mi- NOO-ten.
less than 30 seconds	weniger als dreißig Sekunden.	VAY-ni-ge(r) ahls DRYE- sikh zeh-KOON-den.
She came . . .	Sie kam . . .	zee kahm . . .
• on time.	• rechtzeitig.	• REHKHT-tsye-tikh.
• late.	• spät.	• shpayt.
• early.	• frühzeitig.	• FREW-tsye-tikh.
My watch is fast/slow.	Meine Uhr geht vor/nach.	MINE-eh oor gayt for/nahkh.

THE 24-HOUR CLOCK

In normal conversation, Europeans generally express time the way we do, but for official listings, like transportation schedules, business hours, and theater times, the 24-hour system, our "military time," is used. After 12 noon, just keep counting. 1:00 p.m. becomes 12 plus 1 = 13.00, or *dreizehn Uhr;* 12 midnight becomes 24.00, or *vierundzwanzig Uhr.* Once you pass 12 noon, you can convert official time back to the 12-hour system by subtracting 12. A typical evening show time, 7:30 P.M. would be 19.30, *neunzehn Uhr dreißig.* Note that in place of the colon, a decimal point is used. Use this chart for quick reference:

Official Time Chart

1 A.M.	01.00	**ein Uhr**	ine oor
2 A.M.	02.00	**zwei Uhr**	tsvye oor
3 A.M.	03.00	**drei Uhr**	drye oor
4 A.M.	04.00	**vier Uhr**	veer oor
5 A.M.	05.00	**fünf Uhr**	fewnf oor
6 A.M.	06.00	**sechs Uhr**	zehks oor
7 A.M.	07.00	**sieben Uhr**	ZEE-ben oor
8 A.M.	08.00	**acht Uhr**	ahkht oor
9 A.M.	09.00	**neun Uhr**	noyn oor
10 A.M.	10.00	**zehn Uhr**	tsayn oor
11 A.M.	11.00	**elf Uhr**	ehlf oor
12 noon	12.00	**zwölf Uhr**	tsvu(r)lf oor
1 P.M.	13.00	**dreizehn Uhr**	DRYE-tsayn oor
2 P.M.	14.00	**vierzehn Uhr**	FEER-tsayn oor
3 P.M.	15.00	**fünfzehn Uhr**	FEWNF-tsayn oor
4 P.M.	16.00	**sechzehn Uhr**	ZEHKH-tsayn oor
5 P.M.	17.00	**siebzehn Uhr**	ZEEP-tsayn oor
6 P.M.	18.00	**achtzehn Uhr**	AHKH-tsayn oor
7 P.M.	19.00	**neunzehn Uhr**	NOYN-tsayn oor
8 P.M.	20.00	**zwanzig Uhr**	TSVAHN-tsikh oor
9 P.M.	21.00	**einundzwanzig Uhr**	INE-unt-tsvahn-tsikh oor
10 P.M.	22.00	**zweiundzwanzig Uhr**	TSVYE-unt-tsvahn-tsikh oor
11 P.M.	23.00	**dreiundzwanzig Uhr**	DRYE-unt-tsvahn-tsikh oor
12 midnight	24.00	**vierundzwanzig Uhr**	FEER-unt-tsvahn-tsikh oor

20

2/AT THE AIRPORT

Willkommen in Deutschland! Welcome to Germany! Customs formalities at German, Austrian, and Swiss airports are minimal and, as a rule, take little time. After your passport has been checked and you have collected your luggage, you will notice that customs clearance is divided into two sections, one marked by a green arrow: *ANMELDEFREIE WAREN* (Nothing to declare); the other by a red arrow: *ANMELDEPFLICHTIGE WAREN* (Goods to declare). Personal clothing and other items intended for personal use are duty-free, but tobacco and alcoholic beverages above certain amounts are taxed.

Customs officials at major airports in the German-speaking countries generally have a working knowledge of English, but you may find the following dialogue and phrases helpful.

DIALOGUE: CUSTOMS AND IMMIGRATION (*PAβKONTROLLE*)

Zollbeamtin:	**Guten Tag. Darf ich bitte Ihren Paβ sehen?**	GOO-ten taak. dahrf ikh BIT-teh EE-ren pahs ZAY-en?
Reisender:	**Ja bitte, hier ist er.**	yaa BIT-teh, heer ist ehr.
Zollbeamtin:	**Sind Sie Amerikaner?**	zint zee ah-meh-ri-KAH-ne(r)?
Reisender:	**Ja, bin ich.**	yaa, bin ikh.
Zollbeamtin:	**Wie lange bleiben Sie im Lande?**	vee LAHNG-eh BLYE-ben zee im LAHN-deh?
Reisender:	**Ich werde zwei Wochen hier sein.**	ikh VEHR-deh tsvye VOKH-en heer zine.

AT THE AIRPORT

21

Customs Official:	Hello. May I please see your passport?
Traveler:	Yes, please. Here it is.
Customs Official:	Are you an American?
Traveler:	Yes, I am.
Customs Official:	How long will you be staying in the country?
Traveler:	I'll be here for two weeks.

CLEARING CUSTOMS (*ZOLLABFERTIGUNG*)

What nationality are you?	**Welche Staatsangehörigkeit haben Sie?**	VEHL-kheh SHTAHTS-ahn-geh-HU(R)-rikh-kite HAA-ben zee?
I'm	**Ich bin . . .**	ikh bin . . .
• American.	• **Amerikaner(in).**	• ah-meh-ri-KAH-ne(r) {-rin}.
• Canadian.	• **Kanadier(in).**	• kah-NAH-deer {-rin}.
• English.	• **Engländer(in).**	• EHN-glehn-de(r) {-rin}.
What's your name?	**Wie heißen Sie?**	vee HICE-en zee
My name is . . .	**Ich heiße . . .**	ikh HICE-eh . . .
Where will you be staying?	**Wo bleiben Sie?**	voh BLYE-ben zee?
I'm staying at the ——— Hotel.	**Ich bleibe im Hotel ———.**	ikh BLYE-beh im ho-TEL ———.
Is this a vacation trip?	**Machen Sie eine Urlaubsreise?**	MAHKH-en zee INE-eh OOR-lowps-rye-zeh?
I'm just passing through.	**Ich bin auf der Durchreise.**	ikh bin owf dehr DURKH-RYE-zeh.
I'm here on a business trip.	**Ich bin auf Geschäftsreise.**	ikh bin owf geh-SHEHFTS-RYE-zeh.
I'll be here for . . .	**Ich werde hier für ——— sein.**	ikh VEHR-deh heer fewr ——— zine.
• a few days.	• **ein paar Tage**	• ine paar TAA-geh

22

• a week.	• eine Woche	• INE-eh VOKH-eh
• several weeks.	• einige Wochen	• INE-i-geh VOKH-en
• a month.	• einen Monat	• INE-en MOH-naat
Your passport, please.	Ihren Paß, bitte.	EE-ren pahs, BIT-teh.
Do you have anything to declare?	Haben Sie etwas zu verzollen?	HAA-ben zee EHT-vahs tzoo vehr-TSO-len?
No, I have nothing to declare.	Nein, ich habe nichts zu verzollen.	nine, ikh HAA-beh nikhts tzoo vehr-TSOL-len.
Please open this bag.	Bitte, öffnen Sie diese Tasche.	BIT-teh, U(R)F-nen zee DEE-zeh TAHSH-eh.
On these items you'll have to pay duty.	Auf diese Artikel müssen Sie Zoll zahlen.	owf DEE-zeh ahr-TEE-kel MEWS-sen zee tsol TSAA-len.
But they're . . .	Aber sie sind . . .	AH-be(r) zee zint . . .
• for personal use.	• zum persönlichen Gebrauch.	• tsoom pehr-ZU(R)N-likh-en geh-BROWKH.
• gifts.	• Geschenke.	• geh-SHEHN-keh.
Have a pleasant stay!	Angenehmer Aufenthalt!	AHN-geh-neh-meh(r) OW-fehnt-HAHLT!

LUGGAGE AND PORTERS

Larger airports and train stations usually have porters, but they are becoming scarce these days, so you may prefer to use a luggage cart, available at most airports in the baggage claim area and usually free of charge.

I need . . .	Ich brauche . . .	ikh BROW-kheh . . .
• a porter.	• einen Gepäckträger.	• INE-en geh-PEHK-tray-ge(r).
• a luggage cart.	• einen Kofferkuli.	• INE-en KOF-fe(r)-koo-lee.
Here's my luggage.	Hier ist mein Gepäck.	heer ist mine geh-PEHK.
Please take my bags . . .	Bitte, bringen Sie mein Gepäck . . .	BIT-teh, BRING-en zee mine geh-PEHK . . .

23

to the taxi stand.	zum Taxistand.	tsoom TAHK-see-shtahnt.
to the bus stop.	zur Bushaltestelle.	tsoor BUS-hahl-teh-shtehl-leh.
to the metro/train.	zur U-Bahn/S-Bahn.	tsoor OO-baan/EHS-baan.
to the luggage lockers.	zu den Schließfächern.	tsoo dehn SHLEES-feh-khe(r)n.
Please be careful with this suitcase.	Vorsicht bitte mit diesem Koffer.	FOR-zikht BIT-teh mit DEE-zem KOF-fe(r).
How much do I owe you?	Wieviel macht das?	VEE-feel mahkht dahs?

AIRPORT TRANSPORTATION AND SERVICES

Where is/are . . .	Wo ist/sind . . .	voh ist/zint . . .
the car rental agencies?	die Agenturen zur Autovermietung?	dee ah-gehn-TOO-ren tsoor OW-toh-fehr-mee-tung?
taxis?	Taxis?	TAHK-sees?
buses/trains to the city?	Busse/Züge in die Stadt?	BUS-eh/TSEW-geh in dee shtaht?
the information booth?	die Auskunft?	dee OWS-koonft?
the ticket counter?	der Fahrkarten-schalter?	dehr FAAR-kahr-ten-shahl-te(r)?
the luggage check-in?	die Gepäckannahme?	dee geh-PEHK-ahn-naa-meh?
the luggage claim area?	die Gepäckausgabe?	dee geh-PEHK-ows-gaa-beh?
the lost and found?	das Fundbüro?	dahs FUNT-bew-roh?
a currency exchange office?	eine Wechselstube?	INE-eh VEHK-sel-SHTOO-beh?
the newsstand?	der Zeitungsstand?	dehr TSYE-tungs-shtahnt?
the post office?	die Post?	dee post?

24

• the restroom?	• **die Toilette?**	• dee toy-LEHT-teh?
• the exit?	• **der Ausgang?**	• dehr OWS-gahng?
• a telephone?	• **ein Telefon?**	• ine tay-lay-FOHN?

FLIGHT ARRANGEMENTS

Is there a direct flight to Zurich?	**Gibt es einen Direktflug nach Zürich?**	gipt ehs INE-en dee-REHKT-flook nahkh TSEW-rikh?
Or do I have to change planes?	**Oder muß ich um-steigen?**	OH-de(r) mus ikh OOM-shtye-gen?
How many stops are there?	**Wieviele Zwischen-landungen gibt es?**	vee-FEEL-eh TSVISH-en-lahn-doon-gen gipt ehs?
Can I make a connection to Stuttgart?	**Habe ich Anschluß nach Stuttgart?**	HAA-beh ikh AHN-shlus nahkh SHTUT-gahrt?
When does it leave?	**Wann fliegt es ab?**	vahn fleegt ehs ahp?
What is the arrival time?	**Was ist die Ankunftszeit?**	vahs ist dee AHN-koonfts-tsite?
Please give me . . .	**Geben Sie mir bitte . . .**	GAY-ben zee meer BIT-teh.
• a one-way ticket.	• **eine Hinflugkarte.**	• INE-eh HIN-floog-kahr-teh.
• a round-trip ticket.	• **eine Hin- und Rückflugkarte.**	• INE-eh HIN unt REWK-floog-kahr-teh.
• a seat in first class.	• **einen Platz in der ersten Klasse.**	• INE-en plahts in dehr EHR-sten KLAHS-seh.
• a seat in tourist/coach class.	• **einen Platz in der zweiten/ Touristen-klasse.**	• INE-en plahts in dehr TSVYE-ten/too-RIS-ten KLAHS-eh.
• a seat for nonsmokers.	• **einen Platz für Nichtraucher.**	• INE-en plahts fewr NIKHT-rowkh-e(r).
• a window seat.	• **einen Fensterplatz.**	• INE-en FEHN-ste(r)-plahts.

25

• an aisle seat.	• einen Platz zum Gang.	• INE-en plahts tsoom gahng.
What's my seat number?	Welche Platznummer habe ich?	VEHL-kheh PLAHTS-num-me(r) HAA-beh ikh?
And the flight number?	Und die Flugnummer?	unt dee FLOOK-num-me(r)?
What gate does it leave from?	Von welchem Flugsteig ist der Abflug?	von VEHL-khem FLOOK-shtike ist dehr AHP-flook?
When do I have to check in?	Wann muß ich mich zum Flug melden?	vahn mus ikh mikh tsoom flook MEHL-den?
I have only hand luggage.	Ich habe nur Handgepäck.	ikh HAA-beh noor HAANT-geh-pehk.
I'd like to check these suitcases.	Ich möchte diese Koffer abgeben.	ikh MU(R)KH-teh DEE-zeh KOF-fe(r) AHP-gay-ben.
I'd like to —— my reservation.	Ich möchte meine Reservier- ung . . .	ikh MU(R)KH-teh MINE-seh reh-zehr-VEE-rung . . .
• confirm	• bestätigen.	• beh-SHTAY-ti-gen.
• change	• umändern.	• OOM-ehn-de(r)n.
• cancel	• stornieren	• shtor-NEE-ren.

COMMON AIRPORT SIGNS AND TERMS

German	Pronunciation	English
Ankunft	AHN-koonft	Arrival
Abflug	AHP-flook	Departure
Inlandflüge	IN-lahnd-flew-geh	Domestic Flights
Auslandflüge	OWS-lahnd-flew-geh	International Flights
Zollabfertigung	TSOL-ahp-fehr-ti-gung	Customs Clearance
Anmeldefreie Waren	AHN-mehl-deh-frye-eh WAH-ren	Nothing to Declare
Anmeldepflichtige Waren	AHN-mehl-deh-pflikh-ti-geh WAH-ren	Goods to Declare
Gepäckannahme	geh-PEHK-ahn-naa-meh	Baggage Check
Gepäckausgabe	geh-PEHK-ows-gaa-beh	Baggage Claim

26

Gepäckschein	geh-PEHK-shine	Baggage Tag
Auskunft	OWS-koonft	Information
Autovermietung/	OW-toh-fehr-mee-tung/	Car Rental
Autoverleih	OW-toh-fehr-lye	

3/FINDING YOUR WAY

DIALOGUE: ON THE STREET (*AUF DER STRAβE*)

Touristin:	**Verzeihung, wie komme ich zum Schloβ Charlottenburg?**	fehr-TSYE-ung, vee KOM-meh ikh tsoom shlos shahr-LOT-ten-boork?
Berliner:	**Ganz einfach. Gehen Sie diese Straβe geradeaus bis zum Ende. Dann sehen Sie links schon das Schloβ.**	gahnts INE-fahkh. GAY-en zee DEE-zeh SHTRAAHS-eh geh-RAA-deh-ows bis tsoom EHN-deh. dahn ZAY-en zee links shohn dahs shlos.
Touristin:	**Kann ich zu Fuβ dahin?**	kahn ikh tsoo foos dah-HIN?
Berliner:	**Sicher. Versäumen Sie auch nicht den schönen Park hinter dem Schloβ.**	ZIKH-e(r). fehr-ZOY-men zee owkh nikht dehn SHU(R)-nen pahrk HIN-te(r) dehm shlos.
Touristin:	**Bestimmt nicht. Danke für den Hinweis.**	beh-SHTIMT nikht. DAHN-keh fewr dehn HIN-vice.
Berliner:	**Viel Spaβ noch in Berlin!**	feel shpahs nohkh in behr-LEEN!

. . . .

Tourist:	Excuse me, how do I get to the Charlottenburg castle?
Berliner:	It's quite simple. Go straight down this street to the end. Then you'll see the castle on your left.
Tourist:	Can I walk there?
Berliner:	Sure. And don't miss the nice park behind the castle.
Tourist:	I'll be sure not to. Thanks for the tip.
Berliner:	Enjoy yourself in Berlin!

FINDING YOUR WAY ON FOOT

In general you will find the large Central European cities much easier to get around in on foot than their American counterparts. These cities are older, and most have maintained an old central core or *Altstadt,* which was designed more or less expressly for foot traffic. Naturally the automobile has made considerable inroads in these cities, but urban planning, even in the newer districts and suburbs, is still relatively *fuβgängerfreundlich* (friendly to pedestrians). Wide sidewalks, pedestrian bridges and tunnels, and *Grünanlagen* (green areas = parks) abound, and nearly all the larger German, Swiss, and Austrian cities now boast impressive new *Fuβgängerzone* (pedestrian zones), centrally located areas in which streets have been closed to vehicles and transformed into attractive shopping centers. *Radwege* (cycling paths) are also quite prevalent, and cycling in general is a much safer means of urban transport here than in U.S. cities.

If you are staying in a city for any length of time, it will be worth your while to purchase a *Stadtplan* (city map), which can be obtained at bookstores, newsstands, or street kiosks. They usually contain a good deal of other useful information about the city. Two of the best-known German publishers of such city map-guides are *Falk-Verlag* and *Reise- und Verkehrsverlag.*

Directions

When providing street directions, Central Europeans do not indicate distance by the number of city blocks, but rather by the number of streets *(Straβen)*, intersections *(Kreuzungen)*, traffic lights *(Ampeln)*, or simply in meters or kilometers. They are also likely to refer to specific landmarks, monuments, and pieces of architecture.

Do you have a map of the city?	**Haben Sie einen Stadtplan?**	HAA-ben zee INE-en SHTAHT-plaan?
Could you show me this on the map, please?	**Könnten Sie mir dies bitte auf dem Plan zeigen?**	KU(R)N-ten zee meer dees BIT-teh owf dehm plaan TSYE-gen?

29

Can I get there on foot?	**Kann ich zu Fuβ dahin?**	kahn ikh tsoo foos dah-HIN?
How far is it?	**Wie weit ist es?**	vee vite ist ehs?
I think I'm lost.	**Ich glaube ich habe mich verlaufen.**	ikh GLOW-beh ikh HAA-beh mikh fehr-LOW-fen.
How do I get to this address?	**Wie komme ich zu dieser Adresse?**	vee KOM-meh ikh tsoo DEE-ze(r) ah-DREHS-seh?
How long will it take on foot?	**Wie lange dauert es zu Fuβ?**	vee LAHNG-eh DOW-ehrt ehs tsoo foos?
Where is . . .	**Wo ist . . .**	voh ist . . .
• the Hotel Kaiser Hof?	• **das Hotel Kaiser Hof?**	• dahs ho-TEL KYE-ze(r) hohf?
• . . . Street?	• **die —— Straβe?**	• dee —— SHTRAAS-eh?
• . . . Square?	• **der —— Platz?**	• dehr —— plahts?
How can I get to . . .	**Wie komme ich . . .**	vee KOM-meh ikh . . .
• the center of town?	• **zum Stadtzentrum?**	• tsoom SHTAHT-tsehn-trum?
• the main train station?	• **zum Hauptbahnhof?**	• tsoom HOWPT-baan-hohf?
• the nearest subway station?	• **zur nächsten U-Bahn-Station?**	• tsoor NAYKH-sten OO-baan staht-SYON?
• the nearest bus stop?	• **zur nächsten Bushaltestelle?**	• tsoor NAYKH-sten BUS-hahl-teh-shtehl-eh?

Responses You'll Hear to Your Requests for Directions:

geradeaus	geh-RAA-deh-ows	straight ahead
links/nach links	links/nahkh links	left, to the left
rechts/nach rechts	rehkhts/nahkh rechts	right, to the right
an der Ecke	ahn dehr EH-keh	on the corner
auf dem Platz	owf dehm plats	on the square
zwei Straβen weiter	tsvye SHTRAAS-sen VITE-e(r)	two blocks further
nach der Ampel	nahkh dehr AHM-pel	after the traffic light

vor der Kreuzung	for dehr KROY-tsung	before the intersection
neben der Bank	NAY-ben dehr bahnk	next to the bank
bei der Post	bye dehr post	near/next to the post office
hinter der Kirche	HIN-te(r) dehr KIR-kheh	behind the church
vor dem Dom	for dehm dohm	in front of the cathedral
in der Nähe des Fluβes	in dehr NAY-eh dehs FLUS-ehs	near the river
über die Brücke	EW-be(r) dee BREW-keh	over the bridge
unter dem Turm	UN-te(r) dehm toorm	under the tower
Es ist zu weit zu Fuβ.	ehs ist tsoo vite tsoo foos.	It's too far to walk.
Es ist gerade um die Ecke.	ehs ist geh-RAA-deh oom dee EH-keh.	It's right around the corner.

PUBLIC TRANSPORTATION

You can go just about anywhere in Europe by public transportation, and the system of trains, buses, and urban mass transit in Germany, Austria, and Switzerland is one of the most efficient in the world. Many of the large German cities (Berlin, Bonn, Cologne, Düsseldorf, Frankfurt, Hamburg, and Munich), as well as Vienna, have modern subway or *U-Bahn* (*Untergrundbahn* = underground train) systems, which can be used in combination with the commuter trains or *S-Bahn* (*Stadtbahn* = city train) to reach the outlying suburbs. *Busse* (buses) are in use everywhere, and some cities still have a tram or *Straβenbahn* (streetcar) system.

In most cities tickets can be used interchangeably on these various systems and usually must be purchased in advance from automats or ticket stands in the stations. Instructions in English for buying and using tickets, as well as overview maps and timetables for these transport systems can also be found in the individual stations. Most of the *U-Bahn*, *S-Bahn*, and *Straβenbahn* networks operate on the "honor system," that is, you can board the trains without a ticket. If you are caught, however,

31

there is a stiff fine for *schwarzfahren* (riding without a ticket). The *U-Bahn* and *S-Bahn* usually stop running from 1 to 5 A.M. Many cities offer discounted prices for blocks of tickets or special unlimited travel passes, which may be worth your while if you travel frequently within a city.

Riding the Subway, Commuter Trains, Streetcars, and Buses

Where is the nearest . . .	**Wo ist die nächste. . . .**	voh ist dee NAYKH-steh
• subway station?	• **U-Bahn-Station?**	• OO-baan-staht-SYON?
• commuter train station?	• **S-Bahn-Station?**	• EHS-bann-staht-SYON?
• streetcar stop?	• **Straßenbahn-haltestelle?**	• shtraahs-sen-baan-HAHL-teh-shtehl-eh?
• bus stop?	• **Bushaltestelle?**	BUS-hahl-teh-shtehl-leh?
Where can I buy a ticket?	**Wo kann ich eine Fahrkarte kaufen?**	voh kahn ikh INE-eh FAAR-kahr-teh KOW-fen?
How much is the fare?	**Wieviel kostet eine Fahrt?**	VEE-feel KOS-tet INE-eh faart?
Is this ticket still valid?	**Ist diese Fahrkarte noch gültig?**	ist DEE-zeh FAAR-kahr-teh nohkh GEWL-tikh?
How much is a one-week tourist pass?	**Wieviel kostet eine Touristen-Woch-enkarte?**	VEE-feel KOS-tet INE-eh too-RIS-ten VOKH-en-kahr-teh?
Which train/bus/line goes to ———?	**Welcher Zug/Bus/Welche Linie fährt nach ———?**	VEHL-khe(r) tsook/bus VEHL-kheh LEEN-yeh fehrt nahkh ———?
Where does this train go?	**Wohin fährt dieser Zug?**	VOH-hin fehrt DEE-ze(r) tsook?
How long does the trip take?	**Wie lange dauert die Fahrt?**	vee LAHNG-eh DOW-ehrt dee faart?
What's the next stop?	**Was ist die nächste Haltestelle?**	vahs ist dee NAYKH-steh HAHL-teh-shtehl-eh?

Where do I have to change trains/buses?	**Wo muß ich umsteigen?**	voh mus ikh OOM-shtye-gen?
Which line do I take then?	**Welche Linie nehme ich dann?**	VEHL-kheh LEEN-yeh NAY-meh ikh dahn?
Please tell me when to get off.	**Sagen Sie mir bitte, wann ich aussteigen muß.**	ZAA-gen zee meer BIT-teh, vahn ikh OWS-shtye-gen mus.

TAKING A CAB

Taxis are not usually hailed in the street, but rather ordered by phone or found at a *Taxistand* (taxi stand). Rates are clearly posted and will also indicate extra charges for luggage and other additional services. A 10–15% tip for the *Taxler* or *Taxifahrer* (taxi driver) is customary but is included in Switzerland.

Is there a taxi stand nearby?	**Gibt es einen Taxistand in der Nähe?**	gipt ehs INE-en TAHK-see-shtahnt in dehr NAY-eh?
Please call me a taxi.	**Rufen Sie mir bitte ein Taxi.**	ROO-fen zee meer BIT-teh ine TAHK-see.
What is the fare to/from the airport?	**Wieviel kostet die Fahrt zum/vom Flughafen?**	VEE-feel KOS-tet dee faart tsoom/fom FLOOK-haa-fen?
I'm in a hurry.	**Ich habe es eilig.**	ikh HAA-beh ehs EYE-likh
How long will the trip take?	**Wie lange dauert die Fahrt?**	vee LAHNG-eh DOW-ehrt dee faart?
And during rush hour?	**Und bei starkem Verkehr?**	unt bye SHTAR-kem fehr-KEHR?
Take me to this address please.	**Fahren Sie mich bitte zu dieser Adresse.**	FAA-ren zee mikh BIT-teh tsoo DEE-ze(r) ah-DREHS-seh.
Please put my bags in the trunk.	**Legen Sie bitte mein Gepäck in den Kofferraum.**	LAY-gen zee BIT-teh mine geh-PEHK in dehn KO-fe(r)-rowm.
Please slow down!	**Fahren Sie langsamer bitte!**	FAA-ren zee LAHNG-sah-me(r) BIT-teh!

Stop at the next corner.	**Halten Sie an der nächsten Ecke.**	HAHL-ten zee ahn dehr NAYKH-sten EH-keh.
Let me off here please.	**Lassen Sie mich bitte hier aussteigen.**	LAHS-sen zee mikh BIT-teh heer OWS-shtye-gen.
How much do I owe you?	**Wieviel macht das?**	VEE-feel mahkht dahs?
Keep the change.	**Das stimmt so.**	dahs shtimt zoh.

TRAVELING BY TRAIN

Germany, Austria, and Switzerland all have extensive, well-run national rail systems. Rail travel is the preferred mode of economical transportation for most Europeans. The trains are fast, reliable, and comfortable. If you are planning to travel much, you may want to inquire with your travel agent about Eurail passes and other kinds of unlimited-travel passes.

Most long-distance trains have first- and second-class compartments, and a *Speisewagen* (dining car), serving full-course meals or snacks at relatively high prices. Overnight trains offer *Schlafwagen* (sleeping cars) to first-class passengers or *Liegewagen* (couchette or bunk-style sleeping cars) for those in second class. Both must be reserved in advance. Certain express trains charge a *Zuschlag* (extra fee, see list below). To reserve a second-class seat on some trains, it may be necessary to purchase a *Platzkarte* (seat ticket) in addition to the ticket itself. Tickets are usually inspected and punched on the train, and not at the gate. Various discounts apply toward children's tickets: in Germany those under age four (six in Switzerland, seven in Austria) ride for free; youngsters under twelve (under sixteen in Austria and Switzerland) pay half fare.

Types of Trains: Germany

TEE	Trans-Europe Express; first-class international service, reservation, and *Zuschlag* (surcharge) required
IC/Intercity	Intercity express trains; some only first class, others with first and second class or surcharge

34

D-Zug	Intermediate- to long-distance express trains; first and second class
City-D-Zug	Short-distance, intercity express trains; surcharge on tickets for trips less than 50 km
Eilzug	Intermediate-distance rapid trains, stopping at large- and medium-size towns
Nahverkehrszug	Local trains, stopping at all stations

Types of Trains: Switzerland and Austria

Städteschnellzug	Austrian equivalent of the Intercity trains
Expreβzug	Austrian equivalent of the *D-Zug*
Schnellzug	Swiss, Austrian equivalent of the *Eilzug*
Personenzug	Austrian local train
Regionalzug	Swiss local train

AT THE STATION

The main stations in some of the larger cities (Frankfurt and Munich, for instance) have computerized timetable machines; otherwise look for posted timetables:

ABFAHRT in yellow is for departures

ANKUNFT in white is for arrivals

Where is/are . . .	**Wo ist/sind . . .**	voh ist/zint . . .
• the train station?	• **der Bahnhof?**	• dehr BAAN-hohf?
• the ticket window?	• **der Fahrkarten-schalter?**	• dehr FAAR-kahr-ten-shahl-te(r)?
• the booking/ reservations office?	• **die Platzreser-vierung?**	• dee PLAHTS-reh-zehr-vee-rung?
• the baggage check?	• **die Gepäckauf-bewahrung?**	• dee geh-PEHK-owf-beh-vaa-rung?

35

• the baggage lockers?	• die Schließfächer?	• dee SHLEES-feh-khe(r)?
• the baggage carts?	• die Kofferkulis?	• dee KOF-fe(r)-koo-lees?
• the lost and found?	• das Fundbüro?	• dahs FUNT-bew-roh?
• the restroom?	• die Toilette?	• dee toy-LEH-teh?
• the waiting room?	• der Wartesaal?	• dehr VAHR-teh-zaal?
• the exit?	• der Ausgang?	• dehr OWS-gahng?
• a telephone?	• ein Telefon?	• ine tay-lay-FOHN?
• platform 2?	• Bahnsteig zwei?	• BAAN-shtike tzvye?
• track 5?	• Gleis fünf?	• glice fewnf?

TICKETS, RESERVATIONS, AND INQUIRIES

I'd like a ticket to Bonn . . .	Ich möchte eine Fahrkarte nach Bonn . . .	ikh MU(R)KH-teh INE-eh FAAR-kahr-teh nakh bohn.
• first class.	• erste Klasse.	• EHR-steh KLAHS-seh.
• second class.	• zweite Klasse.	• TSVYE-teh KLAHS-seh.
• half price.	• zum halben Preis.	• tsoom HAAL-ben price.
• one way.	• einfach.	• INE-fahkh.
• roundtrip.	• hin und zurück.	• hin unt tsoo-REWK.
• on the next train.	• für den nächsten Zug.	• fewr dehn NAYKH-sten tsook.
How much is the ticket?	Was kostet die Fahrkarte?	vahs KOS-tet dee FAAR-kahr-teh?
I'd like to reserve . . .	Ich möchte —— reservieren lassen.	ikh MU(R)KH-teh —— reh-zehr-VEE-ren LAHS-sen.

a (window) seat.	einen (Fenster) platz	INE-en (FEHN-ste(r)) plahts
two nonsmoker seats.	zwei Plätze im Nichtraucherabteil	tsvye PLEH-tseh im NIKHT-row-khe(r)-AHP-tile.
two berths in the sleeping car.	zwei Plätze im Schlafwagen	tsvye PLEH-tseh im SHLAHF-vah-gen
a couchette/bunk.	einen Platz im Liegewagen	INE-en plahts im LEE-geh-vah-gen
I'd like to check these bags.	Ich möchte dieses Gepäck aufgeben.	ikh MU(R)KH-teh DEE-zehs geh-PEHK OWF-GAY-ben.
When does the next train for Salzburg leave?	Wann fährt der nächste Zug nach Salzburg?	vahn fehrt dehr NAYKH-steh tsook nahk ZAHLTS-boork?
Is it a through train?	Ist es ein durchgehender Zug?	ist ehs ine DURKH-gay-ehn-de(r) tsook?
Will it stop in Munich?	Hält der Zug in München?	hehlt dehr tsook in MEWN-khen?
Is there a connection to Graz?	Gibt es einen Anschluß nach Graz?	gipt ehs INE-en AHN-shlus nahk grahts?
Do I have to change trains?	Muß ich umsteigen?	mus ikh OOM-shtye-gen?
When does it arrive in Linz?	Wann kommt er in Linz an?	vahn komt ehr in lints ahn?
Is there —— on the train?	Hat der Zug . . .	haht dehr tsook . . .
a dining car	einen Speisewagen?	INE-en SHPYE-zeh-vah-gen?
a sleeping car	einen Schlafwagen?	INE-en SHLAHF-vah-gen?
a through coach to Vienna	einen Kurswagen nach Wien?	INE-en KOORS-vaa-gen nahk veen?
From which platform does the train to Ulm leave?	Auf welchem Bahnsteig fährt der Zug nach Ulm ab?	owf VEHL-khem BAAN-shtike fehrt dehr tsook nahk oolm ahp?

| At which track does the train from Nurenberg arrive? | **Auf welchem Gleis kommt der Zug aus Nürnberg an?** | owf VEHL-khem glice komt dehr tsook ows NU(R)RN-behrk ahn? |
| Do you have a timetable? | **Haben Sie einen Fahrplan?** | HAA-ben zee INE-en FAAR-plaan? |

ON BOARD

All aboard.	**Einsteigen bitte.**	INE-shtye-gen BIT-teh.
Excuse me. May I get by?	**Entschuldigung. Darf ich vorbei?**	ehnt-SHOOL-di-gung. dahrf ikh for-BYE?
Is this seat free?	**Ist dieser Platz besetzt?**	ist DEE-ze(r) plahts beh-ZEHTST?
I think you're sitting in my seat.	**Ich glaube, Sie sitzen auf meinem Platz.**	ikh GLOW-beh zee ZIT-tsen owf MINE-em plahts.
Could you help me please with my suitcase?	**Könnten Sie mir bitte mit dem Koffer helfen?**	KU(R)N-ten zee meer BIT-teh mit dehm KOF-fe(r) HEHL-fen?
How long will the train stop here?	**Wie lange hält der Zug hier?**	vee LAHNG-eh hehlt dehr tsook heer?
What town is this?	**Wie heißt dieser Ort?**	vee heyst DEE-ze(r) ort?
Where should I change trains/get off?	**Wo soll ich umsteigen/ aussteigen?**	voh zol ikh OOM-shtye-gen/OWS-shtye-gen?

TRAVELING BY BOAT

When does the ship/ferry for Bremerhaven leave?	**Wann fährt das Schiff/ die Fähre nach Bremerhaven?**	vahn fehrt dahs shif/dee FEH-reh nahkh breh-me(r)- HAA-fen?
Will it also stop in Hamburg?	**Legt es auch in Hamburg an?**	laykt ehs owkh in HAAM-boork ahn?
How much does a tour of the harbor cost?	**Wieviel kostet eine Hafenrundfahrt?**	VEE-feel KOS-tet INE-eh HAA-fen-runt-faart?
Where is the point of embarkation?	**Wo ist der Anlegeplatz?**	voh ist dehr AHN-lay-geh-plahts?

38

4/ ACCOMMODATIONS

If you are planning to stay in any of the major tourist centers during the high season (summer or specific holidays), you will need to make hotel or boardinghouse reservations well in advance. At other times you can rely on the referral services of the local *Fremdenverkehrsbüro** (tourist information office), usually located near the main train station in most cities and towns. Ask to see their *Hotelverzeichnis* (hotel guide). Germany has three different catagories of hotels and boarding houses, designated as follows: F for hotels and boardinghouses with breakfast included; G for country inns and boardinghouses with more meals included; H for standard hotels. Each category is rated I, II, or III (adequate, good, very good). In Austria and Switzerland, hotels and inns are rated with one to five stars, similar to the French system.

The terms *Pension* and *Fremdenheim* indicate a boardinghouse, offering either *Vollpension* (full board) or *Halbpension* (half board, meaning breakfast and one other meal). *Hotel Garni* means bed and breakfast only. The sign *Zimmer frei* indicates a room or rooms to rent, often in private homes. *Gasthaus* or *Gasthof* usually refer to a country inn, while *Rasthof* means a motel or wayside lodge with restaurant, located right off the *Autobahn* or main highway. The accommodations of many *Jugendherberge* (youth hostels) are no longer as spartan as they used to be and are often open to seniors and "young at heart" middle-agers. If you are in a larger party and planning to stay longer in a resort area, you may want to investigate renting a *Ferienwohnung* (furnished apartment).

---

*Referred to also as: *Verkehrsverein, Verkehrsamt, Verkehrsverband,* or (in spas) as *Kurkommission.*

DIALOGUE: AT THE RECEPTION DESK (*AN DER REZEPTION*)

Reisender:	**Haben Sie ein Doppelzimmer für eine Nacht?**	HAA-ben zee ine DOP-pehl-tsim-me(r) fewr INE-eh nahkht?
Empfangsdame:	**Moment mal. Ja, wir haben eins mit Doppelbett im dritten Stock zum Hof.**	mo-MEHNT mahl. yaa, veer HAA-ben ines mit DOP-pehl-beht im DRIT-ten shtok tsoom hohf.
Reisender:	**Schön. Ist es ein Zimmer mit Bad?**	shu(r)n. ist ehs ine TSIM-me(r) mit baat?
Empfangsdame:	**Nein, aber es gibt eine Toilette und Dusche.**	nine, AH-be(r) ehs gipt INE-eh toy-LEHT-teh unt DOO-sheh.
Reisender:	**In Ordnung. Darf ich es sehen?**	in ORT-nung. dahrf ikh ehs ZAY-en?
Empfangsdame:	**Selbstverständlich. Folgen Sie mir, bitte.**	zehlpst-fehr-STEHNT-likh. FOHL-gen zee meer, BIT-teh.

. . . .

Traveler:	Do you have a double room for one night?
Receptionist:	One moment. Yes, we have one with a double bed on the third floor* facing the courtyard.
Traveler:	Fine. Does the room have a bath?
Receptionist:	No, but it has a toilet and shower.
Traveler:	That's all right. May I see it?
Receptionist:	Of course. Follow me, please.

*Our first floor is referred to in Germany as the *Erdgeschoß;* our second floor becomes their first, and so forth.

CHECKING IN

Most larger hotels will have staff who speak English, but in smaller ones these phrases may be useful.

I have a reservation in the name of Brown.	**Ich habe auf den Namen Brown ein Zimmer reservieren lassen.**	ikh HAA-beh owf dehn NAA-men Brown ine TSIM-me(r) reh-zehr-VEE-ren LAHS-en.
Here's the confirmation.	**Hier ist die Bestätigung.**	heer ist dee beh-SHTEH-ti-gung.
Do you have any vacancies?	**Haben Sie noch Zimmer frei?**	HAA-ben zee nohkh TSIM-me(r) frye?
Could you recommend another hotel that might not be booked up?	**Können Sie mir ein anderes Hotel empfehlen, das vielleicht nicht ausgebucht ist?**	KU(R)-nen zee meer ine AHN-dehr-ehs ho-TEL ehm-PFAY-len, dahs fee-LYEKHT nikht OWS-geh-bookht ist?
I'd like . . .	**Ich hätte gern . . .**	ikh HEHT-teh gehrn . . .
• a room for two nights.	• **ein Zimmer für zwei Nächte.**	• ine TSIM-me(r) fewr tsvye NEHKH-teh.
• a single room.	• **ein Einzelzimmer.**	• ine INE-tsehl-tsim-me(r).
• a double room.	• **ein Doppelzimmer.**	• ine DOP-pehl-tsim-me(r).
• a room on the ground/top floor.	• **ein Zimmer im Erdgeschoß/ obersten Geschoß.**	• ine TSIM-me(r) im EHRT-geh-shos/OH-behr-sten geh-SHOS.
. . . a room with . . .	**. . . ein Zimmer mit . . .**	. . . ine TSIM-me(r) mit . . .
• a double bed.	• **einem Doppelbett.**	• INE-em DOP-pehl-beht.
• twin beds.	• **zwei Einzelbetten.**	• tsvye INE-tsehl-beht-ten.
• private bath.	• **Privatbad.**	• pri-VAAT-baat.
• shower and toilet.	• **Dusche und WC.**	• DOO-sheh unt VAY-tsay.

41

• a balcony.	• **Balkon.**	• bahl-KOHN.
• a nice view.	• **schönem Ausblick.**	• SHU(R)-nem OWS-blik.
• radio and (color) TV.	• **Radio und (Farb) Fernseher.**	• RAA-dee-oh unt (faarp) FEHRN-zay-e(r).
• air-conditioning.	• **Klimaanlage.**	• KLEE-mah-ahn-laa-geh.
We need a quiet room . . .	**Wir brauchen ein ruhiges Zimmer . . .**	veer BROW-khen ine ROO-i-gehs TSIM-me(r) . . .
• toward the back.	• **zum Hof.**	• tsoom hohf.
• (not) facing the street.	• **(nicht) zur Straße.**	• (nikht) tsoor SHTRAAS-eh.
How much is it . . .	**Wieviel kostet es . . .**	VEE-feel KOS-tet ehs . . .
• per night?	• **pro Nacht?**	• pro nahkht?
• per week?	• **pro Woche?**	• pro VOKH-eh?
• for bed and breakfast?	• **für Übernachtung mit Frühstück?**	• fewr ew-behr-NAHKH-tung mit FREW-shtewk?
• for full board?	• **für Vollpension?**	• fewr FOL-pehn-ziohn?
• for half board?	• **für Halbpension?**	• fewr HAALP-pehn-ziohn?
• without meals?	• **ohne Mahlzeiten?**	• OH-neh MAAL-tsite-en?
Does that include breakfast/tax?	**Ist Frühstück/ Mehrwertsteuer im Preis inbegriffen?**	ist FREW-shtewk/MEHR-vehrt-shtoy-e(r) im price IN-beh-grif-en?
Can you show me the room?	**Können Sie mir das Zimmer zeigen?**	KU(R)-nen zee meer dahs TSIM-me(r) TSYE-gen?
It's fine. I'll take it.	**Gut. Ich nehme es.**	goot. ikh NAY-meh ehs.
No, I don't like it.	**Nein, es gefällt mir nicht.**	nine, ehs geh-FEHLT meer nikht.
Do you have anything . . .	**Haben Sie etwas . . .**	HAA-ben zee EHT-vahs . . .

• larger/better?	• **Größeres/Besser-es?**	• GRU(R)S-eh-rehs/ BEHS-eh-rehs
• less expensive/ quieter?	• **Preiswerteres/ Ruhigeres?**	• PRICE-vehr-teh-rehs/ ROO-i-geh-rehs?
What is my room number?	**Welche Zimmernummer habe ich?**	VEHL-kheh TSIM-me(r)-num-me(r) HAA-beh ikh?
Can I leave the key at the front desk?	**Kann ich den Schlüssel bei der Rezeption lassen?**	kahn ikh dehn SHLEWS-el bye dehr reh-tsehp-TSYOHN LAHS-en?
May I leave this in your safe?	**Darf ich dies in Ihrem Tresor aufbewahren?**	dahrf ikh dees in EE-rem treh-ZOHR OWF-beh-vaa-ren?
Please have my luggage brought to my room.	**Lassen Sie bitte mein Gepäck ins Zimmer bringen.**	LAHS-en zee BIT-teh mine geh-PEHK ins TSIM-me(r) BRIN-gen.
Are there any messages/letters for me?	**Gibt es für mich Nachrichten/ Post?**	gipt ehs fewr mikh NAKH-rikh-ten/post?
Would you please wake me at seven?	**Würden Sie mich bitte um sieben Uhr wecken?**	VEWR-den zee mikh BIT-teh oom ZEE-ben oor VEH-ken?
I wish not to be disturbed.	**Ich will nicht gestört werden.**	ikh vil nikht geh-SHTU(R)T VEHR-den.

REQUESTS FOR HOTEL SERVICES

May I/we have . . .	**Kann ich/können wir ——— haben?**	kahn ikh/KU(R)-nen veer ——— HAA-ben?
• an extra bed?	• **ein zusätzliches Bett**	• ine TSOO-zehts-likh-ehs beht
• an extra pillow?	• **ein extra Kopfkissen**	• ine EHK-straa KOPF-kis-sen
• a blanket?	• **eine Decke**	• INE-eh DEH-keh
• bath towels?	• **Badetücher**	• BAA-deh-tew-khe(r)
• some soap?	• **etwas Seife**	• EHT-vahs ZYE-feh

43

• a roll of toilet paper?	• eine Rolle Toilettenpapier	• INE-eh RO-leh toy-LEHT-ten-paa-peer
• a hair dryer?	• einen Haartrockner	• INE-en HAAR-trohkh-ne(r)
• extra hangers?	• extra Kleiderbügel	• EHK-straa KLYE-dehr-bew-gehl
• some ice cubes?	• Eiswürfel	• ICE-vewr-fel
• an ashtray?	• einen Aschenbecher	• INE-en AH-shehn-beh-khe(r)
Where is . . .	Wo ist . . .	voh ist . . .
• the chambermaid?	• das Zimmer-mädchen?	• dahs TSIM-me(r)-mayt-khen?
• the bellboy?	• der Hotelpage?	• dehr ho-TEL-paa-zheh?
• the receptionist?	• die Empfangsdame/ der Empfangschef?	• dee ehm-PFAHNGS-dah-meh/dehr ehm-PFAHNGS-shef?
• the switchboard operator?	• die Telefonistin?	• dee tay-lay-foh-NIS-tin?
• the manager?	• der Direktor?	• dehr dee-REHK-tor?
• the elevator?	• der Aufzug/ Fahrstuhl?	• dehr OWF-tsook/FAAR-shtool?
• the dining room?	• der Speisesaal?	• dehr SHPYE-zeh-zaal?
• the checkroom?	• die Garderobe?	• dee gahr-deh-ROH-beh?
Could you please mail this for me?	Können Sie das bitte für mich aufgeben?	KU(R)-nen zee dahs BIT-teh fewr mikh OWF-gay-ben?
Could you get me . . .	Können Sie mir—— besorgen?	KU(R)-nen zee meer —— beh-ZOR-gen?
• an iron?	• ein Bügeleisen	• ine BEW-gehl-eye-zen
• a typewriter?	• eine Schreibmaschine	• INE-eh SHRIPE-mah-shee-neh
• a babysitter?	• einen Babysitter	• INE-en ''Babysitter''
What's the voltage here?	Welche Stromspannung gibt es hier?	VEHL-kheh SHTROHM-shpah-nung gipt ehs heer?

44

Can we have breakfast in our room?	**Können wir im Zimmer frühstücken?**	KU(R)-nen veer im TSIM-me(r) FREW-shtew-ken?

PROBLEMS

My room hasn't been made up.	**Mein Zimmer ist nicht gemacht.**	mine TSIM-me(r) ist nikht geh-makht.
The —— doesn't work.	**. . . ist defekt.**	. . . ist deh-FEHKT.
• door lock	• **Das Türschloß**	• dahs TEWR-shlos
• light switch	• **Der Lichtschalter**	• dehr LIKHT-shahl-te(r)
• lamp	• **Die Lampe**	• dee LAHM-peh
• plug	• **Der Stecker**	• dehr SHTEH-ke(r)
• heating	• **Die Heizung**	• dee HYE-tsung
• air-conditioning	• **Die Klimaanlage**	• dee KLEE-mah-ahn-laa-geh
• fan	• **Der Ventilator**	• dehr vehn-tee-LAA-tor
• faucet	• **Der Wasserhahn**	• dehr VAHS-se(r)-haan
The —— is clogged.	**. . . ist verstopft.**	. . . ist fehr-SHTOPFT.
• toilet	• **Die Toilette**	• dee toy-LEHT-teh
• bathtub	• **Die Badewanne**	• die BAA-deh-vahn-neh
• washbasin	• **Das Waschbecken**	• dahs VAHSH-beh-ken
There's no hot water.	**Es gibt kein warmes Wasser.**	ehs gipt kine VAHR-mehs VAHS-se(r).
Can we switch rooms?	**Können wir die Zimmer wechseln?**	KU(R)-nen veer dee TSIM-me(r) VEHK-seln?

CHECKING OUT

We're leaving early tomorrow.	**Wir reisen morgen früh ab.**	veer RYE-zen MOR-gen frew ahp.
Please have our bill ready.	**Bereiten Sie bitte die Rechnung vor.**	beh-RYE-ten zee BIT-teh dee REHKH-nung for.

45

Can I pay with a credit card?	**Kann ich mit Kreditkarte bezahlen?**	kahn ikh mit kray-DEET-kahr-teh beh-TSAA-len?
I think you've made a mistake on my bill.	**Ich glaube, Sie haben sich verrechnet.**	ikh GLOW-beh, zee HAA-ben zikh fehr-REHKH-neht.
Would you please have our luggage brought down?	**Würden Sie bitte unser Gepäck herunterbringen lassen?**	VEWR-den zee BIT-teh UN-ze(r) geh-PEHK heh-RUN-te(r)-bring-en LAHS-en?
Could you order us a taxi?	**Können Sie uns ein Taxi bestellen?**	KU(R)-nen zee uns ine TAHK-see beh-SHTEHL-len?
It's been a very enjoyable stay.	**Der Aufenthalt war sehr angenehm.**	dehr OW-fehnt-hahlt vahr zehr AHN-geh-nehm.

CAMPING

In German-speaking countries, *zelten* (camping) has become a very popular and sophisticated activity, and there are many excellent, well-equipped campsites. Authorized sites are indicated on many maps, and local tourist offices as well as camping guides will also help you to locate them. Many youth hostels provide camping facilities. Should you decide to camp elsewhere, always ask for permission first.

Is there a campsite anywhere near here?	**Gibt es hier in der Nähe einen Campingplatz?**	gipt ehs heer in dehr NAY-eh INE-en KEHM-ping-plahts?
Do you mind if we camp on your property?	**Haben Sie etwas dagegen, wenn wir auf Ihrem Grundstück zelten?**	HAA-ben zee EHT-vahs dah-GAY-gen, vehn veer owf EE-rem GRUNT-shtewk TSEHL-ten?
Does this youth hostel have a campsite?	**Hat diese Jugendherberge einen Zeltplatz?**	haht DEE-ze(r) YOO-gehnt-hehr-behr-geh INE-en TSEHLT-plats?

Is there/Are there . . .	Gibt es . . .	gipt ehs . . .
• electricity?	• Stromanschluß?	• SHTROHM-ahn-shlus?
• drinking water?	• Trinkwasser?	• TRINK-vahs-se(r)?
• showering facilities?	• eine Duschmög-lichkeit?	• INE-eh DOOSH-mu(r)-glikh-kite?
What are the fees . . .	Wie hoch sind die Gebühren . . .	vee hohhk zint dee geh-BEW-ren . . .
• per day?	• pro Tag?	• pro taak?
• per week?	• pro Woche?	• pro VOKH-eh?
• for a tent?	• für ein Zelt?	• fewr ine tsehlt?
• for a trailer?	• für einen Wohnwagen?	• fewr INE-en VOHN-vaa-gen?
Where are the toilets and washroom?	Wo sind die Toiletten und Waschraum?	voh zint dee toy-LEHT-ten unt VAHSH-rowm?
Where can we wash our dishes/clothes?	Wo können wir Geschirr spülen/Wäsche waschen?	voh KU(R)-nen veer geh-SHIR SHPEW-len/VEH-sheh VAHSH-en?
Can we buy butane gas here?	Können wir hier Butangas kaufen?	KU(R)-nen veer heer bu-TAAN-gahs KOW-fen?
Where can we go shopping?	Wo können wir einkaufen?	voh KU(R)-nen veer INE-kow-fen?

5/SOCIALIZING

Meeting people and discovering a new culture through personal contacts can be one of the most rewarding travel experiences. Europeans are generally more reserved than Americans, but with a little patience, good will, and curiosity, behavioral as well as linguistic barriers are easily overcome. A genuine interest in the people and culture of your host country is perhaps the best entrée into the German-speaking world.

When meeting or taking leave, German speakers usually shake hands; close friends often embrace, while women exchange kisses. There is a somewhat complex set of etiquette rules for crossing the threshold of formality by switching from the formal *Sie* to the familiar *du* form of address, and these rules may vary from one locale to another, so to be on the safe side and not risk offending anyone, a foreigner should wait for the native speaker to offer or suggest using the *du* form. (*Warum duzen wir uns nicht?* Why don't we use the *"du"* form with each other?) An exception to this rule of thumb is when adults are addressing children under the age of 16, who are always addressed as *du*.

DIALOGUE: INTRODUCTIONS (*SICH VORSTELLEN*)

Karen Jackson:	**Guten Abend. Darf ich mich vorstellen? Ich heiße Karen Jackson.**	GOO-ten AA-behnt. dahrf ikh mikh FOR-shtehl-len? ikh HICE-seh "Karen Jackson."
Klaus Schulz:	**Sehr erfreut. Ich heiße Klaus Schulz.**	zehr ehr-FROYT. ikh HICE-seh klows shults.
Karen Jackson:	**Ich freue mich sehr, Sie kennenzulernen.**	ikh FROY-eh mikh zehr, zee KEHN-nen-tsoo-lehr-nen.
Klaus Schulz:	**Sind Sie hier in der Schweiz auf Urlaubsreise?**	zint zee heer in dehr shvites owf OOR-lowps-rye-zeh?

Karen Jackson:	**Ja, ich bleibe noch eine Woche.**	yaa, ikh BLYE-beh nohkh INE-eh VOKH-eh.
Klaus Schulz:	**Ich hoffe, Sie amüsieren sich gut. Auf Wiedersehen.**	ikh HOF-feh, zee ah-mew-ZEE-ren sikh goot. owf VEE-de(r)-zay-en.
Karen Jackson:	**Vielen Dank und auf Wiedersehen.**	FEE-len dahnk unt owf VEE-de(r)-zay-en.

. . . .

Karen Jackson:	Good evening. May I introduce myself? My name is Karen Jackson.
Klaus Schulz:	Pleased to meet you. My name is Klaus Schulz.
Karen Jackson:	I am very pleased to meet you.
Klaus Schulz:	Are you here in Switzerland on vacation?
Karen Jackson:	Yes, I'll be here for one more week.
Klaus Schulz:	I hope you have a good time. Good-bye.
Karen Jackson:	Thanks a lot and good-bye.

INTRODUCTIONS

I'd like to introduce you to . . .	**Ich möchte Ihnen ——— vorstellen.**	ikh MU(R)KH-teh EE-nen ——— FOR-shtehl-len.
May I introduce . . .	**Darf ich ——— vorstellen?**	dahrf ikh ——— FOR-shtehl-len?
• my husband?	• **meinen Mann**	• MINE-en mahn
• my wife?	• **meine Frau**	• MINE-eh frow
• my colleague?	• **meinen Kollegen/meine Kollegin**	• MINE-en ko-LAY-gehn/MINE-eh ko-LAY-gin

49

• my friend	• **meinen Freund/meine Freundin***	• MINE-en froynt/MINE-eh FROYN-din
Pleased to meet you.	**Sehr erfreut.**	zehr ehr-FROYT.
May I introduce myself?	**Darf ich mich vorstellen?**	dahrf ikh mikh FOR-shtehl-len?
What's your name?	**Wie heißen Sie?**	vee HICE-sen zee?
My name is . . .	**Ich heiße ——— /Mein Name ist . . .**	ikh HICE-seh ——— /mine NAA-meh ist . . .
How are you?/How do you do?	**Wie geht es Ihnen?**	vee gayt ehs EE-nen?
Fine, thanks, and you?	**Danke, gut. Und Ihnen?**	DAHN-keh, goot. unt EE-nen?
How are you?**	**Wie geht's?****	vee gayts?

*These terms are not used as casually in German as "friend" in English; in male/female relationships, they indicate boyfriend/girlfriend. For more casual relationships, Germans use the word *Bekannte(r)* (acquaintance).
**Informal expression to be used with "du" friends (see page 48).

FIRST CONTACT

Are you German/ Swiss/ Austrian?	**Sind Sie aus Deutschland/ der Schweiz/ Österreich?**	zint zee ows DOYCH-lahnt/dehr shvites/U(R)-steh-ryekh?
Where are you from?	**Woher kommen Sie?**	voh-HEHR KOM-men zee?
I'm from . . .	**Ich bin aus . . .**	ikh bin ows . . .
• the United States.	• **den Vereinigten Staaten.**	• dehn fehr-INE-ikh-ten SHTAA-ten.
• Canada.	• **Kanada.**	• KAH-nah-dah.
• England.	• **England.**	• EHNG-lahnt.
• Australia.	• **Australien.**	• ows-TRAAL-yen.
Where do you live?	**Wo wohnen Sie?**	voh VOH-nen zee?
I live in . . .	**Ich wohne in . . .**	ikh VOH-neh in . . .
• New England.	• **Neuengland.**	• noy-EHNG-lahnt.
• the Middle West.	• **dem Mittelwesten.**	• dehm MIT-tel-vehs-ten.

• Boston.	• **Boston.**	• BOS-ton.
• California.	• **Kalifornien.**	• kah-lee-FORN-yen.
How long have you been here?	**Wie lange sind Sie schon hier?**	vee LAHNG-eh zint zee shohn heer?
We've been here a week.	**Wir sind schon seit einer Woche hier.**	veer zint shohn zite INE-e(r) VOKH-eh heer.
How do you like . . .	**Wie gefällt Ihnen . . .**	vee geh-FEHLT EE-nen . . .
• Germany?	• **Deutschland?**	• DOYCH-lahnt?
• Switzerland?	• **die Schweiz?**	• dee shvites?
• Austria?	• **Österreich?**	• U(R)-steh-ryekh?
I don't know yet.	**Ich weiß noch nicht.**	ikh vice nohkh nikht.
I just arrived.	**Ich bin gerade angekommen.**	ikh bin geh-RAA-deh AHN-geh-kom-men.
I like it a lot here.	**Mir gefällt* es hier sehr gut.**	meer geh-FEHLT ehs heer zehr goot.
I like ——— a lot.	**Mir gefällt/ gefallen* ——— sehr.**	meer geh-FEHLT/geh-FAHL-len ——— zehr.
• the landscape	• **die Landschaft**	• dee LAHNT-shahft
• the cities	• **die Städte**	• dee SHTEH-teh
• the people	• **die Menschen**	• dee MEHN-shen
Everything is so . . .	**Alles ist so . . .**	AH-lehs ist zoh . . .
• interesting.	• **interessant.**	• in-teh-rehs-SAHNT.
• different.	• **anders.**	• AHN-dehrs.
• beautiful.	• **schön.**	• shu(r)n.

*The verb *gefallen* (to please) agrees with the object of the translated English sentence. "*Mir gefallen die Städte*" (I like the cities) means literally: "The cities are pleasing to me."

JOBS AND PROFESSIONS**

What's your occupation?	**Was machen Sie beruflich?**	vahs MAHKH-en zee beh-ROOF-likh?
I'm a businessman/ woman.	**Ich bin Geschäftsmann/ -frau.**	ikh bin geh-SHEHFTS-mahn/-frow.

**For a more complete list of professions and occupations, see page 172 in Chapter 14, General Information.

I'm on a business trip now.	**Ich bin jetzt auf Geschäftsreise.**	ikh bin yehtst owf geh-SHEHFTS-rye-zeh.
I'm retired.	**Ich bin pensioniert.**	ikh bin pehn-zioh-NEERT.

MAKING FRIENDS

May I invite you . . .	**Darf ich Sie ——— einladen?**	dahrf ikh zee ——— INE-laa-den?
• for a cup of tea?	• **zu einer Tasse Tee**	• tsoo INE-e(r) TAHS-seh tay
• for a glass of wine?	• **zu einem Glas Wein**	• tsoo INE-em glaas vine
• to lunch/dinner?	• **zum Mittagessen/ Abendessen**	• tsoom MIT-taak-ehs-sen/AA-behnt-ehs-sen
Can I get you a drink?	**Möchten Sie etwas trinken?**	MU(R)KH-ten zee EHT-vahs TRIN-ken?
Are you married?	**Sind Sie verheiratet?**	zint zee fehr-HYE-raa-tet?
No, I'm . . .	**Nein, ich bin . . .**	nine, ikh bin . . .
• single.	• **ledig.**	• LAY-dikh.
• divorced.	• **geschieden.**	• geh-SHEE-den.
• a widow(er).	• **Witwe/Witwer.**	• VIT-veh/VIT-ve(r).
Are you traveling alone?	**Reisen Sie allein?**	RYE-zen zee ah-LINE?
I'm here with friends.	**Ich bin mit Freunden hier.**	ikh bin mit FROYN-den heer.
My family is traveling with me.	**Meine Familie reist auch mit.**	MINE-eh fah-MEEL-yeh reyst owkh mit.
Are you free this evening/ tomorrow?	**Sind Sie heute abend/morgen frei?**	zint zee HOY-teh AA-behnt/MOR-gen frye?
May I telephone you?	**Darf ich Sie anrufen?**	dahrf ikh zee AHN-roo-fen?
What's your phone number?	**Wie ist Ihre Telefon-num-mer?**	vee ist EE-reh tay-lay-FOHN-num-me(r)?
What's your address?	**Wie ist Ihre Adresse?**	vee ist EE-reh ah-DREHS-seh?

Can you join us for a drink this evening?	**Kommen Sie heute abend auf ein Gläschen zu uns?**	KOM-men zee HOY-teh AA-behnt owf ine GLEHS-khen tsoo uns.
With pleasure, thanks.	**Mit Vergnügen, danke.**	mit fehrk-NEW-gen, DAHN-keh.
Thanks very much, but I have no time.	**Vielen Dank, aber ich habe keine Zeit.**	FEE-len dahnk, AA-be(r) ikh HAA-beh KINE-eh tsite.
Would you like to go with us . . .	**Möchten Sie mit uns ——— gehen?**	MU(R)KH-ten zee mit uns ——— GAY-en?
• to the movies?	**• ins Kino**	• ins KEE-noh
• to a party?	**• zu einer Party**	• tsoo INE-e(r) PAAR-tee
Thanks for the invitation.	**Danke für die Einladung.**	DAHN-keh fewr dee INE-laa-dung.
Great. I'd love to come.	**Prima. Ich komme sehr gerne mit.**	PREE-mah. ikh KOM-meh zehr GEHR-neh mit.
May I bring a friend?	**Darf ich einen Freund/eine Freundin mitbringen?**	dahrf ikh INE-en froynt/INE-eh FROYN-din MIT-brin-gen?
Where shall we meet?	**Wo treffen wir uns?**	voh TREHF-fen veer uns?
I'll wait here for you.	**Ich warte hier auf Sie.**	ikh VAHR-teh heer owf zee.
I'll pick you up at your hotel.	**Ich hole Sie von Ihrem Hotel ab.**	ikh HOH-leh zee fon EE-rem ho-TEL ahp.
It's getting late.	**Es wird spät.**	ehs virt shpayt.
I must be getting back.	**Ich muß schon langsam zurück.**	ikh mus shohn LAHNG-sahm tsoo-REWK.
May I take you home?	**Darf ich Sie nach Hause bringen?**	dahrf ikh zee nahkh HOW-zeh BRIN-gen?
Thanks for everything.	**Vielen Dank für alles.**	FEE-len dahnk fewr AH-lehs.
It's been a wonderful evening.	**Es war ein wunderbarer Abend.**	ehs vahr ine VUN-de(r)-baa-re(r) AA-behnt.

53

THE FAMILY

I'm traveling without/with my family.	**Ich reise ohne die/mit der* Familie.**	ikh RYE-zeh OH-neh dee/mit dehr fah-MEEL-yeh.
My family lives in Milwaukee.	**Meine Familie wohnt in Milwaukee.**	MINE-eh fah-MEEL-yeh vohnt in "Milwaukee."
My family is spread out.	**Meine Familie wohnt weit auseinander.**	MINE-eh fah-MEEL-yeh vohnt vite ows-ine-AHN-de(r).
I have . . .	**Ich habe . . .**	ikh HAA-beh . . .
• a large/small family.	• **eine große/kleine Familie.**	• INE-eh GROHS-seh/KLINE-eh fah-MEEL-yeh.
• many (German) relatives.	• **viele (deutsche) Verwandte.**	• FEE-leh (DOY-cheh) fehr-VAHN-teh.
• a husband/a wife.	• **einen Mann/eine Frau.**	• INE-en mahn/INE-eh frow.
• two children.	• **zwei Kinder.**	• tsvye KIN-de(r).
• a daughter/two daughters.	• **eine Tochter/zwei Töchter.**	• INE-eh TOHKH-te(r)/tsvye TU(R)KH-te(r).
• a son/two sons.	• **einen Sohn/zwei Söhne.**	• INE-nen zohn/tsvye ZU(R)-neh.
• a baby.	• **ein Baby.**	• ine BAY-bee.
• a brother/two brothers.	• **einen Bruder/zwei Brüder.**	• INE-en BROO-de(r)/tsvye BREW-de(r).
• a sister/two sisters.	• **eine Schwester/zwei Schwestern.**	• INE-eh SHVEHS-te(r)/tsvye SHVEHS-te(r)n.
• three siblings.	• **drei Geschwister.**	• drye geh-SHVIS-te(r).
• a mother/ a father/ parents.	• **eine Mutter/ einen Vater/ Eltern.**	• INE-eh MUT-te(r)/INE-en FAA-te(r)/EHL-tern.

*When referring to relatives and parts of the body, German speakers often use the definite article der, die, das (the) instead of the possessive pronouns mein, dein (my, your), etc.

• a grandmother.	• eine Großmutter.	• INE-eh GROHS-MUT-te(r).
• a grandfather.	• einen Großvater.	• INE-en GROHS-faa-te(r).
• grandparents.	• Großeltern.	• GROHS-ehl-tern.
• a grandson/granddaughter.	• einen Enkel/eine Enkelin.	• INE-en EHNG-kel/INE-eh EHNG-keh-lin.
• an aunt/two aunts.	• eine Tante/zwei Tanten.	• INE-eh TAHN-teh/tsvye TAHN-ten.
• an uncle/two uncles.	• einen Onkel/zwei Onkel.	• INE-en ONG-kel/tsvye ONG-kel.
• a cousin (male)	• einen Vetter.	• INE-en FEHT-te(r).
• a cousin (female)	• eine Kusine.	• INE-eh koo-ZEE-neh.
• a niece/a nephew.	• eine Nichte/einen Neffen.	• INE-eh NIKH-teh/INE-en NEH-fehn.
How old are your children?	Wie alt sind Ihre Kinder?	vee aalt zint EE-reh KIN-de(r)?
Peter is five years old.	Peter ist fünf Jahre alt.	PAY-te(r) ist fewnf YAA-reh aalt.
He's older/younger than Paul.	Er ist älter/jünger als Paul.	ehr ist EHL-te(r)/YEWN-ge(r) ahls powl.
He's my oldest/youngest son.	Er ist mein ältester/jüngster Sohn.	ehr ist mine EHL-tehs-te(r)/YEWN-gste(r) zohn.

AT HOME

We have a/an . . .	Wir haben . . .	veer HAA-ben . . .
• apartment/flat.	• eine Wohnung.	• INE-eh VOH-nung.
• condominium.	• eine Eigentums-wohnung.	• INE-eh EYE-gen-tooms-voh-nung.
• house.	• ein Haus.	• ine hows.
• townhouse/row house.	• ein Reihenhaus.	• ine RYE-en-hows.
• vacation house.	• ein Ferienhaus.	• FEHR-yen-hows.
Make yourself at home.	Fühlen Sie sich wie zu Hause.	FEW-len zee zikh vee tsoo HOW-zeh.

Please, take a seat.	Setzen Sie sich, bitte.	ZEHT-sen zee zikh, BIT-teh.
Make yourself comfortable.	Machen Sie es sich bequem.	MAHKH-en zee ehs zikh beh-KVAYM.
What a lovely house you have!	Was für ein schönes Haus haben Sie!	vahs fewr ine SHU(R)-nehs hows HAA-ben zee!
We also like this neighborhood a lot.	Uns gefällt auch diese Nachbarschaft sehr.	uns geh-FEHLT owkh DEE-zeh NAHKH-baar-shahft zehr.
At my house . . .	Bei mir . . .	bye meer . . .
At your house . . .	Bei Ihnen/bei Dir . . .	bye EE-nen/bye deer . . .
At our house . . .	Bei uns* . . .	bye uns . . .
Would you like to see the house?	Möchten Sie das Haus sehen?	MU(R)KH-ten zee dahs hows ZAY-en?
Here is . . .	Hier ist . . .	heer ist . . .
• the living room.	• das Wohnzimmer.	• dahs VOHN-tsim-me(r).
• the dining room.	• das Speisezimmer.	• dahs SHPYE-zeh-tsim-me(r).
• the kitchen.	• die Küche.	• die KEW-kheh.
• the bedroom.	• das Schlafzimmer.	• dahs SHLAHF-tsim-me(r).
• the bathroom.	• das Badezimmer.	• dahs BAA-deh-tsim-me(r).
• the attic.	• der Dachboden.	• dehr DAHKH-boh-den.
• the cellar.	• der Keller.	• dehr KEHL-le(r).
• the study.	• das Arbeitszimmer.	• dahs AHR-bites-tsim-me(r).
• the sofa.	• das Sofa.	• dahs ZOH-fah.
• the armchair.	• der Sessel.	• dehr SEHS-sel.
• the table.	• der Tisch.	• dehr tish.
• the chair.	• der Stuhl.	• dehr shtool.
• the lamp.	• die Lampe.	• dee LAHM-peh.

*This and the preceding two expressions can be understood in a larger geographic sense, that is, ''at home in our country,'' ''in our hometown,'' ''in our neighborhood.''

• the door.	• **die Tür.**	• dee tewr.
• the rug.	• **der Teppich.**	• dehr TEHP-pikh.
• the carpeting.	• **der Teppichboden.**	• dehr TEHP-pikh-boh-den.
• the ceiling.	• **die Decke.**	• dee DEH-keh.
• the floor.	• **der Boden.**	• dehr BOH-den.
Thanks for inviting us to your home.	**Danke für die Einladung, Sie zu Hause zu besuchen.**	DAHN-keh fewr dee INE-lah-dung, zee tsoo HOW-zeh tsoo beh-ZOO-khen.
You must come to visit us sometime.	**Sie müssen uns mal besuchen.**	zee MEWS-sen uns maal beh-ZOO-khen.

TALKING ABOUT LANGUAGE

Do you speak . . .	**Sprechen Sie* . . .**	SHPREH-khen zee . . .
• English?	• **Englisch?**	• EHN-glish?
• Spanish?	• **Spanisch?**	• SHPAHN-ish?
• French?	• **Französisch?**	• frahn-ZU(R)-zish?
I speak only English.	**Ich spreche nur Englisch.**	ikh SHPREH-kheh noor EHN-glish.
I speak only a little German.	**Ich spreche nur ein bißchen Deutsch.**	ikh SHPREH-kheh noor ine BIS-khen doych.
My German is bad/weak.	**Mein Deutsch ist schlecht/ schwach.**	mine doych ist shlehkht/shvahkh.
That's not true. You speak very well.	**Das stimmt nicht. Sie sprechen sehr gut.**	dahs shtimt nikht. zee SHPREH-khen zehr goot.
I'm trying to learn German.	**Ich versuche, Deutsch zu lernen.**	ikh fehr-ZOO-kheh, doych tsoo LEHR-nen.
I (don't) understand.	**Ich verstehe (nicht).**	ikh fehr-SHTEH-eh (nikht).
I understand more than I can speak.	**Ich verstehe mehr als ich sprechen kann.**	ikh fehr-SHTEH-eh mehr ahls ikh SHPREH-khen kahn.

*For a list of languages, see page 172.

Can you understand me?	**Können Sie mich verstehen?**	KU(R)-nen zee mikh fehr-SHTAY-en?
Repeat that, please.	**Wiederholen Sie das, bitte.**	vee-de(r)-HOH-len zee dahs BIT-teh.
Please speak more slowly.	**Bitte, sprechen Sie langsamer.**	BIT-teh SHPRE-khen zee LAHNG-zahm-me(r).
What do you call this/that in German?	**Wie heißt dies/das auf deutsch?**	vee heyst dees/dahs owf doych?
What does that mean?	**Was bedeutet das?**	vahs beh-DOY-tet dahs?
How do you say . . .	**Wie sagt man . . .**	vee zahgt mahn . . .
• in German?	• **auf deutsch?**	• owf doych?
• in English?	• **auf englisch?**	• owf EHN-glish?
Could you translate this for me/us?	**Könnten Sie mir/uns das übersetzen?**	KU(R)N-ten zee meer/uns dahs ew-be(r)-ZEHT-sen?
Is there anyone here who speaks English?	**Gibt es hier jemanden, der Englisch spricht?**	gipt ehs heer YAY-mahn-ten, dehr EHN-glish shprikht?

6/DINING OUT

The selection of restaurants and eating places in the German-speaking countries has become increasingly international during the postwar period, and most of the larger cities now offer an impressive array of enticing exotic cuisines, ranging from those of other Western European countries (especially France, Italy, Greece, and Spain) to the Balkans, the Slavic countries, the Middle East, the Far East, and Latin America. In some cities, one may even have to search for a traditional restaurant featuring *die deutsche Küche* (German cuisine), but in most places they still abound, and the better ones, even for the traveler with a sophisticated palate, are well worth a visit and usually quite reasonably priced.

Traditional German cooking tends to be rich and hearty—its critics would say heavy—with healthy portions of beef, pork, and potatoes. But Germans, like people in the rest of the world, are becoming more diet conscious, and the trend toward low-fat, healthy fare is pronounced. As elsewhere in Europe, every region has its own specialties, a must for the culinary adventurer, and most towns boast their own *Brauerei* (brewery) or *Kellerei* (wine cellars). German beer, bread, and sausage are arguably the best in the world, and the variety of these as well as other traditional staples like smoked and pickled meats and fish is quite remarkable. For lovers of venison and other game dishes, Germany will be a special treat. *Guten Appetit!** (Enjoy your meal).

*Diners exchange this mealtime greeting as they begin the meal. In Austria and Bavaria, the greeting *Mahlzeit* is exchanged both before and after the meal.

DIALOGUE: AT THE RESTAURANT (*IM RESTAURANT*)

Kellnerin:	**Möchten Sie jetzt bestellen?**	MU(R)KH-ten zee yehtzt beh-SHTEHL-len?
Gast:	**Ja, gibt es eine hiesige Spezialität?**	yaa, gipt ehs INE-eh HEE-zi-geh shpeh-tsyah-li-TAYT?

Kellnerin:	**Ich empfehle Ihnen den Hasenpfeffer.**	ikh ehm-PFAY-leh EE-nen dehn HAA-zen-pfehf-fe(r).
Gast:	**Schön. Das nehme ich.**	shu(r)n. dahs NAY-meh ikh.
Kellnerin:	**Etwas zu trinken?**	EHT-vahs tsoo TRIN-ken?
Gast:	**Ja, bringen Sie mir bitte ein Glas Mineralwasser.**	yaa, BRIN-gen zee meer BIT-teh ine glaas mi-neh-RAAL-vahs-e(r).

. . . .

Waitress:	Would you like to order now?
Guest:	Yes, is there a local speciality?
Waitress:	I recommend the spicy rabbit stew.
Guest:	Fine, I'll take that.
Waitress:	Something to drink?
Guest:	Yes, please bring me a glass of mineral water.

TYPES OF EATING AND DRINKING PLACES

Bierhalle [BEER-hahl-eh]

Beer hall serving *Bier vom Faß* (beer from the barrel), hot meals, cold cuts, sausages, and salads. The most famous are located in Munich, home of the world's largest annual beer festival, the *Oktoberfest,* beginning in late September.

Bierstube [BEER-shtoo-beh]

Similar to an American tavern or an English pub, featuring local beers, other alcoholic beverages, and a limited menu of hot and cold dishes.

Café [kah-FAY]

Coffee shop serving coffee and tea in addition to pastries, ice cream, snacks, and drinks. The Swiss version is called *tearoom,* the Austrian, *Kaffeehaus* (KAH-fay-hows). Vienna is famous for its long, rich tradition of *Kaffeehauskultur* (coffee house culture).

Gasthaus/Gasthof [GAHST-hows/GAHST-hohf]

Rustic inn, usually in the country, featuring local specialities, and home-style cooking. Lodging is sometimes also offered. The Austrian equivalent is referred to as a *Beisel* (BYE-zel).

Kneipe [KNYE-peh]

Similar to the *Bierstube,* common in the cities and towns of Northern Germany. Those frequented by students are called *Studentenkneipen.* Berlin has a very famous *Kneipenkultur.*

Konditorei [kon-dee-toh-RYE]

Pastry and sweet shop, usually attached to a salon serving coffee and tea with the pastries. A variation called the *Milchbar* (MILKH-baar) or, in Austria, *Milchstübl* (MILKH-shtew-bil), serves flavored milk drinks and yogurt dishes with pastries.

Raststätte/Rasthof [RAHST-shteht-teh/RAHST-hohf]

Wayside restaurant with lodge, located right off the *Autobahn* or main highway.

61

Ratskeller [RAHTS-kehl-le(r)]

Cellar restaurant in the *Rathaus* (town hall), usually an old, carefully restored building. Often the best place to sample local specialities.

Restaurant [rehs-to-RAHNT]

Urban eating place, usually featuring an extensive menu including both local and foreign specialities. Also called *Gaststätte*.

Schnellbuffet [SHNEHL-bew-fay]

Snack bar, often with self service à la McDonalds, which, along with other fast food establishments, is making considerable inroads all over Europe.

Schnellimbiβ [SHNEHL-im-bis]

Snack bar, also called *Würselstand* (sausage stand) or even "Snack Bar," located outside, serving beer, *Pommes frites* (french fries), sausages, and other meat snacks.

Weinstube [VINE-shtoo-beh]

Similar to the *Bierstube,* but featuring local wines instead of beer. The Austrian version, *Heuriger* (literally: of this year), serves new, rather potent wine and is identified by a wreath of vines over the door. The Viennese suburb of *Grinzing* is famous for its colorful and cozy *Heurige*.

Wirtshaus [VIRTS-hows]

Another name for *Gasthaus*. The proprietor is referred to as *der Wirt*.

MEALTIMES AND EATING HABITS

Frühstück [FREW-shtewk]   Breakfast is served from 7 to
10 A.M. and is usually included
in the price of a hotel room. It
can range from the simple
"continental" style (bread,
butter, jam, and coffee/tea) to
more elaborate buffets,
including fresh fruit, eggs, and
cold cuts.

Mittagessen [MIT-taak-ehs-sen]   Lunch (from 12 to 2 P.M.) is the
main meal of the day and
usually includes soup, meat or
fish, and vegetables.

Kaffee [KAH-fay]   This afternoon snack from 4 to
5 P.M. is a weekend tradition,
especially Sundays, and usually
consists of coffee/tea and cake
or pastries, but can also be
more substantial, including
bread, cheese, and cold cuts. It
also goes by the names
Vesperbrot, Jause (in Austria),
and *Zvieri* (in Switzerland).

Abendessen [AA-behnt-ehs-sen]   Dinner is served from 6 to 9
P.M. and is generally a light
meal of bread, cold cuts, salad,
and cheese. Restaurants,
however, will still serve full
course meals in the evening.

FINDING A RESTAURANT/MAKING RESERVATIONS

I'm hungry/thirsty.	**Ich habe Hunger/Durst.**	ikh HAA-beh HUN-ge(r)/durst.

63

Can you recommend a good restaurant?	**Können Sie mir ein gutes Restaurant empfehlen?**	KU(R)-nen zee meer ine GOO-tes rehs-to-RAHNT ehm-PFAY-len?
I'm looking for a(n) —— restaurant.	**Ich suche ein —— Restaurant.**	ikh ZOO-kheh ine —— rehs-to-RAHNT.
• inexpensive	• **preiswertes**	• PRICE-vehr-tes
• first class	• **erstklassiges**	• EHRST-klahs-ig-ehs
What's the name of the restaurant?	**Wie heißt das Restaurant?**	vee heyst dahs rehs-to-RAHNT?
How do you get there?	**Wie kommt man dahin?**	vee komt mahn dah-HIN?
Do I need reservations?	**Braucht man eine Vorbestellung?**	browkht mahn INE-eh FOR-beh-shteh-lung?
I would like to reserve a table . . .	**Ich möchte einen Tisch —— bestellen.**	ikh MU(R)KH-teh INE-en tish —— beh-SHTEHL-en.
• for four persons.	• **für vier Personen**	• fewr feer pehr-ZOH-nen
• for this evening.	• **für heute abend**	• fewr HOY-teh AA-behnt
• for 8 P.M.	• **für acht Uhr**	• fewr ahkht oor
• near the window.	• **am Fenster**	• ahm FEHN-ste(r)
• outside.	• **im Freien**	• im FRYE-en
• on the terrace.	• **auf der Terrasse**	• owf dehr teh-RAAS-seh
• in the no-smoking section.*	• **in der Nicht-raucherecke**	• in dehr NIKHT-rowkh-e(r)-eh-keh.

*In Europe, restaurants with no-smoking sections are less common than in the United States.

AT THE RESTAURANT/ORDERING

| Waiter/Waitress! | **Herr Ober/ Fräulein, bitte!** | hehr OH-be(r)/FROY-line, BIT-teh |
| The menu, please. | **Die Speisekarte, bitte.** | dee SHPYE-zeh-kahr-teh, BIT-teh. |

64

What would you recommend?	Was würden Sie uns empfehlen?	vahs VEWR-den zee uns ehm-PFAY-len?
Do you have . . .	Haben Sie . . .	HAA-ben zee . . .
• local dishes?	• hiesige Gerichte?	• HEE-zi-geh geh-RIKH-teh?
• a speciality of the day?	• ein Tagesgericht?	• ine TAA-gehs-geh-rikht?
• a set menu of the day?	• ein Tagesgedeck?	• ine TAA-gehs-geh-dehk?
We're ready to order.	Wir möchten bestellen.	veer MU(R)KH-ten beh-SHTEHL-len.
We need more time.	Wir brauchen mehr Zeit.	veer BROW-khen mehr tsite.
We'd like something to drink/eat.	Wir hätten gern etwas zu trinken/essen.	veer HEH-ten gehrn EHT-vahs tsoo TRIN-ken/EHS-sen.
To begin with I'd like . . .	Als erstes möchte ich . . .	ahls EHR-stehs MU(R)KH-teh ikh . . .
Next . . .	Als nächstes . . .	ahls NAYKH-stehs . . .
And finally . . .	Und zum Schluß . . .	unt tsoom shlus . . .
That's all.	Das wäre alles.	dahs VAY-reh AH-lehs.
Will it take long?	Wird es lange dauern?	virt ehs LAHNG-eh DOW-ern?
We're in a hurry.	Wir haben es eilig.	veer HAA-ben ehs EYE-likh.
Where can I wash my hands?	Wo kann ich mir die Hände waschen?	voh kahn ikh meer dee HEHN-deh VAHSH-en?
Where are the restrooms?	Wo sind die Toiletten?	woh zint dee toy-LEHT-ten?

TABLE ACCESSORIES AND CONDIMENTS

We need another . . .	Wir brauchen noch . . .	veer BROW-khen nohkh . . .
• glass.	• ein Glas.	• ine glaas.
• cup.	• eine Tasse.	• INE-eh TAHS-seh.
• plate.	• einen Teller.	• INE-en TEHL-le(r).
• knife.	• ein Messer.	• ine MEHS-se(r).
• fork.	• eine Gabel.	• INE-eh GAA-bel.

65

• spoon.	• **einen Löffel.**	• INE-en LU(R)f-fel.
• set of silverware.	• **ein Besteck.**	• ine beh-SHTEHK.
• napkin.	• **eine Serviette.**	• INE-eh sehr-VYEH-teh.
• ashtray.	• **einen Aschenbecher.**	• INE-en AH-shen-behkh-e(r).
Could you bring me/us some . . .	• **Könnten Sie mir/uns etwas ⸺ bringen?**	• KU(R)N-ten zee meer/uns EHT-vahs ⸺ BRIN-gen?
• tap water?*	• **Leitungswasser**	• LYE-tungs-vahs-se(r)
• bread?	• **Brot**	• broht
• butter?	• **Butter**	• BUT-te(r)
• salt?	• **Salz**	• zahlts
• pepper?	• **Pfeffer**	• PFEHF-fe(r)
• seasoning?	• **Gewürz**	• geh-VEWRTS
• mustard?	• **Senf**	• zehnf
• oil and vinegar?	• **Öl und Essig**	• u(r)l unt EHS-sikh
• sugar?	• **Zucker**	• TSU-ke(r)
• saccharin?	• **Sacharin**	• zah-kah-REEN
• lemon?	• **Zitrone**	• tsi-TROH-neh
• horseradish?	• **Meerrettich**	• MEHR-reht-tikh
• ketchup?	• **Tomatenketchup**	• to-MAA-ten-keh-chup

*Water is not generally supplied in European restaurants, and if you order a glass of water, you'll be charged for mineral water. Always ask if the tap water is drinkable: *Kann man das Leitungswasser trinken?*

SPECIAL REQUESTS

I'm on a diet.	**Ich mache eine Diät.**	ikh MAH-kheh INE-eh dee-AYT.
Do you have vegetarian dishes?	**Haben Sie vegetarische Gerichte?**	HAA-ben zee veh-geh-TAH-rish-eh geh-RIKH-teh?
Are there dishes for diabetics?	**Gibt es Gerichte für Diabetiker?**	gipt ehs geh-RIKH-teh fewr dee-ah-BAY-ti-ke(r)?
I don't eat pork.	**Ich esse kein Schweinefleisch.**	ikh EHS-eh kine SHVINE-eh-flyshe.
I can't eat anything spicy.	**Ich darf nichts scharfes essen.**	ikh dahrf nikhts SHAHR-fes EHS-en.

I shouldn't eat anything containing . . .	**Ich soll nichts essen, was —— enthält.**	ich zol nikhts EHS-sen, vahs —— ehnt-HEHLT.
• salt/sugar.	• **Salz/Zucker**	• zahlts/TSU-ke(r)
• fat/flour.	• **Fett/Mehl**	• feht/mayl
• milk/alcohol.	• **Milch/Alkohol**	• milkh/AHL-koh-hol

PHRASES YOU'LL HEAR

Haben Sie schon einen Tisch bestellt?	HAA-ben zee shohn INE-en tish beh-SHTEHLT?	Did you make reservations?
Wieviele Personen?	vee-FEEL-eh pehr-ZOH-nen?	How many people
Möchten Sie hier sitzen?	MU(R)KH-ten zee heer ZIT-tsen?	Would you like to sit here?
Brauchen Sie einen Kinderstuhl?	BROW-khen zee INE-en KIN-de(r)-shtool?	Do you need a high chair?
Haben Sie schon gewählt?	HAA-ben zee shohn geh-VAYLT?	Are you ready to order?
Was wünschen Sie?	vahs VEWN-shen zee?	What would you like?
Möchten Sie Getränke bestellen?	MU(R)KH-ten zee geh-TREHN-keh beh-SHTEHL-en?	Would you like to order drinks?
Heute ist —— zu empfehlen.	HOY-teh ist——tsoo ehm-PFAY-len.	Today I recommend . . .
Was hätten Sie gern dazu?	vahs HEHT-ten zee gehrn dah-TSOO?	What would you like with it?
Und anschließend?	unt AHN-shlee-sehnt?	And to follow?
Ihr Essen kommt gleich.	eer EHS-en komt glyekh.	Your meal is coming right away.
Was kann ich Ihnen noch bringen?	vahs kahn ikh EE-nen nohkh BRIN-gen?	What else can I bring you?
Hätten Sie gern eine Nachspeise?	HEH-ten zee gehrn INE-eh NAHKH-shpye-zeh?	Would you like to have a dessert?

67

Ist alles in Ordnung?	ist AH-lehs in ORT-nung?	Is everything all right?
Hat's geschmeckt?	hahts geh-SHMEHKT?	Did you enjoy your meal?
Möchten Sie zusammen bezahlen?	MU(R)KH-ten zee tsoo-ZAHM-men beh-TSAA-len?	Would you like a single bill?
Ist hier noch frei?*	ist heer nohkh frye?	Is this seat free?

*In crowded Kneipen and Cafés, strangers may ask to share your table with this question.

COMPLAINTS (REKLAMATIONEN)
May you never have occasion to use these phrases!

Something is missing.	Es fehlt etwas.	ehs faylt EHT-vahs.
Please bring us another glass/set of silverware.	Bringen Sie uns bitte noch ein Glas/Besteck.	BRIN-gen zee uns BIT-teh nohkh ine glaas/beh-SHTEHK.
The table cloth isn't clean/is dirty.	Das Tischtuch ist nicht sauber/ist schmutzig.	dahs TISH-tookh ist nikht ZOW-be(r)/ist SHMUT-tsikh.
Did you forget the soup/drinks?	Haben Sie die Suppe/Getränke vergessen?	HAA-ben zee dee ZOOP-peh/geh-TREHN-keh fehr-GEHS-sen?
There must be a mistake.	Es muß ein Irrtum sein.	ehs mus ine IR-toom zine.
I didn't order this.	Das habe ich nicht bestellt.	dahs HAA-be ikh nikht beh-SHTEHLT.
Could you bring me something else?	Können Sie mir dafür etwas anderes bringen?	KU(R)-nen zee meer daa-FEWR EHT-vahs AHN-deh-rehs BRIN-gen?
The soup/food is cold.	Die Suppe/das Essen ist kalt.	dee ZOOP-peh/dahs EHS-sen ist kahlt.
The butter/milk isn't fresh.	Die Milch/Butter ist nicht frisch.	dee milkh/BUT-te(r) ist nikht frish.

68

THE BILL *(DIE RECHNUNG)*

The bill, please.	**Die Rechnung, bitte.**	dee REHKH-nung, BIT-teh.
May I pay?	**Darf ich zahlen?**	dahrf ikh TSAA-len?
We'd like separate checks.	**Wir möchten getrennt bezahlen.**	veer MU(R)KH-ten geh-TREHNT beh-TSAA-len.
Is service included?	**Ist die Bedienung inbegriffen?**	ist dee beh-DEE-nung IN-beh-grif-en?
Do you accept credit cards/traveler's checks?	**Nehmen Sie Kreditkarten/ Reiseschecks?**	NAY-men zee kray-DEET-kahr-ten/RYE-zeh-shehks?
That is for you.*	**Das ist für Sie.**	dahs ist fewr zee.
The meal was delicious.	**Das Essen war vorzüglich.**	dahs EHS-sen vahr for-TSEWG-likh.
And the service was excellent.	**Und die Bedienung war ausgezeichnet.**	unt dee beh-DEE-nung wahr OWS-geh-tsyekh-neht.

*See page 17 for information on tipping.

DECIPHERING THE MENU

Most restaurants and other eating places will post their *Speisekarte* (menu) outside, so guests can orient themselves before entering. In addition to the usual à la carte entries, many restaurants offer one or more set meals, *Tagesgedeck* or *Tagesmenü.* These meals change daily, include several courses, often feature local dishes, and are usually favorably priced. Restaurants offering traditional fare may announce this with phrases such as *gut bürgerliche Küche* (good, middle-class cooking—often quite refined and elegant) or *gepflegte Küche* (elegant, well-prepared cuisine). The following is a list of common menu terms and phrases with their English equivalents.

Tageskarte	TAA-gehs-kahr-teh	Daily menu
Tagesmenü/ -gedeck	TAA-gehs-meh-new/ -geh-dehk	Set meal of the day
Tagesgericht	TAA-gehs-geh-rikht	Dish of the day
Tagessuppe	TAA-gehs-zoop-peh	Soup of the day

Spezialität des Hauses	shpeh-tsyah-li-TAYT dehs HOW-zehs	Speciality of the house
Heute zu empfehlen	HOY-teh tsoo ehm-PFAY-len	Recommended dishes
Der Küchenchef empfiehlt . . .	dehr KEW-khen-shehf ehm-PFEELT . . .	Our chef recommends . . .
Hausgemacht	HOWS-geh-mahkht	Homemade
Nach ——— Art	nahkh ——— ahrt	In the ——— style
Nach Wahl	nahkh vaal	For your selection
Fertige Speisen	FEHR-ti-geh SHPYE-zen	Prepared meals (not to order)
Nur auf Bestellung	noor owf beh-SHTEHL-lung	Made to order
. . . Minuten Wartezeit	. . . mi-NOO-ten VAHR-teh-tsite	Preparation time
Extraaufschlag	EHK-strah-owf-shlahk	Additional charge
. . . im Preis inbegriffen	. . . im price IN-beh-grif-fen	Included in the price
Alle Preise sind inklusive Bedienung und Mehrwertsteuer (Mwst)	AH-leh PRYE-zeh zint IN-kloo-see-veh beh-DEE-nung unt MEHR-vehrt-shtoy-e(r)	All prices include service and value added tax (VAT).

TYPICAL MENU CATEGORIES

These are the usual headings in the order you'll find them in most menus.

Vorspeisen und kalte Platten	FOR-shpye-zen unt KAHL-teh PLAHT-ten	Appetizers and Cold Cuts
Suppen und Eintopfgerichte	ZOOP-pen unt INE-topf-geh-rikh-teh	Soups and Stews
Hauptgerichte	HOWPT-geh-rikh-teh	Main Dishes
Fleischgerichte	FLYSHE-geh-rikh-teh	Meat Dishes
Fisch und Meeresfrüchte/ Vom Meer	fish unt MAY-rehs-frewkh-teh/fom mayr	Fish and Seafood/From the Sea
Wild und Geflügel	vilt unt geh-FLEW-gel	Game and Poultry

Beilagen, Neben- und Kleingerichte	BYE-laa-gen, NAY-ben- unt KLINE-geh-rikh- teh	Accompaniments, Side and Small Dishes
Salate	zah-LAA-teh	Salads
Gemüsegerichte	geh-MEW-zeh-geh- rikh-teh	Vegetable Dishes
Reis- und Kartoffelgerichte	rice- unt kahr-TOF-el- geh-rikh-teh	Rice and Potato Dishes
Teigwaren und Nudelgerichte	TIKE-vaa-ren unt NOO- del-geh-rikh-teh	Pasta and Noodle Dishes
Eierspeisen	EYE-e(r)-shpye-zen	Egg Dishes
Wurst und Käse	voorst unt KAY-zeh	Sausages and Cheese
Nachtisch/Süß- speisen	NAHKH-tish/ZEWS- shpye-zen	Desserts
Gebäck	geh-BEHK	Pastries
Eis/Glacé	ice/GLAH-say	Ice Cream
Obst und Nüsse	opst unt NEWS-seh	Fruit and Nuts
Getränke	geh-TREHN-keh	Beverages/Drinks
Wein und Bier	vine unt beer	Wine and Beer
Andere alkoholische Getränke	AHN-deh-reh ahl-koh- HOH-lish-eh geh- TREHN-keh	Other Alcoholic Drinks
Alkoholfreie Getränke	ahl-koh-hol-FRYE-eh geh-TREHN-keh	Nonalcoholic Drinks
Warme Getränke	VAAR-meh geh- TREHN-keh	Hot Beverages

METHODS OF COOKING AND PREPARATION

For meat:

gebacken	geh-BAH-ken	baked
geröstet	geh-RU(R)S-tet	roasted
geschmort	geh-SHMOHRT	braised or stewed
gekocht	geh-KOKHT	boiled
in der Pfanne gebraten	in dehr PFAH-neh geh- BRAA-ten	pan fried
im Ofen gebraten	im OH-fen geh-BRAA- ten	oven roasted
gegrillt	geh-GRILT	grilled, broiled
vom Spieß	fom shpees	from the spit

71

gedämpft	geh-DEHMPFT	steamed, stewed
gefüllt	geh-FEWLT	stuffed
blutig	BLOO-tikh	rare, underdone
mittel	MIT-tel	medium
gut durchbraten	goot durkh-BRAA-ten	well-done

For fish:

blau	blow	boiled in bouillon
in Butter geschwenkt	in BUT-te(r) geh-SHVEHNKT	sautéed in butter
im schwimmenden Fett	im SHVIM-en-den feht	deep fried
gebacken	geh-BAH-ken	baked
paniert	pah-NEERT	breaded
mariniert	mah-ri-NEERT	marinated
geräuchert	geh-ROY-khert	smoked

TYPICAL DISHES

The following is a representative listing of well-known dishes served in Germany, Austria, and Switzerland.

Appetizers, Soups, Salads, Vegetables, and Main Dishes

Aal in Gelee [aal in zheh-LAY]	Eel in aspic
Aalsuppe [AAL-zoop-peh]	Eel soup
Ausgebackene Spätzli [OWS-geh-bah-keh-neh SHPEHTST-lee]	Fried dumplings with egg sauce (Swiss)
Bauernfrühstück [BOW-ern-frew-shtewk]	Scrambled eggs with bacon, tomatoes, onions, potatoes
Bauernschmaus [BOW-ern-shmows]	Bacon, pork, sausage, dumplings, with sauerkraut and potatoes (Austrian)
Bauernsuppe [BOW-ern-zoop-peh]	Cabbage and sausage soup
Bayerisches Kraut [BYE-rish-es krowt]	Fresh cabbage cooked with apples, sugar, and wine
Berliner Bouletten/Frikadellen [behr-LEEN-e(r) boo-LEHT-ten/fri-kah-DEHL-len]	Fried meat ball patties/Croquettes (Berlin specialty)

Bismarckheringe [BIS-mahrk-hay-rin-geh] — Marinated herrings with onions

Bohnensuppe [BOH-nen-zoop-peh] — Thick bean soup with bacon

Bouillon/Fleisch-/Hühner-brühe [BOO-yohn/flyshe-/HEW-ne(r)-brew-eh] — Clear soup/Beef-/Chicken broth

Brathähnchen/-hendl [BRAAT-hehn-khen/-hehn-del] — Roast chicken

Bratheringe [BRAAT-hay-rin-geh] — Fried sour herring

Bratkartoffeln [BRAAT-kahr-tof-eln] — Fried potatoes

Bratwurst [BRAAT-voorst] — Fried pork sausage

Bündnerfleisch [BEWND-ne(r)-flyshe] — Thinly sliced, air-dried beef (Swiss)

Dampfnudeln [DAHMPF-noo-deln] — Steamed noodles

Eisbein [ICE-bine] — Pickled pig's knuckle

Emmentaler Schnitzel [EHM-men-taa-le(r) SHNIT-tsel] — Veal cutlets fried between slices of Emmentaler cheese

Entenbraten [EHN-ten-braa-ten] — Roast duck

Erdäpfelknödel [EHR-dehp-fel-knu(r)-del] — Potato and semolina-dumplings (Austrian)

Falscher Hase/Hackbraten [FAHL-she(r) HAA-zeh/HAHK-braa-ten] — Meatloaf

Faschiertes [fah-SHEER-tes] — Minced meat (Austrian)

Fischsuppe [FISH-zoop-peh] — Fish soup

Fondue [fon-DEW] — Melted cheese with white wine, kirsch, and garlic; diners dip bits of bread (or meat) into the pot of cheese

Forelle blau [fo-REHL-leh blow] — Trout boiled in bouillon

Forelle Steiermark [fo-REHL-leh SHTYE-e(r)-mahrk] — Trout fillet with white sauce and bacon strips (Austrian)

Gänsebraten [GEHN-zeh-braa-ten] — Roast goose

Gefülltes Kraut [geh-FEWL-tes krowt] — Cabbage leaves stuffed with ground meat, eggs, rice and bread crumbs; called *Kohlroulade* in Austria

Gemischter Salat [geh-MISH-te(r) zah-LAAT]

Mixed salad

Gemüseplatte [geh-MEW-zeh-plaht-teh]

Mixed vegetables

Geschnetzeltes [geh-SHNEHT-tsehl-tes]

Braised chipped veal in thick white wine sauce (Swiss)

Geselchtes [geh-ZEHLKH-tes]

Smoked, salted pork

Grießnockerlnsuppe [GREES-nok-ehrln-zoop-peh]

Semolina-dumpling soup (Austrian)

Grüner Salat [GREW-ne(r) zah-LAAT]

Fresh lettuce salad with oil and vinegar

Gulasch/Gulaschsuppe [GOO-lahsh/ -zoop-peh]

Beef stew in spicy paprika gravy/Soup version of dish

Gurkensalat [GOOR-ken-zah-laat]

Cucumber salad

Hammelbraten [HAHM-el-braa-ten]

Roast mutton

Hasenpfeffer [HAA-zen-pfehf-fe(r)]

Spicy rabbit stew

Hirschbraten [HEERSH-braa-ten]

Roast venison

Hühnerbraten [HEW-ne(r)-braa-ten]

Roast chicken

Jungfernbraten [YUNG-fehrn-braa-ten]

Roast suckling pig

Kaiserfleisch [KYE-ze(r)-flyshe]

Boiled, smoked pork (Austrian)

Kalbsbraten/-brust [KAHLPS-braaten/-broost]

Roast veal/Breast of veal

Karpfen in Bier [KAHRP-fen in beer]

Carp poached in beer and red wine with onions, and peppercorns

Kartoffelklöße/-knödel [kahr-TOF-fel-klews-eh/-knu(r)-del]

Potato dumplings; *Knödel* is the Austrian word for dumpling

Kartoffelpitte [kahr-TOF-fel-pit-teh]

Baked potatoes with pears, milk, and bacon (Swiss)

Kasseler Rippenspeer [KAHS-eh-le(r) RIP-pen-shpayr]

Pickled, smoked pork chops

Krautsalat [KROWT-zah-laat]

Cabbage salad with caraway seeds

74

Krenfleisch [KRAYN-flyshe]	Pork (headcheese) with horseradish and shredded vegetables (Austrian)
Labskaus [LAAPS-kows]	Thick meat stew with mashed potatoes and vegetables; sailors' version includes herring and onions
Leberkäs [LAY-be(r)-kays]	Meatloaf made of pork liver
Leberknödelsuppe [LAY-be(r)-knu(r)-del-zoop-peh]	Beef broth with liver dumplings (Austria)
Leipziger Allerlei [LIPE-tsig-e(r) AH-lehr-lye]	Vegetable stew with peas, carrots, cauliflower, asparagus, and cabbage
Matjeshering/-filet [MAH-tyehs-hay-ring/-fi-lay]	Salted, young herring in thick sauce with new potatoes
Maultasche [MOWL-tahsh-eh]	Bite-sized pasta sacks filled with veal pork and spinach (Swabian speciality)
Ochsenschwanzsuppe [OKS-en-shvahnts-zoop-peh]	Oxtail soup
Pfannkuchen [PFAHN-koo-khen]	Pancakes
Pickelsteiner Eintopf [PIK-el-shtine-e(r) INE-topf]	Meat (usually beef) and vegetable stew
Pommes frites [pom frit]	French fries
Pökelfleisch [PU(R)-kehl-flyshe]	Marinated pork or beef
Räucheraal/-hering/-lacks [ROY-khe(r)-aal/-hay-ring/-lahks]	Smoked eel, herring, and salmon
Rehrücken [RAY-rew-ken]	Roast saddle of venison
Reibekuchen [RYE-beh-koo-khen]	Potato pancakes
Rinderbraten [RIN-de(r)-braa-ten]	Roast beef
Rippchen mit Sauerkraut [RIP-khen mit SOW-e(r)-krowt]	Pickled pork ribs with sauerkraut
Rollmops [ROL-mops]	Marinated herring filled with diced onions, gherkins, and white peppercorns
Rösti [RU(R)SH-tee]	Hash-brown potatoes (Swiss)
Rühreier [REWR-eye-e(r)]	Scrambled eggs
Sauerbraten [ZOW-e(r)-braa-ten]	Marinated pot roast in spicy gravy

Schinken [SHIN-ken]	Ham
Schinkenröllchen mit Spargel [SHIN-ken-ru(r)l-khen mit SHPAHR-gel]	Ham slices with asparagus filling
Schlachtplatte [SHLAHKHT-plah-teh]	Mixed cold meats and sausages
Schweinebraten/-kotelett [SHVINE-eh-braa-ten/-kot-let]	Roast pork/Pork chops
Semmelsuppe [ZEHM-mehl-zoop-peh]	Dumpling soup (Austrian)
Serbische Bohnensuppe [ZEHR-bish-eh BOH-nen-zoop-peh]	Spicy bean soup
Spanferkel [SHPAAN-fehr-kel]	Roast suckling pig
Spätzle [SHPEHTS-leh]	Thick noodles served with browned butter and bread-crumbs (Swabian speciality)
Spiegeleier [SHPEE-gel-eye-e(r)]	Fried eggs
Strammer Max [SHTRAHM-me(r) mahks]	Spiced, minced pork with fried eggs, onions, and rye bread
Topfenknödel [TOP-fen-knu(r)-del]	Cheese dumplings with fried breadcrumbs (Austria)
Wiener Backhendl [VEE-ne(r) BAHK-hehn-del]	Fried chicken (Viennese speciality)
Wiener Schnitzel [VEE-ne(r) SHNIT-tsel]	Breaded veal cutlet
Wildbraten [VILT-braa-ten]	Roast venison
Wildgulasch [VILT-goo-lahsh]	Spicy game stew
Wildschweinrücken [VILT-shvine-rew-ken]	Roast wild boar saddle
Zigeuner Schnitzel [tsi-GOY-ne(r) SHNIT-tsel]	Pork or veal cutlet in hot, spicy sauce
Zwiebelsuppe [TSVEE-bel-zoop-peh]	Onion soup

Sausages

Wurst (sausage) is perhaps the most typically German food of all. Many dishes, both warm and cold, include *Wurst* in some form, and most restaurants offer a *Wurstplatte* [VOORST-plah-teh] (sausage platter). Many sausages bear the names of the cities or regions they come from, like *Nürnberger Bratwurst*. The best place to sample sausage is a *Metzgerei* [MEHTST-geh-rye] or *Fleischerei* [FLYSHE-eh-rye] (butcher), where you may ask for a *Kostprobe* [KOST-proh-beh] (tasting sample).

Bierwurst [BEER-voorst]	Beer sausage (smoked pork and beef)
Blutwurst [BLOOT-voorst]	Blood sausage
Bockwurst [BOK-voorst]	Large frankfurter sausage
Currywurst [KUH-ree-voorst]	Pork sausage with curry
Jagdwurst [YAAGT-voorst]	Smoked pork with mustard and garlic
Leberwurst [LAY-be(r)-voorst]	Soft liver sausage
Mettwurst [MEHT-voorst]	Spicy, soft sausage spread
Nürnberger Bratwurst [NEWRN-behr-ge(r) BRAAT-voorst]	Fried pork and veal sausage
Regensburger [RAY-gens-boor-ge(r)]	Smoked, highly spiced pork sausage
Weißwurst [VICE-voorst]	White, spiced pork and veal sausage (Munich speciality)
Wienerli [VEE-nehr-lee]	Thin, Vienna-style frankfurter

Cheeses

An assortment of cheeses is usually not a separate course of a meal, as in France, but most German, Swiss, and Austrian restaurants offer a *Käseteller* [KAY-zeh-tehl-le(r)] (cheese platter), including three or four different cheeses. For a much wider selection, visit a *Käsegeschäft* (cheese shop) or the *Feinschmecker* (gourmet) section of a supermarket or department store.

Allgäuer Bergkäse [AHL-goy-e(r) BEHRK-kay-zeh]	Hard, mild cheese with holes, like our Swiss cheese
Altenburger [AHL-ten-boor-ge(r)]	Soft, mild goat's cheese
Bierkäse [BEER-kay-zeh]	Soft, sharp cheese spread
Edamer [AY-dah-me(r)]	Hard, mild cheese, like Dutch original

Edelpilzkäse [AY-del-pilts-kay-zeh]	Sharp, soft cheese (Austrian)
Frischkäse [FRISH-kay-zeh]	Curd cheese (many kinds)
Emmentaler [EHM-men-taa-le(r)]	Hard, mild cheese with holes (Swiss)
Greyerzer [GRAY-yehr-tse(r)]	Similar to Emmentaler, but without the holes; Swiss version of French Gruyère
Kümmelkäse [KEWM-mehl-kay-zeh]	Hard, mild cheese flavored with caraway
Limburger [LIM-boor-ge(r)]	Strong, soft cheese with herbs
Liptauer [LIP-tow-e(r)]	Cream cheese flavored with paprika and herbs (Austrian)
Münster [MEWN-ste(r)]	Strong, hard cheese flavored with caraway
Quark [kvahrk]	Smooth curd cheese spread
Räucherkäse [ROY-khe(r)-kay-zeh]	Smoked cheese, hard and mild
Tilsiter [TIL-zit-e(r)]	Semihard, mild, slightly sour cheese
Topfen [TOP-fen]	Curd cheese (Austrian)

Desserts

If you have a sweet tooth, you'll have plenty of opportunity to indulge it and also be amazed by the array of delicious and delicate pastries and sweets throughout the German-speaking world. Menus will list desserts under various different headings: *Nachtisch, Nachspeise,* or *Süßspeise. Gebäck* or *Mehlspeise* (pastries) and *Eis* or *Glacé* (ice cream) may be listed separately. Calorie counters should beware, especially when they hear the question *"Mit Schlag?"* ("With whipped cream?"), which in Vienna they invariably will.* Here are a few basic types of desserts that you'll find in combination, usually with a fruit like *Apfel* (apple) or *Erdbeer* (strawberry), or a flavor like *Vanille* (vanilla), as in *Mokkatorte* (coffee layer cake).

---

*Austrians also use the word *Schlagobers,* while the Germans prefer *Schlagsahne* and the Swiss, *Schlagrahm.* They all mean the same and can give a perfect dessert the deliciously fattening, final touch.

auflauf [-owf-lowf]	soufflé
creme [-kraym]	pudding
eis/-glacé [-ice/-glah-se(h)]	ice cream
gebäck [geh-behk]	pastry
kompott [-kom-pot]	compote
kuchen [-koo-khen]	cake
pudding [-pu-ding]	pudding
strudel [-shtroo-del]	delicate, thin, flaky pastry
torte [-tor-teh]	tart or layer cake

Some notable, traditional desserts you'll be tempted by:

apfelrösti [AHP-fel-ru(r)sh-tee]	Apple and bread slices fried in butter (Swiss)
apfelstrudel [AHP-fel-shtroo-del]	Strudel filled with sliced apples, raisins, nuts, and jam
berliner [behr-LEE-ne(r)]	Doughnut filled with raspberry
bienenstich [BEE-nen-shtikh]	Almond-honey cake
cremeschnitte [KRAYM-schnit-teh]	Napoleon
götterspeise [GU(R)-te(r)-shpye-zeh]	Fruit gelatin
gugelhupf [GOO-gel-hupf]	Pound cake with raisins and almonds (Austrian, Bavarian)
hefekranz [HAY-feh-krahnts]	Circular coffee cake with almonds and fruit
kaiserschmarren [KYE-ze(r)-shmahrn]	Shredded pancakes with raisins, sugar, cinnamon, and/or syrup (Austrian)
linzertorte [LIN-tse(r)-tor-teh]	Crushed almond cake with raspberry (Austrian)
mohnkuchen [MOHN-koo-khen]	Poppy seed cake
mohrenkopf [MOHR-en-kopf]	Chocolate, whipped-cream-filled meringue
palatschinken [pah-lah-TSHIN-ken]	Crêpes filled with different jams, cheeses, or (as a main course) meats (Austrian)
rote Grütze [ROH-teh GREW-tseh]	Fresh raspberry and currant pudding topped with fresh cream (North German)

Sachertorte [ZAHKH-e(r)-tor-teh]	Apricot jam layer cake with chocolate icing and filling (famous Viennese speciality)
Salzburger Nockerl [ZAHLTS-boor-ge(r) NOK-erl]	Light, sweet soufflé (Austrian)
Schillerlocken [SHIL-le(r)-lok-en]	Pastry filled with vanilla cream
Schwarzwälder Kirschtorte [SHVAHRTS-vehl-de(r) KEERSH-tor-teh]	Creamy, chocolate layer cake with cherries and cherry brandy (famous Black Forest speciality)
Topfenstrudel [TOP-fen-shtroo-del]	Strudel filled with creamy, vanilla-flavored curd cheese (Austrian)
Windbeutel [VINT-boy-tel]	Cream puff (literally: "wind bag")
Zwetschkenknödel [TSVEHTSH-ken-knu(r)-del]	Plum dumplings, boiled and fried in bread crumbs, served warm (Austrian)

WINES

Germany produces mostly white wines, the best known coming from the Rhine and Mosel River valleys. Along the Danube, the Wachau region in Austria is also famous for its white wines, while the Burgenland vineyards near the Hungarian border and those in German-speaking Switzerland produce mostly red wine. The system for catagorizing wine in these countries is based primarily on the percentage of natural grape sugar in the wine; the more sugar, the higher the quality. The better German wines are thus usually sweet and are classified as *Qualitätswein* or *Qualitätswein mit Prädikat* for the best. These wines are enjoyed by themselves or as dessert wines, while *Deutscher Tafelwein* (German table wine), usually a blend of more common dryer wines, traditionally accompanies a meal. Sometimes sugar is added to sweeten a wine, which is then labeled euphemistically *verbessert* (improved); otherwise the terms *Naturwein* or *natur rein* (naturally pure) indicate normal production methods.

Germans are fond of sparkling wine, called *Schaumwein* or *Sekt*, and produce some of the best anywhere. They also enjoy

ew, still fermenting wines, referred to variously, depending on
he region, as *Most, Sauser, Federweißer*, or, in Austria, as
Heuriger. * German wines are named after the region or vineyard
where the grapes are produced, but usually the type of grape is
indicated as well. The most common white wine grapes are
Müller-Thurgau, Sylvaner, and *Riesling.* You will also encounter
the following terms, which denote in ascending order the relative
quality and degree of sweetness according to the time of harvest
and condition of the grapes.

This Austrian wine name is also applied to the establishment where it is
served and consumed. See page 60, Types of Eating and Drinking Places.

Spätlese [SHPAYT-lay-zeh]	Dry wines from grapes harvested later than those used for the normal vintage
Auslese [OWS-lay-zeh]	Semidry wines from selected, very ripe grapes
Beerenauslese [BAY-ren-ows-lay-zeh]	Slightly sweet wines from a special harvest of overripe grapes
Trockenbeerenauslese [TRO-ken-bay-ren-ows-lay-zeh]	Sweet dessert wines from selected dried, raisinlike grapes; similar to French sauternes
Eiswein [ICE-vine]	Very rare honey-sweet, thick, liqueurlike wines from grapes harvested in midwinter; thus, the name "ice wine."

Ordering Wines

May I see the wine list, please?	**Die Weinkarte, bitte.**	dee VINE-kahr-teh, BIT-teh.
Can you recommend a good local wine?	**Können Sie mir einen guten Wein aus dieser Gegend empfehlen?**	KU(R)-nen zee meer INE-en GOO-ten vine ows DEE-ze(r) GAY-gehnt ehm-PFAY-len?

81

Where is this wine from?	Woher kommt dieser Wein?	voh-HEHR komt DEE-ze(r) vine?
Is this a good vintage?	Ist das ein guter Jahrgang?	ist dahs ine GOO-te(r) YAAR-gahng?
Is this wine . . .	Ist dieser Wein . . .	ist DEE-ze(r) vine . . .
• (very) dry?	• (sehr) trocken?	• (zehr) TRO-ken?
• (a little) sweet?	• (etwas) süß?	• (EHT-vahs) zews?
• light/heavy?	• leicht/schwer?	• lyekht/shvehr?
• full-bodied?	• vollmundig?	• VOL-mun-dikh?
I'd like a glass/bottle/ carafe of . . .	Ich möchte ein Glas/eine Flasche/eine Karaffe . . .	ikh MU(R)KH-teh ine glaas/INE-eh FLAHSH-eh/INE-eh kah-RAH-feh . . .
• house wine.	• Hauswein.	• HOWS-vine.
• white wine.	• Weißwein.	• VICE-vine.
• red wine.	• Rotwein.	• ROHT-vine.
• rosé.	• Rosé/Schiller-wein.	• roh-ZAY/SHIL-le(r)-vine.
• sparkling wine.	• Sekt.	• zehkt.
Please bring me another . . .	Bringen Sie mir bitte noch . . .	BRIN-gen zee meer BIT-teh nohkh . . .
• ⅛ liter glass.	• ein Achtel.	• ine AHKH-tel.
• ¼ liter glass.	• ein Viertel.	• ine FEER-tel.
• bottle.	• eine Flasche.	• INE-eh FLAHSH-eh.

BEER

Breweries abound all over German-speaking Europe—even small towns often have their own—and visitors will be amazed by the variety of different local brews. When enjoying this popular beverage "at the source," so to speak, it helps to know some of the terms Germans apply to their favorite drink. The two main categories are *helles* [HEHL-ehs] (light—in color) and *dunkle* [DUNK-lehs] (dark) *Bier*, which can be ordered *vom Faß* (literally: from the barrel) by the glass or, if you're thirsty, by *Maß* (one liter mug). Ordering is easy: *Ein Bier, bitte* (A beer, please). If you want to be more precise:

| I'd like a small/large glass of beer. | Ich hätte gern ein kleines/großes Bier. | ikh HEHT-teh gehrn ine KLINE-es/ GROHS-ehs beer. |

82

Some types of German beer:

Altbier [AHLT-beer]	Bitter, light beer with high hops *(Hopfen)* content
Bockbier, Doppelbock, Märzen-, Starkbier [BOK-beer, DOP-pehl-bok, MEHR-tsen-, SHTAHRK-beer]	Beers high in alcohol and malt content
Malzbier [MAHLTS-beer]	Dark, sweet beer, low in alcohol, high in calories
Pilsener [PIL-zeh-ne(r)]	Light beer with pronounced hops aroma
Radlermaß [RAAD-le(r)-maas]	Light beer with a dash of lemonade; called *Alsterwasser* [AHL-ste(r)-vahs-e(r)] in Northern Germany
Weißbier, Weizenbier [VICE-beer, VITE-sen-beer]	Light ale brewed from wheat, popular in Berlin as a *Berliner Weiße mit Schuß—Weizenbier* with a shot of *Himbeersaft* (raspberry juice)

OTHER BEVERAGES

To cap off your meal, you may want to try a little *Schnaps* [shnahps] or German *Weinbrandt* [VINE-brahnt] (brandy). The many varieties of brandies often have names ending in *-schnaps*, *-wasser*, or *-geist*. Some of the traditional favorites:

Apfelschnaps [AHP-fehl-shnahps]	Apple brandy
Birnenschnaps [BEER-nen-shnahps]	Pear brandy
Bommerlunder, Kümmel [bom-me(r)-LUN-de(r), KEWM-mel]	Caraway-flavored brandies
Doornkaat, Steinhäger [DORN-kaat, SHTINE-hay-ge(r)]	German gin, juniper berry brandies
Himbeergeist [HIM-bayr-geyst]	Raspberry brandy
Kirschwasser [KIRSH-vahs-se(r)]	Cherry brandy

| **Kräuterlikör** [KROY-te(r)-li-ku(r)r] | Herbal liqueur |
| **Zwetschgenwasser** [TSVEHTSH-gen-vahs-se(r)] | Plum brandy |

Should you wish to inquire about local spirits:

| Are there any special alcoholic drinks from this region? | **Gibt es aus dieser Gegend besondere Spirituosen?** | gipt ehs ows DEE-ze(r) GAY-gehnt beh-ZOHN-deh-reh spi-ri-too-OH-zen? |

Some nonalcoholic drinks you may want to order:

I'd like a/an . . .	**Ich hätte gern . . .**	ikh HEHT-teh gehrn . . .
• mineral water.	• **ein Mineralwasser.**	• ine mi-neh-RAAL-vahs-se(r).
• fruit juice.	• **einen Obstsaft.**	• INE-en OPST-zahft.
• apple juice.	• **einen Apfelsaft.**	• INE-en AHP-fehl-zahft.
• orange juice.	• **einen Orangensaft.**	• INE-en o-RAHN-zhehn-zahft.
• lemonade.	• **eine Limonade.**	• INE-eh lee-mo-NAA-deh.
• iced tea.	• **einen Eistee.**	• INE-en ICE-tay.
• Coke/Pepsi.	• **ein Cola/Pepsi Cola.**	• ine KOH-lah/PEHP-si KOH-lah.
• hot chocolate.	• **eine heiße Schokolade**	• INE-eh HICE-seh sho-ko-LAA-deh.
• cup/pot of coffee.	• **eine Tasse/Portion Kaffee.**	• INE-eh TAHS-seh/por-TSIOHN KAH-feh.
• with cream.	• **mit Sahne.**	• mit ZAA-neh.
• black/decaffein-ated coffee.	• **einen schwarzen/koffeinfreien Kaffee.**	• INE-en SHVAHRT-sen/kof-feh-EEN-frey-en KAH-feh.
• espresso.	• **einen Expresso.**	• INE-en ehs-SPREHS-soh.
• tea with lemon/milk.	• **einen Tee mit Zitrone/Milch.**	• INE-en tay mit tsi-TROH-neh/milkh.
• herbal tea.	• **einen Kräutertee.**	• INE-en KROY-te(r)-tay.

84

7/PERSONAL SERVICES

DIALOGUE: AT THE HAIRDRESSER'S (*BEIM DAMENFRISEUR*)

Friseur:	**Was kann ich für Sie tun?**	vahs kahn ikh fewr zee toon?
Kundin:	**Haare schneiden, bitte.**	HAA-reh SHNYE-den, BIT-teh.
Friseur:	**Wie möchten Sie Ihr Haar haben?**	vee MU(R)KH-ten zee eer haar HAA-ben?
Kundin:	**Hinten lang, aber an den Seiten etwas kürzer.**	HIN-ten lahng, AH-be(r) ahn dehn ZITE-en EHT-vahs KEWR-tse(r).
Friseur:	**Schön. Möchten Sie auch eine Dauerwelle haben?**	shu(r)n. MU(R)KH-ten zee owkh INE-neh DOW-e(r)-vehl-leh HAA-ben?
Kundin:	**Nein, aber Waschen und Legen, bitte.**	nine, AH-be(r) VAHSH-en unt LAY-gen, BIT-teh.
Friseur:	**In Ordnung. Diesen Stuhl, bitte.**	in ORT-nung. DEE-zen shtool, BIT-teh.

. . . .

Hairdresser:	What can I do for you?
Client:	A haircut, please.
Hairdresser:	How would you like your hair?
Client:	Long in back, but a little shorter on the sides.
Hairdresser:	Fine. Would you like a permanent too?
Client:	No, but a shampoo and set, please.
Hairdresser:	Fine. Take a seat here, please.

AT THE BARBERSHOP

Is there a barbershop nearby?	**Gibt es hier in der Nähe einen Herrenfriseur?**	gipt ehs heer in dehr NAY-eh INE-en HEH-ren-fri-zur?
I need a haircut, please.	**Würden Sie mir bitte die Haare schneiden.**	WU(R)-den zee meer BIT-teh dee HAA-reh SHNYE-den.
Long in front, (not too) short in back.	**Vorne lang, hinten (nicht zu) kurz.**	FOR-neh lahng, HIN-ten [nikht tsoo] koorts.
Leave it longer/take a little off . . .	**Lassen Sie es _____ länger/ Nehmen Sie _____ etwas weg.**	LAHS-en zee ehs _____ LEHN-ge(r)/NAY-men zee _____ EHT-vahs vehk.
• on top.	• **oben**	• OH-ben
• on the sides.	• **an den Seiten**	• ahn dehn ZITE-en
• on the neck.	• **im Nacken**	• im NAH-ken
That's enough.	**Das genügt.**	dahs geh-NEWKT.
I'd like a shave, please.	**Rasieren, bitte.**	rah-ZEE-ren, BIT-teh.
Please trim my . . .	**Stutzen Sie mir bitte . . .**	SHTUT-sen zee meer BIT-teh . . .
• beard.	• **den Bart.**	• dehn baart.
• moustache.	• **den Schnurbart.**	• dehn SHNOOR-baart.
• sideburns.	• **die Koteletten.**	• dee kot-LEHT-ten.

AT THE BEAUTY PARLOR

Is there a hairdresser's/ beauty parlor in the hotel?	**Gibt's einen Friseur/ Damensalon im Hotel?**	gipts INE-en fri-ZUR/DAA-men-zaa-lon im ho-TEL?
Do I need an appointment?	**Muß ich mich anmelden?**	mus ikh mikh AHN-mehl-den?
Can I make an appointment for today/tomorrow?	**Kann ich für heute/morgen einen Termin haben?**	kahn ikh fewr HOY-teh/MOR-gen INE-en tehr-MEEN HAA-ben?

86

I need a haircut, please.	Haare schneiden, bitte.	HAA-reh SHNYE-den, BIT-teh.
Don't cut it too short.	Nicht zu kurz schneiden.	nikht tsoo koorts SHNYE-den.
Show me photos of new hairstyles, please.	Zeigen Sie mir bitte Fotos von neuen Frisuren.	TSYE-gen zee meer BIT-teh FOH-tohs fon NOY-en fri-ZOOR-en.
I'd like . . .	Ich möchte . . .	ikh MU(R)KH-teh . . .
• just a shampoo and set.	• nur Waschen und Legen.	• noor VAHSH-en unt LAY-gen.
• a permanent.	• eine Dauerwelle.	• INE-eh DOW-e(r)-vehl-leh.
• a new hairdo.	• eine neue Frisur.	• INE-eh NOY-eh fri-ZOOR.
• a touch-up.	• eine Auffrischung.	• INE-eh OWF-frish-ung.
• a manicure.	• eine Maniküre.	• INE-eh MAH-ni-kew-reh.
• a color rinse.	• eine Farbspülung.	• INE-eh FAHRP-shpew-lung.
Do you have a color chart?	Haben Sie eine Farbtabelle?	HAA-ben zee INE-eh FAHRP-tah-beh-leh?
This time I'd like . . .	Diesmal möchte ich . . .	DEES-maal MU(R)KH-teh ikh . . .
• light/dark blond.	• hell-/dunkel-blond.	• HEHL-/DUN-kel-blont.
• brunette/auburn.	• braun/kastanien-braun.	• brown/kah-STAA-nyen-brown.
• a lighter/darker color.	• eine hellere/dunklere Farbe.	• INE-eh HEHL-lehr-eh/DUN-klehr-eh FAHR-beh.
(No) hair spray, please.	(Kein) Haarspray, bitte.	[kine] HAAR-shpray, BIT-teh.
That's fine, thank you.	So ist es schön, danke.	zoh ist ehs shu(r)n, DAHN-keh.

LAUNDRY AND DRY-CLEANING

| Is there ⸺ nearby? | Gibt es ⸺ in der Nähe? | gipt ehs ⸺ in dehr NAY-eh? |

87

• a laundry	• eine Wäscherei	• INE-eh vehsh-eh-RYE
• a dry cleaner's	• eine (chemische) Reinigung	• INE-eh (KHAY-mi-sheh) RYE-ni-gung
• a laundromat	• einen Waschsalon	• INE-en VAHSH-zaa-lon
I want to have these clothes . . .	Ich möchte diese Kleider ——— lassen.	ikh MU(R)KH-teh DEE-zeh KLYE-de(r) ——— LAHS-sen.
• washed.	• waschen	• VAHSH-en
• dry-cleaned.	• reinigen	• RYE-ni-gen
• ironed/pressed.	• bügeln/dampf-bügeln	• BEW-geln/DAHMPF-bew-geln
When will they be ready?	Wann sind sie fertig?	vahn zint zee FEHR-tikh?
I need them . . .	Ich brauche sie . . .	ikh BROW-kheh zee . . .
• as soon as possible.	• so bald wie möglich.	• zoh bahlt vee MU(R)-glikh.
• today/tonight.	• heute/heute abend.	• HOY-teh/HOY-teh AA-behnt.
Can you . . .	Können Sie . . .	KU(R)-nen zee . . .
• sew on this button?	• diesen Knopf annähen?	• DEE-zen knopf AHN-nay-en?
• remove this stain?	• diesen Fleck entfernen?	• DEE-zen flehk ehnt-FEHR-nen?
Is my laundry ready?	Ist meine Wäsche fertig?	ist MINE-eh VEHSH-eh FEHR-tikh?
Something is missing.	Es fehlt etwas.	ehs fehlt EHT-vahs.
This piece isn't mine.	Dieses Stück gehört mir nicht.	DEE-zehs shtewk geh-HU(R)RT meer nikht.

8/HEALTH CARE

To have peace of mind during your travels, be sure you are covered for any medical expenses abroad. Most health insurance companies will issue limited policies for travelers, if you're not already covered by your present policy. Medical facilities and services in Germany, Switzerland, and Austria are generally quite modern and efficient, and for minor problems in most cases you can rely on the advice of the local pharmacist.

DIALOGUE: AT THE PHARMACY (*IN DER APOTHEKE*)

Apotheker:	**Womit kann ich Ihnen dienen?**	voh-MIT kahn ikh EE-nen DEE-nen?
Reisende:	**Haben Sie etwas gegen Husten?**	HAA-ben zee EHT-vahs GAY-gen HOOS-ten?
Apotheker:	**Sicher. Hätten Sie lieber Hustensaft oder Hustenbonbons?**	HEHT-ten zee LEE-be(r) HOOS-ten-zahft OH-de(r) HOOS-ten-bong-bongs?
Reisende:	**Was würden Sie empfehlen?**	vahs VU(R)R-den zee ehm-PFAY-len?
Apotheker:	**Wie schwer ist der Husten?**	vee shvehr ist dehr HOOS-ten?
Reisende:	**Er ist relativ leicht.**	ehr ist ray-lah-TEEF lyekht.
Apotheker:	**Dann probieren Sie diese Bonbons.**	dahn pro-BEER-en zee DEE-zeh bong-BONGS.

. . . .

Pharmacist:	How can I help you?
Traveler:	Do you have something for a cough?
Pharmacist:	Of course. Would you prefer cough syrup or cough drops?

89

Traveler:	What would you recommend?
Pharmacist:	How bad is the cough?
Traveler:	It's relatively light.
Pharmacist:	Then try these drops.

CONSULTING THE PHARMACIST

A typical *Apotheke* (pharmacy) in the German-speaking countries will be more specialized than its American counterpart and will deal primarily with prescription and over-the-counter drugs, as well as other health products, including herbal teas and remedies. You'll find toiletries, household articles, and nonprescription medicines at a *Drogerie* (drug store; see page 150 under Toiletries in Chapter 12). All larger towns have an all-night pharmacy, and the address is posted on the door or window of every pharmacy in town—and in the local phone book.

Where can I find an (all-night) pharmacy?	**Wo finde ich eine Apotheke (mit Nachtdienst)?**	voh FIN-deh ikh INE-eh ah-poh-TAY-keh [mit NAHKHT-deenst]?
When does it open/close?	**Wann öffnet/schließt sie?**	vahn U(R)F-net/shleest zee?
I need something for . . .	**Ich brauche etwas gegen . . .**	ikh BROW-kheh EHT-vahs GAY-gen . . .
• a cold.	• **eine Erkältung.**	• INE-eh ehr-KEHL-tung.
• a sore throat.	• **Halsschmerzen.**	• HAHLS-shmehr-tsen.
• a cough.	• **Husten.**	• HOOS-ten.
• constipation.	• **Verstopfung.**	• fehr-SHTOP-fung.
• diarrhea.	• **Durchfall.**	• DURKH-fahl.
• fever.	• **Fieber.**	• FEE-be(r)
• a hangover.	• **Kater.**	• KAA-te(r).
• hay fever.	• **Heuschnupfen.**	• HOY-shnup-fen.
• headache.	• **Kopfschmerzen.**	• KOPF-shmehr-tsen.

90

• indigestion.	• **Magenverstimm-ung.**	• MAA-gen-fehr-shtim-mung.
• insect bites.	• **Insektenstiche.**	• in-ZEHK-ten-shtikh-eh.
• motion sickness.	• **Reisekrankheit.**	• RYE-zeh-krahnk-hite.
• sunburn.	• **Sonnenbrand.**	• ZON-nen-brahnt.
• a toothache.	• **Zahnschmerzen.**	• TSAAN-shmehrt-sen.
Can you fill this prescription for me?	**Können Sie mir dieses Rezept anfertigen?**	KU(R)-nen zee meer DEE-zehs reh-TSEHPT AHN-fehr-tig-en?
I'll wait for it.	**Ich warte darauf.**	ikh VAAR-teh dah-ROWF.
It's urgent.	**Es ist dringend.**	ehs ist DRING-ent.
I need . . .	**Ich brauche . . .**	ikh BROW-kheh . . .
• an antacid.	• **ein Antiacidum.**	• ine ahn-tee-AA-si-doom.
• an antiseptic.	• **ein Antiseptikum.**	• ine ahn-tee-ZEHP-ti-koom.
• antiseptic cream.	• **Wundsalbe.**	• VUNT-zaal-beh.
• aspirin.	• **Aspirin.**	• ah-spi-REEN.
• bandages.	• **Verbandzeug.**	• fehr-BAHNT-tsoyk.
• Band-Aids.	• **Heftpflaster.**	• HEHFT-pflahs-te(r).
• contact lense solution.	• **Kontaktlinsen-flüßigkeit.**	• kon-TAHKT-lin-zen-flews-ikh-kite.
• contraceptives.	• **Verhütungsmittel.**	• fehr-HEW-tungs-mit-tel.
• corn plasters.	• **Hühneraugen-pflaster.**	• HEW-nehr-ow-gen-pflahs-te(r).
• cotton balls.	• **Watte.**	• VAH-teh.
• cough drops/syrup	• **Hustenbonbons/-saft.**	• HOOS-ten-bong-bo-ngs/-zahft.
• disinfectant.	• **Desinfektions-mittel.**	• deh-sin-fehk-TSIOHNS-mit-tel.
• eardrops.	• **Ohrentropfen.**	• OHR-en-trop-fen.
• eyedrops.	• **Augentropfen.**	• OW-gen-trop-fen.
• insect repellent/spray.	• **Insektenschutz/ Insektizid.**	• in-ZEHK-ten-shuts/ in-zehk-ti-TSEET.
• iodine.	• **Jod.**	• yoht.
• a laxative.	• **ein Abführmittel.**	• ine AHP-fewr-mit-tel.
• mouthwash.	• **Mundwasser.**	• MUNT-vahs-se(r).

91

• nose drops.	• **Nasentropfen.**	• NAA-zen-trop-fen.
• a pain killer/analgesic.	• **ein Schmerzmittel.**	• ine SHMEHRTS-mit-tel.
• sanitary napkins.	• **Damenbinden.**	• DAA-men-bin-den.
• sleeping pills.	• **Schlaftabletten.**	• SHLAAF-tah-bleht-ten.
• suppositories.	• **Zäpfchen.**	• TSEHPF-khen.
• tampons.	• **Tampons.**	• TAHM-pongs.
• a thermometer.	• **ein Thermometer.**	• ine tehr-mo-MAY-te(r).
• throat lozenges.	• **Halspastillen.**	• HAHLS-pahs-til-en.
• a tranquillizer.	• **ein Beruhigungs-mittel.**	• ine beh-ROO-i-gungs-mit-tel.
• vitamins.	• **Vitamine.**	• vee-taa-MEE-neh.

FINDING A DOCTOR

In an emergency, you can call the *ärztlicher Notdienst* (emergency medical service), listed at the beginning of every telephone directory. Otherwise your hotel or the *Fremdenverkehrsbüro* (tourist information office) should be able to refer you to a doctor.

I need a doctor right away.	**Ich brauche schnell einen Arzt.**	ikh BROW-kheh shnehl INE-en ahrtst.
Can you call me a doctor?	**Können Sie mir einen Arzt rufen?**	KU(R)-nen zee meer INE-en ahrtst ROO-fen?
Is there a doctor here who speaks English?	**Gibt es hier einen Arzt, der Englisch spricht?**	gipt ehs heer INE-en ahrtst, dehr EHN-glish shprikht?
Can he/she see me here in the hotel?	**Kann er/sie mich hier im Hotel sehen?**	kahn ehr/zee mikh heer im ho-TEL ZAY-en?
Can you recommend a/an . . .	**Können Sie mir einen ——— empfehlen?**	KU(R)-nen zee meer INE-en ——— ehm-PFAY-len?
• general practitioner?	• **praktischen Arzt**	• PRAHK-tish-en ahrtst

92

• pediatrician?	• **Kinderarzt**	• KIN-de(r)-ahrtst
• gynecologist?	• **Frauenarzt**	• FROW-en-ahrtst
• eye doctor?	• **Augenarzt**	• OW-gen-ahrtst
Where's the doctor's office?	**Wo ist die Arztpraxis?**	voh ist dee AHRTST-prahk-sis?
When are the office hours?	**Wann sind die Sprechstunden?**	vahn zint dee SHPREKH-shtun-den?
Can I have an appointment . . .	**Kann ich ——— einen Termin haben?**	kahn ikh ——— INE-en tehr-MEEN HAA-ben?
• as soon as possible?	• **so bald wie möglich**	• zoh bahlt vee MU(R)G-likh
• today/tomorrow?	• **heute/morgen**	• HOY-teh/MOR-gen

TALKING TO THE DOCTOR

I don't feel well.	**Ich fühle mich nicht wohl.**	ikh FEW-leh mikh nikht vohl.
I'm sick.	**Ich bin krank.**	ikh bin krahnk.
I don't know what's wrong with me.	**Ich weiß nicht, was mir fehlt.**	ikh vice nikht, vahs meer fehlt.
I have a fever/no fever.	**Ich habe (kein) Fieber.**	ikh HAA-beh (kine) FEE-be(r).
I'm dizzy/nauseated.	**Mir ist schwindlig/übel.**	meer ist SHVIND-likh/EW-bel.
I've been vomiting.	**Ich habe mich übergeben.**	ikh HAA-beh mikh ew-be(r)-GAY-ben.
I'm constipated.	**Ich habe Verstopfung.**	ikh HAA-beh fehr-SHTOP-fung.
I have diarrhea.	**Ich habe Durchfall.**	ikh HAA-beh DURKH-fahl.
I can't sleep.	**Ich kann nicht schlafen.**	ikh kahn nikht SHLAA-fen.
I have . . .	**Ich habe . . .**	ikh HAA-beh . . .
• an abscess.	• **einen Abszeß.**	• INE-en ahps-TSEHS.
• asthma.	• **Asthma.**	• AHST-mah.
• backache.	• **Rückenschmerzen.**	• REW-ken-shmehrt-sen.
• a broken leg.	• **einen Beinbruch.**	• INE-en BINE-brukh.
• a bruise.	• **eine Quetschung.**	• INE-eh KVEHTSH-ung.

93

• a burn.	• eine Brandwunde.	• INE-eh BRAHNT-vun-deh.
• a cold.	• eine Erkältung.	• INE-eh ehr-KEHL-tung.
• a cough.	• Husten.	• HOOS-ten.
• cramps.	• Krämpfe.	• KREHM-pfeh.
• a cut.	• eine Schnittwunde.	• INE-eh SHNIT-vun-deh.
• an earache.	• Ohrenschmerzen.	• OHR-en-shmehrt-sen.
• something in my eye.	• etwas im Auge.	• EHT-vahs im OW-geh.
• the flu.	• Grippe.	• GRIP-peh.
• a fracture.	• einen Knochenbruch.	• INE-en KNOKH-en-brukh.
• a headache.	• Kopfschmerzen.	• KOPF-shmehrt-sen.
• a lump/swelling.	• eine Beule/Schwellung.	• INE-eh BOY-leh/SHVEHL-lung.
• rheumatism.	• Rheumatismus.	• roy-mah-TIS-mus.
• a sore throat.	• Halsschmerzen.	• HAHLS-shmehrt-sen.
• a stiff neck.	• einen steifen Nacken.	• INE-en SHTYE-fen NAH-ken.
• a stomachache.	• Magen-schmerzen.	• MAA-gen-schmehrt-sen.
• sunstroke.	• einen Sonnenstich.	• INE-en ZON-nen-shtikh.
• a sty.	• einen Augen-liederbrand.	• INE-en OW-gen-lee-de(r)-brahnt.
I'm (not) allergic to penicillin.	Ich bin gegen Penizillin (nicht) allergisch.	i(h)h bin GAY-gen peh-ni-tsil-LEEN [nikht] ah-LEHR-gish.
I'm a diabetic and take insulin/this medicine.	Ich bin Diabetiker und nehme Insulin/dieses Medikament.	ikh bin dee-ah-BEH-ti-ke(r) unt NAY-meh in-zoo-LEEN/DEE-zehs meh-di-kah-MEHNT.
I have heart trouble.	Ich bin herzkrank.	ikh bin HEHRTS-krahnk.
I had a heart attack four years ago.	Vor vier Jahren erlitt ich einen Herzanfall.	for feer YAA-ren ehr-LIT ikh INE-en HEHRTS-ahn-fahl.

I've had this pain for two days.	**Seit zwei Tagen habe ich diesen Schmerz.**	zite tsvye TAA-gen HAA-beh ikh DEE-zen shmehrts.
I have menstrual pains.	**Ich habe Menstruations-beschwerden.**	ikh HAA-beh mehn-stru-ah-TSIOHNS-beh-shvehr-den.
I'm four months' pregnant.	**Ich bin im vierten Monat schwanger.**	ikh bin im FEER-ten MOH-naat SHVAHNG-e(r).

PARTS OF THE BODY

My ——— hurts.	**Mir tut/tun* ——— weh.**	meer toot/toon ——— vay.
• ankle	• **der Knöchel**	• dehr KNU(R)-khel
• appendix	• **der Blinddarm**	• dehr BLINT-dahrm
• arm	• **der Arm**	• dehr ahrm
• back	• **der Rücken**	• dehr REW-ken
• bladder	• **die Blase**	• dee BLAA-zeh
• bowels	• **der Darm**	• dehr dahrm
• breast	• **die Brust**	• dee broost
• buttocks	• **das Gesäß**	• dahs geh-SEHS
• chest	• **der Brustkorb**	• dehr BROOST-korp
• ear	• **das Ohr**	• dahs ohr
• eye/eyes	• **das Auge/ die Augen**	• dahs OW-geh/dee OW-gen
• face	• **das Gesicht**	• dahs geh-ZIKHT
• finger	• **der Finger**	• dehr FIN-ge(r)
• foot/feet	• **der Fuß/die Füße**	• dehr foos/dee FEWS-seh
• gland	• **die Drüse**	• dee DREW-zeh
• hand	• **die Hand**	• dee hahnt
• head	• **der Kopf**	• dehr kopf
• heart	• **das Herz**	• dahs hehrts
• hip	• **die Hüfte**	• dee HEWF-teh

*Tun is the plural form of the verb, as in *Mir tun die Augen weh* (literally, my eyes hurt me).

• jaw	• **der Kiefer**	• dehr KEE-fe(r)
• joint	• **das Gelenk**	• dahs geh-LEHNK
• kidney(s)	• **die Niere(n)**	• dee NEER-eh/NEER-en
• knee	• **das Knie**	• dahs knee
• leg	• **das Bein**	• dahs bine
• lip	• **die Lippe**	• dee LIP-peh
• liver	• **die Leber**	• dee LAY-be(r)
• lung(s)	• **die Lunge(n)**	• dee LUNG-eh/LUNG-en
• mouth	• **der Mund**	• dehr munt
• muscle	• **der Muskel**	• dehr MUS-kel
• neck	• **der Hals**	• dehr hahls
• nose	• **die Nase**	• dee NAA-zeh
• penis	• **der Penis**	• dehr PAY-nis
• rib(s)	• **die Rippe(n)**	• die RIP-peh/RIP-pen
• shoulder	• **die Schulter**	• dee SHUL-te(r)
• skin	• **die Haut**	• dee howt
• spine	• **die Wirbelsäule**	• dee VEER-bel-zoy-leh
• stomach	• **der Magen**	• dehr MAA-gen
• tendon	• **die Sehne**	• dee ZAY-neh
• thigh	• **der Schenkel**	• dehr SHEHN-kel
• throat	• **der Hals**	• dehr hahls
• thumb	• **der Daumen**	• dehr DOW-men
• toe(s)	• **die Zehe (n)**	• dee TSEH-eh/TSEH-en
• tooth/teeth	• **der Zahn/ die Zähne**	• dehr TSAAN/dee TSAY-neh
• tongue	• **die Zunge**	• dee TSUN-geh
• tonsils	• **die Mandeln**	• dee MAHN-deln
• vagina	• **die Scheide**	• dee SHYE-deh
• vein	• **die Vene**	• dee VAY-neh
• wrist	• **das Handgelenk**	• dahs HAHNT-geh-lehnk

WHAT YOU'LL HEAR FROM THE DOCTOR

Wo haben Sie Schmerzen?	voh HAA-ben zee SHMEHRT-sen?	Where does it hurt?
Seit wie lange haben sie diese Schmerzen?	zite vee LAHNG-eh HAA-ben zee DEE-zeh SHMEHRT-sen?	How long have you had these pains?

96

German	Pronunciation	English
Welche Symptome haben Sie?	VEHL-kheh ZOOMP-toh-meh HAA-ben zee?	What symptoms do you have?
Wie werden Sie behandelt?	vee VEHR-den zee beh-HAHN-delt?	How are you being treated?
Welche Medikamente nehmen Sie?	VEHL-kheh meh-di-kah-MEHN-teh NAY-men zee?	What medicines are you taking?
Ziehen Sie sich aus/an.	TSEE-en zee zikh ows/ahn.	Undress/Get dressed.
Machen Sie den Oberkörper frei.	MAHKH-en zee dehn OH-be(r)-ku(r)r-pe(r) frye.	Undress to the waist.
Legen Sie sich hierhin.	LAY-gen zee zikh heer-HIN.	Lie down here.
Öffnen Sie den Mund.	U(R)F-nen zee dehn munt.	Open your mouth.
Zeigen Sie die Zunge.	TSYE-gen zee dee TSUN-geh.	Stick our your tongue.
Husten Sie.	HOOS-ten zee.	Cough.
Tief durchatmen.	teef DURKH-aht-men.	Breathe deeply.
Zeigen Sie mir, wo es weh tut.	TSYE-gen zee meer, voh ehs vay toot.	Show me where it hurts.
Ich werde —— messen.	ikh VEHR-deh —— MEHS-sen.	I'm going to take . . .
• Ihre Temperatur	• EE-reh tehm-pay-raa-TOOR	• your temperature
• Ihren Blutdruck/Puls	• EE-ren BLOOT-druk/puls	• blood pressure/pulse
Ich brauche eine . . .	ikh BROW-kheh INE-eh . . .	I need a . . .
• Blutprobe.	• BLOOT-proh-beh.	• blood sample.
• Urinprobe.	• oo-REEN-proh-beh.	• urine sample.
• Stuhlprobe.	• SHTOOL-proh-beh.	• stool sample.
Ich gebe Ihnen eine Spritze.	ikh GAY-beh EE-nen INE-eh SHPRIT-seh.	I'm giving you an injection.
Sie müssen . . .	zee MEWS-en . . .	You have to . . .
• sich röntgen lassen.	• zikh RU(R)NT-gen LAHS-sen.	• be X-rayed.
• einen Facharzt sehen.	• INE-en FAHKH-ahrtst ZAY-en.	• see a specialist.

97

• drei Tage im Bett bleiben.	• drye TAA-geh im beht BLYE-ben.	• stay in bed for three days.
• ins Kranken- haus gehen.	• ins KRAHN-ken-hows GAY-en.	• go to the hospital.
Es ist (nicht) ernst.	ehs ist [nikht] ehrnst.	It's (not) serious.
Es ist . . .	ehs ist . . .	It's . . .
• gebrochen.	• geh-BROKH-en.	• broken.
• verrenkt.	• fehr-REHNKT.	• dislocated.
• verstaucht.	• fehr-SHTOWKHT.	• sprained.
• gerissen.	• geh-RIS-sen.	• torn.
• infiziert.	• in-fi-TSEERT.	• infected.
Sie haben (eine) . . .	zee HAA-ben [INE-eh] . . .	You have (a/an) . . .
• Blasenentzün- dung.	• BLAA-zen-ehn-tsewn- dung.	• bladder infection
• Blinddarmentzün- dung.	• BLINT-dahrm-ehn- tsewn-dung.	• appendicitis.
• Gelbsucht.	• GEHLP-sukht.	• jaundice.
• Geschlechts- krankheit.	• geh-SHLEHKHTS- krahnk-hite.	• venereal disease.
• Grippe.	• GRIP-peh.	• the flu.
• Hepatitis.	• heh-pah-TEE-tis.	• hepatitis.
• einen Knochenbruch.	• IFH-nen KNOKH-en- brukh.	• fracture.
• Lebensmittelver- giftung.	• LAY-bens-mi-tel-fehr- gif-tung.	• food poisoning.
• Lungenentzün- dung.	• LUNG-en-ehn-tsewn- dung.	• pneumonia.
• Magenentzün- dung.	• MAA-gen-ehn-tsewn- dung.	• gastritis.
• Masern.	• MAH-zern.	• measles.

PATIENTS' QUESTIONS

Is it serious/ contagious?	**Ist es ernst/ ansteckend?**	ist ehs ehrnst/AHN- shteh-kehnt
What exactly is wrong with me?	**Was genau fehlt mir?**	vahs geh-NOW fehlt meer?
How long should I stay in bed?	**Wie lange soll ich im Bett bleiben?**	vee LAHNG-eh zol ikh im beht BLYE-ben?

When can I travel again?	**Wann kann ich wieder reisen?**	vahn kahn ikh VEE-de(r) RYE-zen?
Do I need a prescription?	**Brauche ich ein Rezept?**	BROW-kheh ikh ine reh-TSEHPT?
Could you please fill out this medical form?	**Könnten Sie mir bitte dieses Krankenkasse-formular aus-füllen?**	KU(R)N-ten zee meer BIT-teh DEE-zehs KRAHN-ken-kahs-seh-for-moo-lahr OWS-few-len?
Can I have a receipt for my insurance?	**Kann ich eine Quittung für meine Krankenkasse haben?**	kahn ikh INE-eh KVIT-tung fewr MINE-eh KRAHN-ken-kahs-seh HAA-ben?

AT THE HOSPITAL/ACCIDENTS

Help me!	**Helfen Sie mir!**	HEHL-fen zee meer!
It's an emergency.	**Es ist ein Notfall.**	ehs ist ine NOHT-fahl.
Call a doctor/ambulance immediately.	**Rufen Sie sofort einen Arzt/ Krankenwagen.**	ROO-fen zee zoh-FORT INE-en ahrtst/KRAHN-ken-vaa-gen.
Get me (him/her) to the hospital as fast as possible.	**Bringen Sie mich (ihn/sie) so schnell wie möglich ins Krankenhaus.**	BRIN-gen zee mikh [een/zee] zoh shnehl vee MU(R)G-likh ins KRAHN-ken-hows.
I was in an accident.	**Ich war in einem Unfall.**	ikh vahr in INE-em UN-fahl.
I need first aid.	**Ich brauche erste Hilfe.**	ikh BROW-kheh EHRS-teh HIL-feh.
I'm (she/he is) bleeding.	**Ich blute (sie/er blutet).**	ikh BLOO-teh [zee/ehr BLOO-tet].
I've (she/he has) lost a lot of blood.	**Ich habe (sie/er hat) viel Blut verloren.**	ikh HAA-beh [zee/ehr haht] feel bloot fehr-LOH-ren.
She's/he's unconscious.	**Sie/er ist bewußtlos.**	zee/ehr ist beh-VUST-lohs.

99

I'm afraid something is broken/dislocated.	Ich fürchte, es ist etwas gebrochen/verrenkt.	ikh FEWRKH-teh, ehs ist EHT-vahs geh-BROKH-en/fehr-REHNKT.
I can't move my arm/leg.	Ich kann den Arm/das Bein nicht bewegen.	ikh kahn dehn ahrm/dahs bine nikht beh-VAY-gen.
She/he burned herself/himself.	Sie/er hat sich verbrannt.	zee/ehr haht zikh fehr-BRAHNT.
I ate something poisonous.	Ich habe mich vergiftet.	ikh HAA-beh mikh fehr-GIF-tet.
Where's the doctor/nurse?	Wo ist der Arzt/die Krankenschwester?	voh ist dehr ahrtst/dee KRAHN-ken-shvehs-te(r)?
I'm in pain.	Ich habe Schmerzen.	ikh HAA-beh SHMEHRT-sen.
I can't eat/sleep.	Ich kann nicht essen/schlafen.	ikh kahn nikht EHS-sen/SHLAA-fen.
How long will I have to stay in the hospital?	Wie lange muß ich im Krankenhaus bleiben?	vee LAHNG-eh mus ikh im KRAHN-ken-hows BLYE-ben?
Please notify my family.	Benachrichtigen Sie bitte meine Familie.	beh-NAHKH-rikh-ti-gen zee BIT-teh MINE-eh fah-MEEL-yeh.
What are the visiting hours?	Wann sind die Besuchszeiten?	vahn zint dee beh-ZOOKS-tsye-ten?

AT THE DENTIST'S

| Can you recommend a good dentist? | Können Sie mir einen guten Zahnarzt empfehlen? | KU(R)-nen zee meer INE-en GOO-ten TSAAN-ahrtst ehm-PFAY-len? |
| I need an (urgent) appointment to see Dr. . . . | Ich brauche einen (dringenden) Termin bei Herrn/Frau Dr. . . . | ikh BROW-kheh INE-en [DRING-en-den] tehr-MEEN bye hehrn/frow DOK-tor . . . |

I have a (terrible) toothache.	Ich habe (furchtbare) Zahnschmerzen.	ikh HAA-beh [FOORKHT-bahr-eh] TSAAN-shmehrt-sen.
My gums are bleeding.	Das Zahnfleisch blutet.	dahs TSAAN-fleysh BLOO-tet.
I've lost a filling/crown.	Ich habe eine Plombe/Krone ver loren.	ikh HAA-beh INE-eh PLOM-beh/KROH-neh fehr-LOH-ren.
I've broken a tooth.	Ich habe einen Zahn ausgebissen.	ikh HAA-beh INE-en tsaan OWS-geh-bis-sen.
Is it . . .	Ist es . . .	ist ehs . . .
• an abcess?	• ein Abszess?	• ine ahps-TSEHS?
• an infection?	• eine Infektion?	• INE-eh in-fehk-TSYOHN?
• a cavity?	• ein Zahn mit Karies?	• ine tsaan mit KAH-ree-ehs?
Can the tooth be saved?	Ist der Zahn noch zu retten?	ist dehr tsaan nohkh tsoo REH-ten?
I don't want to have it pulled.	Ich will ihn nicht ziehen lassen.	ikh vil een nikht TSEE-en LAHS-en.
Can you fix it temporarily?	Können Sie ihn provisorisch behandeln?	KU(R)-nen zee een pro-vi-ZOR-ish beh-HAHN-deln?
Can you fill it with silver/gold?	Können Sie ihn mit Silberamalgam/Gold plombieren?	KU(R)-nen zee een mit ZIL-be(r)-ah-maal-gam/gohlt plom-BEER-en?
Please give me a local anesthetic.	Geben Sie mir bitte eine Spritze.	GAY-ben zee meer BIT-teh INE-eh SHPRIT-seh.
Can you fix my denture/bridge?	Können Sie mein Gebiß/meine Brücke reparieren?	KU(R)-nen zee mine geh-BIS/MINE-eh BREW-keh reh-pah-REE-ren?
Do I need another appointment?	Brauche ich noch einen Termin?	BROW-kheh ikh nohkh INE-en tehr-MEEN?

101

AT THE OPTICIAN'S

Can you repair these glasses?	**Können Sie diese Brille reparieren?**	KU(R)-nen zee DEE-zeh BRIL-leh reh-pah-REER-en?
The frame/one lens is broken.	**Das Gestell/eine Linse ist zerbrochen.**	dahs geh-SHTEHL/INE-eh LIN-zeh ist tsehr-BROKH-en.
I've lost a contact lens.	**Ich habe eine Kontaklinse verloren.**	ikh HAA-beh INE-eh kon-TAHKT-lin-zeh fehr-LOH-ren.
Can you replace it?	**Können Sie sie ersetzen?**	KU(R)-nen zee zee ehr-ZEHT-sen?
How long will it take?	**Wie lange dauert es?**	vee LAHNG-eh DOW-ehrt ehs?
I'd like . . .	**Ich hätte gern . . .**	ikh HEHT-teh gehrn . . .
• contact lens liquid.	• **Kontaktlinsen-flüβigkeit.**	• kon-TAHKT-lin-zen-flews-ikh-kite.
• a pair of sunglasses.	• **eine Sonnenbrille.**	• INE-eh ZON-nen-bril-leh.

9/ON THE ROAD

CAR RENTALS

Most of the major U.S. car rental agencies have branches in the German-speaking countries, and it is easier and usually more economical to make rental arrangements before you arrive in Europe.* Many travel agencies offer attractive fly-drive packages, which insure that the rental car you want will be waiting for you. Once there, you can use your U.S. driver's license to drive and to rent a car, but if you're renting for more than a month, you may need an International Driver's License, available here from AAA at a nominal charge. If you need a car for longer periods, you may want to investigate leasing options.

*Be sure to specify a car with automatic transmission if you don't know how to drive one with a stick shift.

DIALOGUE: AT THE CAR RENTAL AGENCY (*BEI DER AUTOVERMIETUNG*)

Reisender:	**Ich möchte einen preiswerten Kleinwagen mieten.**	ikh MU(R)KH-teh INE-en PRICE-vehr-ten KLINE-vaa-gen MEE-ten.
Angestellte:	**Wir können Ihnen einen VW Golf mit Automatik anbieten.**	veer KU(R)-nen EE-nen INE-en fow vay gohlf mit ow-toh-MAH-tik AHN-bee-ten.
Reisender:	**Kann ich ihn nur über das Wochenende nehmen?**	kahn ikh een noor EW-be(r) dahs VOHKH-en-ehn-deh NAY-men?
Angestellte:	**Sicher. So bekommen Sie einen Sonderpreis, inklusive unbegrenzter Kilometerzahl.**	ZIKH-e(r). zoh beh-KOM-men zee INE-en ZON-de(r)-price, in-klu-SEE-veh un-beh-GREHNTS-te(r) kee-loh-MAY-te(r)-tsaal.
Reisender:	**Wunderbar. Abgemacht.**	VUN-de(r)-baar. AHP-geh-mahkht.

103

Angestellte:	**Schön. Darf ich Ihren Pass und Führerschein sehen?**	shu(r)n. dahrf ikh EE-ren pahs unt FEW-re(r)-shine ZAY-en?

. . . .

Traveler:	I'd like to rent an economical subcompact car.
Employee:	We can offer you a VW Golf with automatic transmission.
Traveler:	Can I take it just for the weekend?
Employee:	Of course. That way you get a special price, including unlimited milage.
Traveler:	Great. It's a deal.
Employee:	Fine. May I see your passport and driver's license?

Is there a car rental agency in this town?	**Gibt es eine Autovermietung in dieser Stadt?**	gipt ehs INE-eh OW-toh-fehr-MEE-tung in DEE-ze(r) shtaht?
I'd like to rent . . .	**Ich möchte —— mieten.**	ikh MU(R)KH-teh —— MEE-ten.
• a small/subcompact car.	• **einen Kleinwagen**	• INE-en KLINE-vaa-gen
• a midsize car.	• **einen Mittelklassewagen**	• INE-en MIT-tel-klahs-se-vaa-gen
• a large car.	• **einen großen Wagen**	• INE-en GROHS-sen VAA-gen
• a station wagon.	• **einen Kombiwagen**	• INE-en KOM-bee-vaa-gen
• a car with automatic transmission.	• **einen Wagen mit Automatik**	• INE-en VAA-gen mit ot-toh-MAH-tik
• your least expensive car.	• **Ihren preiswertesten Wagen**	• EE-ren PRICE-vehr-tehs-ten VAA-gen

104

How much is it per . . .	**Wieviel kostet es pro . . .**	VEE-feel KOS-tet ehs proh . . .
• day/week/month?	• **Tag/Woche/ Monat?**	• taak/VOHKH-eh/ MOH-naat?
• kilometer?	• **Kilometer?**	• kee-loh-MAY-te(r)?
I'd like comprehensive insurance.	**Ich möchte eine Vollkaskover- sicherung.**	ikh MU(R)KH-teh INE- eh VOL-kahs-koh- vehr-sikh-eh-rung.
Does the rental price include unlimited milage?	**Ist unbegrenzte Kilometerzahl im Mietpreis inbegriffen?**	ist un-beh-GREHNTS- teh kee-loh-MAY- te(r)-tsaal im MEET- price IN-beh-grif-en?
Can I leave the car in another city?	**Kann ich den Wagen anderswo zurückgeben?**	kahn ikh dehn VAA- gen AHN-dehrs-voh tsoo-REWK-gay-ben?
Will I be charged extra for this?	**Muß ich dafür extra bezahlen?**	mus ikh DAH-fewr EHKS-trah beh-TSAA- len?
Do you need . . .	**Brauchen Sie . . .**	BROW-khen zee . . .
• my driver's license?	• **meinen Führerschein?**	• MINE-en FEW-re(r)- shine?
• a deposit?	• **eine Kaution?**	• INE-eh kow- TSYOHN?

DRIVING/PARKING

All three German-speaking countries have extensive, well-main-tained highway networks and roads.* To use the *Autobahn* (superhighway) in Switzerland, you must purchase a *Vignette* (sticker) for your windshield. Some Alpine roads and tunnels in Austria charge tolls, while in Germany there are no tolls at all. The speed of some drivers on the German *Autobahn*, where 130 kilometers (80 miles) per hour is only the recommended speed limit, may take your breath away, so you may prefer to plan your route along the more scenic, secondary highways. For more stress-free driving, try to avoid rush hour in and around cities and the seasonal peak traffic periods during school holidays.

*In East Germany the quality of the highways and roads varies considerably.

Besides lots and meters, larger towns and cities also have Blue Zones, where you need a *Parkscheibe* (parking disk), available at no cost from tourist offices, gas stations, automobile clubs, and hotels. This honor-system parking option requires you to set your arrival time on the disk, display it on your windshield, and leave within an allotted time.

Asking Directions*

Excuse me.	**Entschuldigen Sie, bitte.**	ehnt-SHOOL-di-gen zee, BIT-teh.
I've lost my way.	**Ich habe mich verfahren.**	ikh HAA-beh mikh fehr-FAA-ren.
Can you tell me how I get to . . .	**Können Sie mir sagen, wie ich nach —— komme?**	KU(R)-nen zee meer ZAA-gen, vee ikh nahkh —— KOM-meh?
Is this the road to ——?	**Führt diese Straße nach ——?**	fewrt DEE-zeh SHTRAAS-eh nahkh ——?
How far is it to the next town/to ——?	**Wie weit ist es bis zur nächsten Stadt/bis zu ——?**	vee vite ist ehs bis tsoor NAYKH-sten staht/bis tsoo ——?
Is there a better/faster/less congested road?	**Gibt es eine bessere/schnellere/wenig befahrene Straße?**	gipt ehs INE-eh BEHS-seh-reh/SHNEHL-leh-reh/VAY-nikh beh-FAA-reh-neh-SHTRAAS-seh?
Should I drive straight ahead/to the left/right?	**Soll ich geradeaus/links/rechts fahren?**	zol ikh geh-RAA-deh-ows/links/rehkhts FAA-ren?
Where should I turn?	**Wo soll ich abbiegen?**	voh zol ikh AHP-bee-gen?
Where can I get a good road map?	**Wo bekomme ich eine gute Straßenkarte?**	voh beh-KOM-meh ikh INE-eh GOO-teh SHTRAAS-sen-kahr-teh?

*Additional phrases are in Chapter 3, Finding Your Way, page 28.

May I park here?	**Darf ich hier parken?**	dahrf ikh heer PAHR-ken?
Is there a parking lot near here?	**Gibt es in der Nähe einen Parkplatz?**	gipt ehs in dehr NAY-eh INE-en PAHRK-plahts?
Do you have change for the parking meter?	**Haben Sie Kleingeld für die Parkuhr?**	HAA-ben zee KLINE-gehlt fewr dee PAHRK-oor?

DISTANCES AND LIQUID MEASURES

As you are no doubt aware, distances are expressed in kilometers and liquid measures (gas and oil, for example) in liters.* Unless you are a whiz at mental calculating, the switch from one system to another can be hard to get used to. The following conversion formulas and charts should help.

*In Europe, gas mileage is calculated not in miles per gallon, but in liters per 100 kilometers.

MILES/KILOMETERS

1 kilometer (km) = .62 miles	1 mile = 1.61 km (1,61 km)
Kilometers	**Miles**
1	0.62
5	3.1
8	5.0
10	6.2
15	9.3
20	12.4
50	31.0
75	46.5
100	62.0

GALLONS/LITERS

1 liter (l) = .26 gallon	1 gallon = 3.75 liters (3,75 l)
Liters	**Gallons**
10	2.6
15	3.9
20	5.2
30	7.8
40	10.4
50	13.0
60	15.6
70	18.2

AT THE SERVICE STATION

Where's the nearest gas station (with service/with self service)?	**Wo ist die nächste Tankstelle [mit Bedienung/mit Selbstbedienung (SB)]?**	voh ist dee NAYKH-steh TAHNK-shtehl-eh [mit beh-dee-nung/mit ZEHLPST-beh-dee-nung]?
Fill it, please, with . . .	**Volltanken, bitte, mit . . .**	FOL-tahn-ken, BIT-teh, mit . . .
• regular/super.	• **Normal/Super.**	• nor-MAAL/ZOO-pe(r).
• unleaded.	• **bleifreiem Benzin.**	• BLYE-frye-em behn-TSEEN.
• diesel.	• **Diesel.**	• DEE-zel.
Give me 40 liters/marks of super.	**Geben Sie mir vierzig Liter/Mark Super.**	GAY-ben zee meer FEER-tsikh LEE-te(r)/mahrk ZOO-pe(r).
Please check the . . .	**Prüfen Sie bitte . . .**	PREW-fen zee BIT-teh . . .
• oil.	• **den Ölstand.**	• dehn U(R)L-shtahnt.
• water.	• **das Wasser.**	• dahs VAHS-se(r).
• battery.	• **die Batterie.**	• dee bah-teh-REE.
• brake fluid.	• **die Brems-flüβigkeit.**	• dee BREHMS-flews-sikh-kite.

108

• tire pressure.	• **den Reifendruck.**	• dehn REY-fen-druk.
• spare tire.	• **den Ersatzreifen.**	• dehn ehr-ZAHTS-rye-fen.
• lights.	• **die Beleuchtung.**	• dee beh-LOYKH-tung.
Please change the . . .	**Wechseln Sie bitte . . .**	VEHK-seln zee BIT-teh . . .
• oil.	• **das Motoröl.**	• dahs moh-TOHR-u(r)l.
• tire.	• **den Reifen.**	• dehn RYE-fen.
• fan belt.	• **den Keilriemen.**	• dehn KILE-ree-men.
• spark plugs.	• **die Zündkerzen.**	• TSEWNT-kehr-tsen.
• wipers.	• **die Scheiben-wischer.**	• dee SHYE-ben-vish-e(r).
Please clean the windshield.	**Reinigen Sie bitte die Windschutz-scheibe.**	RYE-ni-gen zee BIT-teh dee VINT-shuts-shye-beh.

BREAKDOWN/REPAIRS

Where's the nearest garage (for repairs)?	**Wo ist die nächste Reparatur-werkstatt?**	voh ist dee NAYKH-steh reh-pah-rah-TOOR-vehrk-shtaht?
I need a mechanic/tow truck.	**Ich brauche einen Mechaniker/ Abschlepp-wagen.**	ikh BROW-kheh INE-en meh-KHAH-ni-ke(r)/AHP-shlehp-vaa-gen.
My car has broken down.	**Mein Wagen hat eine Panne.**	mine VAA-gen haht INE-eh PAHN-eh.
It won't start.	**Er springt nicht an.**	ehr shpringt nikht ahn.
The battery is dead.	**Die Batterie ist leer.**	dee bah-teh-REE ist layr.
I have a flat tire.	**Ich habe einen Platten.**	ikh HAA-beh INE-en PLAHT-ten.
The engine overheats.	**Der Motor läuft zu heiß.**	dehr moh-TOHR loyft tsoo hice.
I've run out of gas.	**Der Tank ist leer.**	dehr tahnk ist layr.

109

I've locked the keys inside the car.	Ich habe die Schlüssel im Wagen abgeschlossen.	ikh HAA-beh dee SHLEWS-sel im VAA-gen AHP-geh-shlos-sen.
This is broken.	Das ist kaputt.	dahs ist kah-POOT.
The engine is making a funny sound.	Der Motor macht ein komisches Geräusch.	dehr moh-TOHR mahkht ine KOH-mish-es geh-ROYSH.
Something is wrong with the . . .	. . . ist/sind nicht in Ordnung.	. . . ist/zint nikht in ORT-nung.
• directional signals.	• Die Blinklichter	• dee BLINK-likh-te(r)
• headlights	• Die Scheinwerfer	• dee SHINE-vehr-fe(r)
• the electrical system.	• Die elektrische Anlage	• dee eh-LEHK-trish-eh AHN-laa-geh
• the ignition.	• Die Zündung	• dee TSEWN-dung
• the starter.	• Der Anlasser	• dehr AHN-lahs-se(r)
• carburetor.	• Der Vergaser	• dehr vehr-GAA-ze(r)
• fuel pump.	• Die Benzinpumpe	• dee behn-TSEEN-pum-peh
• brakes.	• Die Bremsen	• dee BREHM-zen
• radiator.	• Der Kühler	• dehr KEW-le(r)
• exhaust pipe.	• Der Auspuff	• dehr OWS-puf
• transmission.	• Das Getriebe	• dahs geh-TREE-beh
• wheels.	• Die Räder	• dee RAY-de(r)
Is it serious?	Ist es etwas Ernstes?	ist ehs EHT-vahs EHRN-stess?
Do you have the parts?	Haben Sie die Ersatzteile?	HAA-ben zee dee ehr-ZAHTS-tile-eh?
Can you repair it temporarily?	Können Sie es provisorisch reparieren?	KU(R)-nen zee ehs pro-vee-ZOH-rish reh-pah-REE-ren?
How long will it take?	Wie lange dauert es?	vee LAHNG-eh DOW-ert ehs?
How much will it cost?	Wieviel wird es kosten?	VEE-feel wirt ehs KOS-ten?
Can I have an itemized bill for my insurance?	Kann ich eine detaillierte Rechnung für meine Versicherung haben?	kahn ikh INE-eh deh-tah-YEER-teh REHKH-nung fewr MINE-eh fehr-ZIKH-eh-rung HAA-ben?

110

ROAD SIGNS

Ausfahrt	Exit
Ausfahrt Frei Halten	Don't Block Exit (Driveway)
Blaue Zone	Blue Parking Zone (requires parking disk)
Durchgangsverkehr	Through Traffic
Einbahnstrasse	One-Way Street
Einfahrt	Entrance
Einordnen	Get in Lane
Ende des Parkverbots	End of No-Parking Zone
Frostschäden	Frost Damage
Fussgängerzone	Pedestrian Zone
Gefährliche Gefälle	Dangerous Descent
Glatteis	Ice Conditions
Halt, Polizei	Stop, Police
Hupen Verboten	No Horn Honking
Kurzparkzone	Limited Parking Zone
Langsam Fahren	Drive Slowly
Lawinengefahr	Avalanche Danger
Links Fahren	Keep Left
LKW	Trucks/Truck Route
Notausfahrt	Emergency Exit
Nur für Anlieger	Access Only for Residents
Parken Verboten	No Parking
Rechts Fahren	Keep Right
Sackgasse	Dead-End Street
Schlechte Fahrbahn	Bad Road Surface
Schule	School
Stadtmitte	Center of Town
Stau	Traffic Jam
Steinschlag	Falling Rocks
Strassenarbeit auf 3 KM	Road Work for the Next 3 km
Umleitung	Detour
Verkehrsstau auf 10 KM	Traffic Backup for the Next 10 km
. . . Verboten	No . . .
Vorfahrt Gewähren	Yield
Vorsicht	Caution
Zoll	Customs/Border Crossing

ONE WAY

MAIN ROAD

PARKING

SUPERHIGHWAY

YIELD

GAS
(10 km ahead)

DANGER AHEAD

DANGEROUS DESCENT

BUMPS

ROAD NARROWS

LEVEL (RAILROAD) CROSSING

TWO-WAY TRAFFIC

SLIPPERY ROAD

CAUTION—SHARP CURVES

PEDESTRIAN CROSSING

NO ENTRY FOR MOTOR VEHICLES

DANGEROUS INTERSECTION AHEAD

STOP

NO ENTRY

MINIMUM SPEED (km/hr)

SPEED LIMIT (km/hr)

DIRECTION TO BE FOLLOWED

OVERHEAD CLEARANCE (meters)

ROTARY

NO PASSING

END OF NO PASSING ZONE

END OF RESTRICTION

NO LEFT TURN

NO U-TURN

NO PARKING

10/COMMUNICATIONS

TELEPHONES

The easiest but most expensive way to make a telephone call is from your hotel. However, public phones are also relatively easy to operate and usually have multilingual instructions posted inside. The phone networks in Germany, Switzerland, and Austria are part of the postal systems, and all post offices have public phones. From these and from most other coin-operated public phones, you can place direct-dial long-distance and international calls. Local calls in Germany now cost 30 *Pfennig*. Newer pay phones make change and also indicate on long-distance calls when you must insert more coins.

Telephone numbers are quoted in pairs, and *zwei* over the phone becomes *zwo* [tsvoh]. When spelling out words over the phone, use the telephone alphabet and method described on pages 6–7.

DIALOGUE: A TELEPHONE CALL (*EIN TELFONGESPRÄCH*)

Birgit Lenz:	**Hallo. Hier spricht Lenz* bei der Firma Beck und Böttger.**	HAH-loh, heer shprikht lehnts bye dehr FIR-mah behk unt BU(R)T-ge(r).
Bernd Pohl:	**Guten Morgen. Hier spricht Bernd Pohl aus Hamburg. Darf ich Herrn Beck sprechen?**	GOO-ten MOR-gen. heer shprikht behrnt pohl ows HAHM-boork. dahrf ikh hehrn behk SHPREHKH-en?
Birgit Lenz:	**Einen Augenblick, bitte. . . . Es tut mir leid, er ist im Moment ausser Haus.**	INE-en OW-gen-blik, BIT-teh . . . ehs toot meer light, ehr ist im mo-MEHNT OWS-e(r) hows.
Bernd Pohl:	**Wann ist er zurück?**	vahn ist ehr tsoo-REWK?
Birgit Lenz:	**Um drei Uhr ungefähr.**	oom drye oor UN-ge-fayr.

Bernd Pohl:	**Sagen Sie ihm bitte, daß ich angerufen habe.**	ZAA-gen zee ihm BIT-teh, dahs ikh AHN-ge-roo-fen HAA-beh.
Birgit Lenz:	**Ich werde es ihm ausrichten. Soll er Sie zurückrufen?**	ikh VEHR-deh ehs ihm OWS-rikh-ten. zol ehr zee tsoo-REWK-roo-fen?
Bernd Pohl:	**Ja, bitte. Die Nummer hat er.**	yaa, BIT-teh. dee NUM-me(r) haht ehr.
Birgit Lenz:	**Es geht in Ordnung. Auf Wiederhören.**	ehs gayt in ORT-nung. owf VEE-de(r)-hu(r)-ren.
Bernd Pohl:	**Vielen Dank und auf Wiederhören.**	FEE-len dahnk unt owf VEE-de(r)-hu(r)-ren.

. . . .

Birgit Lenz:	Hello. This is Birgit Lenz at Beck and Böttger.
Bernd Pohl:	Good morning. This is Bernd Pohl calling from Hamburg. May I speak to Mr. Beck?
Birgit Lenz:	Just a moment. . . . I'm sorry, he's away right now.
Bernd Pohl:	When will be be back?
Birgit Lenz:	Around three.
Bernd Pohl:	Please tell him I called.
Birgit Lenz:	I'll give him the message. Should he call you back?
Bernd Pohl:	Yes, please. He has my number.
Birgit Lenz:	I'll see that he calls you. Good-bye.
Bernd Pohl:	Thank you and good-bye.

*When answering the phone, German speakers usually identify themselves with last names only.

115

Where's a telephone/ telephone directory?	Wo ist ein Telefon/ Telefonbuch?	voh ist ine tay-lay-FOHN/tay-lay-FOHN-bookh?
Is there a phone booth near here?	Gibt es in der Nähe eine Telefonzelle?	gipt ehs in dehr NAY-eh INE-eh tay-lay-FOHN-tsehl-leh?
May I use your phone?	Darf ich Ihr Telefon benutzen?	dahrf ikh eer tay-lay-FOHN beh-NUT-sen?
How much/what coins do I need for a local call?	Wieviel/welche Münzen brauche ich für ein Ortsgespräch?	VEE-feel/VEHL-kheh MEWN-tsen BROW-kheh ikh fewr ine ORTS-geh-shpraykh?
What's the area code for ——?	Welche Vorwahlnummer hat ——?	VEHL-kheh FOHR-vaal-num-me(r) haht ——?
How do I reach the (international) operator?	Wie wähle ich die (internationale) Vermittlung?	vee VAY-leh ikh dee [in tehr-nah-tsyo-NAA-le fehr-MIT-lung?
Hello. I'd like . . .	Guten Tag. Ich möchte . . .	GOO-ten taak. ikh MU(R)KH-teh . . .
• Stuttgart 14-43-70.	• Stuttgart 14-43-70.	• SHTUT-gahrt [FEER-tsayn DRYE-unt-feer-zikh-ZEEP-zikh)
• (international) information.	• die (internationale) Auskunft.	• dee [in-tehr-nah-tsyo NAA-leh] OWS-koonft.
• to place a long-distance call to London.	• ein Ferngespräch nach London.	• ine FEHRN-geh-shpraykh nahkh LON-don.
• a person-to-person call.	• ein Gespräch mit Voranmeldung.	• ine geh-SHPRAYKH mit FOHR-ahn-mehl-dung.
• a collect call.	• ein R-Gespräch.	• ine EHR-geh-shpraykh.
Please help me reach this number.	Helfen Sie mir bitte, diese Nummer zu erreichen.	HEHL-fen zee meer BIT teh, DEE-zeh NUM-me(r) tsoo ehr-RYEKH-en.

116

Operator, can I dial direct?	Fräulein, kann ich durchwählen?	FROY-line, kahn ikh DURKH-vay-len?
Connect me with the number/extension . . .	Verbinden Sie mich mit der Nummer/dem Nebenanschluβ . . .	fehr-BIN-den zee mikh mit dehr NUM-me(r)/dehm NAY-ben-ahn-shlus . . .
You gave me the wrong number.	Sie haben mich falsch verbunden.	zee HAA-ben mikh fahlsh fehr-BUN-den.
The connection is bad.	Die Verbindung ist schlecht.	dee vehr-BIN-dung ist shlehkht.
We were cut off.	Wir sind unterbrochen worden.	veer zint un-te(r)-BROKH-en VOR-den.
May I speak to Mr./Mrs. . . .	Darf ich Herrn/Frau ——— sprechen?	dahrf ikh hehrn/frow ——— SHPREHKH-EN?
Speaking.	Am Apparat.	ahm ah-pah-RAAT.
Please speak louder/more slowly.	Sprechen Sie bitte lauter/langsamer.	SHPREHKH-en zee BIT-teh LOW-te(r)/LAHNG-zaa-me(r).
Please repeat.	Wiederholen Sie, bitte.	vee-de(r)-HOH-len zee BIT-teh.
May I leave a message for Mr./Mrs.———?	Darf ich Herrn/Frau ——— eine Nachricht hinterlassen?	dahrf ikh hehrn/frow ——— INE-eh NAKH-rikht HIN-ter-lahs-sen?

Phrases You'll Hear Over the Phone

German	Pronunciation	English
Wer ist am Apparat?	vehr ist ahm ah-pah-RAAT?	Who's calling?
Wen wollen Sie sprechen?	vehn VOL-len zee SHPREHKH-en?	Whom do you want to speak to?
Bleiben Sie am Apparat.	BLYE-ben zee ahm ah-pah-RAAT.	Hold the line.
Es meldet sich niemand.	ehs MEHL-det zikh NEE-mahnt.	There's no answer.

German	Pronunciation	English
Die Leitung ist besetzt.	dee LYE-tung ist beh-ZEHTST.	The line is busy.
Sie sind falsch verbunden.	zee zint fahlsh fehr-BUN-den.	You have the wrong number.
Ein Anruf für Sie.	ine AHN-roof fewr zee.	You have a call.
Welche Nummer haben Sie gewählt?	VEHL-kheh NUM-me(r) HAA-ben zee geh-VAYLT?	What number did you dial?
Sie/er ist im Moment nicht da.	zee/ehr ist im mo-MEHNT nikht daa.	She/he is not here at the moment.
Kann ich etwas ausrichten?	kahn ikh EHT-vahs OWS-rikh-ten?	Can I take a message?
Können Sie später zurückrufen?	KU(R)-nen zee SHPAY-te(r) tsoo-REWK-roo-fen?	Can you call back later?

THE POST OFFICE

The hours of Germany's *Bundespost* (Federal Postal Service) are from 8 A.M. to 6 P.M.; Saturdays from 8 to 12 noon. Austrian post offices close at 5 P.M. and have a two-hour break at noon; in Switzerland the hours are from 7:30 A.M. to 6:30 P.M. with a break from noon to 1:30 P.M. (Saturdays from 8 to 11 A.M.). Post offices in the main train stations of larger cities have longer hours. Mailboxes in all three countries are yellow, sometimes blue in Austria. Stamps are available at newsstands and kiosks, as well as at post offices in Switzerland and Austria, but in Germany only at post offices and postal stamp automats. All post offices receive and distribute *postlagernd*—in Switzerland *poste restante*—(general delivery) mail.

I want to mail this letter.	**Ich will diesen Brief aufgeben.**	ikh vil DEE-zen breef OWF-gay-ben.
Where's the nearest mail box?	**Wo ist der nächste Briefkasten?**	voh ist dehr NAYKH-steh BREEF-kahs-ten?
I'm looking for the post office.	**Ich suche das Postamt.**	ikh ZOO-kheh dahs POST-ahmt.

Where is the window for . . .	Wo ist der Schalter für . . .	voh ist dehr SHAHL-te(r) fewr . . .
• stamps?	• Briefmarken?	• BREEF-mahr-ken?
• packages?	• Pakete?	• pah-KAY-teh?
• money orders?	• Postanweisung-en?	• POST-ahn-vye-zung-en?
• telegrams?	• Telegramme?	• tay-lay-GRAAM-meh?
• general delivery?	• postlagernde Sendungen?	• POST-laa-gehrn-deh ZEHN-dung-en?
How much postage do I need on ——— to the U.S./ Canada/ England?	Was kostet ——— nach USA/ Kanada/ England?	vahs KOS-tet ——— nahkk oo-ehs-aa/KAA-nah-dah/ EHNG-lahnt?
• a letter	• ein Brief	• ine breef
• a postcard	• eine Postkarte	• INE-eh POST-kahr-teh
• an airmail letter	• ein Luftpostbrief	• ine LUFT-post-breef
• an express (special delivery) letter	• ein Eilbrief	• ine ILE-breef
• a registered letter	• ein Einschrei-benbrief	• ine INE-shrye-ben-breef
• this package	• dieses Paket	• DEE-zehs pah-KAYT
When will it arrive?	Wann wird es ankommen?	vahn virt ehs AHN-kom-men?
I'd like to insure this letter/package.	Ich möchte diesen Brief/dieses Paket versichern lassen.	ikh MU(R)KH-teh DEE-zen breef/DEE-zehs pah-KAYT fehr-ZIKH-ern LAHS-en.
Do you have commemorative stamps for stamp collectors?	Haben Sie Sondermarken für Briefmarken-sammler?	HAA-ben zee ZOHN-de(r)-mahr-ken fewr BREEF-mahr-ken-zahm-le(r)?
May I please have . . .	Geben Sie mir bitte . . .	GAY-ben zee meer BIT-teh . . .
• ten (airmail) stamps.	• zehn (Luftpost) Briefmarken.	• tsayn [LUFT-post] BREEF-mahr-ken.

119

• five aerograms.	• **fünf Aerogramme**	• fewnf eye-roh-GRAAM-meh.
• three envelopes.	• **drei Briefumschläge**	• drye BREEF-oom-shlay-geh.
Is there any mail for me?	**Ist Post für mich da?**	ist post fewr mikh daa?
Here's my passport.	**Hier ist mein Paß.**	heer ist mine pahs.

TELEGRAMS

Telegrams can be sent from some hotels, and by phone, otherwise only from post offices.

I'd like to send a telegram/telex to . . .	**Ich möchte ein Telegram/Telex nach ——— aufgeben.**	ikh MU(R)KH-teh ine tay-lay-GRAAM/TAY-lehks nahkh ——— OWF-gay-ben.
May I have a telegram form, please.	**Ein Telegramm-formular, bitte.**	ine tay-lay-GRAAM-for-moo-LAHR, BIT-teh.
How much is it per word?	**Was kostet es pro Wort?**	vahs KOS-tet ehs proh vort?
Can I send it collect?	**Kann ich es als Nachnahme schicken?**	kahn ikh ehs ahls NAHKH-naa-meh SHIK-en?

THE MEDIA

In the larger cities of German-speaking Europe, newspapers and magazines from all over the world are available, including English-language publications such as *Newsweek, Time, London Times,* the *New York Times,* the *International Herald Tribune,* the *Wall Street Journal,* and the *Christian Science Monitor.* Should you have trouble locating them, look in the Yellow Pages for international or English-language bookstores and newsstands. BBC and AFN (American Forces Network) radio broadcasts can be received all over Europe, and American and British TV programs are becoming increasingly available through cable and satellite hookups. Video rental shops, most of them including a large selection of English-language films, are also proliferating rapidly. You may want to tune in to German-language radio and TV, especially news broadcasts, as this is an excellent way to improve your language skills.

Publications

Do you have ——— in English?	**Haben Sie ——— in Englisch?**	HAA-ben zee ——— in EHNG-lish?
• newspapers	• **Zeitungen**	• TSITE-ung-en
• magazines	• **Zeitschriften**	• TSITE-shrif-ten
• books/publications	• **Bücher/Veröffent- lichungen**	• BEW-khe(r)/fehr-U(R)F-ehnt-likh-ung-en

Radio and TV

Are there any English-language ——— here?	**Gibt es hier englisch-sprachige . . .**	gipt ehs heer EHNG-lish-shprahkh-i-geh . . .
• radio stations	• **Radiosender?**	• RAA-dee-oh-zehn-de(r)?
• TV channels	• **Fernseh-programme?**	• FEHRN-zay-proh-GRAAM-meh?
What is the dial setting/channel number?	**Auf welcher Frequenz?/ Welches Programm?**	owf VEHL-khe(r) fray-KVEHNTS?/VEHL-khess proh-GRAAM?
Do you have a TV guide?	**Haben Sie ein Fernseh-programm?***	HAA-ben zee ine FEHRN-zay-proh-graam?

*The word for TV channel and TV guide is the same in German.

11/SIGHTSEEING

To get the most out of your trip and really take advantage of unique cultural and sightseeing opportunities, we suggest reading beforehand about the places you will be visiting. National tourist offices here in this country and local offices in the countries you visit will also provide information to help you plan your itinerary. For a different and usually very memorable impression of a city, strike out on your own and use public transportation.

DIALOGUE: TOURING THE CITY (*STADTBESICHTIGUNG*)

Reisender:	Was für Sehenswürdigkeiten gibt es in dieser Stadt?	vahs fewr SAY-ens-vewr-dikh-kite-en gipt ehs in DEE-ze(r) shtaht?
Hotelangestellte:	Hier gibt es eine Menge interessante Sachen zu sehen.	heer gipt ehs INE-eh MEHNG-eh in-teh-reh-SAHN-teh ZAHKH-en tsoo ZAY-en.
Reisender:	Und wo liegen sie?	unt voh LEE-gen zee?
Hotelangestellte:	Die meisten liegen in der Altstadt.	dee MICE-ten LEE-gen in dehr AHLT-shtaht.
Reisender:	Ist es leicht, dahin zu kommen?	ist ehs lyekht dah-HIN tsoo KOM-men?
Hotelangestellte:	Ja, sicher. Der dreier Bus, der hier an der Ecke hält, fährt direkt in die Altstadt.	yaa, ZIKH-e(r). dehr DRYE-e(r) bus, dehr heer ahn dehr EH-keh hehlt, fehrt dee-REHKT in dee AHLT-shtaht.
Reisender:	Gibt es da einen Dom?	gipt ehs da INE-en dohm?

Hotelangestellte:	**Ja, sogar einen sehr berühmten spätgotischen Dom und dazu mehrere Museen.**	yaa, zoh-GAHR INE-en zehr beh-REWM-ten SHPAYT-goh-tish-en dohm unt dah-TSOO MEH-rehr-eh moo-ZAY-en.
Reisender:	**Vielen Dank für die Hinweise.**	FEE-len dahnk fewr dee HIN-vye-zeh.

. . . .

Traveler:	What kind of sites worth seeing are there in this town?
Hotel clerk:	There are many interesting things to see here.
Traveler:	And where are they?
Hotel clerk:	Most of them are in the old part of the city.
Traveler:	Is it easy to get there?
Hotel clerk:	Yes, of course. The number three bus that stops here on the corner goes right there.
Traveler:	Is there a cathedral there?
Hotel clerk:	Yes, in fact a very famous late gothic cathedral and several museums as well.
Traveler:	Thanks very much for the tips.

SIGHTSEEING IN TOWN

Where is the tourist office?	**Wo ist das Fremdenverkehrsbüro?**	voh ist dahs FREHM-den-fehr-kehrs-bew-roh?
What are the most important things to see?	**Was sind die wichtigsten Sehenswürdigkeiten?**	vahs zint dee VIKH-tikh-sten ZAY-ens-vewr-dikh-kite-en?

123

Do you have . . .	Haben Sie . . .	HAA-ben zee . . .
• a map of the town?	• einen Stadtplan?	• INE-en SHTAHT-plaan?
• a guidebook for the town/area (in English)?	• einen Stadtführer/ Reiseführer für die Gegend (auf Englisch)?	• INE-en SHTAHT-few-re(r)/RYE-zeh-few-re(r) fewr dee GAY-gehnt [owf EHNG-lish]?
Can you recommend a tour of the town/an excursion?	Können Sie eine Stadtrundfahrt/ einen Ausflug empfehlen?	KU(R)-nen zee INE-eh SHTAHT-runt-faart/ INE-en OWS-floog ehm-PFAY-len?
Does the tour guide speak English?	Spricht der Fremdenführer Englisch?	shprikht dehr FREHM-den-few-re(r) EHNG-lish?
When/Where does the tour start?	Wann/Wo beginnt die Rundfahrt?	vahn/voh beh-GINT dee RUNT-faart?
How long does it last?	Wie lange dauert sie?	vee LAHNG-eh DOW-ert zee?
How much does it cost?	Was kostet sie?	vahs KOS-tet zee?
Does that include lunch?	Ist das Mittagessen inbegiffen?	ist dahs MIT-taag-ehs-sen IN-beh-grif-en?
We'd like an English-speaking guide for . . .	Wir möchten einen englisch-sprechenden Fremdenführer für . . .	veer MU(R)KH-ten INE-en EHNG-lish-shprehkh-en-den FREHM-den-few-re(r) fewr . . .
• an afternoon.	• einen Nachmittag.	• INE-en NAHKH-mit-taak.
• a day.	• einen Tag.	• INE-en taak.
Where is/are the . . .	Wo ist/wo sind . . .	voh ist/voh zint . . .
• abbey?	• die Abtei?	• dee ahp-TYE?
• amusement park?	• der Vergnügungspark?	• dehr fehrg-NEW-gungks-paark?
• aquarium?	• das Aquarium?	• dahs ah-KVAH-ree-oom?
• art galleries?	• die Kunstgalerien?	• die KUNST-gah-leh-ree-en?

artists' quarter?	das Künstlerviertel?	dahs KEWNST-lehr-feer-tel?
botanical gardens?	der Botanische Garten?	dehr bo-TAA-nish-eh GAAR-ten?
castle?	das Schloβ/die Burg?	dahs shlos/dee boork?
cathedral?	der Dom/die Kathedrale?	dehr dohm/dee kaa-tay-DRAA-leh?
caves?	die Höhlen?	dee HU(R)-len?
cemetery?	der Friedhof?	dehr FREET-hohf?
chapel?	die Kapelle?	dee kah-PEHL-leh?
church?	die Kirche?	dee KEER-kheh?
city center/ downtown?	die Stadtmitte/das Zentrum/die Innenstadt?	dee SHTAHT-mit-teh/dahs TSEHN-trum/dee IN-nen-shtaht?
city/town hall?	das Rathaus?	dahs RAAT-hows?
city walls/ ramparts?	die Stadtmauern?	dee SHTAHT-mow-ern?
commercial district?	das Geschäftsviertel?	dahs geh-SHEHFTS-feer-tel?
concert hall?	die Konzerthalle?	dee kon-TSEHRT-hahl-leh?
convent/ monastery?	das Kloster?	dahs KLOHS-te(r)?
convention hall?	die Kongresshalle?	dee kon-GREHS-hahl-leh?
courthouse?	das Gericht?	dahs geh-RIKHT?
exhibition center?	die Ausstellungshalle?	dee OWS-shtehl-lungs-hahl-leh?
factory?	die Fabrik?	dee fah-BRIK?
fair (trade fair)?	die (Handels-)Messe?	dee [HAHN-dels-]MEHS-seh?
flea market?	der Flohmarkt?	dehr FLOH-mahrkt?
fortress?	die Burg?	dee boork?
fountain?	der (Spring-)Brunnen?	dehr [SHPRING-]BRUN-nen?
gardens?	die Gärten/Grünanlagen?	dee GEHR-ten/GREWN-ahn-laa-gen?

125

grave/tomb of ——?	das Grab von ——?	dahs grahp fon ——?
harbor?	der Hafen?	dehr HAA-fen?
library?	die Bibliothek?	dee bib-lee-oh-TAYK?
main square?	der Hauptplatz?	dehr HOWPT-plahts?
market?	der Markt?	dehr mahrkt?
memorial/monument?	das Denkmal?	dahs DEHNK-maal?
museum?	das Museum?	dahs moo-ZAY-um?
old town?	die Altstadt?	dee AHLT-shtaht?
open-air stage?	die Freilichtbühne?	dee FRYE-likht-bew-neh?
opera house?	das Opernhaus/die Oper?	dahs OH-pehrn-hows/dee OH-pe(r)?
palace?	der Palast/das Schloß?	dehr pah-LAHST/dahs shlos?
park?	der Park?	dehr pahrk?
planetarium?	das Planetarium?	dahs plah-neh-TAA-ree-um?
river?	der Fluß?	dehr flus?
ruins?	die Ruinen?	dee roo-EE-nen?
shopping district?	das Einkaufsviertel?	dahs INE-kowfs-feer-tel?
stadium?	das Stadion?	dahs SHTAA-dee-ohn?
statue?	die Statue?	dee SHTAA-too-eh?
stock exchange?	die Börse?	dee BU(R)-zeh?
synagogue?	die Synagoge?	dee zew-nah-GOH-geh?
theater?	das Theater?	dahs tay-AA-te(r)?
tower?	der Turm?	dehr toorm?
university?	die Universität?	dee u-nee-vehr-zi-TAYT?
zoo?	der Zoo?	dehr tsoh?
How old is that building?	Wie alt ist das Gebäude?	vee ahlt ist dahs geh-BOY-deh?
Who built it?	Wer hat es gebaut?	vehr haht ehs geh-BOWT?

| What monument is that? | Was für ein Denkmal ist das? | vahs fewr ine DEHNK-maal ist dahs? |
| Where can I get souvenirs? | Wo kann man Andenken kaufen? | voh kahn mahn AHN-dehn-ken KOW-fen? |

AT THE MUSEUM

When does the museum open/close?	Wann öffnet/schließt das Museum?	vahn U(R)F-net/shleest dahs moo-ZAY-um?
How much is the admission for . . .	Was kostet der Eintritt für . . .	vahs KOS-tet dehr INE-trit fewr . . .
• an adult?	• einen Erwachsenen?	• INE-en ehr-VAHK-seh-nen?
• a child?	• ein Kind?	• ine kint?
• a senior?	• einen Rentner?	• INE-en REHNT-ne(r)?
Is there a group discount?	Gibt es eine Gruppener-mäßigung?	gipt ehs INE-eh GRUP-pen-ehr-MAYS-i-gung?
Do you have . . .	Haben Sie . . .	HAA-ben zee . . .
• a guidebook (in English)?	• einen Museumsführer (in Englisch)?	• INE-en moo-ZAY-ums-few-re(r) [in EHNG-lish]?
• an audiocassette guide to the museum?	• einen Tonband-begleiter für das Museum?	• INE-en TOHN-bahnt-beh-GLITE-e(r) fewr dahs moo-ZAY-um?
May I take (flash) pictures?	Darf man (mit Blitz) fotografieren?	dahrf mahn [mit blits] foh-toh-grah-FEE-ren?
Where can I buy reproductions/catalogs?	Wo kann man Reproduktionen/Kataloge kaufen?	woh kahn mahn ray-pro-duk-TSYOH-nen/kah-tah-LOH-geh KOW-fen?
I'm interested in . . .	Ich interssiere mich für . . .	ikh in-teh-rehs-SEER-reh mikh fewr . . .
• antiques.	• Antiquitäten.	• ahn-tik-vee-TAY-ten.
• anthropology.	• Anthropologie.	• ahn-tro-po-lo-GEE.

127

• archaeology.	• **Archäologie.**	• ahr-keh-o-lo-GEE.
• classical art.	• **klassische Kunst.**	• KLAHS-ish-eh kunst.
• medieval art.	• **mittelalterliche Kunst.**	• MIT-tel-ahl-te(r)-likh-eh kunst.
• Renaissance art.	• **Renaissance* Kunst.**	• ruh-nay-SAH[N]S* kunst.
• modern art.	• **moderne Kunst.**	• mo-DEHR-neh kunst.
• impressionist art.	• **impressionistische Kunst.**	• im-prehs-yoh-NIS-tish-eh kunst.
• expressionist art.	• **expressionistische Kunst.**	• ehk-sprehs-yoh-NIS-tish-eh kunst.
• surrealist art.	• **surrealistische Kunst.**	• sur-reh-aa-LIS-tish-eh kunst.
• ceramics.	• **Keramik.**	• keh-RAA-mik.
• fine arts.	• **bildende Künste.**	• BIL-den-deh KEWN-steh.
• furniture.	• **Möbel.**	• MU(R)-bel.
• geography.	• **Geographie.**	• gay-o-grah-FEE.
• geology.	• **Geologie.**	• gay-o-lo-GEE.
• handicrafts.	• **Kunsthandwerk.**	• KUNST-hahnt-vehrk.
• history.	• **Geschichte.**	• geh-SHIKH-teh.
• musical instruments.	• **musikalische Instrumente.**	• moo-zee-KAH-lish-eh in-stroo-MEHN-teh.
• natural history.	• **Naturkunde.**	• nah-TOOR-kun-deh.
• painting.	• **Malerei.**	• maa-leh-RYE.
• pottery.	• **Töpferei.**	• tu(r)p-feh-RYE.
• sculpture.	• **Bildhauerei.**	• BILT-how-eh-rye.
• zoology.	• **Zoologie.**	• tsoh-o-lo-GEE.
Who is the . . .	**Wer ist der . . .**	vehr ist dehr . . .
• artist?	• **Künstler?**	• KEWNST-le(r)?
• architect?	• **Architekt?**	• ahr-khi-TEHKT?
• painter?	• **Maler?**	• MAA-le(r)?
• sculptor?	• **Bildhauer?**	• BILT-how-e(r)?
Who painted that picture?	**Wer hat das Bild gemalt?**	vehr haht dahs bilt geh-MAALT?
When was it painted?	**Wann wurde es gemalt?**	vahn VOOR-deh ehs geh-MAALT?

---

*German speakers use the French pronunciation, nasalizing the final n.

I think it's . . .	**Ich finde es . . .**	ikh FIN-deh ehs . . .
• beautiful.	• **schön.**	• shu(r)n.
• exceptional.	• **außerordentlich.**	• ows-e(r)-OR-dehnt-lihk.
• impressive.	• **eindrucksvoll.**	• INE-druks-fol.
• (un)interesting.	• **(un)interessant.**	• [UN-] in-teh-rehs-SAHNT.
• strange.	• **merkwürdig.**	• MEHRK-vu(r)-dikh.
• ugly.	• **häßlich.**	• HEHS-likh.

IN THE COUNTRY

Where are the most beautiful/ interesting landscapes?	**Wo sind die schönsten/ interessantesten Landschaften?**	voh zint dee SHU(R)N-sten/in-teh-rehs-SAHN-tehs-ten LAHNT-shahf-ten?
How far is it to ——?	**Wie weit ist es bis ——?**	vee vite ist ehs bis ——?
Is there a bus from here?	**Gibt es von hier einen Bus dahin?**	gipt ehs fon heer INE-en bus dah-HIN?
How long does the trip take?	**Wie lange dauert die Fahrt?**	vee LAHNG-eh DOW-ert dee faart?

COUNTRY SIGHTS

barn	**die Scheune**	dee SHOY-neh
beach	**der Strand**	dehr shtrahnt
bridge	**die Brücke**	dee BREW-keh
cliff	**der Felsen**	dehr FEHL-zen
farm	**der Bauernhof**	dehr BOW-ehrn-hohf
field	**das Feld**	dahs fehlt
flowers	**die Blumen**	dee BLOO-men
footpath	**der Fußweg**	dehr FOOS-vehk
forest/wood	**der Wald**	dehr vahlt
garden	**der Garten**	dehr GAAR-ten
hill	**der Hügel**	dehr HEW-gel
inn	**das Gasthaus**	dahs GAHST-hows
lake	**der See**	dehr zay

meadow	**die Wiese**	dee VEE-zeh
mountain pass	**der Paβ**	dehr pahs
pond	**der Teich**	dehr tyekh
river	**der Fluβ**	dehr flus
sea	**die See/das Meer**	dee zay/dahs mayr
valley	**das Tal**	dahs taal
village	**das Dorf**	dahs dorf
vineyard	**der Weinberg**	dehr VINE-behrk
waterfall	**der Wasserfall**	dehr VAHS-se(r)-fahl

RELIGIOUS SERVICES

Austria and southern Germany are predominantly Roman Catholic, northern Germany is mostly Protestant, and the Swiss population is evenly divided between the two religions; but in the larger cities of all three countries you will find other denominations and religions well represented. Most churches are open to the public, but visitors should be careful not to disturb any services in progress.

Is there a ——— nearby?	**Gibt es eine ——— in der Nähe?**	gipt ehs INE-eh ——— in dehr NAY-eh?
• Protestant church	• **evangelische Kirche**	• ay-vahn-GAY-lish-eh KEER-kheh
• Catholic church	• **katholische Kirche**	• kah-TOH-lish-eh KEER-kheh
• synagogue	• **Synagoge**	• zew-nah-GOH-geh
• mosque	• **Moschee**	• mo-SHAY
When does the mass/service begin?	**Wann beginnt die Messe/der Gottesdienst?**	vahn beh-GINT dee MEHS-eh/dehr GOT-tehs-deenst?
Is there a service in English?	**Gibt es einen Gottesdienst in Englisch?**	gipt ehs INE-en GOT-ehs-deenst in EHNG-lish?
I'm looking for a ——— who speaks English.	**Ich suche einen ———, der Englisch spricht.**	ikh ZOO-kheh INE-en ———, dehr EHNG-lish shprikht.
• minister	• **Pfarrer**	• PFAH-re(r)
• priest	• **Priester**	• PREES-te(r)
• rabbi	• **Rabbiner**	• rah-BEE-ne(r)
• mullah	• **Mullah**	• MOO-lah

12/SHOPPING

12/SHOPPING

In Germany, Switzerland, and Austria, shops usually open at 8 or 9 A.M. and close at 6 or 6:30 P.M. Many close at noon for a lunch break of one to two hours, and on Saturdays most German and Austrian shops close for the day around 2 P.M. while Swiss shops remain open until 4 or 5 P.M., but usually take Monday mornings off. In Germany the first Saturday of each month and the four Saturdays preceding Christmas are known as *langer Samstag* (long Saturday), during which shops remain open until 6 P.M.

On all purchases in Germany, there is a hefty (presently 14.5%) *Mehrwertsteuer* (value-added tax), which is refunded to those living outside Germany, but only if you ask at the place of purchase for the appropriate forms and fill them out. The amount of the tax will then be mailed to your home address.

DIALOGUE: AT THE DEPARTMENT STORE (*IM KAUFHAUS*)

Kunde:	**Guten Tag. Ich suche Schuhe. Bin ich hier richtig?**	GOO-ten taak. ikh ZOO-kheh shoo-eh. bin ikh heer RIKH-tikh?
Verkäuferin:	**Jawohl. Womit kann ich Ihnen dienen?**	yah-VOHL. voh-MIT kahn ikh EE-nen DEE-nen?
Kunde:	**Ich brauche sehr bequeme Schuhe zum Wandern.**	ikh BROW-kheh zehr beh-KVAY-meh SHOO-eh tsoom VAHN-dern.
Verkäuferin:	**Möchten Sie vielleicht Wanderstiefel?**	MU(R)KH-ten zee fee-LYEKHT VAHN-de(r)-shtee-fel?
Kunde:	**Nein, lieber normale Lederschuhe mit Gummisohlen, die ich auch in der Stadt tragen kann.**	nine, LEE-be(r) nor-MAA-leh LAY-der-shoo-eh mit GOO-mee-soh-len, dee ikh owkh in dehr shtaht TRAA-gen kahn.

131

| Verkäuferin: | **Welche Größe? Und welche Farbe hätten Sie gern?** | VEHL-kheh GRU(R)S-eh? unt VEHL-kheh FAHR-beh HEH-ten zee gehrn? |
| Kunde: | **Dreiundvierzig und dunkelbraun, bitte.** | DRYE-unt-feer-tsikh unt DUN-kel-brown, BIT-teh. |

. . . .

Shopper:	Hello, I'm looking for shoes. Am I in the right place?
Salesperson:	Yes, indeed. What can I do for you?
Shopper:	I need very comfortable shoes for hiking.
Salesperson:	Perhaps you'd like hiking boots?
Shopper:	No, I'd rather have normal leather shoes with rubber soles that I can also wear in town.
Salesperson:	What size? And what color would you like?
Shopper:	Forty-three and dark brown, please.

I'm looking for . . .	**Ich suche . . .**	ikh ZOO-kheh . . .
• an antique shop.	• **ein Antiquitätengeschäft.**	• ine ahn-tik-vee-TAY-ten-geh-shehft.
• an art dealer.	• **einen Kunsthändler.**	• INE-en KUNST-hehnt-le(r).
• a bakery.	• **eine Bäckerei.**	• INE-eh beh-keh-RYE.
• a bookstore.	• **eine Buchhandlung.**	• INE-eh BOOKH-hahnt-lung.
• a butcher shop.	• **eine Metzgerei.**	• INE-eh mehts-geh-RYE.
• a camera shop.	• **ein Photogeschäft.**	• ine FOH-toh-geh-shehft.
• a candy store.	• **einen Süßwarenladen.**	• INE-en SEWS-vaa-ren-laa-den
• a cheese shop.	• **ein Käsegeschäft.**	• ine KAY-zeh-geh-shehft.

132

• a china shop.	• **einen Porzellanladen.**	• INE-en por-tsehl-LAAN-laa-den.
• a clothing store.	• **ein Bekleidungsgeschäft.**	• ine beh-KLYE-dungs-geh-shehft.
for women.	**Damenbekleidungsgeschäft.**	DAA-men-beh-KLYE-dungs-geh-shehft.
for men.	**Herrenbekleidungsgeschäft.**	HEH-ren-beh-KLYE-dungs-geh-shehft.
for children.	**Kinderbekleidungsgeschäft.**	KIN-de(r)-beh-KLYE-dungs-geh-shehft.
• a dairy store.	• **ein Milchgeschäft.**	• ine MILKH-geh-shehft.
• a delicatessen.	• **ein Delikatessengeschäft.**	• ine deh-li-kah-TEHS-sen-geh-shehft.
• a department store.	• **ein Kaufhaus.**	• ine KOWF-hows.
• a drugstore.	• **eine Drogerie/ Apotheke.***	• INE-eh dro-geh-REE/ah-poh-TAY-keh.
• a drycleaner's.	• **eine chemische Reinigung.**	• INE-eh KHAY-mish-eh RYE-ni-gung.
• an electrical (applicance) store.	• **ein Elektrogeschäft.**	• ine ay-LEHK-troh-geh-shehft.
• a fish store.	• **eine Fischhandlung.**	• INE-eh FISH-hahnt-lung.
• a flea market.	• **einen Flohmarkt.**	• INE-en FLOH-mahrkt.
• a flower shop.	• **ein Blumengeschäft.**	• ine BLOO-men-geh-shehft.
• a furrier.	• **ein Pelzgeschäft.**	• ine PEHLTS-geh-shehft.
• a furniture store.	• **ein Möbelgeschäft.**	• ine MU(R)-bel-geh-shehft.
• a gourmet grocery.	• **ein Feinkostgeschäft.**	• ine FINE-kost-geh-shehft.

*A *Drogerie* specializes in nonprescription drugs and toiletries, an *Apotheke* in prescription medicines; see page 90 under Consulting the Pharmacist in Chapter 8, Health Care.

133

• a grocery store.	• ein Lebensmittelgeschäft.	• ine LAY-bens-mit-tel-geh-sheft.
• a hardware store.	• eine Eisenwarenhandlung.	• INE-eh EYE-zen-vaa-ren-hahnt-lung.
• a health food store.	• ein Reformhaus.	• ine ray-FORM-hows.
• a jewelry store.	• einen Juwelier.	• INE-en yu-veh-LEER.
• a laundromat.	• einen Waschsalon.	• INE-en VAHSH-zaa-long.
• a laundry.	• eine Wäscherei.	• INE-eh vehsh-eh-RYE.
• a liquor store.	• eine Spirituosenhandlung.	• INE-eh shpee-ree-tu-OH-zen-hahnt-lung.
• a market.	• einen Markt.	• INE-en mahrkt.
• a newsstand.	• einen Zeitungsstand.	• INE-en TSYE-tungs-shtahnt.
• an optician.	• einen Optiker.	• INE-en OP-tik-e(r).
• a pastry shop.	• eine Konditorei.	• INE-eh kon-dee-to-RYE.
• a photographer.	• einen Fotografen.	• INE-en foh-toh-GRAA-fen
• a produce shop.	• eine Gemüsehandlung.	• INE-eh geh-MEW-zeh-hahnt-lung.
• a record store.	• ein Schallplattengeschäft.	• ine SHAHL-plah-ten-geh-shehft.
• a secondhand shop.	• einen Gebrauchtwarenladen.	• INE-en geh-BROWKHT-vaa-ren-laa-den.
• a shoe repair shop.	• einen Schuhmacher.	• INE-en SHOO-mahkh-e(r).
• a shoe store.	• ein Schuhgeschäft.	• ine SHOO-geh-shehft.
• a shopping center.	• ein Einkaufszentrum.	• ine INE-kowfs-tsehn-trum.
• a souvenir (gift) shop.	• einen Andenkenladen.	• INE-en AHN-dehn-ken-laa-den.
• a sporting goods shop.	• ein Sportgeschäft.	• ine SHPORT-geh-shehft.
• a stationery shop.	• ein Schreibwarengeschäft.	• ine SHRYEP-vaa-ren-geh-shehft.

• a supermarket.	• einen Supermarkt.	• INE-en ZOO-pe(r)-mahrkt.
• a tailor.	• einen Schneider.	• INE-en SHNYE-de(r).
• a tobacco shop.	• einen Tabakladen.	• INE-en tah-BAHK-laa-den.
• a toy shop.	• ein Spielwarengeschäft.	• ine SHPEEL-vaa-ren-geh-shehft.
• a travel agency.	• ein Reisebüro.	• ine RYE-zeh-bew-roh.
• a watchmaker.	• einen Uhrmacher.	• INE-en OOR-mahkh-e(r).
• a wine shop.	• eine Weinhandlung.	• INE-eh VINE-hahnt-lung.

GENERAL SHOPPING EXPRESSIONS

Where can I find . . .	Wo finde ich . . .	voh FIN-deh ikh . . .
Can you help me?	Können Sie mir helfen?	KU(R)-nen zee meer HEHL-fen?
I'm just browsing.	Ich schaue mich nur um.	ikh SHOW-eh mikh noor oom.
I'd like to buy . . .	Ich möchte —— kaufen.	ikh MU(R)KH-teh —— KOW-fen.
Do you sell/stock ——?	Verkaufen/Führen Sie ——?	fehr-KOW-fen/FEW-ren zee ——?
Where is the —— department?	Wo ist die ——-abteilung?	voh ist dee ——-ahp-tile-ung?
Can you show me . . .	Können Sie mir —— zeigen?	KU(R)-nen zee meer —— TSYE-gen?
• this/that?	• das da/das dort	• dahs daa/dahs dort
• the one in the window/in the display case?	• das im Schaufenster/in der Vitrine	• dahs im SHOW-fehn-ste(r)/in dehr vi-TREE-neh
• some more?	• noch andere	• nohkh AHN-deh-reh
• something less costly/cheaper?	• etwas Preiswerteres/Billigeres	• EHT-vahs PRICE-vehr-teh-rehs/BIL-likh-e(r)-rehs
• something better?	• etwas Besseres	• EHT-vahs BEHS-seh-rehs

135

• something larger/smaller?	• etwas Größeres/ Kleineres	• EHT-vahs GRU(R)S-eh-rehs/KLINE-eh-rehs
I prefer something . . .	Ich hätte lieber etwas . . .	ikh HEHT-teh LEE-ber EHT-vahs . . .
• handmade.	• Handgemachtes.	• HAHNT-geh-mahkh-tehs.
• more typical.	• Typischeres.	• TEW-pish-eh-rehs.

DECIDING AND PAYING

How much is this (in dollars)?	Wieviel kostet das (in Dollar)?	VEE-feel KOS-tet dahs [in DOL-lahr]?
Please write it down.	Schreiben Sie es bitte auf.	SHRYE-ben zee ehs BIT-teh owf.
I'll take it/two.	Ich nehme es/zwei.	ikh NAY-meh ehs/tsvye.
Do you have it in stock?	Haben Sie es auf Lager?	HAA-ben zee ehs owf LAA-ge(r)?
Can you please . . .	Können Sie es mir bitte . . .	KU(R)-nen zee ehs meer BIT-teh . . .
• order it for me?	• bestellen?	• beh-SHTEHL-len?
• send it to me?	• schicken?	• SHIK-en?
• deliver it to my hotel?	• ins Hotel liefern?	• ins ho-TEL LEE-fern?
How long will it take?	Wie lange dauert es?	vee LAHNG-eh DOW-ert ehs?
Where do I pay?	Wo ist die Kasse?	voh ist dee KAHS-seh?
Can I pay with . . .	Kann ich mit ——— bezahlen?	kahn ikh mit ——— beh-TSAA-len?
• traveler's checks?	• Reisechecks	• RYE-zeh-shehks
• this credit card?	• dieser Kreditkarte	• DEE-ze(r) kray-DEET-kahr-teh
• dollars/pounds?	• Dollar/Pfund	• DOL-lahr/pfunt
Do I have to pay the value-added tax?	Muß ich die Mehrwertsteuer bezahlen?	mus ikh dee MEHR-vehrt-shtoy-e(r) beh-TSAA-len?
Do you have forms for the return of this tax?	Haben Sie Formulare für die Rückgabe dieser Steuer?	HAA-ben zee for-moo-LAH-reh fewr dee REWK-gaa-beh DEE-ze(r) SHTOY-e(r)?

136

May I please have a bag/plastic sack?	**Kann ich bitte eine Tragetasche/ Plastiktüte haben?**	kahn ikh BIT-teh INE-eh TRAA-geh-tahsh-eh/PLAHS-tik-tew-teh HAA-ben?
Could you please giftwrap this?	**Können Sie das bitte als Geschenk einwickeln?**	KU(R)-nen zee dahs BIT-teh ahls geh-SHEHNK INE-vi-keln?
Can I exchange this?	**Kann ich das umtauschen?**	kahn ikh dahs OOM-tow-shen?
I'd like to return this.	**Ich möchte das zurückgeben.**	ikh MU(R)KH-teh dahs tsoo-REWK-gay-ben.
Here's my receipt.	**Hier ist die Quittung.**	heer ist dee KVIT-tung.

WOMEN'S AND MEN'S CLOTHING AND ACCESSORIES
(DAMEN- UND HERRENBEKLEIDUNG UND ZUBEHÖR)

I'd like a/an/ some . . .	**Ich hätte gern . . .**	i(h)h HEHT-teh gehrn . . .
• a bathrobe.	• **einen Bademantel.**	• INE-en BAA-deh-mahn-tel.
• a bathing cap.	• **eine Badekappe.**	• INE-eh BAA-deh-kah-peh.
• a bathing suit.	• **einen Badeanzug.**	• INE-en BAA-deh-ahn-tsook.
• belt.	• **einen Gürtel.**	• INE-en GEWR-tel.
• blouse.	• **eine Bluse.**	• INE-eh BLOO-zeh.
• bow tie.	• **eine Fliege.**	• INE-eh FLEE-geh.
• brassiere.	• **einen Büstenhalter.**	• INE-en BEWS-ten-hahl-te(r).
• cap.	• **eine Mütze.**	• INE-eh MEW-tseh.
• coat.	• **einen Mantel.**	• INE-en MAHN-tel.
• dress.	• **ein Kleid.**	• ine klite.
• dressing gown.	• **einen Morgenrock.**	• INE-en MOR-gen-rok.
• evening dress/gown.	• **ein Abendkleid.**	• ine AA-behnt-klite.
• fur coat.	• **einen Pelzmantel.**	• INE-en PEHLTS-mahn-tel.

137

• girdle.	• einen Hüfthalter.	• INE-en HEWFT-hahl-te(r).
• gloves.	• Handschuhe.	• HAHNT-shoo-eh.
• handbag.	• eine Handtasche.	• INE-eh HAHNT-tahsh-eh.
• handkerchief.	• ein Taschentuch.	• ine TAHSH-en-tookh.
• hat.	• einen Hut.	• INE-en hoot.
• jacket.	• eine Jacke.	• INE-en YAH-keh.
• jeans.	• Jeans.	• ''jeans.''
• leather pants.	• eine Lederhose.	• INE-eh LAY-de(r)-hoh-zeh.
• lingerie.	• Damenunter-wäsche.	• DAA-men-un-te(r)-vehsh-eh.
• overalls.	• eine Überziehhose.	• INE-eh EW-be(r)-tsee-hoh-zeh.
• panties.	• einen Schlüpfer.	• INE-en SHLEWP-fe(r).
• pants/trousers.	• eine Hose.	• INE-eh HOH-zeh.
• panty hose.	• eine Strumpfhose.	• INE-eh SHTRUMPF-hoh-zeh.
• pullover. turtleneck V-neck	• einen Pullover. mit Rollkragen mit V-Ausschnitt	• INE-en pu-LOH-ve(r). mit ROL-kraa-gen mit FOW-ows-shnit
• pajamas.	• einen Pyjama.	• INE-en pi-JAA-maa.
• raincoat.	• einen Regenmantel.	• INE-en RAY-gen-mahn-tel.
• scarf.	• ein Halstuch.	• ine HAHLS-tookh.
• shirt. with long/ short sleeves sleeveless shirt	• ein Hemd. mit langen/ kurzen Ärmeln ein ärmelloses Hemd	• ine hehmt. mit LAHN-gen/koort-sen EHR-meln ine EHR-mehl-loh-zehs hehmt
• (a pair of) shoes.	• (ein Paar) Schuhe.	• [ine paar] SHOO-eh.
• shorts.	• Shorts.	• ''shorts.''
• skirt.	• einen Rock.	• INE-en rok.
• slip.	• einen Unterrock.	• INE-en UN-te(r)-rok.
• socks.	• Socken.	• ZOK-en.
• sports coat/jacket.	• einen Sportsakko.	• INE-en SHPORT-zah-koh.
• stockings.	• Strümpfe.	• SHTREWM-pfeh.
• suit (man's).	• einen Anzug.	• INE-en AHN-tsook.

• suit (woman's).	• **ein Kostüm.**	• ine kos-TEWM.
• suspenders/ braces.	• **Hosenträger.**	• HOH-zen-tray-ge(r).
• sweater.	• **einen Pullover.**	• INE-en pull-OH-ver.
• sweater blouse.	• **eine Strickbluse.**	• INE-eh SHTRIK-bloo-zeh.
• swimming trunks.	• **eine Badehose.**	• INE-eh BAA-deh-hoh-zeh.
• tie.	• **eine Krawatte.**	• INE-eh krah-VAHT-teh.
• tights.	• **eine Strumpfhose.**	• INE-eh SHTRUMPF-hoh-zeh.
• trench coat.	• **einen Trenchcoat.**	• INE-en "trench coat."
• umbrella.	• **einen Regenschirm.**	• INE-en RAY-gen-sheerm.
• underpants.	• **eine Unterhose.**	• INE-eh UN-te(r)-hoh-zeh.
• undershirt.	• **ein Unterhemd.**	• ine UN-te(r)-hehmt.
• underwear.	• **Unterwäsche.**	• UN-te(r)-vehsh-eh.
• vest.	• **eine Weste.**	• INE-eh VEHS-teh.

MATERIALS AND FABRICS

I don't like this material.	**Der Stoff gefällt mir nicht.**	dehr shtof geh-fehlt meer nikht.
I prefer natural fibers.	**Ich hätte lieber etwas aus natürlichen Fasern.**	ikh HEHT-teh LEE-be(r) EHT-vahs ous nah-TEWR-likh-en FAA-zern.
Is this fabric . . .	**Ist dieser Stoff . . .**	ist DEE-ze(r) shtof . . .
• pure wool?	• **reine Wolle?**	• RINE-eh VOL-leh?
• synthetic?	• **aus Kunststoff?**	• ows KUNST-shtof?
• wash and wear?	• **bügelfrei?**	• BEW-gel-frye?
• shrinkproof?	• **nicht einlaufend?**	• nikht INE-low-fehnt?
I want something . . .	**Ich möchte etwas . . .**	ikh MU(R)KH-teh EHT-vahs . . .
• thicker/thinner.	• **Dickeres/Dünneres.**	• DIK-eh-rehs/DEWN-neh-rehs.
• of better quality.	• **von besserer Qualität.**	• fon BEHS-eh-re(r) kvah-li-TAYT.

139

Do you have anything in . . .	**Haben Sie etwas in . . .**	HAA-ben zee EHT-vahs in . . .
• corduroy?	• **Kordsamt?**	• KORT-zahmt?
• cotton?	• **Baumwolle?**	• BOWM-vol-leh?
• crepe?	• **Krepp?**	• krehp?
• denim?	• **Drillich?**	• DRIL-likh?
• felt?	• **Filz?**	• filts?
• flannel?	• **Flanell?**	• flah-NEHL?
• gabardine?	• **Gabardine?**	• GAH-bahr-din?
• lace?	• **Spitze?**	• SHPIT-seh?
• leather?	• **Leder?**	• LAY-de(r)?
• linen?	• **Leinen?**	• LINE-en?
• nylon?	• **Nylon?**	• NYE-lon?
• poplin?	• **Popline?**	• po-peh-LEEN?
• rayon?	• **Kunstseide?**	• KUNST-zye-deh?
• satin?	• **Satin?**	• zah-TEHNG?
• silk?	• **Seide?**	• ZYE-deh?
• suede?	• **Wildleder?**	• VILT-lay-de(r)?
• velvet?	• **Samt?**	• zahmt?
• wool?	• **Wolle?**	• VO-leh?

COLORS AND PATTERNS

I'd like something . . .	**Ich möchte etwas . . .**	ikh MU(R)KH-teh EHT-vahs . . .
• lighter/darker.	• **Helleres/ Dunkleres**	• HEHL-leh-rehs/ DUNK-leh-rehs.
• in a different color.	• **in einer anderen Farbe.**	• in INE-e(r) AHN-deh-ren FAHR-beh.
• to match this.	• **hierzu Passendes.**	• HEER-tsoo PAHS-sen-dehs.
• color fast.	• **Farbechtes.**	• FAHRP-ehkh-tehs.
Do you have it in . . .	**Haben Sie es in . . .**	HAA-ben zee ehs in . . .
• beige?	• **beige?**	• bayzh?
• black?	• **schwarz?**	• shvahrts?
• blue?	• **blau?**	• blow?
• brown?	• **braun?**	• brown?
• gray?	• **grau?**	• grow?
• green?	• **grün?**	• grewn?

- orange? • orange? • o-RAHNG-zheh?
- pink? • rosa? • ROH-zah?
- purple? • violett? • vee-oh-LEHT?
- red? • rot? • roht?
- silver? • silbern? • ZIL-bern?
- white? • weiß? • vice?
- yellow? • gelb? • gehlp?

I'd rather have it . . . Ich hätte es lieber . . . ikh HEHT-teh ehs LEE-be(r) . . .

- in a solid color. • uni. • U-nee.
- with stripes. • gestreift. • geh-SHTRYEFT.
- with polka dots. • mit • mit PUNKT-mus-te(r).
- in plaid. • kariert. • kah-REERT.
- checkered. • gewürfelt. • geh-VEWR-fehlt.

SIZES AND FITTING

I'm a size 40. | Ich trage Größe vierzig. | ikh TRAA-geh GRU(R)S-eh FEER-tsikh.
I don't know my size. | Ich kenne meine Größe nicht. | ikh KEH-neh MINE-eh GRU(R)S-seh nikht.
Can I try it on? | Kann ich es anprobieren? | kahn ikh ehs AHN-pro-beer-en
Is there a mirror? | Gibt es einen Spiegel? | gipt ehs INE-en SHPEE-gel?
It fits very well. | Es paßt/sitzt sehr gut. | ehs pahst/zitst zehr goot.
It doesn't fit. | Es paßt nicht. | ehs pahst nikht.
Can you alter it? | Können Sie es ändern? | KU(R)-nen zee ehs EHN-dern?

SHOES

I need a pair of . . . | Ich brauche ein Paar . . . | ikh BROW-kheh ine paar . . .

- boots/rain boots. • Stiefel/Regenstie-fel. • SHTEE-fel/RAY-gen-shtee-fel.
- flats. • flache Schuhe. • FLAH-kheh SHOO-eh.

141

• high heels.	• **Schuhe mit hohen Absätzen.**	• SHOO-eh mit HOH-en AHP-zeht-sen.
• sandals/shoes.	• **Sandalen/ Schuhe.**	• zahn-DAA-len/ SHOO-eh.
• slippers.	• **Hausschuhe.**	• HOWS-shoo-eh.
• sneakers.	• **Turnschuhe.**	• TURN-shoo-eh.
Do you have any with leather/rubber soles?	**Haben Sie welche mit Leder-/ Gummisohlen?**	HAA-ben zee VEHL-kheh mit LAY-de(r)-/ GOOM-mee-zoh-len?
These are too . . .	**Diese sind zu . . .**	DEE-zeh zint tsoo . . .
• small/large.	• **klein/groβ.**	• kline/grohs.
• narrow/wide.	• **eng/weit.**	• ehng/vite.

WOMEN'S CLOTHING SIZES

Coats, dresses, suits, skirts, slacks

U.S.	4	6	8	10	12	14	16
Europe	36	38	40	42	44	46	48

Blouses/Sweaters

U.S.	32/6	34/8	36/10	38/12	40/14	42/16
Europe	38/2	40/3	42/4	44/5	46/6	48/7

Shoes

U.S.	4	4½	5	5½	6	6½	7	7½	8	8½	9	9½	10
Europe	35	35	36	36	37	37	38	38	39	39	40	40	41

MEN'S CLOTHING SIZES

Suits/Coats

U.S.	34	36	38	40	42	44	46	48
Europe	44	46	48	50	52	54	56	58

Sweaters

U.S.	XS/36	S/38	M/40	L/42	XL/44
Europe	42/2	44/3	46–48/4	50/5	52–54/6

Shirts

U.S.	14	14½	15	15½	16	16½	17	17½	18
Europe	36	37	38	39	40	41	42	43	44

Slacks

U.S.	30	31	32	33	34	35	36	37	38	39
Europe	38	39–40	41	42	43	44–45	46	47	48–49	50

Socks							
U.S.	9½	10	10½	11	11½	12	13
Europe	36–37	38–39	40–41	42–43	44–45	46–47	48–49

Shoes								
U.S.	7	7½	8	8½	9	9½	10	10½	11
Europe	39	40	41	42	43	43	44	44	45

AT THE JEWELER'S *(BEIM JUWELIER)*

What kind of jewelry/watches do you have?	**Was für Schmucksachen/ Uhren haben Sie?**	vahs fewr SHMUK-zahkh-en/OOR-en HAA-ben zee?
I'm looking for a/an/some . . .	**Ich suche . . .**	ikh ZOO-kheh . . .
• alarm clock.	• **einen Wecker.**	• INE-en VEHK-e(r).
• antique jewelry.	• **alten Schmuck.**	• AHL-ten shmuk.
• bracelet.	• **ein Armband.**	• ine AHRM-bahnt.
• brooch.	• **eine Brosche.**	• INE-eh BROSH-eh.
• chain.	• **eine Kette.**	• INE-eh KEHT-teh.
• cufflinks.	• **Manschetten-knöpfe.**	• mahn-SHEHT-ten-knu(r)p-feh.
• earrings.	• **Ohrringe.**	• OHR-ring-eh.
• gem.	• **einen Edelstein.**	• INE-en AY-del-shtine.
• jewelry box	• **ein Schmuck-kästchen.**	• ine SHMUK-kehst-khen.
• necklace.	• **eine Halskette.**	• INE-eh HAHLS-keht-teh.
• pin.	• **eine Anstecknadel.**	• INE-eh AHN-shtehk-naa-del.
• ring.	• **einen Ring.**	• INE-en ring.
• engagement ring.	• **einen Verlobungsring.**	• INE-en fehr-LOH-bungs-ring.
• wedding ring.	• **einen Ehering.**	• INE-en AY-eh-ring.
• tie pin.	• **eine Krawattennadel.**	• INE-eh krah-VAHT-ten-naa-del.
• wristwatch.	• **eine Armbanduhr.**	• INE-eh AHRM-bahnt-oor.

143

What do you have in . . .	Was haben Sie in . . .	vahs HAA-ben zee in . . .
• gold?	• Gold?	• golt?
• platinum?	• Platin?	• plah-TEEN?
• silver?	• Silber?	• ZIL-be(r)?
• stainless steel?	• Edelstahl?	• AY-del-shtahl?
What's this made of?	Aus welchem Metall ist das?	ows VEHL-khem meh-TAHL ist dahs?
Is this solid gold or just gold plate?	Ist das massives Gold oder nur vergoldet?	ist dahs mah-SEE-vehs golt OH-de(r) noor fehr-GOL-det?
How many carats is it?	Wieviel Karat hat es?	VEE-feel kah-RAAT haht ehs?
Can you repair this watch/jewelry?	Können Sie diese Uhr/dieses Schmuckstück reparieren?	KU(R)-nen zee DEE-zeh oor/DEE-zehs SHMUK-shtewk reh-pah-REE-ren?
Show me please your selection of . . .	Zeigen Sie mir bitte Ihre Auswahl von . . .	TSYE-gen zee meer BIT-teh EE-reh OWS-vaal fon . . .
• amber.	• Bernstein.	• BEHRN-shtine.
• amethyst.	• Amethyst.	• ah-meh-TEWST.
• crystal.	• Kristall.	• kris-TAHL.
• diamonds.	• Diamanten.	• dee-ah-MAHN-ten.
• emeralds.	• Smaragden.	• smah-RAHK-ten.
• hematite.	• Blutstein.	• BLOOT-shtine.
• ivory.	• Elfenbein.	• EHL-fen-bine.
• jade.	• Jade.	• YAA-deh.
• onyx.	• Onyx.	• OH-niks.
• pearls.	• Perlen.	• PEHR-len.
• rubies.	• Rubinen	• ru-BEE-nen.
• sapphires.	• Saphiren.	• zah-FEE-ren.
• topazes.	• Topasen.	• toh-PAA-zen.
• turquoises.	• Türkisen.	• tewr-KEE-zen.

THE PHOTO SHOP *(DAS FOTOGESCHÄFT)*

I need film for this camera/movie camera.	Ich brauche einen Film für diese Kamera/Film-kamera.	ikh BROW-kheh INE-en film fewr DEE-zeh KAH-meh-raa/FILM-kah-meh-raa.

144

I'd like a roll of . . .	Ich möchte einen . . .	ikh MU(R)KH-teh INE-en . . .
• 35-mm color film.	• fünfunddreißig Millimeter Farbfilm.	• FEWNF-unt-drye-sikh mi-lee-MAY-te(r) FAHRP-film.
• black and white film.	• Schwarzweiß-film.	• shvahrts-VICE-film.
• color slide film.	• Film für Farbdias.	• film fewr FAHRP-dee-ahs.
• daylight film.	• Tageslichtfilm.	• TAA-gehs-likht-film.
• artificial light film.	• Kunstlichtfilm.	• KUNST-likht-film.
24/36 exposures, please.	Vierundzwanzig/ sechsunddreißig Aufnahmen, bitte.	FEER-unt-TSVAHN-tsikh/zehks-unt-drye-sikh OWF-naa-men, BIT-teh.
How much does developing cost?	Was kostet das Entwickeln?	vahs KOS-tet dahs ehnt-VIK-eln?
I'd like . . .	Ich möchte . . .	ikh MU(R)KH-teh . . .
• one/two prints of each negative.	• einen Abzug/zwei Abzüge von jedem Negativ.	• INE-en AHP-tsook/tsvye AHP-tsew-geh fon YEH-dem NEH-gah-teef.
• matt/glossy prints.	• matt/Hochglanz-abzüge.	• maht/HOHKH-glahnts-AHP-tzew-geh.
• enlargements.	• Vergrößerungen.	• fehr-GRU(R)S-eh-rung-en.
When will they be ready?	Wann sind sie fertig?	vahn zint see FEHR-tikh?
Do you sell ——— cameras?	Verkaufen Sie ——— Kameras?	fehr-KOW-fen zee ——— KAH-meh-raas?
• automatic	• automatische	• ow-to-MAH-ti-sheh
• simple	• einfache	• INE-fah-khe
• single lens reflex	• Spiegelreflex	• SHPEE-gel-reh-flehks
• movie	• Film	• film
Do you carry . . .	Führen Sie . . .	FEW-ren zee . . .
• batteries?	• Batterien?	• bah-teh-REE-en?
• filters?	• Filter?	• FIL-te(r)?
• lens caps?	• Objektivdeckel?	• ob-yehk-TEEF-deh-kel?

145

THE BOOKSTORE *(DIE BUCHHANDLUNG)*

Larger book stores in the German-speaking countries will often stock English-language and other foreign-language publications. Newspapers, magazines, and postcards are readily available at a newsstand *(Zeitungsstand* or *Kiosk).*

Where can I find English-language . . .	**Wo finde ich englisch-sprachige . . .**	voh FIN-deh ikh EHNG-lish-shprahkh-i-geh . . .
• newspapers?	• **Zeitungen?**	• TSITE-ung-en?
• magazines?	• **Zeitschriften?**	• TSITE-shrif-ten?
• books/publications?	• **Bücher/Veröffent-lich ungen?**	• BEW-khe(r)/fehr-U(R)F-ehnt-likh-ung-en?
Where's the section for . . .	**Wo stehen die . . .**	voh SHTAY-en dee . . .
• books in English?	• **Bücher in Englisch?**	• BEW-khe(r) in EHNG-lish?
• dictionaries?	• **Wörterbücher?**	• VUR-te(r)-bew-khe(r)?
• guide books?	• **Reiseführer?**	• RYE-zeh-few-re(r)?
• secondhand books?	• **antiquarischen Bücher?**	• ahn-ti-KVAA-rish-en-BEW-khe(r)?
Do you have . . .	**Haben Sie . . .**	HAA-ben zee . . .
• a German-English pocket dictionary?	• **ein deutsch-englisches Taschen-wörterbuch?**	• ine doych-EHNG-lish-ehs TAHSH-en-vur-te(r)-bookh?
• the novel ——— by ——— in English?	• **den Roman ——— von ——— in Englisch?**	• dehn roh-MAAN ——— fon ——— in EHNG-lish?

THE STATIONERY SHOP *(DAS SCHREIBWARENGESCHÄFT)*

I'd like a/an/some . . .	**Ich möchte . . .**	ikh MU(R)KH-teh . . .
• adhesive tape.	• **Klebeband.**	• KLAY-beh-bahnt.
• ballpoint pen.	• **einen Kugel-schreiber.**	• INE-en KOO-gel-shrye-be(r).

- calendar.
- carbon paper.

- crayons.
- drawing paper.

- envelopes.

- eraser.

- felt-tip.
- fountain pen.

- glue.
- ink.
- labels.
- notebook.

- paperclips.

- pencil.
- pencil sharpener.

- playing cards.
- pocket calculator.

- postcards.

- ruler.
- Scotch tape.
- stapler.

- staples.

- string.
- (airmail) stationery.

- einen Kalender.
- Kohlepapier.

- Buntstifte.
- Zeichenpapier.

- Briefumschläge.

- einen Radiergummi.

- einen Filzstift.
- einen Füllfederhalter.

- Leim.
- Tinte.
- Etiketten.
- ein Notizheft.

- Büroklammern.

- einen Bleistift.
- einen Bleistiftspitzer.

- Spielkarten.
- einen Taschenrechner.

- Ansichtskarten.

- ein Lineal.
- Tesafilm.
- eine Drahtheftmaschine.

- Heftklammern.

- Schnur.
- (Luftpost) Briefpapier.

- INE-en kah-LEHN-de(r).
- KOH-leh-pah-peer.

- BUNT-shtif-teh.
- TSYE-khen-pah-peer.

- BREEF-oom-shlay-geh.

- INE-en rah-DEER-goom-mee.

- INE-en FILTS-shtift.
- INE-en FEWL-fay-de(r)-hahl-te(r).

- lime.
- TIN-teh.
- eh-ti-KEH-tehn.
- ine no-TEETS-hehft.

- bew-ROH-klahm-mern.

- INE-en BLYE-shtift.
- INE-en BLYE-shtift-shpit-se(r).

- SHPEEL-kahr-ten.
- INE-en TAHSH-en-rehkh-ne(r).

- AHN-zikhts-kahr-ten.

- ine lee-neh-AAL.
- TAY-zah-film.
- INE-eh DRAHT-heft-mah-shee-neh.

- HEHFT-klahm-mern.

- shnoor.
- [LUFT-post] BREEF-pah-peer.

147

• thumbtacks.	• **Reißzwecken.**	• RICE-tsveh-ken.
• typing paper.	• **Schreibmachi-nenpapier.**	• SHRIPE-mah-shee-nen-pah-peer.
• writing pad.	• **einen Schreibblock.**	• INE-en SHRIPE-blok.

ELECTRICAL APPLIANCES *(ELEKTROGERÄTE)*

Standard household current throughout continental Europe is 220 volts, 50-cycle A.C. Many appliances are now equipped with dual-voltage capacity. Make sure about this before you buy an appliance overseas; otherwise you will need a transformer, as well as adapter plugs, to use it in the United States.

What's the voltage on this appliance?	**Welche Spannung hat dieses Gerät?**	VEHL-kheh SHPAHN-nung haht DEE-zehs geh-RAYT?
Show me please how it works.	**Zeigen Sie mir bitte, wie es funktioniert.**	TSYE-gen zee meer BIT-teh, vee ehs funk-tsyo-NEERT.
Do you have batteries for this?	**Haben Sie hierfür Batterien?**	HAA-ben zee HEER-fewr bah-teh-REE-en?
It's broken. Can you fix it?	**Es ist kaputt. Können Sie es reparieren?**	ehs ist kah-PUT. KU(R)-nen zee ehs reh-pah-REE-ren?
I need a/an/ some . . .	**Ich brauche . . .**	ikh BROW-kheh . . .
• adapter plug.	• **einen Zwischenstecker.**	• INE-en TSVISH-en-shteh-ke(r).
• bulb.	• **eine Glühbirne.**	• INE-eh GLEW-beer-neh.
• cassette recorder.	• **einen Kassetten-recorder.**	• INE-en kah-SEHT-ten-reh-kor-de(r).
• clock radio.	• **einen Radiowecker.**	• INE-en RAA-dee-oh-veh-ke(r).
• extension cord.	• **eine Ver-längerungs schnur.**	• INE-eh fehr-LEHNG-eh-rungs-shnoor.

148

- hair dryer.
  - **ein Haartrockner.**
  - ine HAAR-trok-ne(r).

- travel iron.
  - **ein Reisebügeleisen.**
  - ine RYE-zeh-bew-gel-eye-zen.

- lamp.
  - **eine Lampe.**
  - INE-eh LAHM-peh.

- plug.
  - **einen Stecker.**
  - INE-en SHTEH-ke(r).

- (portable) radio.
  - **ein (Koffer-) Radio.**
  - ine [KO-fe(r)-] RAA-dee-oh.

- record/CD player.
  - **einen Platten-/ CD-Spieler.**
  - INE-en PLAHT-ten-/ TSAY-DAY-shpee-le(r).

- shaver.
  - **einen Rasierapparat.**
  - INE-en rah-ZEER-ah-pah-raat.

- tape recorder.
  - **ein Tonbandgerät.**
  - ine TOHN-bahnt-geh-rayt.

- (color) TV.
  - **einen (Farb-) Fernseher.**
  - INE-en [FAHRP-] FEHRN-zay-e(r).

- transformer.
  - **einen Transformator.**
  - INE-en trahns-for-MAA-tor.

- VCR.
  - **einen Videorecorder.**
  - INE-en VEE-deh-oh-reh-kor-de(r).

RECORDS/CASSETTES *(SCHALLPLATTEN/KASSETTEN)*

Do you have any recordings by ——?	**Haben Sie Aufnahmen von ——?**	HAA-ben zee OWF-naa-men fon ——?
May I listen to this record?	**Darf ich diese Platte hören?**	dahrf ikh DEE-zeh PLAHT-teh HU(R)-en?
Do you sell . . .	**Verkaufen Sie . . .**	fehr-KOW-fen zee . . .
• audiocassettes?	• **Kassetten?**	• kah-SEHT-ten?
• videocassettes?	• **Videokassetten?**	• VEE-deh-oh-kah-seht-ten?
• compact discs?	• **Compact Discs?**	• "compact discs"?
• LPs (33 rpm)?	• **Langspiel-platten?**	• LAHNG-shpeel-plaht-ten?
Where's the section for . . .	**Wo finde ich . . .**	voh FIN-deh ikh . . .
• chamber music?	• **die Kammermusik?**	• dee KAHM-me(r)-moo-zeek?

149

• classical music?	• **die klassische Musik?**	• dee KLAHS-sish-eh moo-ZEEK?
• folk music/folk songs?	• **die Volksmusik/ Volkslieder?**	• dee FOLKS-moo-zeek/FOLKS-lee-de(r)?
• jazz?	• **den Jazz?**	• dehn jazz?
• opera?	• **die Opermusik?**	• dee OH-pe(r)-moo-zeek?
• pop music/hits?	• **die Popmusik/ Schlager?**	• dee POP-moo-zeek/SHLAA-ge(r)?

TOILETRIES *(TOILETTENARTIKEL)*

The following list of items can be found at a *Drogerie* (drug store) or department store. Prescription medicines are available only at an *Apotheke* (pharmacy; see page 90 under Consulting the Pharmacist, in Chapter 8).

I'd like a/an/ some . . .	**Ich hätte gern . . .**	ikh HEHT-teh gehrn . . .
• after-shave lotion.	• **ein Rasierwasser.**	• ine rah-ZEER-vahs-se(r).
• bobby pins.	• **Haarnadeln.**	• HAAR-naa-dehln.
• bath salts.	• **Badesalz.**	• BAA-deh-zahlts.
• bubble bath.	• **ein Schaumbad.**	• ine SHOWM-baat.
• cleansing cream.	• **eine Reinigungs-creme.**	• INE-eh RYE-ni-gungs-kraym.
• cologne.	• **ein Kölnisch Wasser.**	• ine KU(R)L-nish VAHS-se(r).
• condoms.	• **Kondome.**	• kon-DOH-meh.
• comb.	• **einen Kamm.**	• INE-en kahm.
• curlers.	• **Lockenwickler.**	• LOK-en-vik-le(r).
• deodorant.	• **ein Desodorans.**	• ine deh-zoh-doh-RAHNS.
• (disposable) diapers.	• **(wegwerfbare) Windeln.**	• [VEHK-vehrf-baa-reh] VIN-deln.
• emery board.	• **eine Nagelpfeile.**	• INE-eh NAA-gel-pfye-leh.

• eyebrow pencil.	• **einen Augenbrauenstift.**	• INE-en OW-gen-brow-en-shtift.
• eyeliner.	• **einen Lidstift.**	• INE-en LEET-shtift.
• eye shadow.	• **einen Lidschatten.**	• INE-en LEET-shaht-ten.
• face powder.	• **Gesichtspuder.**	• geh-ZIKHTS-poo-de(r).
• foot powder.	• **Fußpuder.**	• FOOS-poo-de(r).
• hairbrush.	• **eine Haarbürste.**	• INE-eh HAAR-bewr-steh.
• hair spray.	• **einen Haarspray.**	• INE-en HAAR-shpray.
• hand cream.	• **Handcreme.**	• HAHNT-kraym.
• lipsalve.	• **eine Lippenpomade.**	• INE-eh LIP-pen-po-maa-deh.
• lipstick.	• **einen Lippenstift.**	• INE-en LIP-pen-shtift.
• mascara.	• **Wimperntusche.**	• VIM-pern-tush-eh.
• mirror.	• **einen Spiegel.**	• INE-en SHPEE-gel.
• moisturizing cream.	• **Feuchtigkeitscreme.**	• FOYKH-tikh-kites-kraym.
• mouthwash.	• **ein Mundwasser.**	• ine MUNT-vahs-se(r).
• nail clippers.	• **eine Nagelzange.**	• INE-eh NAA-gel-tsahng-eh.
• nail polish (remover).	• **Nagellack (-entferner).**	• NAA-gel-lahk [-ehnt-fehr-ne(r)].
• nail scissors.	• **eine Nagelschere.**	• INE-eh NAA-gel-shay-reh.
• perfume.	• **ein Parfüm.**	• ine pahr-FEWM.
• razor.	• **einen Rasierapparat.**	• INE-en rah-ZEER-ahp-pah-raat.
• razor blades.	• **Rasierklingen.**	• rah-ZEER-kling-en.
• rouge.	• **Rouge/Schminke.**	• roozh/SHMIN-keh.
• safety pins.	• **Sicherheitsnadeln.**	• ZIKH-e(r)-hites-NAA-deln.
• sanitary napkins.	• **Damenbinden.**	• DAA-men-bin-den.
• scissors.	• **eine Schere.**	• INE-eh SHAY-reh.
• setting lotion.	• **einen Haarfestiger.**	• INE-en HAAR-fehs-ti-ge(r).

• shampoo.	• **ein Haarwasch-mittel.**	• ine HAAR-vahsh-mit-tel.
• shaving cream.	• **Rasiercreme.**	• rah-ZEER-kraym.
• soap.	• **eine Seife.**	• INE-en ZYE-feh.
• sponge.	• **einen Schwamm.**	• INE-en shvahm.
• suntan lotion/oil.	• **Sonnencreme/-öl.**	• ZON-en-kraym/-u(r)l.
• talcum powder.	• **Talkumpuder.**	• TAAL-kum-poo-de(r).
• tampons.	• **Tampons.**	• TAHM-pongs.
• tissues.	• **Papiertücher.**	• pah-PEER-tew-khe(r).
• toilet paper.	• **Toilettenpapier.**	• toy-LEHT-ten-pah-peer.
• toilet water.	• **ein Toilettenwasser.**	• ine toy-LEHT-ten-vahs-se(r).
• toothbrush.	• **eine Zahnbürste.**	• INE-eh TSAAN-bewr-steh.
• tooth paste.	• **Zahnpasta.**	• TSAAN-pahs-tah.
• towels.	• **Handtücher.**	• HAHNT-tew-khe(r).
• tweezers.	• **eine Pinzette.**	• INE-eh pin-TSEHT-teh.

SHOPPING FOR GROCERIES *(EINKAUF IM LEBENSMITTELGESCHÄFT)*
The standard unit of weight for purchasing produce, cheese, and sausage is the kilogram *(Kilo)*, fractions thereof, or 100-gram units *(einhundert, zweihundert Gramm,* etc.) for smaller amounts. You'll also hear the term *Pfund* (pound), which is equal to half a kilo or 500 grams. Take along your own shopping bag or basket, since not all shops and markets provide bags.

I'd like a loaf of dark bread, please.	**Ich hätte gern ein Bauernbrot, bitte.**	ikh HEHT-teh gehrn ine BOW-ern-broht, BIT-teh.
May I have a tasting sample of this cheese/sausage?	**Darf ich eine Kostprobe von diesem Käse/dieser Wurst haben?**	dahrf ikh INE-eh KOST-proh-beh fon DEE-zem KAY-zeh/DEE-ze(r) voorst HAA-ben?

152

May I help myself?	**Darf ich mich selbst bedienen?**	dahrf ikh mikh zehlpst beh-DEE-nen?
Please give me . . .	**Geben Sie mir, bitte . . .**	GAY-ben zee meer, BIT-teh . . .
• a kilo of potatoes.	• **ein Kilo Kartoffeln.**	• ine KEE-loh kahr-TOF-feln.
• half a kilo of tomatoes.	• **ein halbes Kilo Tomaten.**	• ine HAHL-behs KEE-loh to-MAA-ten.
• a pound (500 grams) of butter.	• **ein Pfund Butter.**	• ine pfunt BUT-te(r).
• 200 grams of cheese.	• **zweihundert Gramm Käse.**	• TSVYE-hun-dert graam KAY-zeh.
• 100 grams of liverwurst.	• **hundert Gramm Leberwurst.**	• HUN-dert gram LAY-be(r)-voorst.
• three slices of ham.	• **drei Scheiben Schinken.**	• drye SHYE-ben SHIN-ken.
• half a dozen eggs.	• **ein halbes Dutzend Eier.**	• ine HAHL-behs DUT-sehnt EYE-e(r).
• a liter of milk.	• **einen Liter Milch.**	• INE-en LEE-te(r) milkh.
• a bottle of fruit juice.	• **eine Flasche Obstsaft.**	• INE-eh FLAHS-eh OPST-sahft.
• a package of coffee.	• **eine Packung Kaffee.**	• INE-eh PAHK-ung KAH-fay.
• a jar of jam.	• **ein Glas Marmelade.**	• ine glaas mahr-meh-LAA-deh.
• a can of beans.	• **eine Büchse Bohnen.**	• INE-eh BEWK-seh BOH-nen.
• a cup of yogurt.	• **einen Becher Yogurt.**	• INE-en BEHKH-e(r) YO-gurt.

153

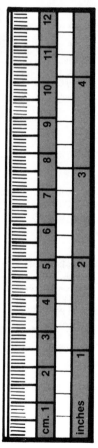

WEIGHTS AND MEASURES

Metric Weight	**U.S.**
1 gram (g)	0.035 ounce
28.35 grams	1 ounce
100 grams	3.5 ounces
454 grams	1 pound
1 kilogram (kilo)	2.2 pounds

Liquids	**U.S.**
1 liter (l)	4.226 cups
1 liter	2.113 cups
1 liter	1.056 quarts
3.785 liters	1 gallon

Dry Measures	**U.S.**
1 liter	0.908 quart
1 decaliter	1.135 pecks
1 hectoliter	2.837 bushel

One inch = 2.54 centimeters
One centimeter = .39 inch

	inches	feet	yard
1 mm	0.039	0.003	0.00
1 cm	0.39	0.03	0.01
1 dm	3.94	0.32	0.10
1 m	39.40	3.28	1.09

.39 (# of centimeters) = (# of inches)
2.54 (# of inches) = (# of centimeters)

	mm	cm	m
1 in.	25.4	2.54	0.025
1 ft.	304.8	30.48	0.304
1 yd.	914.4	91.44	0.914

13/ENTERTAINMENT AND SPORTS

The possibilities for entertainment in German-speaking Europe are practically limitless, even for those not fluent in the language. On the lighter, more social side, the larger cities offer a variety of nightclubs, discos, cabarets, and gambling casinos. In terms of cultural entertainment and diversions, such as theater, cinema, opera, ballet, musical concerts, and festivals, the richness and high quality of the productions from this part of the world are difficult to match. Those traveling with children will find the German-speaking world quite *"kinderfreundlich"* (friendly to children) and be amazed over the number of modern, well-kept playgrounds, amusement parks, children's museums, aquariums, and zoos. Berlin and Hamburg boast two of the world's most famous zoos that will delight not only the children. A special treat for young and old are the many marionette and puppet shows, part of a long and rich German tradition and usually performed outdoors during the summer.

Sports enthusiasts will enjoy traveling in Germany, Austria, and Switzerland, since all three countries offer a wide array of sports activities, both spectator and participatory.

DIALOGUE: LET'S GO SWIMMING (*GEHEN WIR BADEN*)

Helmut:	**Die Sonne sticht heute! Mir ist wahnsinnig heiß.**	dee ZON-eh shtikht HOY-teh! meer ist WAAN-zin-nikh hice.
Linda:	**Mir auch. Gehen wir baden.**	meer owkh. GAY-en veer BAA-den.
Helmut:	**Gute Idee. Gehen wir ins Schwimmbad oder zum Strand?**	GOO-teh ee-DAY. GAY-en veer ins SHVIM-baat OH-de(r) tsoom shtrahnt?
Linda:	**Lieber zum Strand. Ich mag das Chlor-wasser im Schwimmbad nicht.**	LEE-be(r) tsoom shtrahnt. ikh mahk dahs KLOR-vahs-se(r) im SHVIM-baat nikht.

Helmut:	**Wie wär's denn mit dem Strand am Waldsee?**	vee vehrs den mit dehm shtrahnt ahm VAHLT-zee?
Linda:	**Schön. Treffen wir uns da in einer halben Stunde.**	shu(r)n. TREHF-en veer uns daa in INE-e(r) HAHL-ben SHTUN-deh.
Helmut:	**Abgemacht. Vergiß dein Sonnenöl nicht. Sonst bekommst du* einen Sonnenbrand.**	AHP-geh-mahkht. fehr-GIS dine ZON-en-u(r)l nikht. zonst beh-KOMST doo INE-en ZON-en-brahnt.

. . . .

Helmut:	The sun is so strong today! I'm really hot.
Linda:	Me too. Let's go swimming.
Helmut:	Good idea. Shall we go to a swimming pool or to the beach?
Linda:	I'd prefer the beach. I don't like the chlorinated water in the pool.
Helmut:	How about the beach at the forest lake?
Linda:	Fine. Let's meet there in half an hour.
Helmut:	Agreed. Don't forget your suntan oil. Otherwise you'll get sunburned.

*Note here the use of the familiar form of address *du*. For the rules regarding its use, see pages 48 and 183.

PARTICIPATORY SPORTS

Swimming

Is there a swimming pool/thermal pool (spa) near here?	**Gibt es ein Schwimmbad/ Thermalbad in der Nähe?**	gipt ehs ine SHVIM-baat/tayr-MAAL-baat in dehr NAY-eh?

156

Is it . . .	Ist es . . .	ist ehs . . .
• outdoors/indoors?	• ein Freibad/ Hallenbad?	• ine FRYE-baat/HAHL-en-baat
• heated/crowded?	• geheizt/über-füllt?	• geh-HYETST/ew-be(r)-FEWLT?
Is there a lifeguard?	Gibt es einen Rettungsdienst?	gipt ehs INE-en REHT-tungs-deenst?

At the Beach

Can you swim in this lake/ pond/river?	Kann man in diesem See/Teich/Fluβ baden?	kahn mahn in DEE-zem zee/tyekh/flus BAA-den?
Is it dangerous for children?	Ist es für Kinder gefährlich?	ist ehs fewr KIN-de(r) geh-FEHR-likh?
Can you recommend a . . .	Können Sie uns (einen) ——— empfehlen?	KU(R)-nen zee uns [INE-en] ——— ehm-PFAY-len?
• sandy beach?	• Sandstrand	• ZAHNT-shtrahnt
• quiet beach?	• ruhigen Strand	• ROO-i-gen shtrahnt
• nudist beach?	• FKK* Strand	• EHF-KAH-KAH shtrahnt
• beach resort?	• ein Strandbad	• ine SHTRAHNT-baat
• seaside resort?	• ein Seebad	• ine ZEE-baat
How are the waves/surf?	Wie ist der Wellengang/die Brandung?	vee ist dehr VEHL-len-gahng/dee BRAHN-dung?
Is the water cold/warm?	Ist das Wasser kalt/warm?	ist dahs VAHS-se(r) kahlt/vahrm?
Where can I rent/buy . . .	Wo kann ich ——— mieten/kaufen?	voh kahn ikh ——— MEE-ten/KOW-fen?
• an air mattress?	• eine Luftmatratze	• INE-eh LUFT-mah-traht-seh
• a beach chair?	• einen Liegestuhl	• INE-en LEE-geh-shtool
• a beach towel?	• ein Strandtuch	• ine SHTRAHNT-tookh

*FKK = abbreviation of *Freikörperkultur*, which means, literally, free body culture. This nudist movement has a long tradition in Germany, and its beaches are quite popular, especially in the north.

157

• a canopied beach chair?	• einen Strandkorb	• INE-en SHTRAHNT-korp
• a rowboat?	• ein Ruderboot	• ine ROO-de(r)-boht
• a sailboat?	• ein Segelboot	• ine ZAY-gel-boht
• skin-diving equipment?	• eine Taucher-ausrüstung	• INE-eh TOW-khe(r)-ows-rews-tung
• a surfboard?	• ein Surfbrett	• ine SURF-breht
• an umbrella?	• einen Sonnenschirm	• INE-en ZON-en-shirm
• waterskis?	• Wasserschier	• VAHS-se(r)-shee-e(r)
• a windsurfer?	• einen Windsurfer	• INE-en VINT-sur-fe(r)

What's the fee per hour/day/week?
Was kostet es pro Stunde/Tag/Woche?
vahs KOS-tet ehs proh SHTUN-deh/taak/VOKH-eh?

Other Active Sports

My favorite sports are . . .
Meine Lieblings-sportarten sind . . .
MINE-eh LEEP-lings-shport-ahr-ten zint . . .

• basketball	• Basketball	• BAAS-keht-bahl
• bowling	• Kegeln	• KAY-geln
• boxing	• Boxen	• BOKS-en
• cycling	• Radfahren	• RAAT-faa-ren
• golf	• Golf	• golf
• horseback riding	• Reiten	• RYE-ten
• mountain climbing	• Bergsteigen	• BEHRK-shtye-gen
• skiing	• Skifahren	• SHEE-faa-ren
• soccer	• Fußball	• FOOS-bahl
• swimming	• Schwimmen	• SHVIM-men
• tennis	• Tennis	• TEHN-is
• volleyball	• Volleyball	• VOL-lee-bahl

I'm looking for . . . **Ich suche . . .** ikh ZOO-kheh . . .

• a golf course.	• einen Golfplatz.	• INE-en GOLF-plahts.
• a soccer field.	• ein Fußballfeld.	• ine FOOS-bahl-fehlt.
• tennis courts.	• Tennisplätze.	• TEHN-nis-pleht-seh.

Are there rackets for rent?
Gibt es Tennisschläger zu mieten?
gipt ehs TEHN-is-shlay-ge(r) tsoo MEE-ten?

We also need balls.	**Wir brauchen auch Bälle.**	veer BROW-khen owkh BEHL-leh.
You play very well.	**Sie spielen sehr gut.**	zee SHPEE-len zehr goot.

Winter Sports

How far is the nearest ski area?	**Wie weit ist das nächste Skigebiet?***	vee vite ist dahs NAYKH-steh SHEE-geh-beet?
Can you get there by train?	**Kann man mit der Bahn dahin?**	kahn mahn mit dehr baan dah-HIN?
What are the skiing conditions like now?	**Wie sind jetzt die Skiverhältnisse?**	vee zint yehtst dee SHEE-fehr-hehlt-nis-seh?
Are there . . .	**Gibt es . . .**	gipt ehs . . .
• ski lifts?	• **Skilifts?**	• SHEE-lifts?
• beginners' slopes?	• **Pisten für Anfänger?**	• PIS-ten fewr AHN-fehn-ge(r)?
• skiing lessons?	• **Skiunterricht?**	• SHEE-un-tehr-rikht?
• cross-country ski trails?	• **Wege für Langlaufskifahrer?**	• VAY-geh fewr LAHNG-lowf-shee-faa-re(r)?
Is there an (artificial) skating rink there?	**Gibt es dort eine (Kunst-) Eisbahn?**	gipt ehs dort INE-eh [KUNST-] ICE-baan?
Can you rent . . .	**Kann man ——— mieten?**	kahn mahn ——— MEE-ten?
• skiing equipment?	• **eine Skiausrüstung?**	• INE-eh SHEE-ows-rews-tung?
• downhill skis?	• **Abfahrtsskier?**	• AHP-faarts-shee-e(r)?
• cross-country skis?	• **Langlaufskier?**	• LAHNG-lowf-shee-e(r)?
• poles/boots?	• **Skistöcke/ Stiefel?**	• SHEE-shtu(r)-keh/ SHTEE-fel?
• skates?	• **Schlittschuhe?**	• SHLIT-shoo-eh?
• a sled?	• **einen Schlitten?**	• INE-en SHLIT-ten?

*In German, ski is sometimes spelled *Schi,* and always pronounced [SHEE].

159

ENTERTAINMENT

SPECTATOR SPORTS

Is there a soccer game this weekend?	**Gibt es am Wochenende ein Fußballspiel?**	gipt ehs ahm VOKH-en-ehn-deh ine FOOS-bahl-shpeel?
Which teams are playing?	**Welche Mannschaften spielen?**	VEHL-kheh MAHN-shahf-ten SHPEE-len?
Where's the stadium?	**Wo ist das Stadion?**	voh ist dahs SHTAA-dee-ohn?
When does the game start?	**Wann beginnt das Spiel?**	vahn beh-GINT dahs shpeel?
How much are the tickets?	**Was kosten die Eintrittskarten?**	vahs KOS-ten dee INE-trits-kahr-ten?
Can you get me a ticket?	**Können Sie mir eine Karte besorgen?**	KU(R)-nen zee meer INE-eh KAHR-teh beh-ZOR-gen?
I'd like to see . . .	**Ich habe Lust, ―――― zu sehen.**	ikh HAA-beh loost, ―――― tsoo ZAY-en.
• a boxing match.	• **einen Boxkampf**	• INE-en BOKS-kahmpf
• car racing.	• **ein Autorennen**	• ine OW-toh-rehn-nen
• a golf tournament.	• **ein Golfturnier**	• ine GOLF-toor-neer
• horse racing.	• **ein Pferderennen**	• ine PFEHR-deh-rehn-nen
• a tennis tournament.	• **ein Tennisturnier**	• ine TEHN-nis-toor-neer

CULTURAL DIVERSIONS

Cinema (Movies)

Foreign films are usually dubbed into German, but some movie houses will show them at certain times with the original sound track and German subtitles. This will be indicated by the letters O.F. (*Originalfassung* = original version). Films are shown on a fixed schedule, so tickets can be purchased in advance.

160

Let's go to the movies tonight.	**Gehen wir heute abend ins Kino.**	GAY-en veer HOY-teh AA-behnt ins KEE-noh.
I want to see the new film by —— with ——.	**Ich will den neuen Film von —— mit —— sehen.**	ikh vil dehn NOY-en film fon —— mit —— ZAY-en.
What kind of film is it?	**Was für ein Film ist es?**	vahs fewr ine film ist ehs?
Is it dubbed?	**Ist er synchronisiert?**	ist ehr sin-kro-nee-ZEERT?
Who is the leading actor/actress?	**Wer spielt die Hauptrolle?**	vehr shpeelt dee HOWPT-rol-leh?
Who's the director?	**Wer ist der Regisseur?**	vehr ist dehr reh-zhis-SUR?
Where/When is it playing?	**Wo/Wann spielt er?**	voh/vahn shpeelt ehr?
I'd rather see . . .	**Ich möchte lieber —— sehen.**	ikh MU(R)KH-teh LEE-be(r) —— ZAY-en.
• the original version with subtitles.	• **die Originalfassung mit Untertiteln**	• dee o-ri-gi-NAAL-fahs-sung mit UN-te(r)-tee-teln
• a comedy.	• **eine Komödie**	• INE-eh ko-MU(R)-dyeh
• a musical.	• **ein Musical**	• ine "musical"
• a thriller.	• **einen Krimi**	• INE-en KREE-mee
• a Western.	• **einen Western**	• INE-en VEHST-ern
I'd like tickets (now) for this evening.	**Ich möchte jetzt Karten für heute abend.**	ikh MU(R)KH-teh yehtst KAHR-ten fewr HOY-teh AA-behnt.

Theater, Opera, Ballet, and Concert Halls

Non-German operas, operettas, and stage plays are usually performed in German translations. The same is true even for well-known non-German musicals. Music, dance, and pantomime performances are of course the most accessible for non-German speakers, but those with an interest in theater and some grasp of German may find it worthwhile to venture into theater and

161

opera productions in German. Often the music, sets, and staging are so impressive that they can be enjoyed in and of themselves.

Can you recommend a/an . . .	Können Sie mir —— empfehlen?	KU(R)-nen zee meer —— ehm-PFAY-len?
• ballet?	• ein Ballett	• ine bah-LEHT
• concert?	• ein Konzert	• ine kon-TSEHRT
• opera	• eine Oper	• INE-eh OH-pe(r)
• operetta	• eine Operette	• INE-eh oh-peh-REHT-teh
• play	• ein Theaterstück	• ine tay-AA-te(r)-shtewk
Where's the theater/opera house/concert hall?	Wo ist das Theater/das Opernhaus/die Konzerthalle?	voh ist dahs tay-AA-te(r)/dahs OH-pern-hows/dee kon-TSEHRT-hahl-eh?
What's being performed?	Was wird gegeben?	vahs virt geh-GAY-ben?
Who's it by?	Von wem ist das?	fon vehm ist dahs?
Which orchestra is playing?	Welches Orchester spielt?	VEHL-khes or-KEHS-te(r) shpeelt?
Who's conducting/ singing/ dancing?	Wer dirigiert/ singt/ tanzt?	vehr di-ree-GEERT/zinkt/tahntst?
I'd like . . .	Ich möchte . . .	ikh MU(R)KH-teh . . .
• an orchestra seat toward the middle.	• einen Platz im Parkett in der Mitte.	• INE-en plahts im pahr-KEHT in dehr MIT-teh.
• a balcony seat not too far back.	• einen Platz im Balkon nicht zu weit hinten.	• INE-en plahts im baal-KON nikht tsoo vite HIN-ten.

NIGHTCLUBS AND DISCOS

Is there —— in this town?	Gibt es in dieser Stadt ——	gipt ehs in DEE-ze(r) shtaht . . .
• a good disco	• eine gute Diskothek?	• INE-eh GOO-teh dis-koh-TAYK?

162

• an interesting nightclub	• ein interessantes Nachtlokal?	• ine in-teh-rehs-SAHN-tehs NAHKHT-loh-kaal?
Is there a floor show?	Gibt es Attraktionen?	gipt ehs aht-trahk-TSYOH-nen?
Are reservations necessary?	Muβ man reservieren lassen?	mus mahn reh-zeh-VEER-en LAHS-en?
Is evening dress required?	Wird Abendgarderobe verlangt?	virt AA-behnt-gaar-deh-roh-beh fehr-LAHNKT?
Is there a cover charge?	Gibt es eine Mindestgebühr?	gipt ehs INE-eh MIN-dehst-geh-bewr?
Would you like to dance?	Möchten Sie tanzen?	MU(R)KH-ten zee TAHN-tsen?

14/GENERAL INFORMATION

DAYS, MONTHS, AND SEASONS

Days of the Week *(Tage der Woche)*

(on) Monday	**(am) Montag**	[ahm] MOHN-taak
Tuesday	**Dienstag**	DEENS-taak
Wednesday	**Mittwoch**	MIT-vokh
Thursday	**Donnerstag**	DON-nehrs-taak
Friday	**Freitag**	FRYE-taak
Saturday	**Samstag/Sonnabend**	ZAHMS-taak/ZON-aa-behnt
Sunday	**Sonntag**	ZON-taak

Months of the Year *(Monate des Jahres)*

January	**Januar/Jänner** (Austrian)	YAH-noo-aar/YEH-ne(r)
February	**Februar**	FAY-broo-aar
March	**März**	mehrts
April	**April**	ah-PRIL
May	**Mai**	mye
June	**Juni**	YOO-nee
July	**Juli**	YOO-lee
August	**August**	ow-GUST
September	**September**	zehp-TEHM-be(r)
October	**Oktober**	ok-TOH-be(r)
November	**November**	no-VEHM-be(r)
December	**Dezember**	deh-TSEHM-be(r)

The Four Seasons *(Die vier Jahreszeiten)*

(in the) winter	**(im) Winter/der Winter**	[im] VIN-te(r)/dehr VIN-te(r)
spring	**der Frühling**	dehr FREW-ling
summer	**der Sommer**	dehr ZOM-me(r)
autumn	**der Herbst**	dehr hehrpst

THE DATE

| What is today's date? | **Der wievielte ist heute?** | dehr vee-FEEL-teh ist HOY-teh? |

164

What day is it today?	**Welchen Tag haben wir heute?**	VEHL-khen taak HAA-ben veer HOY-teh?
Today is Friday, April 13.	**Heute ist Freitag, der dreizehnte (13e) April.**	HOY-teh ist FRYE-taak, dehr DRYE-tsayn-teh ah-PRIL.
It's Wednesday, July 11, 1990.	**Es ist Mittwoch, der elfte Juli, neunzehnhun-dertneunzig.**	ehs ist MIT-vokh, dehr EHLF-teh YOO-lee, NOYN-tsayn-hun-dert-NOYN-tsikh.

AGE

How old are you?	**Wie alt sind Sie?**	vee ahlt zint zee?
I'm forty years old.	**Ich bin vierzig Jahre alt.**	ikh bin VEER-tsikh YAA-reh ahlt.
How old is he/she?	**Wie alt ist er/sie?**	vee ahlt ist ehr/zee?
He/she is thirty.	**Er/Sie ist dreißig.**	ehr/zee ist DRYE-sikh.
I'm older/younger than she is.	**Ich bin älter/jünger als sie.**	ikh bin EHL-te(r)/YEWN-ge(r) ahls zee.
I was born in 1950.	**Ich bin neunzehn-hundertfünfzig geboren.**	ikh bin NOYN-tsayn-hun-dert-FEWNF-tsikh geh-BOH-ren.
When's her birthday?	**Wann hat sie Geburtstag?**	vahn haht zee geh-BURTS-taak?
Her birthday is March 15	**Ihr Geburtstag ist am fünfzehnten März**	eer geh-BURTS-taak ist ahm FEWNF-tsayn-ten mehrts

TIME EXPRESSIONS

now	**jetzt**	yehtst
earlier	**früher**	FREW-e(r)
later	**später**	SHPAY-te(r)
before	**vor/vorher**	for/FOR-hehr
after/afterward	**nach/nachher**	nahkh/NAHKH-hehr
soon	**bald**	bahlt
once	**einmal**	INE-maal
in the morning	**morgens**	MOR-gens

165

at noon	**um Mittag**	oom MIT-taag
in the afternoon	**nachmittags**	NAHKH-mit-taags
in the evening	**abends**	AA-behnts
at night	**nachts**	nahkhts
at midnight	**um Mitternacht**	oom MIT-te(r)-nahkht
tomorrow	**morgen***	MOR-gen
yesterday	**gestern**	GEHS-tern
the day after tomorrow	**übermorgen**	EW-be(r)-mor-gen
the day before yesterday	**vorgestern**	FOR-gehs-tern
this week	**diese Woche**	DEE-zeh VOKH-eh
next week	**nächste Woche**	NAYKH-steh VOKH-eh
last week	**vorige Woche**	FOR-i-geh VOKH-eh
every day	**jeden Tag**	YAY-den taak
in three days	**in drei Tagen**	in drye TAA-gen
two days ago	**vor zwei Tagen**	for tsye TAA-gen
on Saturdays	**Samstags/Sonnabends**	ZAHMS-taags/ZON-aa-behnts
on weekends	**an den Wochenenden**	ahn den VOKH-en-ehn-den
on weekdays	**wochentags**	VOKH-en-taags
during the week	**während der Woche**	VAY-rehnt dehr VOKH-eh
a working day	**ein Arbeitstag**	ine AHR-bites-taak
a day off	**ein freier Tag**	ine FRYE-e(r) taak
in January	**im Januar**	im YAH-noo-aar
last January	**im vorigen Januar**	im FOR-i-gen YAH-noo-aar
next January	**im nächsten Januar**	im NAYKH-sten YAH-noo-aar
since July	**seit Juli**	zite YOO-lee
before/after June	**vor/nach Juni**	for/nahkh YOO-nee
during May	**während des Monats Mai**	VAY-rehnt dehs MOH-naats mye
(not) until March	**(nicht) bis März**	(nikht) bis mehrts
the beginning of August	**Anfang August**	AHN-fahng OW-gust

*When capitalized, Morgen means morning, as in Guten Morgen (good morning).

166

the middle of November	**Mitte November**	MIT-teh no-VEHM-be(r)
the end of December	**Ende Dezember**	EHN-deh deh-TSEHM-be(r)
each/every month	**jeden Monat**	YAY-den MOH-naat
this month	**in diesem Monat**	in DEE-zem MOH-naat
next month	**im nächsten Monat**	im NAYKH-sten MOH-naat
last month	**im letzten Monat**	im LEHT-sten MOH-naat
this year	**dieses Jahr**	DEE-zehs yaar
next year	**nächstes Jahr**	NAYKH-stehs yaar
last year	**letztes Jahr**	LEHT-stehs yaar
every year	**jedes Jahr**	YAY-dehs yaar
in what year	**in welchem Jahr**	in VEHL-khem yaar
in the 19th century	**im neunzehnten Jahrhundert**	im NOYN-tsayn-ten yaar-HUN-dert
in the forties	**in den vierziger Jahren**	in dehn VEER-tsikh-e(r) YAA-ren
in 1980	**(im Jahre) 1980***	[im YAA-reh] NOYN-tsayn-hun-dert-AHKH-tsikh

*im Jahre (in the year) is optional; just the date 1980 by itself already means "in 1980."

PUBLIC HOLIDAYS

January 1	New Year's Day	**Neujahr****
January 6	Epiphany	**Dreikönigstag** (Austria only)
April–May	Good Friday	**Karfreitag** (not Austria)
	Easter	**Ostern**
	Easter Monday	**Ostermontag**
May 1	May Day (Labor Day)	**Tag der Arbeit** (not Switzerland)

**As elsewhere, most of the celebrating is done on New Year's Eve, *Sylvesterabend*.

May–June	Ascension Day	**Christi Himmelfahrt**
	Pentecost (Whit-monday)	**Pfingstmontag**
	Corpus Christi Day	**Fronleichnam** (Austria only)
August 1	National Day	**Nationalfeiertag** (Switzerland only)
August 15	Assumption Day	**Mariä Himmelfahrt** (Austria only)
October 26	National Day	**Nationalfeiertag** (Austria only)
November 1	All Saints' Day	**Allerheiligen** (Austria only)
December 8	Immaculate Conception	**Mariä Empfängnis** (Austria only)
December 25	Christmas Day	**Weihnachten**
December 26	St. Stephen's Day	**Weihnachtstag**

Merry Christmas!	**Fröhliche Weihnachten!**	FRU(R)-likh-eh VYE-nahkh-ten
Happy New Year!	**Glückliches Neues Jahr!**	GLEWK-likh-ehs NOY-ehs yaar!
Happy Easter!	**Frohe Ostern!**	FROH-eh OHS-tern!
Happy Holidays!	**Frohe Feiertage!**	FROH-eh FYE-e(r)-taa-geh!
Happy Birthday!	**Alles Gute zum Geburtstag!**	AH-lehs GOO-teh tsoom geh-BURTS-taak!
Congratulations!	**Herzlichen Glückwunsch!**	HEHRTS-likh-en GLEWK-voonsh!

168

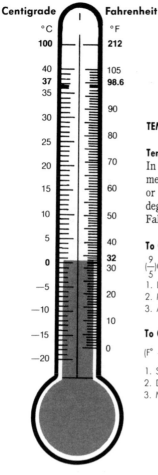

Centigrade
°C
100
40
37
35
30
25
20
15
10
5
0
−5
−10
−15
−20

Fahrenheit
°F
212
105
98.6
90
80
70
60
50
40
32
30
20
10
0

TEMPERATURE CONVERSIONS

Temperature Conversions
In Europe, temperature is measured in degrees Celsius, or centigrade. To convert degrees Celsius into degrees Fahrenheit, use this formula:

To Convert Centigrade to Fahrenheit

$(\frac{9}{5})C° + 32 = F°$

1. Divide by 5.
2. Multiply by 9.
3. Add 32.

To Convert Fahrenheit to Centigrade

$(F° - 32)\frac{5}{9} = C°$

1. Subtract 32.
2. Divide by 9.
3. Multiply by 5.

THE WEATHER

What wonderful/terrible weather!	Was für ein schönes/ furchtbares Wetter!	vahs fewr ine SHU(R)-nehs/FOORKHT-baa-rehs VEH-te(r)!
A lovely day, isn't it?	Ein herrlicher Tag, nicht wahr?	ine HEHR-likh-e(r) taak, nikht waar?
How hot/cold it is today!	Wie heiß/kalt es heute ist!	vee hice/kahlt ehs HOY-teh ist!
Is it always this warm?	Ist es immer so warm?	ist ehs IM-me(r) zoh vahrm?
What's the weather forecast?	Wie ist die Wettervor- hersage?	vee ist dee VEHT-te(r)-for-hehr-zaa-geh?
What do you think?	Was meinen Sie?	vahs MINE-en zee?
Will it ——— tomorrow?	Wird es morgen . . .	virt ehs MOR-gen . . .
• be nice	• schön sein?	• shu(r)n zine?
• rain	• regnen?	• REHG-nen?
• snow	• schneien?	• SHNYE-en?
• be cloudy	• bewölkt sein?	• beh-WU(R)LKT zine?
• be sunny	• sonnig sein?	• ZON-nikh zine?
• be windy	• windig sein?	• VIN-dikh zine?
• be stormy	• stürmisch sein?	• SHTEWR-mish zine?

CONTINENTS AND COUNTRIES

Where are you from?	Woher kommen Sie?	voh-HEHR KO-men zee?
I'm from . . .	Ich komme aus* . . .	ikh KOM-eh ows . . .
Africa	Afrika	AAF-ree-kah
Asia	Asien	AHZ-yen
Australia	Australien	ow-STRAA-lyen
Europe	Europa	oy-ROH-pah
North America	Nordamerika	NORT-ah-meh-ri-kah

*Because of the preposition aus (from), which requires the dative case, those countries taking a definite article, like die Schweiz (Switzerland), will appear different in this construction: Ich komme aus der Schweiz.

170

South America	**Südamerika**	ZEWT-ah-meh-ri-kah
Argentina	**Argentinien**	ahr-gehn-TEEN-yen
Austria	**Österreich**	U(R)-stehr-ryekh
Belgium	**Belgien**	BEHL-gyen
Brazil	**Brasilien**	brah-ZEEL-yen
Canada	**Kanada**	KAH-nah-dah
China	**China**	KHEE-nah
Czechosolovakia	**die Tschecho-slowakei**	dee tsheh-khoh-sloh-vah-KYE
Denmark	**Dänemark**	DAY-neh-mahrk
England	**England**	EHNG-lahnt
Finland	**Finnland**	FIN-lahnt
France	**Frankreich**	FRAHNK-ryekh
Germany	**Deutschland**	DOYCH-lahnt
Great Britian	**Großbritannien**	grohs-bri-TAHN-yen
Greece	**Griechenland**	GREE-khen-lahnt
Holland/the Netherlands	**Holland/die Niederlande**	HOL-lahnt/dee NEE-de(r)-lahn-deh
Hungary	**Ungarn**	UN-gahrn
India	**Indien**	IN-dyen
Ireland	**Irland**	EER-lahnt
Israel	**Israel**	IS-rah-el
Italy	**Italien**	ee-TAAL-yen
Japan	**Japan**	YAA-pahn
Korea	**Korea**	ko-RAY-ah
Liechtenstein	**Liechtenstein**	LEEKH-ten-shtine
Luxembourg	**Luxemburg**	LUK-sehm-boork
Mexico	**Mexiko**	MEHK-see-koh
New Zealand	**Neuseeland**	noy-ZAY-lahnt
Norway	**Norwegen**	NOR-vay-gen
Poland	**Polen**	POH-len
Portugal	**Portugal**	POR-too-gaal
Russia/Soviet Union	**Rußland/Sowjet-union**	RUS-lahnt/sov-YET-oo-nyohn
Scotland	**Schottland**	SHOT-lahnt
South Africa	**Südafrika**	ZEWT-aaf-ree-kah
Spain	**Spanien**	SHPAH-nyen
Sweden	**Schweden**	SHVAY-den
Switzerland	**die Schweiz**	dee shvites
Turkey	**die Türkei**	dee tewr-KYE

171

| United States | **die Vereinigten Staaten** | dee fehr-EYE-nikh-ten SHTAA-ten |
| Yugoslavia | **Jugoslawien** | yoo-goh-SLAA-vyen |

LANGUAGES

Do you speak . . .	**Sprechen Sie . . .**	SHPREHKH-en zee .
Arabic?	**Arabisch?**	ah-RAA-bish?
Chinese?	**Chinesisch?**	khee-NAY-zish?
English?	**Englisch?**	EHNG-lish?
French?	**Französisch?**	frahn-ZO(R)-zish?
German?	**Deutsch?**	doych?
Japanese?	**Japanisch?**	yaa-PAH-nish?
Portuguese?	**Portugiesisch?**	por-too-GEE-zish?
Russian?	**Russisch?**	ROO-sish?
Spanish?	**Spanisch?**	SHPAH-nish?

PROFESSIONS AND OCCUPATIONS*

accountant	**der Buchhalter**	dehr BOOKH-hahl-te(r)
architect	**der Architekt**	dehr ahr-khee-TEHKT
artist	**der Künstler**	dehr KEWNST-le(r)
baker	**der Bäcker**	dehr BEH-ke(r)
butcher	**der Metzger/ Fleischer**	dehr MEHTS-ge(r)/FLYE-she(r)
cardiologist	**der Kardiologe**	dehr kahr-dyoh-LOH-geh
carpenter	**der Tischler**	dehr TISH-le(r)
cook	**der Koch**	dehr kokh
dentist	**der Zahnarzt**	dehr TSAAN-ahrtst
doctor	**der Arzt**	dehr ahrtst
electrician	**der Elektriker**	dehr eh-LEHK-tri-ke(r)
engineer	**der Ingenieur**	dehr in-zheh-NYUR
eye doctor	**der Augenarzt**	dehr OW-gen-ahrtst
lawyer	**der Rechtsanwalt**	dehr REHKHTS-ahn-vahlt

*The feminine forms are derived in most cases by adding the suffix -in and by placing an umlant over the main vowel; for example, der Arzt, die Ärztin (doctor); der Koch, die Köchin (cook). As with nationalities, here too the indefinite article ein(e) is not used; for example, Ich bin Lehrer (I'm a teacher).

maid	**das Dienstmädchen**	dahs DEENST-mayt-khen
nurse	**die Krankenschwester**	dee KRAHN-ken-shvehs-te(r)
painter	**der Maler**	dehr MAA-le(r)
plumber	**der Klempner**	dehr KLEHMP-ne(r)
salesperson	**der Verkäufer**	dehr fehr-KOY-fe(r)
secretary	**der Sekretär**	dehr zeh-kreh-TAYR
	die Sekretärin	dee zeh-kreh-TAYR-in
shopkeeper	**der Ladenbesitzer**	dehr LAA-den-beh-zits-e(r)
teacher	**der Lehrer**	dehr LEHR-e(r)
waiter	**der Kellner**	dehr KEHL-ne(r)
waitress	**die Kellnerin**	dee KEHL-neh-rin
writer	**der Schriftsteller**	dehr SHRIFT-shtehl-le(r)

EMERGENCY EXPRESSIONS

Watch out!	**Paß auf!**	pahs owf!
Be careful!	**Vorsicht!**	FOR-zikht!
Fire!	**Feuer!**	FOY-e(r)!
Help/Get help!	**Hilfe/Holen Sie Hilfe!**	HIL-feh/HOH-len zee HIL-feh!
Hurry!	**Schnell!**	shnehl!
I'm lost.	**Ich habe mich verirrt.**	ikh HAA-beh mikh fehr-EERT.
I'm sick.	**Ich bin krank.**	ikh bin krahnk.
Call a doctor/the police/the fire department!	**Rufen Sie einen Artzt/die Polizei/die Feuerwehr!**	ROO-fen zee INE-en ahrtst/dee po-lee-TSYE/dee FOY-e(r)-vehr!
It's an emergency.	**Es ist ein Notfall.**	ehs ist ine NOHT-fahl.
Stop!	**Halt!**	hahlt!
Stop that thief/man/woman!	**Haltet den Dieb/Mann/die Frau!**	HAHL-tet dehn deep/mahn/dee frow!
Leave me alone!	**Lassen Sie mich in Ruhe!**	LAHS-en zee mikh in ROO-eh!
. . . was stolen!	**. . . wurde gestohlen!**	. . . VUR-deh geh-SHTOH-len!
• My camera	**• Meine Kamera**	• MINE-eh KAH-meh-raa

173

• My wallet	• **Meine Brieftasche**	• MINE-eh BREEF-tahsh-eh
Who speaks English here?	**Wer spricht hier Englisch?**	vehr sprikht heer EHNG-lish?

EMERGENCY TELEPHONE NUMBERS

Police	**Polizei** [po-lee-TSYE]	110 (Germany)
		117 (Switzerland)
		133 (Austria)
Fire	**Feuerwehr** [FOY-e(r)-vehr]	112 (Germany)
		118 (Switzerland)
		122 (Austria)
Ambulance	**Krankenwagen** [KRAHN-ken-vaa-gen]	112 (Germany)
		144 (Austria)

SIGNS AND ANNOUNCEMENTS

Achtung	Attention/Caution
Angebot	Sale (of a specific item)
Aufzug	Elevator/Lift
Ausfahrt	Highway Exit
Ausgang	Pedestrian Exit
Auskunft	Information
Außer Betrieb	Out of Order
Ausverkauf	Clearance Sale
Ausverkauft	Sold Out
Belegt	No Vacancies/Full
Besetzt	Occupied
Betreten des Rasens Verboten	Keep Off the Grass
Bitte Klingeln	Please Ring
Bitte Nicht Stören	Please Do Not Disturb
Damen	Ladies
Drücken	Push/Press
Einfahrt	Highway Entrance
Eingang	Pedestrian Entrance
Eintreten Ohne zu Klopfen	Enter Without Knocking
Eintritt Frei	No Admission Charge

Frei	Vacant/Free
Frisch Gestrichen	Wet Paint
Für Unbefugte Verboten	No Trespassing
Gefahr	Danger
Geöffnet von —— bis ——	Open from —— to ——
Geschlossen	Closed
Geschlossene Gesellschaft	Private Party
Heiß	Hot
Kalt	Cold
Herren	Men
Kasse	Cashier
Kein Zutritt	No Entry
Lebensgefahr	Mortal Danger
Lift	Elevator/Lift
Nicht Berühren	Do Not Touch
Nichtraucher	No Smoking Section
Notausgang	Emergency Exit
Notruf	Emergency Telephone
Nur für Anlieger	Residents Only
Privatstrand	Private Beach
Privatweg	Private Road
Radweg	Cycling Path
Rauchen Verboten	No Smoking
Raucher	Smoking Section/Compartment
Reserviert	Reserved
Schlußverkauf	Clearance Sale
Unbefugtes Betreten Verboten	No Trespassing
. . . Verboten	. . . Prohibited
Vorsicht	Caution
Vorsicht, Bissiger Hund	Beware of Dog
Ziehen	Pull
Zimmer Frei	Vacancies/Room(s) to Let
Zu Verkaufen	For Sale
Zu Vermieten	For Rent/To Let

COMMON ABBREVIATIONS

Abt.	Abteilung	compartment
ACS	Automobil-Club der Schweiz	Automobile Association of Switzerland
ADAC	Allgemeiner Deutscher Automobil-Club	General Automobile Association of Germany
a.M.	am Main	on the Main River
a.Rh.	am Rhein	on the Rhine River
Bhf.	Bahnhof	railway station
BRD	Bundesrepublik Deutschland	Federal Republic of Germany (W. Germany)
BMW	Bayerische Motorenwerke	Bavarian Motor Works
bzw.	beziehungsweise	or/respectively
CDU	Christlich-Demokratische Union	Christian Democratic Union Party
DB	Deutsche Bundesbahn	Federal German Railways
DBP	Deutsche Bundespost	Federal German Postal Service
DDR	Deutsche Demokratische Republik	German Democratic Republic (E. Germany)
d.h.	das heißt	i.e. (that is)
DIN	Deutsche Industrie-Norm	German Industrial Standard
e.V.	eingetragener Verein	registered association
FKK	Freikörperkultur	Free Body Culture (nudism)
Frl.	Fräulein	Miss
Fr.	Frau	Mrs.
GmbH	Gesellschaft mit beschränkter Haftung	limited company
Hbf.	Hauptbahnhof	main railway station
Hr.	Herr	Mr.
JH	Jugendherberge	youth hostel
LKW	Lastkraftwagen	truck/lorry
MEZ	Mitteleuropäische Zeit	Central European Time
Mio.	Million	million
Mrd.	Milliarde	billion

Mwst.	Mehrwertsteuer	value-added tax
n. Chr.	nach Christus	A.D.
ÖAMTC	Österreichischer Automobil-Motorrad- und Touring-Club	Austrian Automobile, Motorcycle, and Touring Association
ÖBB	Österreichische Bundesbahn	Austrian Federal Railways
PKW	Personenkraftwagen	passenger car
Pl.	Platz	square
PS	Pferdestärke	horsepower
PTT	Post, Telephon, Telegraph	Posta, Telephone, and Telegraph Office
SBB	Schweizerische Bundesbahn	Swiss Federal Railways
SPD	Sozialdemokratische Partei Deutschlands	Social Democratic Party of Germany
St.	Stock	floor
Str.	Straße	street
TCS	Touring-Club der Schweiz	Touring Association of Switzerland
usw.	und so weiter	etc.
v.	von	of, from
v.Chr.	vor Christus	B.C.
z.B.	zum Beispiel	e.g. (for example)
z.Z.	zur Zeit	at present

15/GRAMMAR IN BRIEF

NOUNS AND ARTICLES

All German nouns begin with a capital letter and fall into one of three gender catagories: masculine, feminine, or neuter. Although there are some rules to determine grammatical gender from the spelling and meaning of a word, it is largely unpredictable and should be learned together with the noun in question. The definite articles, *der, die, das* (the), and the indefinite articles, *ein, eine* (a/an), are determined by the gender of a noun. The changes from singular to plural noun forms are complex and include the addition of umlauts and the endings *-e, -er, -en, -s;* in some cases, there is no change at all. The plural definite article is the same for all three genders.

Definite Articles:

Singular

masculine	**der Vater**	the father
feminine	**die Mutter**	the mother
neuter	**das Mädchen**	the girl

Plural

masculine	**die Väter**	the fathers
feminine	**die Mütter**	the mothers
neuter	**die Mädchen**	the girls

Indefinite Articles:

Singular

masculine	**ein Tisch**	a table
feminine	**eine Tasse**	a cup
neuter	**ein Messer**	a knife

Singular

masculine	**kein Tisch**	no table
feminine	**keine Tasse**	no cup
neuter	**kein Messer**	no knife

Plural

masculine	**keine Tische**	no tables
feminine	**keine Tassen**	no cups
neuter	**keine Messer**	no knives

Note: the indefinite article *ein* has no plural form. To translate "I need (some) cups," you would say *"Ich brauche Tassen."* The negative *kein* does have a plural form and takes the same endings in the singular as the indefinite article.

ADJECTIVES AND DECLENSIONS

Predicate adjectives like *neu* in this sentence, *Der Wagen ist <u>neu</u>* (the car is new), are not declined, that is, they have no endings and appear as in the dictionary. When they precede the noun they modify, as in *Der <u>neue</u> Wagen fährt gut* (the new car drives well), adjectives take endings, like articles, according to the gender of the noun and its case or use in the sentence. The four cases are: subject (nominative), direct object (accusative), indirect object (dative), and possessive (genitive). The following charts illustrate how articles, adjectives and nouns are declined.

	Masculine Singular	Masculine Plural
subject	**der alte Freund**	**die alten Freunde**
	(the old friend)	
direct object	**den alten Freund**	**die alten Freunde**
indirect object	**dem alten Freund**	**den alten Freunden**
possessive	**des alten Freundes**	**der alten Freunde**

	Feminine Singular	Feminine Plural
subject	**die schwarze Katze**	**die schwarzen Katzen**
	(the black cat)	
direct object	**die schwarze Katze**	**die schwarzen Katzen**
indirect object	**der schwarzen Katze**	**den schwarzen Katzen**
possessive	**der schwarzen Katze**	**der schwarzen Katzen**

179

	Neuter Singular	Neuter Plural
subject	**das kleine Buch**	**die kleinen Bücher**
	(the small book)	
direct object	**das kleine Buch**	**die kleinen Bücher**
indirect object	**dem kleinen Buch**	**den kleinen Büchern**
possessive	**des kleinen Buches**	**der kleinen Bücher**

When the adjective is preceded by the indefinite article, the adjective endings are somewhat different.

	Masculine Singular	Feminine Singular
subject	**ein alter Freund**	**eine schwarze Katze**
	(an old friend)	(a black cat)
direct object	**einen alten Freund**	**eine schwarze Katze**
indirect object	**einem alten Freund**	**einer schwarzen Katze**
possessive	**eines alten Freundes**	**einer schwarzen Katze**

	Neuter Singular	Negative Plural
subject	**ein kleines Buch**	**keine* kleinen Bücher**
	(a small book)	(no small books)
direct object	**ein kleines Buch**	**keine kleinen Bücher**
indirect object	**einem kleinen Buch**	**keinen kleinen Büchern**
possessive	**eines kleinen Buches**	**keiner kleinen Bücher**

*See Note, under Nouns and Articles, page 179.

When modifying adjectives are not preceded by an article, they have the same endings as the definite article, except for the seldom-occurring masculine and neuter singular possessives, which become -en instead of -es. More common examples: *Er trinkt nur kaltes Bier* (He drinks only cold beer); *Mir gefällt starke Sonne* (I like strong sun).

GRAMMAR

Demonstrative Adjectives

Referred to sometimes as "der words," the demonstrative adjectives *dieser* (this), *jener* (that), *jeder* (every), *mancher* (some), *welcher* (which) follow the same declension as the definite article, *der, die, das*. Examples: *Dieses Brot schmeckt gut* (This bread tastes good); *Mit welchem Bus fahren Sie?* (With which bus are you traveling?). In conversation *jener* (that) is usually replaced by the definite article, which is then given special stress. Example: *Dieser Sessel ist bequem, der Stuhl aber gar nicht.* (This armchair is comfortable, but that chair isn't comfortable at all.)

Possessive Adjectives

The endings on these parts of speech agree with the gender and number of the noun they modify, regardless of the speaker's gender. Examples: *ihr Vater* (her father), *seine Mutter* (his mother). In the singular possessive, adjectives are declined like the indefinite article, *ein* and are thus sometimes called "ein words." The plural forms follow the declension pattern of the definite article.

mein	my	**unser**	our
dein	your (familiar singular)	**euer**	your (familiar plural)
Ihr	your (polite singular)	**Ihr**	your (polite plural)
ihr	her	**ihr**	their
sein	his/its		

Note that *Ihr,* the polite form of your, is capitalized and the same in both singular and plural, while *ihr* can mean either her or their—only context will clarify which; for example, *Anna verwöhnt ihr Kind* (Anna spoils her child); *Die Eltern verwöhnen ihr Kind.* (The parents spoil their child.)

Comparative and Superlative Adjective Forms

The comparative is formed by adding *-er*, the superlative by adding *-st* or *-est* to the adjective. Single syllable adjectives usually add an umlaut where possible. For example:

hart (hard)	**härter** (harder)	**härtest** (hardest)
aggressiv (aggressive)	**aggressiver** (more aggresive)	**aggressivst** (most aggressive)
groß (large)	**größer** (larger)	**größt** (largest)

Regular adjective endings are added to these forms: *das härteste Holz* (the hardest wood), *mit dem aggressiveren Spieler* (with the more aggressive player). Predicate superlatives take this form: *Dieser Baum ist am größten.* (This tree is the largest.)

ADVERBS

Most adverbs are derived from adjectives in their undeclined form; for example, *Sie ist schön* (She is beautiful), *Sie singt schön* (She sings beautifully). The suffix *-lich* corresponds to our *-ly* ending. As in English, however, some of the most commonly used adverbs have unique forms and must be learned individually; for example: *fast* = almost, *sehr* = very, *ziemlich* = rather.

PERSONAL PRONOUNS

These pronouns are declined as follows:

Subject	Direct Object	Indirect Object
ich (I)	**mich** (me)	**mir** (to me)
du (you, familiar singular)	**dich** (you)	**dir** (to you)
er (he/it)	**ihn** (him/it)	**ihm** (to him/it)
sie (she/it)	**sie** (her/it)	**ihr** (to her/it)
es (it)	**es** (it)	**ihm** (to it/him/her)
wir (we)	**uns** (us)	**uns** (to us)
ihr (you, familiar plural)	**euch** (you)	**euch** (to you)
sie (they)	**sie** (them)	**ihnen** (to them)
Sie (you, polite plural and singular)	**Sie** (you)	**Ihnen** (to you)

Examples:

Er leiht es mir (He lends it to me);
Wir schicken ihn euch (We send him/it to you).

182

When both direct and indirect objects are pronouns, as above, the direct object precedes the indirect. When both are nouns (*Wir schicken Hans den Brief*—We send Hans the letter), the order is reversed. When they are mixed, the pronoun precedes the noun:

Wir schicken ihn Hans (We send it to Hans).
Wir schicken ihm den Brief (We send him the letter).

As with the possessive adjectives, the polite forms of you *(Sie, Ihnen)* are capitalized to distinguish them from *sie* (she, her, they, them) and *ihnen* (to them). Other pronouns with identical forms (e.g., *ihm* [to him, or, to it]) can be differentiated only through context. Personal pronouns reflect the grammatical gender of the nouns they replace.

The familiar you forms, *du* and *ihr*, should be used only when addressing relatives, close friends, young children, and animals. For all others, use *Sie;* otherwise, you may offend the person.

Reflexive Pronouns

These pronouns are used in combination with reflexive verbs to express the idea of "oneself." They have the same forms as the personal pronouns, except for the third person singular *(er, sie, es)*, plural *(sie)*, and polite second person *(Sie)*, which as direct and indirect objects all take the reflexive form *sich*. Reflexive verbs are usually listed in the dictionary together with this pronoun *sich*. Examples:

sich setzen (to sit down), *Er setzt sich* (He sits [himself] down).
sich putzen (to clean oneself), *Ich putze mir die Zähne* (I clean my teeth).

VERBS

German, like English, has regular and irregular verbs; some of the latter follow the same vowel shift patterns as their English cognates: *trinken, trank, getrunken* (drink, drank, drunk). In English perfect tenses are formed with the auxiliary verb "have," while German uses two different ones. Most verbs are conjugated with *haben* (to have), but those of motion or change of state (e.g.,

183

laufen [to run], *wachsen* [to grow]) take *sein* (to be). Future tense uses the auxiliary *werden* (to become).

There is no equivalent in German for the continuous tenses in English. The present continuous, I am working, is rendered by the simple present: *Ich arbeite.* The past continuous, I was working, by either the simple past, *Ich arbeitete* (I worked) or the present perfect, *I habe gearbeitet* (I have worked). The latter two tenses are equivalent in German, but in conversation, where English speakers would use the simple past, such as "I spoke," Germans prefer the present perfect: *Ich habe gesprochen* (I have spoken). As in English, the German present tense is often used to express the future: *Wir fahren morgen ab* (We leave [will leave] tomorrow). Here are the conjugations of two regular and two irregular verbs in four of the most frequently used tenses.

Regular			Irregular	
Infinitive:	sagen	arbeiten	denken	fahren
	(to say)	(to work)	(to think)	(to travel)

Present

ich	sage	arbeite	denke	fahre
du	sagst	arbeitest	denkst	fährst
es/sie/es	sagt	arbeitet	denkt	fährt
wir	sagen	arbeiten	denken	fahren
ihr	sagt	arbeitet	denkt	fahrt
sie/Sie	sagen	arbeiten	denken	fahren

Past (Imperfect)

ich	sagte	arbeitete	dachte	fuhr
du	sagtest	arbeitetest	dachtest	fuhrst
er/sie/es	sagte	arbeitete	dachte	fuhr
wir	sagten	arbeiteten	dachten	fuhren
ihr	sagtet	arbeitetet	dachtet	fuhrt
sie/Sie	sagten	arbeiteten	dachten	fuhren

Present Perfect (auxiliary <u>haben</u>) (auxiliary <u>sein</u>)

ich	**habe** gesagt	<u>gearbeitet</u>	<u>gedacht</u>	**bin** gefahren
du	**hast** gesagt	gearbeitet	gedacht	**bist** gefahren
er/sie/es	**hat** gesagt	gearbeitet	gedacht	<u>ist</u> gefahren
wir	**haben** gesagt	gearbeitet	gedacht	**sind** gefahren
ihr	**habt** gesagt	gearbeitet	gedacht	**seid** gefahren
sie/Sie	**haben** gesagt	gearbeitet	gedacht	**sind** gefahren

Future (auxiliary <u>werden</u>)

ich	**werde** sagen	arbeiten	denken	fahren
du	**wirst** sagen	arbeiten	denken	fahren
er/sie/es	**wird** sagen	arbeiten	denken	fahren
wir	**werden** sagen	arbeiten	denken	fahren
ihr	**werdet** sagen	arbeiten	denken	fahren
sie/Sie	**werden** sagen	arbeiten	denken	fahren

Note that in the endings of *arbeiten* and other regular verbs whose stem ends in *-t* or *-d* (e.g., *reden* = to talk, *retten* = to save), extra *e*'s are added for reasons of pronunciation in the first three tenses. The verb *denken* has a mixture of regular and irregular traits: the vowel and stem change from present to past, from *denk* to *dach,* is irregular, but the past participle, *gedacht,* has a regular form, that is, the ending is *-t* instead of *-en.* Other verbs that follow this same pattern are: *brennen* (to burn), *bringen* (to bring), *nennen* (to name), *rennen* (to run), *senden* (to send). The so-called modal verbs, *dürfen* (to be allowed), *können* (to be able to), *mögen* (to like), *müssen* (to have to), and *sollen* (to be supposed to), also belong to this hybrid category.

Separable Prefixes

Certain verbs can be combined with prefixes, which are separated from the main verb in simple tenses. Example: *ziehen* (to pull) has these reflexive forms: *sich anziehen* (to dress oneself), *sich ausziehen* (to undress oneself), *sich umziehen* (to change dress), *Ich ziehe mich um* (I'm changing).

The past participle of such verbs is formed by inserting the *ge-*syllable between the two parts of the verb: *Ich habe mich umgezogen* (I have changed).

WORD ORDER

German sentences follow the same basic pattern as English—subject, verb, predicate—but the second position of the verb in German is more fixed, so that if anything besides the subject precedes it, the subject-verb order is reversed:

Heute sprechen wir Deutsch (Today we speak German).

Suspended word order, with the verb or parts of the verb at the end of a clause, occurs often in subordinate clauses:

Ich glaube, daß der Preis zu hoch ist (I think that the price is too high).

And with participle and infinitive constructions:

Er hat den Film schon gesehen (He has already seen the film).
Er möchte den Film morgen sehen (He would like to see the film tomorrow).

Questions and Commands

Here the normal word order is simply reversed:

Gehen Sie ins Kino? (Do you go/Are you going to the movies?)
Gehen Sie ins Kino! (Go to the movies!)
Gehen Sie nicht ins Kino! (Don't go to the movies!)

In German there is no equivalent for the English auxiliary verb "do" in questions and commands.

Negatives

Sentences are negated by either *nicht* or *kein. Nicht* is often suspended at the end of the sentence:

Ich verstehe die Frage nicht (I don't understand the question).
Er will mich nicht verstehen (He doesn't want to understand me).
Ich habe keine Fragen (I have no questions).

186

List of Abbreviations
m. masculine
f. feminine
n. neuter
l. plural

a, an ein(-e) *[ine, INE-eh]*

abbey Abtei, f. *[ahp-TYE]*

abbreviation Abkürzung, f. *[AHP-kewrt-sung]*

able, to be kann *[kahn]*; können *[KU(R)-nen]*

about ungefähr *[UN-geh-fayr]*

above oben *[OH-ben]*

abroad im Ausland *[im OWS-lahnt]*

abscess Abszeß, m. *[ahps-TSEHS]*

absolutely unbedingt *[UN-beh-dinkt]*

accelerator Gaspedal, n. *[GAHS-peh-daal]*

accept, to annehmen *[AHN-nay-men]*

accident Unfall, m. *[UN-fahl]*

accommodation Unterkunft, f. *[UN-te(r)-kunft]*

accompany, to begleiten *[beh-GLYE-ten]*

account Konto, n. *[KON-toh]*

ache Schmerz, m. *[shmehrts]*

acid Säure, f. *[ZOY-reh]*

acquaintance Bekannte, m., f. *[beh-KAHN-teh]*

across (movement) über *[EW-be(r)]*; durch *[durkh]*

across gegenüber *[gay-gen-EW-be(r)]*

actually eigentlich *[EYE-gehnt-likh]*

address Adresse, f. *[ah-DREHS-seh]*

adhesive tape Heftpflaster, n. *[HEHFT-pflahs-te(r)]*

adjust, to einstellen *[INE-shtehl-len]*

admire, to bewundern *[beh-VOON-dern]*

admission Eintritt, m. *[INE-trit]*; Zutritt, m. *[TSOO-trit]*

admission fee Eintrittsgeld, n. *[INE-trits-gehlt]*

adult Erwachsene, m./f. *[ehr-VAHK-seh-neh]*

advertising Werbung, f. *[VEHR-bung]*

afraid of something, to be vor etwas Angst haben *[for EHT-vahs ahngst HAA-ben]*

after nach *[nahkh]*

afternoon Nachmittag, m. *[NAHKH-mit-taak]*

afterward nachher *[NAHKH-hehr]*

after-shave lotion Raiserwasser, n. *[rah-ZEER-vahs-se(r)]*

again noch einmal [nohkh INE-maal]; wieder [VEE-de(r)]
against gegen [GAY-gen]
age Alter, n. [AHL-te(r)]
agency Büro, n. [bew-ROH]
ago vor [for]
agreed einverstanden [INE-fehr-shtahn-den]
air Luft, f. [luft]
air-conditioned klimatisiert [klee-mah-ti-ZEERT]
air conditioner Klimaanlage, f. [KLEE-mah-ahn-laa-geh]
airline Fluggesellschaft, f. [FLOOK-geh-zehl-shahft]
airmail mit Luftpost [mit LUFT-post]
air mattress Luftmatraze, f. [LUFT-mah-trah-tseh]
airplane Flugzeug, n. [FLOOK-tsoyk]
airport Flughafen, m. [FLOOK-haa-fen]
alarm clock Wecker, m. [VEH-ke(r)]
all alle(-s) [AH-leh(s)]
all right in Ordnung [in ORT-nung]
allergic allergisch [ah-LEHR-gish]
allowed erlaubt [ehr-LOWPT]
almond Mandel, f. [MAHN-del]
almost fast [fahst]
alone allein [ah-LINE]
aloud laut [lowt]
Alps Alpen, pl. [AHL-pen]
already schon [shon]
also auch [owkh]
always immer [IM-me(r)]

A.M. vormittags [FOR-mit-tahks]
amazing erstaunlich [ehr-SHTOWN-likh]
ambulance Krankenwagen m. [KRAHN-ken-vaa-gen]
America Amerika, n. [ah-MEH-ri-kah]
American Amerikaner(-in), m., f. [ah-meh-ri-KAH-ne(r), {-neh-rin}]
American amerikanisch [ah-meh-ri-KAH-nish]
among unter [UN-te(r)]; zwischen [TSVISH-en]
amount Betrag, m. [beh-TRAHK]
amuse, to unterhalten [un-te(r)-HAAL-ten]; vergnügen [fehrk-NEW-gen]
and und [unt]
angel Engel, m. [EHN-gel]
angry wütend [VEW-tehnt]; böse [BU(R)-zeh]
animal Tier, n. [teer]
ankle Knöchel, m. [KNU(R)-khel]
annoy ärgern [EHR-gern]
another ein anderer [ine AHN-deh-re(r)]; noch ein(-e) [nohkh ine/INE-eh]
answer Antwort, f. [AHNT-vort]
answer, to antworten [AHNT-vor-ten]
antibiotic Antibioticum, n. [ahn-ti-bee-OH-ti-koom]
antique Antiquität, f. [ahn-tik-vee-TAYT]
antiseptic Antisepticum, n. [ahn-ti-ZEHP-ti-koom]

188

any etwas [EHT-vahs]; einige [INE-i-geh]

anybody, anyone (irgend)jemand [(IR-gehnt) YAY-mahnt]

anything (irgend)etwas [(IR-gehnt)EHT-vahs]

anyway jedenfalls [YAY-den-fahls]

anywhere irgendwo [IR-gehnt-voh]

apartment Wohnung, f. [VOH-nung]

apology Entschuldigung, f. [ehnt-SHOOL-di-gung]

apologize, to sich entschuldigen [zikh ehnt-SHOOL-di-gen]

appendicitis Blinddarment-zündung, f. [BLINT-dahrm-ehnt-tsewn-dung]

appetizer Vorspeise, f. [FOR-shpye-zeh]

apple Apfel, m. [AHP-fel]

appliance Gerät, n. [geh-RAYT]

appointment Verabredung, f. [fehr-AHP-ray-dung]

approximately ungefähr [UN-geh-fayr]

apricot Aprikose, f. [ahp-ri-KOH-zeh]

April April, m. [ah-PRIL]

area Gebiet, n. [geh-BEET]; Gegend, f. [GAY-gehnt]

area code Vorwahlnummer, f. [FOR-vaal-num-me(r)]

arrest, to verhaften [fehr-HAHF-ten]

arm Arm, m. [ahrm]

armchair Sessel, m. [ZEHS-sel]

around um [um]; herum [heh-RUM]

arrival Ankunft, f. [AHN-kunft]

arrive, to ankommen [AHN-kom-men]

art Kunst, f. [kunst]

article Artikel, m. [ahr-TEE-kel]

artificial künstlich [KEWNST-likh]

artist Künstler, m. [KEWNST-le(r)]

as als [ahls]; wie [vee]

ashtray Aschenbecher, m. [AHSH-en-behkh-e(r)]

ask, to fragen [FRAA-gen]; bitten [BIT-ten]

asparagus Spargel, m. [SHPAHR-gel]

aspirin Aspirin, n. [ahs-pi-REEN]

asthma Asthma, n. [AHST-mah]

at an [ahn]; bei [bye]

at least mindestens [MIN-dehs-tens]

at once sofort [zoh-FORT]

attention Achtung, f. [AHKH-tung]; Aufmerksamkeit, f. [OWF-mehrk-saam-kite]

attorney Rechtsanwalt, m. [REHKHTS-ahn-vahlt]

attraction (sightseeing) Sehenswürdigkeit, f. [ZAY-ens-vewr-dikh-kite]

attractive schön [shu(r)n]; anziehend [AHN-tsee-ent]

189

August August, m. *[ow-GUST]*

aunt Tante, f. *[TAHN-teh]*

Austria Österreich, n. *[U(R)S-teh-ryekh]*

Austrian Österreicher(-in), m., f. *[U(R)S-teh-ryekh-e(r), {-eh-rin}]*

Austrian österreichisch *[U(R)S-teh-rye-ish]*

automatic automatisch *[ow-toh-MAH-tish]*

autumn Herbst, m. *[hehrpst]*

avenue Allee, f. *[ah-LAY]*

average durchschnittlich *[DURKH-shnit-likh]*

avoid, to vermeiden *[fehr-MYE-den]*

away weg *[vehk]*

awful scheußlich *[SHOYS-likh]*; schrecklich *[SHREHK-likh]*

B

baby Baby, n. *[BAY-bee]*

baby food Säuglingsnahrung, f. *[SOYK-lings-naa-rung]*

babysitter Babysitter, m. *[BAY-bee-sit-e(r)]*

back (body part) Rücken, m. *[REWK-en]*

back (direction) zurück *[tsoo-REWK]*

back, to be zurück sein *[tsoo-REWK zine]*

backache Rückenschmerzen, pl. *[REWK-en-shmehrt-sen]*

bacon Speck, m. *[shpehk]*

bad schlecht *[shlehkht]*

bag Tasche, f. *[TAHSH-eh]*; Tüte, f. *[TEW-teh]*

baggage Gepäck, n. *[geh-PEHK]*

baggage car Gepäckwagen, m. *[geh-PEHK vaa-gen]*

baggage check Gepäckkontrolle, f. *[geh-PEHK-kon-trol-leh]*

baggage checkroom Gepäckaufbewahrung, f. *[geh-PEHK-owf-beh-vaa-rung]*

baggage claim Gepäckausgabe, f. *[geh-PEHK-ows-gaa-beh]*

baggage locker Schließfach, n. *[SHLEES-fahkh]*

bake, to backen *[BAH-ken]*

baked gebacken *[geh-BAH-ken]*

bakery Bäckerei, f. *[beh-keh-RYE]*

balcony Balkon, m. *[bahl-KON]*

ball Ball, m. *[bahl]*

ballet Ballett, n. *[bah-LEHT]*

band Musikkapelle, f. *[moo-ZEEK-kah-pehl-leh]*

bandage Verband, m. *[fehr-BAHNT]*

bank (finance) Bank, f. *[bahnk]*

banknote Schein, m. *[shine]*

barber Friseur, m. *[fri-ZUR]*

bargain Sonderangebot, n. *[ZON-de(r)-ahn-geh-boht]*

basement Untergeschoß, n. *[UN-te(r)-geh-shos]*

basket Korb, m. *[korp]*
bath, bathroom Bad, n. *[baat]*
bath, to baden *[BAA-den]*
bathing suit Badeanzug, m. *[BAA-deh-ahn-tsook]*
bathtub Badewanne, f. *[BAA-deh-vah-neh]*
battery Batterie, f. *[bah-teh-REE]*
be, to sein *[zine]*
beach Strand, m. *[shtrahnt]*
bean Bohne, f. *[BOH-neh]*
beard Bart, m. *[bahrt]*
beautiful schön *[shu(r)n]*
beauty salon Schönheitssalon, m. *[SHU(R)N-hites-zah-lohng]*
because weil *[vile]*
bed Bett, n. *[beht]*
bed and breakfast Übernachtung mit Frühstück *[ew-be(r)-NAHKH-tung mit FREW-shtewk]*
bedroom Schlafzimmer, n. *[SHLAHF-tsim-me(r)]*
beef Rindfleisch, n. *[RINT-flyshe]*
beer Bier, n. *[beer]*
beer garden Biergarten, m. *[BEER-gahr-ten]*
beer stein Bierkrug, m. *[BEER-krook]*
beet (root) rote Bete, f. *[ROH-teh BAY-teh]*
before vor *[for]*
begin, to beginnen *[beh-GIN-nen]*
beginner Anfänger, m. *[AHN-fehn-ge(r)]*

beginning Anfang, m. *[AHN-fahng]*
behind hinten *[HIN-ten]*
believe, to glauben *[GLOW-ben]*
bell (door) Klingel, f. *[KLING-el]*
bellboy Hoteljunge, m. *[ho-TEL-yun-geh]*
belong, to gehören *[geh-HU(R)-en]*
below unten *[UN-ten]*
belt Gürtel, m. *[GEWR-tel]*
beside neben *[NAY-ben]*
best beste *[BEHS-teh]*
bet, to wetten *[VEHT-ten]*
better besser *[BEHS-se(r)]*
beverage Getränk, n. *[geh-TREHNK]*
between zwischen *[TSVISH-en]*
beyond jenseits *[YEHN-zites]*
bicycle Fahrrad, n. *[FAAR-raat]*
big groß *[grohs]*
bill (restaurant) Rechnung, f. *[REHKH-nung]*
billion Milliarde, f. *[mil-YAAR-deh]*
binoculars Fernglas, n. *[FEHRN-glaas]*
bird Vogel, m. *[FOH-gel]*
birthday Geburtstag, m. *[geh-BURTS-taak]*
bite, to beißen *[BICE-sen]*
bitter bitter *[BIT-te(r)]*
black schwarz *[shvahrts]*
bladder Blase, f. *[BLAA-zeh]*
blade (razor) Klinge, f. *[KLING-eh]*
blanket Decke, f. *[DEH-keh]*

191

bleed, to bluten *[BLOO-ten]*
blond blond *[blont]*
blood Blut, n. *[bloot]*
blood pressure Blutdruck, m. *[BLOOT-druk]*
blouse Bluse, f. *[BLOO-zeh]*
blue blau *[blow]*
boardinghouse Pension, f. *[pehn-ZYON]*
boarding pass Bordkarte, f. *[BOHRT-kahr-teh]*
boat Schiff, n. *[shif]*; Boot, n. *[boht]*
body Körper, m. *[KU(R)R-pe(r)]*
boiled gekocht *[geh-KOKHT]*
bone Knochen, m. *[KNOKH-en]*
book Buch, n. *[bookh]*
book, to reservieren lassen *[reh-zehr-VEER-en LAHS-sen]*
bookstore Buchhandlung, f. *[BOOKH-hahnd-lung]*
boots Stiefel, pl. *[SHTEE-fel]*
booth Telefonzelle, f. *[tay-lay-FON-tsehl-leh]*
border Grenze, f. *[GREHN-tseh]*
born geboren *[geh-BOR-en]*
borrow, to borgen *[BOR-gen]*
boss Chef, m. *[shehf]*
botanical garden Botanischer Garten, m. *[bo-TAA-nish-e(r) GAAR-ten]*
both beide, *[BYE-deh]*
bother, to ärgern *[EHR-gern]*
bottle Flasche, f. *[FLAHSH-eh]*
box Schachtel, f. *[SHAHKH-tel]*

box office Kasse, f. *[KAHS-seh]*
boy Junge, m. *[YUN-geh]*
bra BH, m. *[bay-hah]*; Büstenhalter, m. *[BEWS-ten-hal-te(r)]*
bracelet Armband, n. *[AHRM-bahnt]*
brain Gehirn, n. *[geh-HEERN]*
brakes Bremsen, pl. *[BREHM-zen]*
bread Brot, n. *[broht]*
break, to zerbrechen *[tsehr-BREHKH-en]*
breakdown Panne, f. *[PAHN-eh]*
breakfast Frühstück, n. *[FREW-shtewk]*
breast Brust, f. *[broost]*
breathe, to atmen *[AAT-men]*
bridge Brücke, f. *[BREW-keh]*
briefcase Aktentasche, f. *[AAK-ten-tah-sheh]*
bring, to bringen *[BRIN-gen]*
British Brite; Britin, m./f. *[BRI-teh; BRI-tin]*
broil, to grillen *[GRIL-len]*
broken gebrochen *[geh-BROKH-en]*; kaputt *[kah-PUT]*
brooch Broche, f. *[BRO-sheh]*
brother Bruder, m. *[BROO-de(r)]*
brother-in-law Schwager, m. *[SHVAA-ge(r)]*
brown braun *[brown]*
bruise Quetschung, f. *[KVEHT-chung]*
brush Bürste, f. *[BEWR-steh]*
brush, to bürsten *[BEWR-sten]*
buckle Schnalle, f. *[SHNAHL-leh]*

building Gebäude, n. [geh-BOY-deh]

bulb (electric) (Glüh)birne, f. [{GLEW}-BEER-neh]

bump, to stoßen [SHTOHS-sen]

bumper (car) Stoßstange, f. [SHTOHS-shtahng-eh]

burn Brandwunde, f. [BRAHNT-vun-deh]

burn, to brennen [BREHN-nen]

bus Bus, m. [bus]

bus stop Bushaltestelle, f. [BUS-hahl-teh-shtehl-leh]

bus tour Rundfahrt, f. [RUNT-faart]

business Geschäft, n. [geh-SHEHFT]

business trip Geschäftsreise, f. [geh-SHEHFTS-rye-zeh]

busy beschäftigt [beh-SHEHF-tikht]

but aber [AA-be(r)]

butcher Fleischer, m. [FLYE-she(r)]; Metzger, m. [MEHTS-ge(r)]

butcher shop Fleischerei, f. [flye-sheh-RYE]; Metzgerei, f. [mehts-geh-RYE]

butter Butter, f. [BUT-te(r)]

button Knopf, m. [knopf]

buy, to kaufen [KOW-fen]

by durch [durkh]; von [fon]

C

cab Taxi, n. [TAHK-see]

cabbage Kohl, m. [kohl]

cable (telegram) Telegramm, n. [tay-lay-GRAAM]

café Café, n. [kah-FAY]

cake Kuchen, m. [KOO-khen]

call (telephone) Anruf, m. [AHN-roof]

call, to (telephone) anrufen [AHN-roo-fen]

calm ruhig [ROO-ikh]

camera Fotoapparat, m. [FOH-toh-ah-pah-raat]

camp, to zelten [TSEHL-ten]

camp site Campingplatz, m. [KAHM-ping-plahts]

can (container) Dose, f. [DOH-zeh]; Büchse, f. [BEWK-seh]

can (to be able) können [KU(R)-nen]

can opener Büchsenöffner, m. [BEWK-sen-u(r)f-ne(r)]

cancel, to absagen [AHP-zaa-gen]

candle Kerze, f. [KEHRT-seh]

candy Bonbon, n. [bong-BONG]

cap Kappe, f. [KAH-peh]; Mütze, f. [MEWT-seh]

capital Hauptstadt, f. [HOWPT-shtaht]

car Wagen, m. [VAA-gen]; Auto, n. [OW-toh]

car breakdown Autopanne, f. [OW-toh-pahn-neh]

car rental agency Autovermietung, f. [OW-toh-fehr-mee-tung]

carburetor Vergaser, m. [fehr-GAA-ze(r)]

card (Post)karte, f. [{POST}-KAHR-teh]

careful! Vorsicht! *[FOR-zikht]*

careful, to be aufpassen *[OWF-pahs-sen]*

careful sorgfältig *[ZORK-fehl-tikh]*

carpet Teppich, m. *[TEHP-pikh]*

carrot Karotte, f. *[kah-ROT-teh]*

carry, to tragen *[TRAA-gen]*

carry-on luggage Handgepäck, n. *[HAHNT-geh-pehk]*

cash Bargeld, n. *[BAAR-gehlt]*

cash, to einlösen *[INE-lu(r)-zen]*

cash desk Kasse, f. *[KAHS-seh]*

castle Schloß, n. *[shlos]*

cat Katze, f. *[KAHT-seh]*

catch, to fangen *[FAHNG-en]*

cathedral Dom, m. *[dohm]*; Kathedrale, f. *[kah-teh-DRAAL-eh]*

Catholic katholisch *[kah-TOH-lish]*

cauliflower Blumenkohl, m. *[BLOO-men-kohl]*

caution Vorsicht, f. *[FOR-zikht]*

cave Höhle, f. *[HU(R)-leh]*

ceiling Decke, f. *[DEH-keh]*

celery Sellerie, m. *[ZEHL-eh-ree]*

cell Zelle, f. *[TSEHL-leh]*

cemetery Friedhof, m. *[FREET-hohf]*

center Zentrum, n. *[TSEHN-trum]*

century Jahrhundert, n. *[YAAR-hun-dert]*

194

certain sicher *[ZIKH-e(r)]*; gewiß *[geh-VIS]*

certainly bestimmt *[beh-SHTIMT]*; sicher *[ZIKH-e(r)]*

certificate Zeugnis, n. *[TSOYK-nis]*

chain Kette, f. *[KEHT-teh]*

chair Stuhl, m. *[shtool]*

change (money) Kleingeld, n. *[KLINE-gehlt]*

change, to wechseln *[VEHK-seln]*

change, to (bus, train) umsteigen *[OOM-shtye-gen]*

chapel Kapelle, f. *[kah-PEHL-leh]*

charge Gebühr, f. *[ge-BEWR]*

charge, to berechnen *[beh-REHKH-nen]*

cheap billig *[BIL-likh]*

check Scheck, m. *[shehk]*; Rechnung, f. *[REHKH-nung]*

check, to (über)prüfen *[{EW-be(r)}-PREW-fen]*

check, to (luggage) aufgeben *[OWF-gay-ben]*

checkbook Scheckbuch, n. *[SHEHK-bookh]*

checkroom Gepäckaufbewahrung, f. *[geh-PEHK-owf-beh-vaa-rung]*

checkroom (theater) Garderobe, f. *[gar-deh-ROH-beh]*

cheek Wange, f. *[VAHN-geh]*

cheese Käse, m. *[KAY-zeh]*

cherry Kirsche, f. *[KIR-sheh]*

chest (part of body) Brust, f. *[broost]*

chestnut Kastanie, f. *[kah-STAHN-yeh]*

chewing gum Kaugummi, m. [KOW-goom-mee]

chicken Huhn, n. [hoon]

child Kind, n. [kint]

chill, to kühlen [KEW-len]

chin Kinn, n. [kin]

chocolate Schokolade, f. [sho-ko-LAA-deh]

choice Wahl, f. [vaal]

choose, to (aus)wählen [{OWS}-VAY-len]

chop Kotelett, n. [kot-LEHT]

Christmas Weihnachten, f. [VYE-nahkh-ten]

church Kirche, f. [KIR-kheh]

cider Apfelmost, m. [AHP-fehl-mohst]

cigar Zigarre, f. [tsi-GAA-reh]

cigarette Zigarette, f. [tsi-gaa-REHT-teh]

cigarette lighter Feuerzeug, n. [FOY-e(r)-tsoyk]

cinema Kino, n. [KEE-noh]

citizen Bürger, m. [BEWR-ge(r)]

city Stadt, f. [shtaht]

city hall Rathaus, n. [RAAT-hows]

class Klasse, f. [KLAHS-seh]

classic klassisch [KLAHS-sish]

clean sauber [ZOW-be(r)]

clean, to reinigen [RYE-ni-gen]

cleaner's Reinigung, f. [RYE-ni-gung]

clear klar [klahr]

clear (not blocked) frei [frye]

client Kund(-e), (-in), m./f. [KUN-deh; KUN-din]

cliff Felsen, m. [FEHL-zen]

climb steigen [SHTYE-gen]

clock Uhr, f. [oor]

close (near) nahe [NAA-heh]

close, to schließen [SHLEES-sen]

closed geschloßen [geh-SHLOS-sen]

closet Schrank, m. [shrahnk]

cloth Stoff, m. [shtof]

clothes Kleider, pl. [KLIDE-e(r)]

cloud Wolke, f. [VOL-keh]

cloudy bewölkt [beh-VU(R)KT]

club Klub, m. [kloop]

clutch (car) Kupplung, f. [KUP-lung]

coach Bus, m. [bus]

coast Küste, f. [KEWS-teh]

coat Mantel, m. [MAHN-tel]

coffee Kaffee, m. [KAH-feh]

coin Münze, f. [MEWN-tseh]

cold kalt [kahlt]

cold (sick) erkältet [ehr-KEHL-tet]

collar Kragen, m. [KRAA-gen]

collect, to sammeln [ZAHM-eln]

colleague Kolleg(-e), (-in), m., f. [kol-LAY-geh; kol-LAY-gin]

collect call R-Gespräch, n. [EHR-geh-shpraykh]

color Farbe, f. [FAHR-beh]

color film Farbfilm, m. [FAHRP-film]

comb Kamm, m. [kahm]

come, to kommen [KOM-men]

come back, to zurückkommen [tsoo-REWK-kom-men]

195

comedy Komödie, f. [ko-MU(R)-dyeh]

comfortable bequem [beh-KVEHM]

commission Gebühr, f. [geh-BEWR]

company Gesellschaft, f. [geh-ZEHL-shahft]

compare, to vergleichen [vehr-GLYE-khen]

compartment Abteil, n. [AHP-tile]

complaint Reklamation, f. [reh-klah-mah-TSIOHN]; Beschwerde, f. [beh-SHVEHR-deh]

concert Konzert, n. [kon-TSEHRT]

conductor (orchestra) Dirigent, m. [di-ri-GEHNT]

confirm, to bestätigen [beh-SHTAY-ti-gen]

connection (train) Anschluß, m. [AHN-shloos]

confused verwirrt [fehr-VIRT]

consulate Konsulat, n. [kon-zu-LAHT]

contact lenses Kontaktlinsen, pl. [kon-TAHKT-lin-zen]

contents Inhalt, m. [IN-hahlt]

continue, to fortsetzen [FORT-zeht-sen]

convent Kloster, n. [KLOH-ste(r)]

conversation Gespräch, n. [geh-SHPRAYKH]

cook, to kochen [KOKH-en]

cooked gekocht [geh-KOKHT]

cookies Kekse, pl. [KAYK-seh]

cool kühl [kewl]

196

copper Kupfer, n. [KUP-fe(r)]

corduroy Kordsamt, m. [KORT-zahmt]

corkscrew Korkenzieher, m. [KOR-ken-tsee-e(r)]

corn Mais, m. [mice]

corn (foot) Hühnerauge, n. [HEW-ne(r)-ow-geh]

corner Ecke, f. [EH-keh]

costs Kosten, pl. [KOS-ten]

cost, to kosten [KOS-ten]

cotton Baumwolle, f. [BOWM-vol-leh]

cotton wool Watte, f. [VAHT-teh]

cough Husten, m. [HOOS-ten]

cough, to husten [HOOS-ten]

could könnte [KU(R)N-teh]

count, to zählen [TSAY-len]

country Land, n. [lahnt]

countryside Landschaft, f. [LAHNT-shahft]

course (meal) Gang, m. [gahng]

court Gericht, n. [geh-RIKHT]

courtyard Hinterhof, m. [HIN-te(r)-hohf]

cousin Kusine, f. [koo-ZEE-neh]; Vetter, m. [FEHT-te(r)]

cover, to (be)decken [{beh}-DEHK-en]

cramp Krampf, m. [krahmpf]

cranberry Preiselbeere f. [PRICE-ehl-bay-reh]

crazy verrückt [fehr-REWKT]

cream Sahne, f. [ZAA-neh]

cream (cosmetic) Creme, f. [kraym]

credit card Kreditkarte, f. [kray-DEET-kahr-teh]

crime Verbrechen, n. *[fehr-BREHKH-en]*

crisp knusprig *[KNOOS-prikh]*

cross Kreuz, n. *[kroyts]*

cross, to überqueren *[ew-be(r)-KVAY-ren]*

crossroads Kreuzung, f. *[KROY-tsung]*

crosswalk Zebrastreifen, m. *[TSAY-brah-shtrye-fen]*

crust Kruste, f. *[KROOS-teh]*

cry, to weinen *[VINE-en]*

cucumber Gurke, f. *[GOOR-keh]*

cuisine Küche, f. *[KEW-kheh]*

cup Tasse, f. *[TAHS-seh]*

curl Locke, f. *[LO-keh]*

curler Lockenwickler, m. *[LO-ken-vik-le(r)]*

currency Währung, f. *[VAY-rung]*

currency exchange office Wechselstube, f. *[VEHK-sehl-shtoo-beh]*

curtain Vorhang, m. *[FOR-hahng]*

curve Kurve, f. *[KOOR-veh]*

customer Kunde, m. *[KUN-deh]*

customs Zoll, m. *[tsol]*

cut (wound) Schnittwunde, f. *[SHNIT-vun-deh]*

cut, to schneiden *[SHNYE-den]*

cutlet Kotelett, n. *[kot-LEHT]*

cycling Radfahren, n. *[RAAT-faa-ren]*

Czechoslovakia Tschechoslowakei, f. *[cheh-kho-slo-vah-KYE]*

D

daily täglich *[TAYG-likh]*

daily (newspaper) Tageszeitung, f. *[TAA-gehs-tsye-tung]*

dairy Molkerei, f. *[mohl-keh-RYE]*

damp feucht *[foykht]*

dance Tanz, m. *[tahnts]*

dance, to tanzen *[TAHN-tsen]*

danger Gefahr, f. *[geh-FAAR]*

dangerous gefährlich *[geh-FEHR-likh]*

dark dunkel *[DUN-kel]*

date (calendar) Datum, n. *[DAA-tum]*

daughter Tochter, f. *[TOKH-te(r)]*

day Tag, m. *[taak]*

day after tomorrow übermorgen *[EW-be(r)-mor-gen]*

day before yesterday vorgestern *[FOR-gehs-tern]*

dead tot *[toht]*

dead end Sackgasse, f. *[ZAHK-gaas-seh]*

deaf taub *[towp]*

death Tod, m. *[toht]*

dear lieb *[leep]*

debt Schuld, f. *[shoolt]*

decade Jahrzehnt, n. *[YAAR-tsehnt]*

decaffinated koffeinfrei *[kof-feh-EEN-frye]*

December Dezember, m. *[deh-TSEHM-be(r)]*

decide, to entscheiden *[ehnt-SHIDE-en]*

declare, to (custom) verzollen *[fehr-TSOL-len]*

deep tief *[teef]*

delay Verspätung, f. *[fehr-SHPAY-tung]*

delicatessen Feinkostgeschäft, n. *[FINE-kost-geh-shehft]*

delicious köstlich *[KU(R)ST-likh]*

deliver, to liefern *[LEE-fern]*

delivery Lieferung, f. *[LEE-feh-rung]*

demand, to verlangen *[fehr-LAHNG-en]*

Denmark Dänemark, n. *[DEH-neh-mahrk]*

dentist Zahnarzt, m. *[TSAAN-ahrtst]*

denture Gebiß, n. *[geh-BIS]*

department Abteilung, f. *[ahp-TILE-ung]*

department store Kaufhaus, n. *[KOWF-hows]*

departure Abflug, m. *[AHP-flook]*; Abfahrt, f. *[AHP-faart]*

desire Wunsch, m. *[voonsh]*

desk Schreibtisch, m. *[SHRIPE-tish]*

despite trotz *[trots]*

dessert Nachtisch, m. *[NAHKH-tish]*

detour (traffic) Umleitung, f. *[OOM-lye-tung]*

develop, to entwickeln *[ehnt-VIK-eln]*

devil Teufel, m. *[TOY-fel]*

diabetes Zuckerkrankheit, f. *[TSU-ke(r)-krahnk-hite]*

diabetic Diabetiker, m. *[dee-ah-BAY-ti-ke(r)]*

dial, to wählen *[VAY-len]*

diaper Windel, f. *[VIN-del]*

diarrhea Durchfall, m. *[DURKH-fahl]*

dictionary Wörterbuch, n. *[VU(R)-te(r)-bookh]*

diesel fuel Dieselöl, n. *[DEE-zel-u(r)]*

diet Diät, f. *[dee-AYT]*

different verschieden *[fehr-SHEE-den]*

difficult schwer *[shvehr]*

difficulty Schwierigkeit, f. *[SHVEE-rikh-kite]*

dining car Speisewagen, m. *[SHPYE-zeh-vaa-gen]*

dining room Eßzimmer, n. *[EHS-tsim-me(r)]*; Speisesaal, m. *[SHPYE-zeh-zaal]*

dinner Abendessen, n. *[AA-behnt-ehs-sen]*

direct direkt *[dee-REHKT]*

direction Richtung, f. *[RIKH-tung]*

directions, to give den Weg zeigen *[dehn vehk TSYE-gen]*

directory (telephone) Telefonbuch, n. *[tay-lay-FON-bookh]*

dirty schmutzig *[SHMUT-tsikh]*

disabled Behinderte, m., f. *[beh-HIN-dehr-teh]*

disappointed enttäuscht *[ehnt-TOYSHT]*

discount Rabatt, m. *[raa-BAHT]*

discover, to entdecken *[ehnt-DEHK-en]*

disease Krankheit, f. *[KRAHNK-hite]*

dish (food) Gericht, n. *[geh-RIKHT]*

198

disinfect, to desinfizieren *[dehs-in-fi-TSEE-ren]*

dissatisfied unzufrieden *[UN-tsoo-free-den]*

distance Entfernung, f. *[ehnt-FEHR-nung]*

district Bezirk, m. *[beh-TSIRK]*

disturb, to stören *[SHTU(R)-en]*

divorced geschieden *[geh-SHEE-den]*

dizzy schwindlig *[SHVINT-likh]*

do, to tun *[toon]*

dock Hafenanlage, f. *[HAA-fen-ahn-laa-geh]*

doctor Arzt, m. *[ahrtst]*; Ärztin, f. *[EHR-stin]*

document Dokument, n. *[do-koo-MEHNT]*

dog Hund, m. *[hunt]*

doll Puppe, f. *[PUP-peh]*

dollar Dollar, m. *[DOL-lahr]*

door Tür, f. *[tewr]*

doorman Portier, m. *[por-TYAY]*

double bed Doppelbett, n. *[DOP-pehl-beht]*

double room Doppelzimmer, n. *[DOP-pehl-tsim-me(r)]*

down hinunter *[hin-UN-te(r)]*

downstairs unten *[UN-ten]*

downtown Zentrum, n. *[TSEHN-trum]*

dozen Dutzend, n. *[DUT-sehnt]*

drama Drama, n. *[DRAA-mah]*

drawer Schublade, f. *[SHOOP-laa-deh]*

drawing paper Zeichenpapier, n. *[TSYE-khen-pah-peer]*

dress Kleid, n. *[klite]*

dress, to (oneself) sich anziehen *[zikh AHN-tsee-en]*

dressing gown Morgenrock, m. *[MOR-gen-rok]*

dried getrocknet *[geh-TROK-net]*

drink Getränk, n. *[geh-TREHNK]*

drink, to trinken *[TRIN-ken]*

drinking water Trinkwasser, n. *[TRINK-vahs-se(r)]*

drive, to fahren *[FAA-ren]*

driver Fahrer, m. *[FAA-re(r)]*

driver's license Führerschein, m. *[FEWR-e(r)-shine]*

drops Tropfen, pl. *[TROP-fen]*

drug Medikament, n. *[meh-di-kah-MEHNT]*

drugstore Drogerie, f. *[dro-geh-REE]*

drunk betrunken *[beh-TRUN-ken]*

dry trocken *[TRO-ken]*

dry-cleaning chemische Reinigung, f. *[KHAY-mish-eh RYE-ni-gung]*

duck Ente, f. *[EHN-teh]*

during während *[VAY-rehnt]*

dust Staub, m. *[shtowp]*

duty (customs) Zoll, m. *[tsol]*

duty-free zollfrei *[TSOL-frye]*

dye Farbstoff, m. *[FAHRP-shtof]*

E

each jede(-r, -s) *[YAY-deh {-e(r), -ehs}]*

ear Ohr, n. *[ohr]*

earache Ohrenschmerzen, pl. *[OH-ren-shmehrt-sen]*

early früh *[frew]*

earn, to verdienen *[fehr-DEE-nen]*

earring Ohrring, m. *[OHR-ring]*

east Osten, m. *[OS-ten]*

Easter Ostern, pl. *[OS-tern]*

East Germany DDR, f. *[day-day-ehr]*

easy leicht *[lyekht]*

eat, to essen *[EHS-sen]*

eel Aal, m. *[aal]*

eggs Eier, pl. *[EYE-e(r)]*

eggplant Aubergine, f. *[o-ber-ZHEE-neh]*

eight acht *[ahkht]*

eighteen achtzehn *[AHKH-tsayn]*

eighth achte(-r; -s) *[AHKH-teh {-te(r), -tehs}]*

eighty achtzig *[AHKH-tsikh]*

elbow Ellbogen, m. *[EHL-boh-gen]*

electric elektrisch *[eh-LEHK-trish]*

elevator Lift, m. *[lift]*

eleven elf *[ehlf]*

embassy Botschaft, f. *[BOHT-shahft]*

emergency Notfall, m. *[NOHT-fahl]*

emergency exit Notausgang, m. *[NOHT-ows-gahng]*

empty leer *[lehr]*

end Ende, n. *[EHN-deh]*

end, to beenden *[beh-EHN-den]*

engaged (betrothed) verlobt *[fehr-LOHPT]*

engine Motor, m. *[moh-TOHR]*

England England, n. *[EHNG-lahnt]*

English englisch *[EHNG-lish]*

enjoy genießen *[geh-NEES-sen]*

enlargement Vergrößerung, f. *[fehr-GRU(r)s-eh-rung]*

enough genug *[geh-NOOK]*

entrance Eingang, m. *[INE-gahng]*

entrance fee Eintrittsgeld, n. *[INE-trits-gehlt]*

envelope Umschlag, m. *[OOM-shlahk]*

environment Umwelt, f. *[OOM-vehlt]*

equal gleich *[glyekh]*

equipment Ausrüstung, f. *[OWS-rews-tung]*

error Fehler, m. *[FAY-le(r)]*

escalator Rolltreppe, f. *[ROL-trehp-peh]*

especially besonders *[beh-ZON-dehrs]*

estimate, to schätzen *[SHEHTS-en]*

Europe Europa *[oy-ROH-pah]*

even selbst *[zehlpst]*

evening Abend, m. *[AA-behnt]*

evening gown Abendkleid, n. *[AA-behnt-klite]*

ever jemals *[YAY-maals]*

every jede(-r, -s) *[YAY-deh {-de(r), -dehs}]*

everything alles *[AH-lehs]*

200

everywhere überall *[EW-be(r)-ahl]*

example Beispiel, n. *[BYE-shpeel]*

excellent ausgezeichnet *[OWS-geh-tsyekh-net]*

exchange Austausch, m. *[OWS-towsh]*

exchange, to wechseln *[VEHK-seln]*

exchange rate Wechselkurs, m. *[VEHK-sel-koors]*

excursion Ausflug, m. *[OWS-flook]*

excuse Ausrede, f. *[OWS-ray-deh]*

excuse, to entschuldigen *[ehnt-SHOOL-di-gen]*

exhaust (car) Abgase, pl. *[AHP-gaa-zeh]*

exhausted erschöpft *[ehr-SHU(R)PFT]*

exhibition Ausstellung, f. *[OWS-shtehl-lung]*

exit Ausgang, m. *[OWS-gahng]*

expect, to erwarten *[ehr-VAAR-ten]*

expenses Spesen, pl. *[SHPAY-zen]*

expensive teuer *[TOY-e(r)]*

experience Erfahrung, f. *[ehr-FAA-rung]*

explain, to erklären *[ehr-KLEHR-en]*

express train Schnellzug, m. *[SHNEHL-tsook]*

extra zusätzlich *[TSOO-zehts-likh]*; extra *[EHK-strah]*

eye Auge, n. *[OW-geh]*

eyebrow Augenbraue, f. *[OW-gen-brow-eh]*

eyeglasses Brille, f. *[BRIL-leh]*

eyelash Augenwimper, f. *[OW-gen-vim-pe(r)]*

eyelid Augenlid, n. *[OW-gen-leet]*

F

fabric Stoff, m. *[shtof]*

face Gesicht, n. *[ge-ZIKHT]*

face cream Gesichtscreme, f. *[geh-ZIKHTS-kraym]*

factory Fabrik, f. *[fah-BREEK]*

fall (autumn) Herbst, m. *[hehrpst]*

fall, to fallen *[FAHL-len]*

false falsch *[fahlsh]*

familiar with, to be vertraut sein mit *[fehr-TROWT zine mit]*

family Familie, f. *[fah-MEEL-yeh]*

fan Ventilator, m. *[vehn-ti-LAA-tor]*

far weit *[vite]*

fare (fee) Fahrpreis, m. *[FAAR-price]*

farm Bauernhof, m. *[BOW-ehrn-hohf]*

fashion Mode, f. *[MOH-deh]*

fast schnell *[shnehl]*

fat dick; Fett, n. *[dik; feht]*

father Vater, m. *[FAA-te(r)]*

father-in-law Schwiegervater, m. *[SHVEE-ge(r)-faa-te(r)]*

faucet Wasserhahn, m. *[VAHS-se(r)-hahn]*

favor Gefallen, m. *[geh-FAHL-len]*

fear Angst, f. *[ahngst]*

fear, to Angst haben *[ahngst HAA-ben]*

February Februar, m. *[FAY-broo-aar]*

feel, to sich fühlen *[zikh FEW-len]*

felt (cloth) Filz, m. *[filts]*

fender Kotflügel, m. *[KOHT-flew-gel]*

ferry Fähre, f. *[FEH-reh]*

festival Fest, n. *[fehst]*

fever Fieber, n. *[FEE-be(r)]*

few wenige; einige *[VEH-ni-geh; INE-i-geh]*

field Feld, n. *[fehlt]*

fifteen fünfzehn *[FEWNF-tsayn]*

fifty fünfzig *[FEWNF-tsikh]*

fig Feige, f. *[FYE-geh]*

file Feile, f. *[FYE-leh]*

fill in, to ausfüllen *[OWS-fewl-len]*

fill up, to volltanken *[FOL-tahn-ken]*

fillet Filet, n. *[fee-LAY]*

filling (tooth) Plombe, f. *[PLOM-beh]*

filling station Tankstelle, f. *[TAHNK-shtehl-leh]*

film Film, m. *[film]*

find, to finden *[FIN-den]*

fine (quality) fein *[fine]*

fine (penalty) Geldstrafe, f. *[GEHLT-shtrah-feh]*

fine arts bildende Künste, pl. *[BIL-den-deh KEWN-steh]*

finger Finger, m. *[FIN-ge(r)]*

finish, to erledigen *[ehr-LAY-di-gen]*

fire Feuer, n. *[FOY-e(r)]*

fire department Feuerwehr, f. *[FOY-e(r)-vehr]*

first erste (-r, -s) *[EHR-steh {-ste(r), -stehs}]*

first aid kit Verbandkasten, m. *[fehr-BAHNT-kahs-ten]*

fish Fisch, m. *[fish]*

fish, to angeln *[AHN-geln]*

five fünf *[fewnf]*

fit, to passen *[PAHS-sen]*

fix, to reparieren *[reh-pah-REE-ren]*

flash (on camera) Blitzlicht, n. *[BLITS-likht]*

flashlight Taschenlampe, f. *[TAHSH-en-lahm-peh]*

flat flach *[flahkh]*

flat tire Reifenpanne, f. *[RYE-fen-pahn-neh]*

flavor Geschmack, m. *[geh-SHMAHK]*

flea market Flohmarkt, m. *[FLOH-mahrkt]*

flight Flug, m. *[flook]*

floor Boden, m. *[BOH-den]*; Stock, m. *[shtok]*

florist's Blumengeschäft, n. *[BLOO-men-geh-shehft]*

flour Mehl, n. *[mayl]*

flow fließen *[FLEES-sen]*

flower Blume, f. *[BLOO-meh]*

flu Grippe, f. *[GRIP-peh]*

fluid Flüssigkeit, f. *[FLEWS-sikh-kite]*

fly, to fliegen *[FLEE-gen]*

fog Nebel, m. *[NAY-bel]*

folding chair Klappstuhl, m. *[KLAHP-shtool]*

folk music Volksmusik, f. *[FOLKS-moo-zeek]*

follow, to folgen *[FOL-gen]*

food Essen, n. *[EHS-sen]*
foot Fuß, m. *[foos]*
footpath Fußweg, m. *[FOOS-vehk]*
foot powder Fußpuder, m. *[FOOS-poo-de(r)]*
for für *[fewr]*
forbidden verboten *[fehr-BOH-ten]*
forehead Stirn, f. *[shteern]*
foreign fremd *[frehmt]*
foreigner Ausländer, (-in), m., f. *[OWS-lehn-de(r), {-deh-rin}]*
forest Wald, m. *[vahlt]*
forget, to vergessen *[fehr-GEHS-sen]*
fork Gabel, f. *[GAA-bel]*
form Formular, n. *[for-moo-LAHR]*
format Format, n. *[for-MAAT]*
fortress Burg, f. *[boork]*; Festung, f. *[FEHS-tung]*
fortune Vermögen, n. *[fehr-MU(R)-gen]*
forty vierzig *[FEER-tsikh]*
forward vorwärts *[FOR-vehrts]*
fountain Brunnen, m. *[BRUN-nen]*
fountain pen Füllfederhalter, m. *[FEWL-fay-de(r)-hahl-te(r)]*
four vier *[feer]*
fourteen vierzehn *[FEER-tsayn]*
fourth vierte (-r, -s) *[FEER-teh {-te(r),-tehs}]*
fowl Geflügel, n. *[geh-FLEW-gel]*
fox Fuchs, m. *[fooks]*

fracture Bruch, m. *[brukh]*
frame Rahmen, m. *[RAA-men]*
France Frankreich, n. *[FRAHNK-ryekh]*
free frei *[frye]*
freeze, to frieren *[FREE-ren]*
frequent häufig *[HOY-fikh]*
fresh frisch *[frish]*
Friday Freitag, m. *[FRYE-taak]*
fried gebraten *[geh-BRAA-ten]*
friend Freund, (-in), m., f. *[FROYNT, FROYN-din]*
friendly freundlich *[FROYNT-likh]*
frog Frosch, m. *[frohsh]*
from von *[fon]*
front vorne *[FOR-neh]*
frost Frost, m. *[frost]*
frozen gefroren *[geh-FROH-ren]*
fruit Obst, n. *[opst]*
fry, to braten *[BRAA-ten]*
full voll *[fol]*
fun, to have Spaß haben *[shpahs HAA-ben]*
funny komisch *[KOH-mish]*
furniture Möbel, pl. *[MU(R)-bel]*
furs Pelze, pl. *[PEHL-tseh]*
future Zukunft, f. *[TSOO-kunft]*

G

gallery Galerie, f. *[gah-leh-REE]*
gain weight, to zunehmen *[TSOO-nay-men]*
game Spiel, n. *[shpeel]*
gamble, to spielen *[SHPEE-len]*

203

garage Garage, f. *[gah-RAH-zheh]*

garbage Abfall, m. *[AHP-fahl]*

garden Garten, m. *[GAAR-ten]*

garlic Knoblauch, m. *[KNOH-blowkh]*

gas Gas, n. *[gahs]*

gasoline Benzin, n. *[behn-TSEEN]*

gas station Tankstelle, f. *[TAHNK-shtehl-leh]*

gear (car) Gang, m. *[gahng]*

general allgemein *[AHL-geh-mine]*

general delivery postlagernd *[POST-laa-gehrnt]*

generous großzügig *[GROHS-tsew-gikh]*

gentleman Herr, m. *[hehr]*

genuine echt *[ehkht]*

German deutsch *[doych]*

Germany Deutschland, n. *[DOYCH-lahnt]*

get, to (obtain) bekommen *[beh-KOM-men]*

get, to (fetch) holen *[HOH-len]*

get back, to zurück sein *[tsoo-REWK zine]*

get dressed, to sich anziehen *[zikh AHN-tsee-en]*

get off (out), to aussteigen *[OWS-shtye-gen]*

get up, to aufstehen *[OWF-shteh-en]*

gift Geschenk, n. *[geh-SHEHNK]*

gin (drink) Gin, m. *[jin]*

ginger Ingwer, m. *[ING-vehr]*

girl Mädchen, n. *[MAYT-khen]*

give, to geben *[GAY-ben]*

glad froh *[froh]*

gladly gern *[gehrn]*

glass Glas, n. *[glaas]*

glasses (eye) Brille, f. *[BRIL-leh]*

glove Handschuh, m. *[HAHNT-shoo]*

go, to gehen *[GAY-en]*

go away, to weggehen *[VEHK-gay-en]*

go home, to nach Hause gehen *[nahkh HOW-zeh GAY-en]*

god Gott, m. *[got]*

gold Gold, n. *[golt]*

golf course Golfplatz, m. *[GOLF-plahts]*

good gut *[goot]*

good-bye auf Wiedersehen *[owf VEE-de(r)-zay-en]*

goose Gans, f. *[gahns]*

gourmet Feinschmecker, m. *[FINE-shmehk-e(r)]*

gram Gramm, n. *[graam]*

grammar Grammatik, f. *[grah-MAH-tik]*

grandparents Großeltern, pl. *[GROHS-ehl-tern]*

grape (Wein)traube, f. *[{VINE} TROW-beh]*

grapefruit Pampelmuse, f. *[pahm-pehl-MOO-zeh]*

grass Gras, n. *[grahs]*

grave Grab, n. *[grahp]*

gray grau *[grow]*

great groß *[grohs]*

green grün *[grewn]*

greeting Gruß, m. *[groos]*

204

grilled gegrillt [geh-GRILT]
grocery store
Lebensmittelgeschäft, n.
[LAY-bens-mit-tel-geh-shehft]
ground Boden, m. [BOH-den]
ground floor Erdgeschoβ,
n. [EHRT-geh-shos]
guidebook Reiseführer,
m. [RYE-zeh-few-re(r)]
guided tour Führung,
f. [FEW-rung]

H

habit Gewohnheit, f. [geh-
VOHN-hite]
hair Haar, n. [haar]
hair dryer Haartrockner,
m. [HAAR-trok-ne(r)]
hairbrush Haarbürste,
f. [HAAR-bewr-steh]
haircut Frisur, f. [fri-ZOOR]
hairdresser Friseur, m. [fri-
ZUR]
hairpin Haarnadel,
f. [HAAR-naa-dehl]
half Hälfte, f. [HEHLF-teh];
halb [hahlp]
hall Halle, f. [HAHL-leh]
ham Schinken, m. [SHIN-ken]
hammer Hammer,
m. [HAHM-me(r)]
hand Hand, f. [hahnt]
handbag Handtasche,
f. [HAHNT-tahsh-eh]
handicapped behindert [beh-
HIN-dert]
handkerchief Taschentuch,
n. [TAHSH-en-took]
handmade
handgearbeitet [HAHNT-geh-
ahr-bye-tet]

hanger (clothes)
Kleiderbügel, m. [KLIDE-e(r)-
bew-gel]
hangover Kater, m. [KAA-
te(r)]
happy glücklich [GLEWK-likh]
harbor Hafen, m. [HAA-fen]
hard (difficult)
schwer [shvehr]
hard (tough) hart [hahrt]
hardware store
Eisenwarenhandlung, f. [EYE-
zen-vaa-ren-hahnt-lung]
harmful schädlich [SHAYT-
likh]
hat Hut, m. [hoot]
hay fever Heuschnupfen,
m. [HOY-shnup-fen]
have, to haben [HAA-ben]
he er [ehr]
head Kopf, m. [kopf]
headache Kopfschmerzen,
pl. [KOPF-shmehrt-sen]
headlight Scheinwerfer,
m. [SHINE-vehr-fe(r)]
head waiter Oberkellner,
m. [OH-be(r)-kehl-ne(r)]
health Gesundheit, f. [geh-
ZUNT-hite]
health food store
Reformhaus, n. [reh-FORM-
hows]
health insurance
Krankenkasse, f. [KRAHN-ken-
kahs-seh]
hear, to hören [HU(R)-en]
heart Herz, n. [hehrts]
heart trouble
Herzkrankheit, f. [HEHRTS-
krahnk-hite]
heat Hitze, f. [HIT-seh]

205

heater Heizgerät, n. [HITES-geh-rayt]

heaven Himmel, m. [HIM-mel]

heavy schwer [shvehr]

heel Ferse, f. [FEHR-zeh]

heel (of shoe) Absatz, m. [AHP-zahts]

height Höhe, f. [HU(R)-eh]

hell Hölle, f. [HU(R)-leh]

hello! (phone) Hallo! [HAH-loh]

help Hilfe, f. [HIL-feh]

help, to helfen [HEHL-fen]

herbs Kräuter, pl. [KROY-te(r)]

here hier [heer]

high hoch [hohkh]

high school Oberschule, f. [OH-be(r)-shoo-leh]

high tide Flut, f. [floot]

highway Landstraße, f. [LAHNT-shtrahs-seh]

hike Wanderung, f. [VAHN-deh-rung]

hill Hügel, m. [HEW-gel]

hip Hüfte, f. [HEWF-teh]

hire, to (rent) mieten [MEE-ten]

history Geschichte, f. [geh-SHIKH-teh]

hit, to schlagen [SHLAA-gen]

hitchhiker Anhalter, m. [AHN-hahl-te(r)]

hold, to halten [HAAL-ten]

hole Loch, n. [lohkh]

holiday Feiertag, m. [FYE-e(r)-taak]

holidays Ferien, pl. [FEHR-yen]; Urlaub, m. [OOR-lowp]

holy heilig [HYE-likh]

home Heim, n. [hime]; Haus, n. [hows]

home address Heimatadresse, f. [HYE-maat-ah-drehs-seh]

home, to go nach Hause gehen [nahkh HOW-zeh GAY-en]

(at) home zu Hause [tsoo HOW-zeh]

honey Honig, m. [HOH-nikh]

hope Hoffnung, f. [HOF-nung]

horn (car) Hupe, f. [HOO-peh]

horse Pferd, n. [pfehrt]

hospital Krankenhaus, n. [KRAHN-ken-hows]

hospitality Gastfreundschaft, f. [GAHST-froynt-shahft]

host Gastgeber, m. [GAHST-gay-be(r)]

hot heiß [hice]

hotel Hotel, n. [ho-TEL]

hour Stunde, f. [SHTUN-deh]

house Haus, n. [hows]

how wie [vee]

how much wieviel [VEE-feel]

hundred hundert [HUN-dert]

Hungary Ungarn, n. [UN-gahrn]

hunger Hunger, m. [HUN-ge(r)]

hungry, to be Hunger haben [HUN-ge(r) HAA-ben]

hurry, to eilen [EYE-len]

hurry, to be in a es eilig haben [ehs EYE-likh HAA-ben]

hurt, to weh tun [vay toon]; schmerzen [SHMEHRT-sen]

hurt, to (oneself) sich verletzen *[zikh fehr-LEHT-sen]*

husband Mann, *m.* *[mahn]*; Ehemann, *m.* *[AY-eh-mahn]*

hut Hütte, *f.* *[HEW-teh]*

I

ice Eis, *n.* *[ice]*

ice cream Eis, *n.* *[ice]*

ice cube Eiswürfel, *m.* *[ICE-vewr-fel]*

identity card Ausweis, *m.* *[OWS-vice]*

if wenn *[vehn]*; ob *[op]*

ignition Zündung, *f.* *[TSEWN-dung]*

ill krank *[krahnk]*

illness Krankheit, *f.* *[KRAHNK-hite]*

immediately sofort *[zoh-FORT]*

important wichtig *[VIKH-tikh]*

impossible unmöglich *[un-MU(R)-glikh]*

impressive eindrucksvoll *[INE-druks-fol]*

in in *[in]*

included inbegriffen *[IN-beh-grif-fen]*

increase, to erhöhen *[ehr-HU(R)-en]*

indigestion Magenverstimm-ung, *f.* *[MAA-gen-fehr-shtim-ung]*

inexpensive preiswert *[PRICE-vehrt]*

infection Infektion, *f.* *[in-fehk-TSYOHN]*

inflation Inflation, *f.* *[in-flah-TSYOHN]*

information Auskunft, *f.* *[OWS-kunft]*

injection Spritze, *f.* *[SHPRI-tseh]*

injure, to verletzen *[fehr-LEHT-sen]*

ink Tinte, *f.* *[TIN-teh]*

inn Gasthaus, *n.* *[GAHST-hows]*

insect repellent Insekten-schutz, *m.* *[in-ZEHK-ten-shuts]*

inside drinnen *[DRIN-nen]*

instead of statt *[shtaht]*

insurance Versicherung, *f.* *[fehr-ZIKH-eh-rung]*

interest Interesse, *n.* *[in-teh-REHS-seh]*

interested in, to be sich interessieren für *[zikh in-teh-rehs-SEE-ren fewr]*

interesting interessant *[in-teh-rehs-SAHNT]*

intersection Kreuzung, *f.* *[KROY-tsung]*

introduce, to vorstellen *[FOR-shtehl-len]*

invite einladen *[INE-laa-den]*

iodine Jod, *n.* *[yoht]*

iron (metal) Eisen, *n.* *[EYE-zen]*

iron (flatiron) Bügeleisen, *n.* *[BEW-gel-eye-zen]*

iron, to bügeln *[BEW-geln]*

island Insel, *f.* *[IN-zel]*

ivory Elfenbein, *n.* *[EHL-fen-bine]*

J

jack (car) Wagenheber, *m.* *[VAA-gen-hay-be(r)]*

207

jacket Jacke, f. *[YAH-keh]*
jam Marmelade, f. *[mahr-meh-LAA-deh]*
January Januar, m. *[YAH-noo-aar]*
Japan Japan, n. *[YAH-pahn]*
jar Glas, n. *[glaas]*
jaw Kiefer, m. *[KEE-fe(r)]*
jeweler Juwelier, m. *[yoo-veh-LEER]*
jewelry Schmuck, m. *[shmuk]*
Jewish jüdisch *[YEW-dish]*
job (employment) Stelle, f. *[SHTEHL-leh]*
job (task) Aufgabe, f. *[OWF-gaa-beh]*
joint Gelenk, n. *[geh-LEHNK]*
joke Witz, m. *[vits]*
journey Fahrt, f. *[faart]*
joy Freude, f. *[FROY-deh]*
juice Saft, m. *[zahft]*
July Juli, m. *[YOO-lee]*
June Juni, m. *[YOO-nee]*
just (only) nur *[noor]*

K

keep, to behalten *[beh-HAAL-ten]*
key Schlüssel, m. *[SHLEWS-sel]*
kidney Niere, f. *[NEE-reh]*
kilogram Kilo(gramm), n. *[KEE-loh {GRAAM}]*
kilometer Kilometer, m. *[kee-loh-MAY-te(r)]*
kind (nice) nett *[neht]*
kind (type) Art, f. *[ahrt]*
kiss Kuß, m. *[kus]*
kiss, to küssen *[KEWS-sen]*
kitchen Küche, f. *[KEW-kheh]*
knee Knie, n. *[knee]*

knife Messer, m. *[MEHS-se(r)]*
knock, to klopfen *[KLOP-fen]*
know, to (be familiar with) kennen *[KEHN-nen]*
know, to (facts) wissen *[VIS-sen]*
kosher koscher *[KOH-she(r)]*

L

label Etikett, f. *[eh-ti-KEHT]*
lace Spitze, f. *[SHPIT-seh]*
laces (shoe) Schuhbänder, pl. *[SHOO-behn-de(r)]*
ladder Leiter, f. *[LITE-e(r)]*
ladies' room Damentoilette, f. *[DAA-men-toy-leh-teh]*
lady Dame, f. *[DAA-meh]*
lake See, m. *[zay]*
lamb Lammfleisch, n. *[LAHM-flyshe]*
lamp Lampe, f. *[LAHM-peh]*
land Land, n. *[lahnt]*
land, to landen *[LAHN-den]*
landscape Landschaft, f. *[LAHNT-shahft]*
language Sprache, f. *[SHPRAHKH-eh]*
large groß *[grohs]*
last letzte *[LEHTS-teh]*
last, to dauern *[DOW-ern]*
late spät *[shpayt]*
laugh, to lachen *[LAHKH-en]*
laundromat Waschsalon, m. *[VAHSCH-zaa-long]*
laundry Wäscherei, f. *[veh-sheh-RYE]*
lawyer Rechtsanwalt, m. *[REHKHTS-ahn-vahlt]*
lawn Rasen, m. *[RAA-zen]*
laxative Abführmittel, n. *[AHP-fewr-mit-tel]*

lead, to führen *[FEW-ren]*
lead (stage) Hauptrolle, f. *[HOWPT-rol-leh]*
leak, to lecken *[LEHK-en]*
learn, to lernen *[LEHR-nen]*
least, at wenigstens *[VAY-nikh-stens]*
leather Leder, n. *[LAY-de(r)]*
leave, to (behind) lassen *[LAHS-sen]*
leave, to (depart) abfahren *[AHP-faa-ren]*
left links *[links]*
leg Bein, n. *[bine]*
lemon Zitrone, f. *[tsi-TROH-neh]*
lemonade Limonade, f. *[lee-moh-NAA-deh]*
lend, to leihen *[LYE-en]*
length Länge, f. *[LEHNG-eh]*
lens (camera) Objektiv, n. *[op-yehk-TEEF]*
lens (glasses) Glas, n. *[glaas]*
less weniger *[VAY-neh-ge(r)]*
lesson Aufgabe, f. *[OWF-gaa-beh]*
let, to lassen *[LAHS-sen]*
letter Brief, m. *[breef*
letterbox Briefkasten, m. *[BREEF-kahs-ten]*
lettuce Kopfsalat, m. *[KOPF-zah-laat]*
level Ebene, f. *[AY-beh-neh]*
library Bibliothek, f. *[bib-lee-oh-TAYK]*
license (driver's) Führer-schein, m. *[FEW-re(r)-shine]*
lie, to (down) sich hinlegen *[zikh HIN-lay-gen]*
life Leben, n. *[LAY-ben]*

lifeguard Rettungsschwim-mer, m. *[REH-tungs-shvim-me(r)]*
lift, to heben *[HAY-ben]*
light (weight) leicht *[lyekht]*
light, n. *[likht]*
light, to anzünden *[AHN-tsewn-den]*
lighter Feuerzeug, n. *[FOY-e(r)-tsoyk]*
lighting Blitz, m. *[blits]*
like (as) wie *[vee]*
like, to gern haben *[gehrn HAA-ben]*; mögen *[MU(R)-gen]*; gefallen *[geh-FAHL-len]*
lime Limone, f. *[li-MOH-neh]*
limit Begrenzung, f. *[beh-GREHN-tsung]*
line Linie, f. *[LEEN-yeh]*
line (of people) Schlange, f. *[SHLAHNG-eh]*
linen Leinen, n. *[LINE-en]*
lip Lippe, f. *[LIP-peh]*
lipstick Lippenstift, m. *[LIP-pen-shtift]*
liqueur Likör, m. *[li-KUR]*
liquor Alkohol, m. *[AHL-koh-hol]*
list Liste, f. *[LIS-teh]*
listen, to (zu)hören *[{TSOO}HU(R)-ren]*
liter Liter, m. *[LEE-te(r)]*
little klein *[kline]*
live, to leben *[LAY-ben]*
liver Leber, f. *[LAY-be(r)]*
living room Wohnzimmer, n. *[VOHN-tsim-me(r)]*
lobby Eingangshalle, f. *[INE-gahngs-hahl-leh]*
lobster Hummer, m. *[HUM-me(r)]*
local hiesig *[HEE-zikh]*

local train Nahverkehrszug, m. [NAA-fehr-kehrs-tsook]

local phone call Ortsgespräch, n. [ORTS-geh-spraykh]

lock, to abschließen [AHP-shlees-en]

long lang [lahng]

long-distance call Ferngespräch, n. [FEHRN-geh-spraykh]

look at, to ansehen [AHN-zay-en]

look for, to suchen [ZOO-khen]

look out, to aufpassen [OWF-pahs-sen]

lose, to verlieren [fehr-LEER-en]

lose weight, to abnehmen [AHP-nay-men]

loss Verlust, m. [fehr-LOOST]

lost verloren [fehr-LOR-en]

lost and found Fundbüro, n. [FUNT-bew-roh]

a lot eine Menge [INE-eh MEHNG-eh]

lotion Lotion, f. [loh-TSYOHN]

love Liebe, f. [LEE-beh]

love, to lieben [LEE-ben]

low niedrig [NEE-drikh]

low tide Ebbe, f. [EHB-eh]

luck Glück, n. [glewk]

good luck viel Glück [feel glewk]

luggage Gepäck, n. [geh-PEHK]

lunch Mittagessen, n. [MIT-taak-ehs-sen]

lung Lunge, f. [LUNG-eh]

luxury Luxus, m. [LUKS-us]

210

M

machine Maschine, f. [mah-SHEE-neh]

magazine Zeitschrift, f. [TSITE-shrift]

maid Zimmermädchen, n. [TSIM-e(r)-mayt-khen]

mail Post, f. [post]

mail, to aufgeben [OWF-gay-ben]

mailbox Briefkasten, m. [BREEF-kahs-ten]

make, to machen [MAHKH-en]

man Mann, m. [mahn]

manager Geschäftsführer, m. [geh-SHEHFTS-few-re(r)]

manicure Maniküre, f. [mah-ni-KEW-reh]

many viele [FEE-leh]

map Karte, f. [KAHR-teh]; Plan, m. [plaan]

March März, m. [mehrts]

market Markt, m. [mahrkt]

married verheiratet [fehr-HYE-raa-tet]

mass (church) Messe, f. [MEHS-seh]

massage Massage, f. [mah-SAA-zheh]

match Streichholz, n. [SHTRYEKH-hohlts]

material (fabric) Stoff, m. [shtof]

mattress Matratze, f. [mah-TRAHT-tseh]

May Mai, m. [mye]

maybe vielleicht [fee-LYEKHT]

meal Mahlzeit, f. [MAAL-tsite]

mean, to bedeuten [beh-DOY-ten]

meaning Bedeutung, f. [beh-DOY-tung]

means Mittel, n. [MIT-tel]

measure, to messen [MEHS-sen]

meat Fleisch, n. [flyshe]

mechanic Mechaniker, m. [meh-KHAH-ni-ke(r)]

medical ärztlich [EHRTS-likh]

medicine Medikament, n. [meh-di-kah-MEHNT]

meet, to treffen [TREHF-fen]

meeting Versammlung, f. [fehr-ZAHM-lung]

melon Melone, f. [meh-LOH-neh]

mend, to flicken [FLIK-en]

men's room Herrentoilette, f. [HEHR-ren-toy-leht-teh]

menstrual pains Menstruationsbeschwerden, pl. [mehn-stru-ah-TSYOHNS-beh-shvehr-den]

mention, to erwähnen [ehr-VAY-nen]

menu Speisekarte, f. [SHPYE-zeh-kahr-teh]

merry fröhlich [FRU(R)-likh]

mess Unordnung, f. [UN-ort-nung]

message Nachricht, f. [NAKHK-rikht]

meter (length) Meter, m. [MAY-te(r)]

middle Mitte, f. [MIT-teh]

middle-class bürgerlich [BEWR-ge(r)-likh]

midnight Mitternacht, f. [MIT-te(r)-nahkht]

mild mild [milt]

milk Milch, f. [milkh]

million Million, f. [mil-YOHN]

mind Geist, m. [geyst]

never mind macht nichts [mahkht nikhts]

mineral water Mineralwasser, n. [mi-neh-RAAL-vahs-se(r)]

minister (clergyman) Pfarrer, m. [PFAHR-e(r)]

mint Minze, f. [MIN-tseh]

minute Minute, f. [mi-NOO-teh]

mirror Spiegel, m. [SHPEE-gel]

Miss Fräulein, n. [FROY-line]

miss, to versäumen [fehr-ZOY-men]

missing, to be verschwunden sein [fehr-SHVUN-den zine]

mistake Irrtum, m. [EER-toom]

modern modern [mo-DEHRN]

moment Augenblick, m. [OW-gen-blik]

monastery Kloster, n. [KLOHS-te(r)]

Monday Montag, m. [MOHN-taak]

money Geld, n. [gehlt]

money order Postanweisung, f. [POST-ahn-vye-zung]

month Monat, m. [MOH-naat]

monument Denkmal, n. [DEHNK-maal]

moon Mond, f. [mohnt]

more mehr [mehr]

morning Morgen, m. [MOR-gen]

211

mosque Moschee, f. [mo-SHAY]

mother Mutter, f. [MUT-te(r)]

mother-in-law Schwiegermutter, f. [SHVEE-ge(r)-MUT-te(r)]

motion sickness Reisekrankheit, f. [RYE-zeh-krahnk-hite]

motor Motor, m. [moh-TOHR]

motorcycle Motorrad, n. [moh-TOHR-raat]

mountain Berg, m. [behrk]

mountain pass Paß, m. [pahs]

mouth Mund, m. [munt]

mouthwash Mundwasser, n. [MUNT-vahs-se(r)]

move (to change residence) umziehen [OOM-tsee-en]

movie Film, m. [film]

movie theater Kino, n. [KEE-noh]

Mr. Herr, m. [hehr]

Mrs., Ms. Frau, f. [frow]

much viel [feel]

muscle Muskel, m. [MUS-kel]

museum Museum, n. [moo-ZAY-um]

mushroom Pilz, m. [pilts]

music Musik, f. [moo-ZEEK]

mussels Muscheln, pl. [MOO-shehln]

must, to müssen [MEWS-sen]

mustache Schnurrbart, m. [SHNOOR-bahrt]

mustard Senf, m. [zehnf]

myself selbst [zehlpst]

N

nail (finger) Nagel, m. [NAA-gel]

nail polish Nagellack, m. [NAA-gel-lahk]

naked nackt [nahkt]

name Name, m. [NAA-meh]

named, to be heißen [HICE-sen]

napkin Serviette, f. [sehr-VYEHT-teh]

narrow eng [ehng]

nationality Staatsangehörigkeit, f. [SHTAATS-ahn-geh-hu(r)-rikh-kite]

native einheimisch [INE-hye-mish]

nature Natur, f. [nah-TOOR]

nausea Übelkeit, f. [EW-bel-kite]

near nah [naa]

nearby in der Nähe [in dehr NAY-eh]

nearly fast [fahst]

necessary nötig [NU(R)-tikh]

neck Hals, m. [hahls]

necklace Halskette, f. [HAHLS-keht-teh]

necktie Krawatte, f. [krah-VAHT-teh]

need, to brauchen [BROW-khen]

needle Nadel, f. [NAA-del]

neighbor Nachbar, m. [NAHKH-baar]

neighborhood Nachbarschaft, f. [NAHKH-baar-shahft]

nerve Nerv, m. [nehrf]

never nie [nee]

new neu [noy]

New Year Neujahr, n. [NOY-yaar]

newspaper Zeitung, f. [TSITE-ung]

newspaper stand
Zeitungsstand, m. [TSITE-ungs-shtahnt]
next nächst [naykhst]
nice nett [neht]
night Nacht, f. [nahkht]
nightclub Nachtlokal, n. [NAHKHT-loh-kaal]
nightgown Nachthemd, n. [HAHKHT-hehmt]
nine neun [noyn]
nineteen neunzehn [NOYN-tsayn]
ninety neunzig [NOYN-tsikh]
ninth neunte [NOYN-teh]
no nein [nine]
no one niemand [NEE-mahnt]
noise Lärm, m. [lehrm]
noisy laut [lowt]
none kein [kine]
nonsmoker Nichtraucher, m. [NIKHT-row-khe(r)]
noodles Nudeln, pl. [NOO-deln]
noon Mittag, m. [MIT-taak]
north Norden, m. [NOR-den]; nördlich [NU(R)RT-likh]
nose Nase, f. [NAA-zeh]
not nicht [nikht]
not at all gar nicht [gaar nikht]
notebook Notizheft, n. [no-TEETS-hehft]
nothing nichts [nikhts]
notice Anzeige, f. [AHN-tsye-geh]
notice, to bemerken [beh-MEHR-ken]
novel Roman, m. [roh-MAAN]
November November, m. [no-VEHM-be(r)]

now jetzt [yehtst]
number Nummer, f. [NUM-me(r)]
nurse Krankenschwester, f. [KRAHN-ken-shvehs-te(r)]
nut Nuß, m. [noos]

O
object Gegenstand, m. [GAY-gen-shtahnt]
obtain, to bekommen [beh-KOM-men]
occupation Beruf, m. [beh-ROOF]
occupied besetzt [beh-ZEHTST]
ocean Ozean, m. [OH-tsay-ahn]
October Oktober, m. [ok-TOH-be(r)]
odd (number) ungerade [UN-geh-raa-deh]
of von [fon]
of course natürlich [nah-TEWR-likh]
offer, to anbieten [ahn-BEE-ten]
office Büro, n. [bew-ROH]; Amt, n. [ahmt]
often oft [oft]
oil Öl, n. [u(r)l]
okay okay [o-kay]
old alt [ahlt]
olive Olive, f. [o-LEE-veh]
omelet Omelett, n. [om-LEHT]
on an [ahn]; auf [owf]
on foot zu Fuß [tsoo foos]
on time pünktlich [PEWNKT-likh]
once einmal [INE-maal]

one eins *[ines]*
one-way ticket einfache Fahrkarte, f. *[INE-fahkh-eh FAAR-kahr-teh]*
one-way street Einbahnstraße, f. *[INE-baan-shtrahs-eh]*
onion Zwiebel, f. *[TSVEE-bel]*
only nur *[noor]*
open offen *[OF-fen]*
open, to öffnen *[U(R)F-nen]*; aufmachen *[OWF-mahkh-en]*
opera Oper, f. *[OH-pe(r)]*
operation Operation, f. *[o-peh-rah-TSYOHN]*
operator (phone) Vermittlung, f. *[fehr-MIT-lung]*
opportunity Gelegenheit, f. *[geh-LAY-gen-hite]*
opposite Gegenteil, n. *[GAY-gen-tile]*
opposite (across from) gegenüber *[gay-gen-EW-be(r)]*
optician Optiker, m. *[OP-ti-ke(r)]*
or oder *[OH-de(r)]*
orange Orange, f. *[oh-RAHN-zheh]*
orange juice Orangensaft, m. *[oh-RAHN-zhen-sahft]*
orchestra Orchester, n. *[or-KEHS-te(r)]*
order Bestellung, f. *[beh-SHTEH-lung]*
order, to bestellen *[beh-SHTEHL-len]*
ordinary gewöhnlich *[geh-VU(R)N-likh]*
other andere *[AHN-deh-reh]*
otherwise sonst *[zonst]*
out aus *[ows]*

out of order außer Betrieb *[OWS-se(r) beh-TREEP]*
outdoors draußen *[DROWS-sen]*
outlet (electrical) Steckdose, f. *[SHTEHK-doh-zeh]*
outfit Ausrüstung, f. *[OWS-rews-tung]*
outside of außerhalb *[OWS-se(r)-hahlp]*
oven Ofen, m. *[OH-fen]*
over (above) über *[EW-be(r)]*
over (finished) aus *[ows]*; zu Ende *[tsoo EHN-deh]*
overcoat Mantel, m. *[MAHN-tel]*
overdone zu stark gebraten *[tsoo shtahrk geh-BRAA-ten]*
overdose Überdosis, f. *[EW-be(r)-doh-zis]*
overheat, to (motor) heißlaufen *[HICE-low-fen]*
overnight (stay) eine Nacht *[INE-eh nahkht]*
overrun überlaufen *[ew-be(r)-LOW-fen]*
overtime Überstunden, pl. *[EW-be(r)-shtun-den]*
owe, to schulden *[SHOOL-den]*
own, to besitzen *[beh-ZIT-sen]*
owner Besitzer, m. *[beh-ZIT-se(r)]*
oyster Auster, f. *[OW-ste(r)]*

P
pack, to packen *[PAH-ken]*
package Paket, n. *[pah-KAYT]*
pain Schmerz, m. *[shmehrts]*

214

painter Maler, m. [MAA-le(r)]
painting Bild, n. [bilt];
  Gemälde, n. [geh-MEHL-deh]
painted gemalt [geh-MAALT]
pair Paar, n. [paar]
pajamas Pyjama, m. [pi-JAA-maa]
palace Palast, m. [pah-LAHST]; Schloß, m. [shlos]
pancake Pfannkuchen,
  m. [PFAHN-koo-khen]
panties Schlüpfer,
  m. [SHLEWP-fer]
pants Hose, f. [HOH-zeh]
panty hose Strumpfhose,
  f. [SHTRUMPF-hoh-zeh]
paper Papier, n. [pah-PEER]
parcel Paket, n. [pah-KAYT]
pardon Verzeihung, f. [fehr-TSYE-ung]; Wie bitte? [vee BIT-teh]
park Park, m. [pahrk]
park, to parken [PAHR-ken]
parking disk Parkscheibe,
  f. [PAHRK-shye-beh]
parking lot Parkplatz,
  m. [PAHRK-plahts]
parking meter Parkuhr,
  f. [PAHRK-oor]
parking prohibited Parken
  verboten [PAHR-ken fehr-BOH-ten]
parsley Petersilie, f. [pay-te(r)-ZEEL-yeh]
part Teil, m. [tile]
part, to (separate)
  trennen [TREHN-en]
party (celebration) Party,
  f. [PAHR-tee]
pass (permit) Ausweis,
  m. [OWS-vice]

pass, to (car) überholen [EW-be(r)-hoh-len]
passenger Fahrgast,
  m. [FAAR-gahst]
passport (Reise-)Paß,
  m. [{RYE-zeh-}pahs]
past Vergangenheit, f. [fehr-GAHNG-en-hite]
pasta Teigwaren, pl. [TIKE-vaa-ren]
pastry Gebäck, n. [geh-BEHK]
pastry shop Konditorei,
  f. [kon-dee-to-RYE]
path Pfad, m. [pfaat]
pay, to bezahlen [beh-TSAA-len]
pea Erbse, f. [EHRP-seh]
peach Pfirsich, m. [PFIR-zikh]
peak Gipfel, m. [GIP-fel]
pear Birne, f. [BEER-neh]
pedestrian Fußgänger,
  m. [FOOS-gehng-e(r)]
pedestrian zone
  Fußgängerzone, f. [FOOS-gehng-e(r)-tsoh-neh]
pediatrician Kinderarzt,
  m. [KIN-de(r)-ahrtst]
pen (ball point)
  Kugelschreiber, m. [KOO-gel-shrye-be(r)]
penknife Taschenmesser,
  n. [TAHSH-en-mehs-se(r)]
pencil Bleistift, m. [BLYE-shtift]
people Leute, pl. [LOY-teh]
pepper Pfeffer, m. [PFEH-fe(r)]
perfect perfekt [pehr-FEHKT]
performance Vorstellung,
  f. [for-SHTEHL-lung]
perfume Parfüm, n. [pahr-FEWM]

215

perhaps vielleicht [fee-LYEKHT]

period (menstrual) Periode, f. [peh-ree-OH-deh]

permanent wave Dauerwelle, f. [DOW-e(r)-vehl-leh]

permit (pass) Genehmigung, f. [geh-NAY-mi-gung]

permit, to erlauben [ehr-LOW-ben]

person Person, f. [pehr-ZOHN]

personal persönlich [pehr-ZU(R)N-likh]

personal check Barscheck, m. [BAAR-shehk]

person-to-person call Gespräch mit Voranmeldung [geh-SHPRAYKH mit FOHR-ahn-mehl-dung]

persuade, to überzeugen [ew-be(r)-TSOY-gen]

pharmacy Apotheke, f. [ah-poh-TAY-keh]

phone Telefon, n. [tay-lay-FON]

photocopy Fotokopie, f. [fot-toh-koh-PEE]

photograph Foto, n. [FOH-toh]

photograph, to fotographieren [fot-toh-grah-FEE-ren]

phrase Ausdruck, m. [OWS-druk]

piano Klavier, n. [klah-VEER]

pickle saure Gurke, f. [SOW-reh GOOR-keh]

216

pick up, to abholen [AHP-hoh-len]

picnic Picknick, n. [PIK-nik]

picture Bild, n. [bilt]

pie Torte, f. [TOR-teh]

piece Stück, n. [shtewk]

pier Pier, m. [peer]

pig Schwein, n. [shvine]

pigeon Taube, f. [TOW-beh]

pill Pille, f. [PIL-eh]

pillow Kopfkissen, n. [KOPF-kis-sen]

pillowcase Kopfkissenbezug, m. [KOPF-kis-sen-beh-tsook]

pilot Pilot, m. [pee-LOHT]

pin Stecknadel, f. [SHTEHK-naa-del]

pineapple Ananas, f. [AH-nah-nahs]

pink rosa [ROH-zah]

pipe Pfeife, f. [PFIFE-eh]

pipe tobacco Pfeifentabak, m. [PFIFE-en-tah-bahk]

pitcher Krug, m. [krook]

pity!, what a wie schade! [vee SHAA-deh]

place Platz, m. [plahts]; Ort, n. [ort]

place, to stellen [SHTEHL-len]

plan Plan, m. [plaan]

plan, to planen [PLAA-nen]

planetarium Planetarium, n. [plah-neh-TAH-ree-oom]

plate Teller, m. [TEHL-le(r)]

platform (station) Bahnsteig, m. [BAAN-shtyek]

play (stage) Stück, n. [shtewk]

play, to spielen [SHPEE-len]

playground Spielplatz, m. [SHPEEL-plahts]

playing cards Spielkarten, pl. [SHPEEL-kahr-ten]
pleasant angenehm [AHN-geh-naym]
please bitte [BIT-teh]
pleasure Vergnügen, n. [fehrk-NEW-gen]
pliers Zange, f. [TSAHNG-eh]
plug (electrical) Steckdose, f. [SHTEHK-doh-zeh]
plum Pflaume, f. [PFLOW-meh]
pocket Tasche, f. [TAHSH-eh]
pocketbook Brieftasche, f. [BREEF-tahsh-eh]
point, to zeigen [TSYE-gen]
poison Gift, n. [gift]
Poland Polen, n. [POH-len]
police Polizei, f. [po-lee-TSYE]
police station Polizeiwache, f. [po-lee-TSYE-vahkh-eh]
policeman Polizist, m. [po-lee-TSIST]
polish, to polieren [po-LEE-ren]
polite höflich [HU(R)F-likh]
pond Teich, m. [tyekh]
pool (game) Billard, n. [BIL-yahrt]
poor arm [ahrm]
pork Schweinefleisch, n. [SHVINE-eh-flyshe]
port Hafen, m. [HAA-fen]
porter Gepäckträger, m. [geh-PEHK-tray-ge(r)]
portion Portion, f. [por-TSYOHN]
possible möglich [MU(R)G-likh]
postage Porto, n. [POR-toh]

postcard Postkarte, f. [POST-kahr-teh]
post office Postamt, n. [POST-ahmt]
post office box Postfach, n. [POST-fahkh]
potato Kartoffel, f. [kahr-TOF-fel]
pottery Keramik, f. [keh-RAH-mik]
pour, to einschenken [INE-shehn-ken]
powder Puder, m. [POO-de(r)]; Pulver, n. [PUL-ve(r)]
powerful kräftig [KREHF-tikh]
practical praktisch [PRAHK-tish]
practice, to üben [EW-ben]
prefer, to vorziehen [FOR-tsee-en]; lieber haben [LEE-be(r) HAA-ben]
pregnant schwanger [SHVAHNG-e(r)]
prepare, to vorbereiten [FOR-beh-rye-ten]
prescription Rezept, n. [reh-TZEHPT]
present (gift) Geschenk, n. [geh-SHEHNK]
present, to übergeben [ew-be(r)-GAY-ben]
press (media) Presse, f. [PREHS-seh]
press, to drücken [DREWK-en]
pressure Druck, m. [druk]
pretty hübsch [hewpsh]
price Preis, m. [price]
price range Preisskala, f. [PRICE-skah-lah]
priest Priester, m. [PREES-te(r)]

217

print (photo) Abzug, m. *[AHP-tsook]*

print, to drucken *[DRUK-en]*

private privat *[pri-VAAT]*

private lessons Privatunterricht, m. *[pri-VAAT-un-teh-rikht]*

profession Beruf, m. *[beh-ROOF]*

prohibit, to verbieten *[fehr-BEE-ten]*

program Programm, n. *[proh-GRAAM]*

promise, to versprechen *[fehr-SHPREHKH-en]*

pronounciation Aussprache, f. *[OWS-shprahkh-eh]*

property Besitz, m. *[beh-ZITS]*; Grundstück, n. *[GROONT-shtewk]*

protect, to beschützen *[beh-SHEWT-sen]*

Protestant evangelisch *[ay-fahn-GAY-lish]*

prune Backpflaume, f. *[BAHK-pflow-meh]*

public öffentlich *[U(R)F-ehnt-likh]*

pull, to ziehen *[TSEE-en]*

pump (fuel) Pumpe, f. *[PUM-peh]*

puncture Reifenpanne, f. *[RIFE-en-pahn-eh]*

purchases Einkäufe, pl. *[INE-koy-feh]*

purple violett *[vee-oh-LEHT]*

purse Handtasche, f. *[HAHNT-tahsh-eh]*

push, to (a car) schieben *[SHEE-ben]*

push, to (a button) drücken *[DREWK-en]*

put, to stellen *[SHTEHL-len]*

put on, to (dress) anziehen *[AHN-tsee-en]*

Q

quality Qualität, f. *[kvah-li-TAYT]*

quantity Menge, f. *[MEHNG-eh]*

quarter Viertel, n. *[FEER-tel]*

question Frage, f. *[FRAA-geh]*

quiche Quiche, f. *[keesh]*

quick(ly) schnell *[shnehl]*

quiet ruhig *[ROO-ikh]*

quite ziemlich *[TSEEM-likh]*

R

rabbi Rabbiner, m. *[rah-BEE-ne(r)]*

rabbit Kaninchen, s. *[kah-NEEN-khen]*; Hase, f. *[HAA-zeh]*

rabies Tollwut, f. *[TOL-voot]*

race track Rennbahn, f. *[REHN-baan]*

radiator Heizkörper, m. *[HITES-ku(r)-pe(r)]*; (car) Kühler, m. *[KEW-le(r)]*

radio Radio, n. *[RAA-dee-oh]*

radish Radieschen, n. *[raa-DEES-khen]*

railroad Eisenbahn, f. *[EYE-zen-baan]*

railroad station Bahnhof, m. *[BAAN-hohf]*

rain Regen, m. *[RAY-gen]*

raincoat Regenmantel, m. *[RAY-gen-mahn-tel]*

raisins Rosinen, pl. [roh-ZEE-nen]

rare selten [ZEHL-ten]

rare (uncooked) blutig [BLOO-tikh]

raspberry Himbeere, f. [HIM-bay-reh]

rate Tarif, m. [tah-REEF]

rate of exchange Wechselkurs, m. [VEHK-sel-koors]

rather lieber [LEE-be(r)]

rather (quite) ziemlich [TSEEM-likh]

raw roh [roh]

razor Rasierapparat, n. [rah-ZEER-ah-pah-raat]

razor blade Rasierklinge, f. [rah-ZEER-kling-eh]

read, to lesen [LAY-zen]

ready bereit [beh-RITE]

ready, to be fertig sein [FEHR-tikh zine]

real echt [ehkht]

really wirklich [VIRK-likh]

rear hinten [HIN-ten]

reason Grund, m. [groont]

reasonable vernünftig [fehr-NEWNF-tikh]

receipt Quittung, f. [KVIT-tung]

receive, to erhalten [ehr-HAAL-ten]; empfangen [ehm-PFAHNG-en]

receiver (letter) Empfänger, m. [ehm-PFEHNG-e(r)]

receiver (phone) Hörer, m. [HU(R)-e(r)]

recently kürzlich [KEWRTS-likh]

recommend, to empfehlen [ehm-PFAY-len]

record (disc) Schallplatte, f. [SHAHL-plaht-teh]

record player Plattenspielern, m. [PLAHT-ten-shpee-le(r)]

recording Aufnahme, f. [OWF-naa-meh]

recover, to sich erholen [zikh ehr-HOH-len]

red rot [roht]

reduction (price) Ermäßigung, f. [ehr-MAYS-si-gung]

refreshing erfrischend [ehr-FRISH-ent]

refund Rückerstattung, f. [REWK-ehr-shtaht-tung]

refuse, to ablehnen [AHP-lay-nen]

regards Grüße, pl. [GREWS-seh]

register, to sich eintragen [zikh INE-traa-gen]

registered mail per Einschreiben [pehr INE-shrye-ben]

regret, to bedauern [beh-DOW-ern]

regular normal [nor-MAAL]; regelmäßig [RAY-gel-mays-ikh]

relative Verwandte, m., f. [fehr-VAHN-teh]

religion Religion, f. [ray-li-GYOHN]

religious service Gottesdienst, m. [GOT-tehs-deenst]

remain, to bleiben [BLYE-ben]

219

remedy Heilmittel, n. [HILE-mit-tel]

remember, to sich erinnern [zikh eh-RIN-ern]

rent Miete, f. [MEE-teh]

rent, to vermieten [fehr-MEE-ten]

repair Reparatur, f. [reh-pah-rah-TOOR]

repair, to reparieren [reh-pah-REE-ren]

repeat, to wiederholen [vee-de(r)-HOH-len]

replace, to ersetzen [ehr-ZEHT-sen]

represent, to vertreten [fehr-TRAY-ten]

request, to bitten [BIT-ten]

require, to verlangen [fehr-LAHNG-en]

resemble, to ähneln [AY-neln]

reservation Reservierung, f. [reh-zehr-VEE-rung]

reserve, to reservieren (lassen) [reh-zehr-VEE-ren {LAHS-en}]

reserved vorbestellt [FOR-beh-shtehlt]

responsibility Verantwortung, f. [fehr-AHNT-vor-tung]

resort (place) Ferienort, m. [FEHR-yen-ort]

rest Ruhe, f. [ROO-eh]

rest, to sich ausruhen [zikh OWS-roo-en]

restaurant Restaurant, n. [rehs-to-RAHNT]

restroom Toilette, f. [toy-LEHT-teh]

result Ergebnis, n. [ehr-GAYP-nis]

retirement Ruhestand, m. [ROO-eh-shtahnt]

return, to (something) zurückgeben [tsoo-REWK-gay-ben]

return to, (come back) zurückkommen [tsoo-REWK-kom-men]

rib Rippe, f. [RIP-peh]

ribbon Band, n. [bahnt]

rice Reis, m. [rice]

rich reich [ryekh]

ride Fahrt, f. [faart]

ride, to fahren [FAA-ren]

ride, to (a horse) reiten [RITE-en]

right (correct) richtig [RIKH-tikh]

right (direction) rechts [rehkhts]

right, to be Recht haben [rehkht HAA-ben]

right away gleich [glyekh]

right-handed rechtshändig [REHKHTS-hehn-dikh]

ring Ring, m. [ring]

ring, to klingeln [KLING-eln]

rinse, to spülen [SHPEW-len]

risk Risiko, n. [REE-zee-koh]

river Fluß, m. [floos]

road Straße, f. [SHTRAHS-seh]

road map Straßenkarte, f. [SHTRAHS-sen-kahr-teh]

roast, to braten [BRAA-ten]

roasted gebraten [geh-BRAA-ten]

220

robbery Raub, m. *[rowp]*

robe Bademantel, m. *[BAA-deh-mahn-tel]*

roll (film) Filmrolle, f. *[FILM-rol-leh]*

roll (stage) Rolle, f. *[ROL-leh]*

roll, to rollen *[ROL-len]*

rolls (bread) Brötchen, pl. *[BRU(R)T-khen]*

roof Dach, n. *[dahkh]*

room Zimmer, n. *[TSIM-me(r)]*

room service Zimmerbedienung, f. *[TSIM-me(r)-beh-dee-nung]*

root Wurzel, f. *[VUR-tsel]*

rope Seil, n. *[zile]*

rose Rose, f. *[ROH-zeh]*

rosé wine Rosé, m. *[roh-ZAY]*

rouge Rouge, n. *[roozh]*

round rund *[runt]*

round-trip ticket Rückfahrkarte, f. *[REWK-faar-kahr-teh]*

row (theatre) Reihe, f. *[RYE-eh]*

rowboat Ruderboot, n. *[ROO-de(r)-boht]*

rubber Gummi, m. *[GOOM-mee]*

rubber eraser Radiergummi, m. *[rah-DEER-goom-mee]*

rubber band Gummiband, n. *[GOOM-mee-bahnt]*

rug Teppich, m. *[TEHP-pikh]*

ruins Ruinen, pl. *[roo-EE-nen]*

rule Regel, f. *[RAY-gel]*

ruler Lineal, n. *[lee-nay-AAL]*

run, to laufen *[LOW-fen]*

running water fließendes Wasser, n. *[FLEES-sen-dehs VAHS-se(r)]*

runway (plane) Piste, f. *[PIS-teh]*

rush hour Stoßzeit, f. *[SHTOHS-tsite]*

rye bread Roggenbrot, n. *[ROG-gen-broht]*

S

sad traurig *[TROW-rikh]*

safe sicher *[ZIKH-e(r)]*

safety pin Sicherheitsnadel, f. *[ZIKH-e(r)-hites-naa-del]*

salad Salat, m. *[zah-LAAT]*

sale Verkauf, m. *[fehr-KOWF]*

sale (low prices) Ausverkauf, m. *[OWS-fehr-kowf]*

salesman Verkäufer, m. *[fehr-KOY-fe(r)]*

saleswoman Verkäuferin, f. *[fehr-KOY-feh-rin]*

salt Salz, n. *[zahlts]*

salty salzig *[ZAHL-tsikh]*

same selbe *[ZEHL-beh]*; gleiche *[GLYE-kheh]*

sand Sand, m. *[zahnt]*

sandwich Sandwich, n. *[SAHNT-vitch]*

sanitary napkin Damenbinde, f. *[DAA-men-bin-deh]*

Saturday Samstag, m. *[ZAHMS-taak]*; Sonnabend, m. *[ZON-aa-behnt]*

sauce Soße, f. *[ZOH-zeh]*

saucer Untertasse, f. *[UN-te(r)-tahs-seh]*

221

sausage Wurst, f. [voorst]

save, to (money) sparen [SHPAA-ren]

save, to (person) retten [REHT-ten]

say, to sagen [ZAA-gen]

scarf Schal, m. [shahl]

scenic route landschaftlich schöne Straße, f. [LAHNT-shahft-likh SHU(R)-neh SHTRAHS-eh]

schedule Fahrplan, m. [FAAR-plaan]

school Schule, f. [SHOO-leh]

scissors Schere, f. [SHAY-reh]

scrambled eggs Rührei, er, pl. [REWR-eye-e(r)]

screwdriver Schraubenzieher, m. [SHROW-ben-tsee-e(r)]

sculpture Skulptur, f. [skulp-TOOR]

sea Meer, n. [mayr]

seafood Meeresfrüchte, pl. [MAY-rehs-frewkh-teh]

seasick seekrank [ZAY-krahnk]

season Jahreszeit, f. [YAA-rehs-tsite]

seasoning Würze, pl. [VEWR-tseh]

seat Platz, m. [plahts]

seatbelt Sicherheitsgurt, m. [ZIKH-e(r)-hites-gurt]

second zweite [TSVITE-teh]

second (time) Sekunde, f. [zeh-KOON-deh]

second hand gebraucht [geh-BROWKHT]

secretary Sekretär(in), m./f. [zeh-kreh-TAYR{-in}]

see, to sehen [ZAY-en]

seem, to scheinen [SHINE-en]

selection Auswahl, f. [OWS-vaal]

sell, to verkaufen [fehr-KOW-fen]

send, to schicken [SHIK-en]; senden [ZEHN-den]

sender (mail) Absender, m. [AHP-zehn-de(r)]

senior citizen's pass Seniorenpaß, m. [zehn-YOR-en-pahs]

sentence (grammar) Satz, m. [zahts]

September September, m. [zehp-TEHM-be(r)]

serious ernst [ehrnst]

serve, to dienen [DEE-nen]; servieren [zehr-VEE-ren]

service Bedienung, f. [beh-DEE-nung]

service station Tankstelle, f. [TAHNK-shtehl-leh]

seven sieben [ZEE-ben]

seventeen siebzehn [ZEEP-tsayn]

seventh siebte [ZEEP-teh]

seventy siebzig [ZEEP-tsikh]

several mehrere [MEH-reh-reh]

sew, to nähen [NAY-en]

shade, shadow Schatten, m. [SHAHT-ten]

shampoo Haarwaschmittel, n. [HAAR-vahsh-mit-tel]; Shampoo, n. [shahm-POO]

share, to teilen [TILE-en]

shave, to rasieren [rah-ZEE-ren]

shaving cream Rasiercreme, f. [rah-ZEER-kraym]

222

shaver Rasierapparat, n. [rah-ZEER-ah-pah-raat]

shawl Tuch, n. [tookh]

she sie [zee]

sheep Schaf, n. [shahf]

sheet Bettlaken, n. [BEHT-lah-ken]

shelf Regal, n. [ray-GAAL]

shell Schale, f. [SHAH-leh]

shine, to (shoes) putzen [PUT-sen]; polieren [po-LEE-ren]

ship Schiff, n. [shif]

ship, to verschiffen [fehr-SHIF-fen]

shirt Hemd, n. [hehmt]

shoe Schuh, m. [shoo]

shoelaces Schnürsenkel, pl. [SHNEWR-zehn-kel]

shop Geschäft, n. [geh-SHEHFT]; Laden, m. [LAA-den]

shopping, to go einkaufen gehen [INE-kow-fen GAY-en]

shopping center Einkaufszentrum, n. [INE-kowfs-tsehn-trum]

short kurz [koorts]

shorts (underwear) Unterhosen, pl. [UN-te(r)-hoh-zen]

shoulder Schulter, f. [SHOO-te(r)]

show (art) Ausstellung, f. [OWS-shtehl-lung]

show (performance) Vorstellung, f. [FOR-shtehl-lung]

show, to zeigen [TSYE-gen]

show window Schaufenster, n. [SHOW-fehn-ste(r)]

shower Dusche, f. [DOO-sheh]

shrimp Garnele, f. [gahr-NAY-leh]

shrink, to einlaufen [INE-low-fen]

shut, to schließen [SHLEES-sen]

shutter Fensterladen, m. [FEHN-ste(r)-laa-den]

shutter (camera) Verschluß, m. [fehr-SHLUS]

sick krank [krahnk]

sickness Krankheit, f. [KRAHNK-hite]

side Seite, f. [ZITE-eh]

sidewalk Bürgersteig, m. [BEWR-ge(r)-shtike]

sightseeing Besichtigung, f. [beh-ZIKH-ti-gung]

sign Schild, n. [shilt]

sign, to unterschreiben [un-te(r)-SHRYE-ben]

silk Seide, f. [ZYE-deh]

silver Silber, n. [ZIL-be(r)]

silverwear Besteck, n. [beh-SHTEHK]

since seit [zite]

sincerely (yours) mit freundlichen Grüßen [mit FROYNT-likh-en GREWS-en]

sing, to singen [ZING-en]

single (unmarried) ledig [LAY-dikh]

single room Einzelzimmer, n. [INE-tsel-tsim-me(r)]

sink Waschbecken, n. [VAHSH-beh-ken]

sister Schwester, f. [SHVEHS-te(r)]

223

sister-in-law Schwägerin, f. *[SHVAY-geh-rin]*

sit down, to sich setzen *[zikh ZEHT-sen]*

site Stelle, f. *[SHTEHL-leh]*

six sechs *[zehks]*

sixteen sechzehn *[ZEHKH-tsayn]*

sixty sechzig *[ZEHKH-tsikh]*

size Größe, f. *[GRU(R)S-eh]*

skating rink Eisbahn, f. *[ICE-baan]*

ski Ski, m. *[shee]*

ski equipment Skiausrüstung, f. *[SHEE-ows-rews-tung]*

ski lift Skilift, m. *[SHEE-lift]*

skiing skifahren *[SHEE-faa-ren]*

skiing, cross-country langlaufskifahren *[LAHNG-lowf-shee-faa-ren]*

skin Haut, f. *[howt]*

skirt Rock, m. *[rok]*

sky Himmel, m. *[HIM-mel]*

sleep, to schlafen *[SHLAH-fen]*

sleeping bag Schlafsack, m. *[SHLAHF-zahk]*

sleeping car Schlafwagen, m. *[SHLAHF-vaa-gen]*

sleeve Ärmel, m. *[EHR-mel]*

slice Scheibe, f. *[SHYE-beh]*

slide (photo) Dia, n. *[DEE-ah]*

slip Unterrock, m. *[UN-te(r)-rok]*

slippers Hausschuhe, pl. *[HOWS-shoo-eh]*

slippery rutschig *[RUT-shikh]*

slow(ly) langsam *[LAHNG-zahm]*

slow down, to langsam fahren *[LAHNG-zahm FAA-ren]*

small klein *[kline]*

smile, to lächeln *[LEH-kheln]*

smoke, to rauchen *[ROW-khen]*

smoked geräuchert *[geh-ROY-khert]*

smoking section Raucherabteil *[ROW-khe(r)-ahp-tile]*

smooth glatt *[glaht]*

snack bar Schnellimbiss, m. *[SHNEHL-im-bis]*

snail Schnecke, f. *[SHNEH-keh]*

snow Schnee, m. *[shnay]*

snow, to schneien *[SHNYE-en]*

soap Seife, f. *[ZYE-feh]*

sober nüchtern *[NEWKH-tern]*

soccer Fußball, m. *[FOOS-bahl]*

socks Socken, pl. *[ZO-ken]*

sofa Sofa, n. *[ZOH-fah]*

soft weich *[vyekh]*

soft drink alkoholfreies Getränk, n. *[AHL-koh-hohl-frye-ehs geh-TREHNK]*

sold out ausverkauft *[OWS-fehr-kowft]*

sole (shoe) Sohle, f. *[ZOH-leh]*

solid massiv *[mah-SEEF]*

some einige *[INE-eh-geh]*; etwas *[EHT-vahs]*

someone jemand *[YAY-mahnt]*

something etwas *[EHT-vahs]*

sometimes
manchmal [MAHNCH-maal]
somewhere irgendwo [EER-gehnt-voh]
son Sohn, m. [zohn]
song Lied, n. [leet]
soon bald [bahlt]
sore throat Halsschmerzen, pl. [HAHLS-shmehrt-sen]
sorrow Leid, n. [lite]
I am sorry es tut mir leid [ehs toot meer lite]
sort (type) Sorte, f. [ZOR-teh]
soup Suppe, f. [ZOOP-peh]
sour sauer [ZOW-e(r)]
south Süden, m. [ZEW-den]
souvenir Andenken, n. [AHN-dehn-ken]
spa Kurort, m. [KOOR-ort]
spare parts Ersatzteile, pl. [ehr-ZAHTS-tile-eh]
spare tire Ersatzreifen, m. [ehr-ZAHTS-rye-fen]
spark plug Zündkerze, f. [TSEWNT-kehr-tseh]
sparkling wine Schaumwein, m. [SHOWM-vine]
speak, to sprechen [SHPREHKH-en]
speaker (stereo) Lautsprecher, m. [LOWT-sprehkh-e(r)]
special besondere [beh-ZON-deh-reh]
specialty Spezialität, f. [shpeh-tsee-ah-lee-TAYT]
speed Geschwindigkeit, f. [geh-SHVIN-dikh-kite]

speed limit Geschwindig-keitsbegrenzung, f. [geh-SHVIN-dikh-kites-beh-GREHN-tsung]
spell, to buchstabieren [bookh-shtah-BEE-ren]
spend, to (money) ausgeben [OWS-gay-ben]
spend, to (time) verbringen [fehr-BRIN-gen]
spice Gewürz, n. [geh-VEWRTS]
spinach Spinat, m. [shpi-NAAT]
sponge Schwamm, m. [shvahm]
spoon Löffel, m. [LU(R)F-el]
spouse Gatte, m. [GAHT-teh]; Gattin, f. [GAHT-tin]
sprain, to verstauchen [fehr-SHTOW-khen]
spring (mechanical) Feder, f. [FAY-de(r)]
spring (season) Frühling, m. [FREW-ling]
spring (of water) Quelle, f. [KVEHL-leh]
square (geometric) Quadrat, n. [kvah-DRAHT]
square (town) Platz, m. [plahts]
stadium Stadion, n. [SHTAA-dee-ohn]
stain Fleck, m. [flehk]
staircase Treppenhaus, n. [TREHP-pen-hows]
stairs Treppe, f. [TREHP-peh]
stamp (postage) Briefmarke, f. [BREEF-mahr-keh]

225

stand, to stehen [SHTAY-en]

stand up, to aufstehen [OWF-shtay-en]

stand in line, to Schlange stehen [SHLAHNG-eh shtay-en]

star Stern, m. [shtehrn]

starch (laundry) Stärke, f. [SHTEHR-keh]

start, to beginnen [beh-GIN-nen]

start, to (a car) anspringen [AHN-spring-en]

starter (car) Anlasser, m. [AHN-lahs-se(r)]

state Staat, m. [shtaat]

station Bahnhof, m. [BAAN-hohf]

stationery Schreibwaren, pl. [SHRIPE-vaa-ren]

statue Statue, f. [SHTAH-too-eh]

stay Aufenthalt, m. [OWF-ehnt-hahlt]

stay, to (lodge) übernachten [EW-be(r)-nahkh-ten]

stay, to (remain) bleiben [BLYE-ben]

steak Steak, m. [shtayk]

steal, to stehlen [SHTEH-len]

steel Stahl, m. [shtahl]

steering wheel Lenkrad, n. [LEHNK-raat]

stew Eintopf, m. [INE-topf]

stewardess Stewardeß, f. [SHTOO-ahr-dehs]

stick (pole) Stock, m. [shtok]

still noch [nokh]

stock exchange Börse, f. [BU(R)-zeh]

stocking Strumpf, m. [shtrumpf]

stomach Magen, m. [MAA-gen]

stomachache Magenschmer-zen, pl. [MAA-gen-shmehr-tsen]

stone Stein, m. [shtine]

stop (along the way) anhalten [AHN-hahl-ten]

stop, to stehenbleiben [SHTAY-en-blye-ben]

stoplight Ampel, m. [AHM-pel]

store Laden, m. [LAA-den]; Geschäft, n. [geh-SHEHFT]

storm Sturm, m. [shtoorm]

story (floor) Etage, f. [eh-TAH-zheh]

story (tale) Erzählung, f. [ehr-TSAY-lung]

straight gerade [geh-RAA-deh]

strange seltsam [ZEHLT-zahm]

strap Riemen, m. [REE-men]

straw Stroh, n. [shtroh]

strawberry Erdbeere, f. [EHRT-bay-reh]

street Straße, f. [SHTRAHS-eh]

streetcar Straßenbahn, f. [SHTRAHS-sen-baan]

string Schnur, f. [shnoor]

stripe Streifen, m. [SHTRIFE-en]

strong stark [shtahrk]

student Student, m. [shtu-DEHNT]

study, to studieren [shtu-DEE-ren]

style (fashion) Stil, m. [shteel]

suburb Vorort, m. [FOR-ort]

subway Untergrundbahn, f. [UN-te(r)-grunt-baan]

subway station U-bahnstation, f. [OO-baan-shtah-tsyohn]

success Erfolg, m. [ehr-FOLK]

suddenly plötzlich [PLU(R)TS-likh]

suede Wildleder, n. [VILT-lay-de(r)]

sugar Zucker, m. [TSU-ke(r)]

suit Anzug, m. [AHN-tsook]

suitcase Koffer, m. [KOF-fe(r)]

sum Summe, f. [ZOOM-meh]

summer Sommer, m. [ZOM-me(r)]

sun Sonne, f. [ZON-nen]

Sunday Sonntag, m. [ZON-taak]

sunglasses Sonnenbrille, f. [ZON-nen-bril-leh]

sunny sonnig [ZON-nikh]

suntan lotion Sonnenöl, n. [ZON-nen-u(r)l]

supermarket Supermarkt, m. [ZOO-pe(r)-mahrkt]

supper Abendessen, n. [AA-behnt-ehs-sen]

suppository Zäpfchen, n. [TSEHPF-khen]

sure sicher [ZIKH-e(r)]

surgery Chirurgie, f. [khee-roor-GEE]

swallow schlucken [SHLUK-en]

sweater Pullover, m. [pul-LOH-ve(r)]

sweet süß [zews]

swell, to anschwellen [AHN-shvehl-len]

swim, to schwimmen [SHVIM-men]

swimming suit Badeanzug, m. [BAA-deh-ahn-tsook]

swimming pool Schwimmbad, n. [SHVIM-baat]

Swiss schweizerisch [SHVYE-tseh-rish]

switch Schalter, m. [SHAHL-te(r)]

Switzerland die Schweiz [dee shvites]

swollen angeschwollen [AHN-geh-shvol-len]

symptom Symptom, n. [zewmp-TOHM]

synagogue Synagoge, f. [zew-nah-GOH-geh]

syrup (cough) Sirup, m. [ZEE-rup]

system System, n. [zews-TAYM]

T

table Tisch, m. [tish]

tablecloth Tischdecke, f. [TISH-deh-keh]

tablespoon Eßlöffel, m. [EHS-lu(r)-fel]

tailor Schneider, m. [SHNYE-de(r)]

take, to nehmen [NAY-men]

take a photo, to ein Foto machen [ine FOH-toh MAHKH-en]

take time, to dauern [DOW-ern]

ENGLISH/GERMAN

227

talk, to reden *[RAY-den]*
tall groß *[grohs]*
tan hellbraun *[HEHL-brown]*
tangerine Mandarine, f. *[mahn-dah-REE-neh]*
tap Wasserhahn, m. *[VAHS-se(r)-haan]*
tape Band, n. *[bahnt]*
tape recorder Tonbandgerät, n. *[TOHN-bahnt-geh-rayt]*
taste, to schmecken *[SHMEHK-en]*
tasty schmackhaft *[SHMAHK-hahft]*
tax-free steuerfrei *[STOY-e(r)-frye]*
taxi Taxi, n. *[TAHK-see]*
tea Tee, m. *[tay]*
team Mannschaft, f. *[MAHN-shahft]*
teaspoon Teelöffel, m. *[TAY-lu(r)-fel]*
teach, to lehren *[LEHR-en]*
tear, to reißen *[RICE-sen]*
telegram Telegram, n. *[tay-lay-GRAAM]*
telephone Telefon, n. *[tay-lay-FON]*
telephone, to anrufen *[AHN-roo-fen]*
telephone booth Telefonzelle, f. *[tay-lay-FON-tsehl-leh]*
telephone directory Telefonbuch, n. *[tay-lay-FON-bookh]*
television (set) Fernseher, m. *[FEHRN-zay-e(r)]*
telex, to ein Telex schicken *[ine TAY-lehks SHIK-en]*

tell, to erzählen *[ehr-TSAY-len]*
teller (bank) Kassierer, (-in), m., f. *[kah-SEE-re(r), {-reh-rin}]*
temple Tempel, m. *[TEHM-pel]*
temporary provisorisch *[pro-vee-ZOH-rish]*
ten zehn *[tsayn]*
tender zart *[tsahrt]*
tense gespannt *[geh-SHPAHNT]*
tent Zelt, n. *[tsehlt]*
tenth zehnte *[TSAYN-teh]*
than als *[ahls]*
thank, to danken *[DAHN-ken]*
thank you very much vielen Dank *[FEE-len dahnk]*
that jene (-r, -s) *[YEH-neh, {-ne(r), -nehs}]*
that (which) daß *[dahs]*
the der, die, das *[dehr, dee, dahs]*
theater Theater, n. *[tay-AA-te(r)]*
then dann *[dahn]*
there da *[daa]*; dort *[dort]*
there are (is) es gibt *[ehs gipt]*
therefore also *[AHL-zoh]*
thermometer Thermometer, n. *[tehr-mo-MAY-te(r)]*
they sie *[zee]*
thick dick *[dik]*
thief Dieb, m. *[deep]*
thigh Schenkel, m. *[SHEHN-kel]*
thin dünn *[dewn]*
thing Ding, n. *[ding]*; Sache, f. *[ZAHKH-eh]*
think, to denken *[DEHN-ken]*

think, to (belive)
glauben *[GLOW-ben]*
third dritte, -r, -s *[DRIT-teh,
{-te(r), -tehs}]*
thirsty, to be Durst
haben *[durst HAA-ben]*
thirteen dreizehn *[DRYE-
tsayn]*
thirty dreißig *[DRYE-sikh]*
this, these diese *[DEE-zeh,
{-ze(r), -zehs}]*
thousand tausend *[TOW-
zehnt]*
thread Faden, m. *[FAA-den]*
three drei *[drye]*
throat Hals, m. *[hahls]*
through durch *[durkh]*
thumb Daumen, m. *[DOW-
men]*
thunder Donner, m. *[DON-
ne(r)]*
Thursday Donnerstag,
m. *[DON-nehrs-taak]*
ticket Karte, f. *[KAHR-teh]*
tie Krawatte, f. *[krah-VAHT-
teh]*
tights Strumpfhose,
f. *[SHTRUMPF-hoh-zeh]*
till bis *[bis]*
time Zeit, f. *[tsite]*; Mal,
n. *[maal]*
timetable Fahrplan,
m. *[FAAR-plaan]*
tip Trinkgeld, m. *[TRINK-gehlt]*
tire (car) Reifen, m. *[RIFE-en]*
tired müde *[MEW-deh]*
tissue Papiertuch, n. *[pah-
PEER-tookh]*
to zu *[tsoo]*; nach *[nahkh]*
toast Toast, m. *[tohst]*

tobacco Tabak, m. *[TAH-
bahk]*
tobacco shop Tabakladen,
m. *[tah-BAHK-laa-den]*
today heute *[HOY-teh]*
toe Zehe, f. *[TSEH-eh]*
together zusammen *[tsoo-
ZAHM-men]*
toilet Toilette, f. *[toy-LEHT-teh]*
toilet paper Toilettenpapier,
n. *[toy-LEHT-ten-pah-peer]*
toll Gebühr, f. *[geh-BEWR]*
tomato Tomate, f. *[toh-MAH-
teh]*
tomb Grab, n. *[grahp]*
tomorrow morgen *[MOR-
gen]*
tongue Zunge, f. *[TSUN-geh]*
tonight heute abend *[HOY-
teh AA-behnt]*
too (also) auch *[owkh]*
too bad! schade! *[SHAA-deh]*
tool Werkzeug, n. *[VEHRK-
tsoyk]*
tooth Zahn, m. *[tsaan]*
toothache Zahnschmerzen,
pl. *[TSAAN-shmehrt-sen]*
toothbrush Zahnbürste,
f. *[TSAAN-bewr-steh]*
toothpaste Zahnpasta,
f. *[TSAAN-pahs-tah]*
top Spitze, f. *[SHPIT-seh]*
touch, to berühren *[beh-REW-
ren]*
tough zäh *[tsay]*
tour Rundfahrt, f. *[RUNT-
faart]*
tourism Tourismus, m. *[too-
RIS-moos]*
tourist Tourist, m. *[too-RIST]*

229

tourist office
Fremdenverkehrsbüro,
n. *[FREHM-den-fehr-kehrs-bew-roh]*

toward(s) gegen *[GAY-gen]*

towel Handtuch, n. *[HAHNT-tookh]*

tower Turm, m. *[toorm]*

town Stadt, f. *[shtaht]*

town hall Rathaus, n. *[RAAT-hows]*

toy Spielzeug, n. *[SHPEEL-tsoyk]*

toy shop Spielwarenladen,
n. *[SHPEEL-vaa-ren-laa-den]*

track (train) Gleis, n. *[glice]*

traffic Verkehr, m. *[fehr-KEHR]*

traffic jam Stau, m. *[shtow]*

traffic light Ampel, f. *[AHM-pel]*

trailer Wohnwagen,
m. *[VOHN-vaa-gen]*

train Zug, m. *[tsook]*

train station Bahnhof,
m. *[BAAN-hohf]*

transfer, to überweisen *[ew-be(r)-VYE-zen]*

translate, to übersetzen *[ew-be(r)-ZEHT-sen]*

transmission Getriebe,
n. *[geh-TREE-beh]*

trash Abfall, m. *[AHP-fahl]*

travel, to reisen *[RYE-zen]*

travel agency Reisebüro,
n. *[RYE-zeh-bew-roh]*

traveler's check
Reisescheck, m. *[RYE-zeh-shehk]*

treasure Schatz, m. *[shahts]*

treat, to behandeln *[beh-HAHN-deln]*

treatment Behandlung,
f. *[beh-HAHNT-lung]*

tree Baum, m. *[bowm]*

trip Reise, f. *[RYE-zeh]*

trousers Hose, f. *[HOH-zeh]*

trout Forelle, f. *[fo-REHL-leh]*

truck Lastwagen, m. *[LAHST-vaa-gen]*

true wahr *[vaar]*

trunk (car) Kofferraum,
m. *[KOF-fe(r)-rowm]*

try, to versuchen *[fehr-ZOO-khen]*; probieren *[pro-BEER-en]*

try on, to anprobieren *[AHN-pro-beer-en]*

tube Tube, f. *[TOO-beh]*

Tuesday Dienstag,
m. *[DEENS-taak]*

turkey Truthahn, m. *[TROOT-haan]*

turn Kurve, f. *[KOOR-veh]*

turn, to drehen *[DREH-en]*

turn, to (direction)
abbiegen *[AHP-bee-gen]*

turn signal Blinker,
m. *[BLIN-ke(r)]*

tuxedo Smoking, m. *[SMOH-king]*

twelve zwölf *[tsvu(r)lf]*

twenty zwanzig *[TSVAHN-tsikh]*

twice zweimal *[TSVYE-maal]*

two zwei *[tsvye]*

type (sort) Art, f. *[ahrt]*;
Sorte, f. *[ZOR-teh]*

typewriter Schreibmaschine,
f. *[SHRIPE-mah-shee-neh]*

typical typisch *[TEW-pish]*

U

ugly häßlich *[HEHS-likh]*

ulcer Geschwür, n. *[geh-SHVEWR]*

umbrella Regenschirm, m. *[RAY-gen-shirm]*

uncle Onkel, m. *[OHN-kel]*

uncomfortable unbequem *[UN-beh-kvaym]*

unconscious bewußtlos *[beh-VUST-lohs]*

under unter *[UN-te(r)]*

underdone nicht durchgebraten *[nikht durkh-geh-BRAA-ten]*

underpants Unterhose, f. *[UN-te(r)-hoh-zeh]*

undershirt Unterhemd, n. *[UN-te(r)-hehmt]*

understand, to verstehen *[fehr-SHTAY-en]*

underwear Unterwäsche, f. *[UN-te(r)-veh-sheh]*

unfortunately leider *[LYE-de(r)]*

unhappy unglücklich *[UN-glewk-likh]*

unique einzigartig *[INE-tsikh-ahr-tikh]*

United Kingdom das Vereinigte Königreich *[dahs fehr-eye-nikh-teh KU(R)-nikh-ryekh]*

United States die Vereinigten Staaten (von Amerika) *[dee fehr-EYE-nikh-ten SHTAA-ten {fon ah-MEH-ri-kah}]*

university Universität, f. *[u-nee-vehr-zi-TAYT]*

until bis *[bis]*

up oben *[OH-ben]*; hinauf *[hin-OWF]*

upper obere *[OH-beh-reh]*

upside down verkehrt herum *[vehr-KEHRT hehr-ROOM]*

upset stomach Magenverstimmung, f. *[MAA-gen-fehr-shtim-nung]*

urgent dringend *[DRING-ent]*

use (purpose) Verwendung, f. *[fehr-VEHN-dung]*

use, to benutzen *[beh-NUT-sen]*

used gebraucht *[geh-BROWKHT]*

useful nützlich *[NEWTS-likh]*

usual gewöhnlich *[geh-VU(R)N-likh]*

V

vacant frei *[frye]*

vacation Ferien, pl. *[FEHR-yen]*

valid gültig *[GEWL-tikh]*

valley Tal, n. *[taal]*

value Wert, m. *[vehrt]*

valuable wertvoll *[VEHRT-fol]*

value-added-tax Mehrwertsteuer, f. *[MEHR-vehrt-shtoy-e(r)]*

veal Kalbfleisch, n. *[KAHLP-flyshe]*

vegetable Gemüse, n. *[geh-MEW-zeh]*

vegetarian vegetarisch *[veh-geh-TAH-rish]*

velvet Samt, m. *[zahmt]*

verify, to bestätigen *[beh-SHTAY-tig-en]*

vertical senkrecht *[ZEHNK-rehkht]*

231

very sehr *[zehr]*
vest Weste, f. *[VEHS-teh]*
veterinarian Tierarzt, m. *[TEER-ahrtst]*
via über *[EW-be(r)]*
Vienna Wien, n. *[veen]*
vice versa umgekehrt *[OOM-geh-kehrt]*
view Aussicht, f. *[OWS-zikht]*
village Dorf, n. *[dorf]*
vinegar Essig, m. *[EHS-sikh]*
vineyard Weinberg, m. *[VINE-behrk]*
visa Visum, n. *[VEE-zoom]*
visit Besuch, m. *[beh-ZOOKH]*
visit, to besuchen *[beh-ZOO-khen]*
voice Stimme, f. *[SHTIM-meh]*
voltage Stromspannung, f. *[SHTROHM-shpah-nung]*
vomit, to sich erbrechen *[zikh ehr-BREHKH-en]*

W

wait, to warten *[VAAR-ten]*
waiter Kellner, m. *[KEHL-ner]*
waiting room Wartesaal, m. *[VAAR-teh-zaal]*
waitress Kellnerin, f. *[KEHL-neh-rin]*
wake, to wecken *[VEHK-en]*
wake up, to aufwachen *[OWF-vahkh-en]*
walk Spaziergang, m. *[shpah-TSEER-gahng]*
walk, to (zu Fuß) gehen *[{tsoo foos} GAY-en]*
wall (exterior) Mauer, f. *[MOW-e(r)]*
wall (interior) Wand, f. *[vahnt]*

wallet Brieftasche, f. *[BREEF-tahsh-eh]*
want, to wollen *[VOL-len]*
war Krieg, m. *[kreek]*
warm warm *[vahrm]*
wash, to waschen *[VAHSH-en]*
wash and wear bügelfrei *[BEW-gel-frye]*
washbasin Waschbecken, n. *[VAHSH-beh-ken]*
waste of time Zeitverschwendung, f. *[TSITE-vehr-shvehn-dung]*
watch Uhr, f. *[oor]*
watchmaker Uhrmacher, m. *[OOR-mahkh-e(r)]*
watch, to beobachten *[beh-OH-bahkh-ten]*
watch out, to aufpassen *[OWF-pahs-sen]*
water Wasser, n. *[VAHS-e(r)]*
waterfall Wasserfall, m. *[VAHS-se(r)-fahl]*
waterproof wasserdicht *[VAHS-se(r)-dikht]*
wave Welle, f. *[VEHL-leh]*
way Weg, m. *[vehk]*
we wir *[veer]*
weak schwach *[shvahkh]*
wear, to tragen *[TRAA-gen]*
weather Wetter, n. *[VEHT-te(r)]*
weather forecast Wetterbericht, m. *[VEHT-te(r)-beh-rikht]*
wedding Hochzeit, f. *[HOKH-tsite]*
Wednesday Mittwoch, m. *[MIT-vokh]*
week Woche, f. *[VOKH-eh]*

weekend Wochenende, n. *[VOKH-en-ehn-deh]*

weigh, to wiegen *[VEE-gen]*

weight Gewicht, n. *[geh-VIKHT]*

well gut *[goot]*; wohl *[vohl]*

well Brunnen, m. *[BRUN-nen]*

well-done (meat) gut durchgebraten *[goot durkh-geh-BRAA-ten]*

well-known bekannt *[beh-KAHNT]*

west West(en), m. *[VEHST {-en}]*

West Germany Bundesrepublik, f. *[BUN-dehs-reh-poo-bleek]*

wet naβ *[nahs]*

what was *[vahs]*

wheel Rad, n. *[raat]*

when wann *[vahn]*; wenn *[vehn]*

where wo *[voh]*

which welche (-r, -s) *[VEHL-kheh, {-khe(r), -khehs}]*

white weiβ *[vice]*

who wer *[vehr]*

whole ganz *[gahnts]*

why warum *[vah-ROOM]*

wide breit *[brite]*; weit *[vite]*

widow Witwe, f. *[VIT-veh]*

widower Witwer, m. *[VIT-ve(r)]*

wife Frau, f. *[frow]*; Ehefrau, f. *[AY-eh-frow]*

wild wild *[vilt]*

win, to gewinnen *[geh-VIN-nen]*

wind Wind, m. *[vint]*

window Fenster, n. *[FEHN-ste(r)]*

windshield Windschutz-scheibe, f. *[VINT-shuts-shye-beh]*

wine Wein, m. *[vine]*

wine list Weinkarte, f. *[VINE-kahr-teh]*

wine shop Weinladen, m. *[VINE-laa-den]*

wing Flügel, m. *[FLEW-gel]*

winter Winter, m. *[VIN-te(r)]*

wire Draht, m. *[draht]*

wish Wunsch, m. *[voonsh]*

wish, to wünschen *[VEWN-shen]*

with mit *[mit]*

without ohne *[OH-neh]*

woman Frau, f. *[frow]*

wonderful wunderbar *[VUN-de(r)-baar]*

wood Holz, n. *[holts]*

wool Wolle, f. *[VOL-leh]*

word Wort, n. *[vort]*

work Arbeit, f. *[AHR-bite]*

work, to arbeiten *[AHR-bite-en]*

workday Arbeitstag, m. *[AHR-bites-taak]*

world Welt, f. *[vehlt]*

worry Sorge, f. *[ZOR-geh]*

worse schlechter *[SHLEHKH-te(r)]*

worthless wertlos *[VEHRT-lohs]*

would würde *[VU(R)-deh]*

would like möchten *[MU(R)KH-ten]*

wound Wunde, f. *[VUN-deh]*

wrap, to einwickeln *[INE-vi-keln]*

wrist Handgelenk, n. *[HAHNT-geh-lehnk]*

233

wristwatch Armbanduhr,
f. *[AHRM-bahnt-oor]*
write, to schreiben *[SHRYE-ben]*
writer Schriftsteller,
m. *[SHRIFT-shtehl-le(r)]*
wrong falsch *[fahlsh]*

X

X ray Röntgenaufname,
f. *[RU(R)NT-gen-owf-naa-meh]*

Y

year Jahr, n. *[yaar]*
yellow gelb *[gehlp]*
yes ja *[yaa]*
yesterday gestern *[GEHS-tern]*

yet noch *[nohkh]*
yield, to (traffic) Vorfahrt
gewähren *[FOR-faart geh-VAY-ren]*
you du, Sie, ihr *[doo, zee, eer]*
young jung *[yung]*
youth hostel
Jugendherberge, f. *[YOO-gehnt-hehr-behr-geh]*

Z

zero null *[nul]*
zip code Postleitzahl,
f. *[POST-lite-tsaal]*
zipper Reißverschluß,
m. *[RICE-fehr-shlus]*
zoo Zoo, m. *[tsoh]*;
Tierpark, m. *[TEER-pahrk]*

GERMAN-ENGLISH DICTIONARY

List of Abbreviations
m. masculine
f. feminine
n. neuter
pl. plural

A

Aal, m. *[aal]* eel

abbiegen *[AHP-bee-gen]* to turn (direction)

Abend, m. *[AA-behnt]* evening

Abendessen, n. *[AA-behnt-ehs-sen]* dinner; supper

Abendkleid, n. *[AA-behnt-klite]* evening gown

aber *[AA-be(r)]* but

abfahren *[AHP-faa-ren]* to leave (depart)

Abfahrt, f. *[AHP-faart]* departure

Abfall, m. *[AHP-fahl]* garbage; trash

Abflug, m. *[AHP-flook]* departure

Abführmittel, n. *[AHP-fewr-mit-tel]* laxative

Abgase, pl. *[AHP-gaa-zeh]* exhaust (car)

abholen *[AHP-hoh-len]* to pick up

Abkürzung, f. *[AHP-kewr-tsung]* abbreviation

ablehnen *[AHP-lay-nen]* to refuse

abnehmen *[AHP-nay-men]* to lose weight

absagen *[AHP-zaa-gen]* to cancel

Absatz, m. *[AHP-zahts]* heel

abschließen *[AHP-shlees-sen]* to lock

Absender, m. *[AHP-zehn-de(r)]* sender (mail)

Abszeß, m. *[ahps-TSEHS]* abscess

Abtei, f. *[ahp-TYE]* abbey

Abteil, n. *[AHP-tile]* compartment

Abteilung, f. *[ahp-TYE-lung]* department

Abzug, m. *[AHP-tsook]* print (photo)

acht *[ahkht]* eight

achte (-r, -s) *[AHKH-teh {-te(r), -tehs}]* eighth

Achtung, f. *[AHKH-tung]* attention

achtzehn *[AHKH-tsayn]* eighteen

achtzig *[AHKH-tsikh]* eighty

Adresse, f. *[ah-DREHS-seh]* address

ähneln *[AY-neln]* to resemble

Aktentasche, f. *[AAK-ten-tahsh-eh]* briefcase

Alkohol, m. *[AHL-koh-hol]* liquor

alkoholfreies Getränk, n. *[AHL-koh-hohl-frye-ehs geh-TREHNK]* soft drink

alle *[AH-leh]* all

235

Allee, f. *[ah-LAY]* avenue
allein *[ah-LINE]* alone
allergisch *[ah-LEHR-gish]* allergic
alles *[AH-lehs]* everything
alles Gute! *[AH-lehs GOO-teh]* best wishes!
allgemein *[AHL-geh-mine]* general
Alpen, pl. *[AHL-pen]* Alps
als *[ahls]* as; than
also *[AHL-zoh]* therefore
alt *[ahlt]* old
Alter, n. *[AHL-te(r)]* age
Amerikaner(in), m., f. *[ah-meh-ri-KAH-ne(r) {neh-rin}]* American
Amerika, n. *[ah-MEH-ri-kah]* America
amerikanisch *[ah-meh-ri-KAH-nish]* American
Ampel, f. *[AHM-pel]* traffic light
Amt, n. *[ahmt]* office
an *[ahn]* at; on
Ananas, f. *[AH-nah-nahs]* pineapple
anbieten *[ahn-BEE-ten]* to offer
Andenken, n. *[AHN-dehn-ken]* souvenir
andere *[AHN-deh-reh]* other
Anfang, m. *[AHN-fahng]* beginning
anfangen *[AHN-fahng-en]* to begin
Anfänger, m. *[AHN-fehn-ge(r)]* beginner
angeln *[AHN-geln]* to fish
angenehm *[AHN-geh-naym]* pleasant

angeschwollen *[AHN-geh-shvol-len]* swollen
Angst, f. *[ahngst]* fear
Angst haben *[ahngst HAA-ben]* to fear
Angst haben vor etwas *[ahngst HAA-ben for EHT-vahs]* to be afraid of something
anhalten *[AHN-hahl-ten]* stop (along the way)
Anhalter, m. *[AHN-hahl-te(r)]* hitchhiker
ankommen *[AHN-kom-men]* to arrive
Ankuft, f. *[AHN-kunft]* arrival
Anlasser, m. *[AHN-lahs-se(r)]* starter (car)
annehmen *[AHN-nay-men]* to accept
anprobieren *[AHN-pro-beer-en]* to try on
Anruf, m. *[AHN-roof]* call (telephone)
anrufen *[AHN-roo-fen]* to call (telephone)
Anschluβ, m. *[AHN-shloos]* connection (train)
anschwellen *[AHN-shvehl-len]* to swell
ansehen *[AHN-zay-en]* to look at
anspringen *[AHN-shpring-en]* to start (a car)
Antibioticum, n. *[ahn-ti-bee-OH-ti-koom]* antibiotic
Antiquität, f. *[ahn-tik-vee-TAYT]* antique
Antisepticum, n. *[ahn-ti-ZEHP-ti-koom]* antiseptic
Antwort, f. *[AHNT-vort]* answer

antworten [AHNT-vor-ten] to answer

Anzeige, f. [AHN-tsye-geh] notice

anziehen [AHN-tsee-en] to put on (dress)

sich anziehen [zikh AHN-tsee-en] to dress oneself; to get dressed

anziehend [AHN-tsee-ent] attractive

Anzug, m. [AHN-tsook] suit

anzünden [AHN-tsewn-den] to light

Apfel, m. [AHP-fel] apple

Apfelsaft, m. [AHP-fehl-zahft] cider

Apotheke, f. [ah-poh-TAY-keh] pharmacy

Aprikose, f. [ahp-ri-KOH-zeh] apricot

April, m. [ah-PRIL] April

Arbeit, f. [AHR-bite] work

arbeiten [AHR-bite-en] to work

Arbeitsstunden, pl. [AHR-bites-shtun-den] working hours

Arbeitstag, m. [AHR-bites-taak] workday

ärgern [EHR-gern] to annoy; to bother

Arm, m. [ahrm] arm

arm [ahrm] poor

Armband, n. [AHRM-bahnt] bracelet

Armbanduhr, f. [AHRM-bahnt-oor] wristwatch

Ärmel, m. [EHR-mel] sleeve

Art, f. [ahrt] kind (type); type (sort)

Artikel, m. [ahr-TEE-kel] article

Arzt, m. [ahrtst]; **Ärztin,** f. [EHRTS-tin] doctor

ärztlich [EHRTS-likh] medical

Aschenbecher, m. [AHSH-en-behkh-e(r)] ashtray

Aspirin, n. [ahs-pi-REEN] aspirin

Asthma, n. [AHST-mah] asthma

atmen [AAT-men] to breathe

Aubergine, f. [o-ber-ZHEE-neh] eggplant

auch [owkh] also; too (also)

auf [owf] on

Aufenthalt, m. [OWF-ehnt-hahlt] stay

Aufgabe, f. [OWF-gaa-beh] job (task); lesson

aufgeben [OWF-gay-ben] to check (luggage); to mail

aufmachen [OWF-mahkh-en] to open

Aufmerksamkeit, f. [OWF-mehrk-saam-kite] attention

Aufnahme, f. [OWF-naa-meh] recording

aufpassen [OWF-pahs-sen] to be careful; to look out; to watch out

aufstehen [OWF-shteh-en] to get up; to stand up

aufwachen [OWF-vahkh-en] to wake up

Auge, n. [OW-geh] eye

Augenblick, m. [OW-gen-blik] moment

Augenbraue, f. [OW-gen-brow-eh] eyebrow

Augenlid, n. *[OW-gen-leet]* eyelid

Augenwimper, f. *[OW-gen-vim-pe(r)]* eyelash

August, m. *[ow-GUST]* August

aus *[ows]* over (finished); out

Ausdruck, m. *[OWS-druk]* phrase

Ausflug, m. *[OWS-flook]* excursion

ausfüllen *[OWS-fewl-len]* to fill in

Ausgang, m. *[OWS-gahng]* exit

ausgeben *[OWS-gay-ben]* to spend (money)

ausgezeichnet *[OWS-geh-tsyekh-net]* excellent

Auskunft, f. *[OWS-kunft]* information

Ausland, n. *[im OWS-lahnt]* abroad

Ausländer (-in), m., f. *[OWS-lehn-de(r) {-deh-rin}]* foreigner

Ausrede, f. *[OWS-ray-deh]* excuse

sich ausruhen *[zikh OWS-roo-en]* to rest

Ausrüstung, f. *[OWS-rews-tung]* equipment; outfit

außerhalb *[OWS-se(r)-hahlp]* outside of

Aussicht, f. *[OWS-zikht]* view

Aussprache, f. *[OWS-shprahkh-eh]* pronunciation

aussteigen *[OWS-shtye-gen]* to get off; to get out

Ausstellung, f. *[OWS-shtehl-lung]* exhibition

Austausch, m. *[OWS-towsh]* exchange

Auster, f. *[OW-ste(r)]* oyster

Ausverkauf, m. *[OWS-fehr-kowf]* sale (low prices)

ausverkauft *[OWS-fehr-kowft]* sold out

Auswahl, f. *[OWS-vaal]* selection

auswählen *[OWS-vay-len]* to choose

Ausweis, m. *[OWS-vice]* identity card; pass (permit)

Auto, n. *[OW-toh]* car

automatisch *[ow-toh-MAH-tish]* automatic

Autopanne, f. *[OW-toh-pahn-neh]* car breakdown

Autovermietung, f. *[OW-toh-fehr-mee-tung]* car rental agency

B

Baby, n. *[BAY-bee]* baby

Babysitter, m. *[BAY-bee-sit-e(r)]* babysitter

backen *[BAH-ken]* to bake

Bäckerei, f. *[beh-keh-RYE]* bakery

Backpflaume, f. *[BAHK-pflow-meh]* prune

Bad, n. *[baat]* bath, bathroom

Badeanzug, m. *[BAA-deh-ahn-tsook]* bathing suit

Bademantel, m. *[BAA-deh-mahn-tel]* robe

baden *[BAA-den]* to bath

Badewanne, f. *[BAA-deh-vah-neh]* bathtub

Bahnhof, m. *[BAAN-hohf]*
train station

Bahnsteig, m. *[BAAN-shtike]*
platform (station)

bald *[bahlt]* soon

Balkon, m. *[BAHL-kon]*
balcony

Ball, m. *[bahl]* ball

Ballett, n. *[bah-LEHT]* ballet

Band, n. *[bahnt]* ribbon; tape

Bank, f. *[bahnk]* bank
(finance)

Bargeld, n. *[BAAR-gehlt]* cash

Barscheck, m. *[BAAR-shehk]*
personal check

Bart, m. *[bahrt]* beard

Batterie, f. *[bah-teh-REE]*
battery

Bauernhof, m. *[BOW-ehrn-
hohf]* farm

Baum, m. *[bowm]* tree

Baumwolle, f. *[BOWM-vol-leh]*
cotton

bedauern *[beh-DOW-ern]* to
regret

bedeuten *[beh-DOY-ten]* to
mean

Bedeutung, f. *[beh-DOY-tung]*
meaning

Bedienung, f. *[beh-DEE-nung]*
service

beenden *[beh-EHN-den]* to
end

beginnen *[beh-GIN-nen]* to
start

begleiten *[beh-GLYE-ten]* to
accompany

Begrenzung, f. *[beh-GREHN-
tsung]* limit

behalten *[beh-HAHL-ten]* to
keep

behandeln *[beh-HAHN-deln]*
to treat

Behandlung, f. *[beh-HAHNT-
lung]* treatment

behindert *[beh-HIN-dert]*
handicapped

Behinderte, m., f. *[beh-HIN-
dehr-teh]* disabled

bei *[bye]* at

beide *[BYE-deh]* both

Bein, n. *[bine]* leg

Beispiel, n. *[BYE-shpeel]*
example

beißen *[BICE-sen]* to bite

bekannt *[beh-KAHNT]* well-
known

Bekannte, m., f. *[beh-KAHN-
teh]* acquaintance

bekommen *[beh-KOM-men]*
to get (fetch); to obtain

bemerken *[beh-MEHR-ken]* to
notice

benutzen *[beh-NUT-sen]* to
use

Benzin, n. *[behn-TSEEN]*
gasoline

beobachten *[beh-OH-bahkh-
ten]* to watch

bequem *[beh-KVEHM]*
comfortable

berechnen *[beh-REHKH-nen]*
to charge

bereit *[beh-RITE]* ready

Berg, m. *[behrk]* mountain

Beruf, m. *[beh-ROOF]*
occupation; profession

berühren *[beh-REW-ren]* to
touch

beschäftigt *[beh-SHEHF-tikht]*
busy

beschützen [beh-SHEWT-sen] to protect

Beschwerde, f. [beh-SHVEHR-deh] complaint

besetzt [beh-ZEHTST] occupied

Besichtigung, f. [beh-ZIKH-ti-gung] sightseeing

Besitz, m. [beh-ZITS] property

besitzen [beh-ZIT-sen] to own

Besitzer, m. [beh-ZIT-se(r)] owner

besondere [beh-ZON-deh-reh] special

besonders [beh-ZON-dehrs] especially

besser [BEHS-se(r)] better

bestätigen [beh-SHTAY-ti-gen] to confirm; to verify

beste [BEHS-teh] best

Besteck, n. [beh-SHTEHK] silverwear

bestellen [beh-SHTEHL-len] to order

Bestellung, f. [beh-SHTEHL-lung] order

bestimmt [beh-SHTIMT] certainly

Besuch, m. [beh-ZOOKH] visit

besuchen [beh-ZOO-khen] to visit

Bete, f. [BAY-teh] beet

Betrag, m. [beh-TRAHK] amount

außer Betrieb [OWS-se(r) beh-TREEP] out of order

betrunken [beh-TRUN-ken] drunk

Bett, n. [beht] bed

Bettlaken, n. [BEHT-lah-ken] sheet

bewölkt [beh-VU(R)KT] cloudy

bewundern [beh-VOON-dern] to admire

bewußtlos [beh-VUST-lohs] unconscious

bezahlen [beh-TSAA-len] to pay

Bezirk, m. [beh-TSIRK] district

BH (Büstenhalter), m. [bay-hah, BEWS-ten-hahl-te(r)] bra

Bibliothek, f. [bib-lee-oh-TAYK] library

Bier, n. [beer] beer

Biergarten, m. [BEER-gahr-ten] beer garden

Bierkrug, m. [BEER-krook] beer stein

Bild, n. [bilt] painting; picture

bildende Künste, pl. [BIL-den-deh KEWN-steh] fine arts

Billard, n. [BIL-yahrt] pool (game)

billig [BIL-likh] cheap

Birne, f. [BEER-neh] pear

bis [bis] until; till

bitte [BIT-teh] please

Wie bitte? [vee BIT-teh] pardon

bitten [BIT-ten] to ask; to request

bitter [BIT-te(r)] bitter

Blase, f. [BLAA-zeh] bladder

blau [blow] blue

bleiben [BLYE-ben] to stay (remain)

Bleistift, m. [BLYE-shtift] pencil

Blinddarmentzündung, f. [BLINT-dahr-mehnt-tsewn-dung] appendicitis

Blinker, m. [BLIN-ke(r)] turn signal

Blitz, m. *[blits]* lighting

Blitzlicht, n. *[BLITS-likht]* flash (on camera)

blond *[blont]* blond

Blume, f. *[BLOO-meh]* flower

Blumengeschäft, n. *[BLOO-men-geh-shehft]* florist's

Blumenkohl, m. *[BLOO-men-kohl]* cauliflower

Bluse, f. *[BLOO-zeh]* blouse

Blut, n. *[bloot]* blood

Blutdruck, m. *[BLOOT-druk]* blood pressure

bluten *[BLOO-ten]* to bleed

blutig *[BLOO-tikh]* rare (uncooked)

Boden, m. *[BOH-den]* floor; ground

Bohne, f. *[BOH-neh]* bean

Bonbon, n. *[bong-BONG]* candy

Boot, n. *[boht]* boat

Bordkarte, f. *[BOHRT-kahr-teh]* boarding pass

borgen, *[BOR-gen]* to borrow

Börse, f. *[BU(R)-zeh]* stock exchange

böse *[BU(R)-zeh]* angry

botanischer Garten, m. *[bo-TAA-nish-e(r) GAAR-ten]* botanical garden

Botschaft, f. *[BOHT-shahft]* embassy

Brandwunde, f. *[BRAHNT-vun-deh]* burn

braten *[BRAA-ten]* to fry; to roast

brauchen *[BROW-khen]* to need

braun *[brown]* brown

breit *[brite]* wide

Bremsen, pl. *[BREHM-zen]* brakes

brennen *[BREHN-nen]* to burn

Brief, m. *[breef]* letter

Briefkasten, m. *[BREEF-kahs-ten]* letterbox; mailbox

Briefmarke, f. *[BREEF-mahr-keh]* stamp (postage)

Brieftasche, f. *[BREEF-tahsh-eh]* pocketbook; wallet

Brille, f. *[BRIL-leh]* eyeglasses

bringen *[BRIN-gen]* to bring

Brite, Britin, m.,f. *[BRI-teh, BRI-tin]* British

Broche, f. *[BRO-sheh]* brooch

Brot, n. *[broht]* bread

Brötchen, pl. *[BRU(R)T-khen]* rolls (bread)

Bruch, m. *[brukh]* fracture

Brücke, f. *[BREW-keh]* bridge

Bruder, m. *[BROO-de(r)]* brother

Brunnen, m. *[BRUN-nen]* fountain; well

Brust, f. *[broost]* breast; chest (part of body)

Buch, n. *[bookh]* book

Buchhandlung, f. *[BOOKH-hahnd-lung]* bookstore

Büchse, f. *[BEWK-seh]* can (container)

Büchsenöffner, m. *[BEWK-sen-u(r)f-ne(r)]* can opener

buchstabieren *[bookh-shtah-BEE-ren]* to spell

Bügeleisen, n. *[BEW-gel-eye-zen]* iron (flatiron)

bügelfrei *[BEW-gel-frye]* wash and wear

bügeln *[BEW-geln]* to iron

Bundesrepublik Deutschland, f. *[BUN-dehs-reh-poo-bleek DOYCH-lahnt]* West Germany

Burg, f. *[boork]* fortress

Bürger *[BEWR-ge(r)]* citizen

bürgerlich *[BEWR-ge(r)-likh]* middle-class

Bürgersteig, m. *[BEWR-ge(r)-shtike]* sidewalk

Büro, n. *[bew-ROH]* agency; office

Bürste, f. *[BEWR-steh]* brush

bürsten *[BEWR-sten]* to brush

Bus, m. *[bus]* bus; coach

Bushaltestelle, f. *[BUS-hahl-teh-shtehl-leh]* bus stop

Butter, f. *[BUT-te(r)]* butter

C

Café, n. *[kah-FAY]* café

Campingplatz, m. *[KAHM-ping-plahts]* camp site

Chef, m. *[shehf]* boss

chemische Reinigung, f. *[KHAY-mish-eh RYE-ni-gung]* dry-cleaning

Chirurgie, f. *[khee-roor-GEE]* surgery

Creme, f. *[kraym]* cream (cosmetic)

D

da *[daa]* there

Dach, n. *[dahkh]* roof

Dame, f. *[DAA-meh]* lady

Damenbinde, f. *[DAA-men-bin-deh]* sanitary napkin

Damentoilette, f. *[DAA-men-toy-leht-teh]* ladies' room

Dänemark, n. *[DEH-neh-mahrk]* Denmark

vielen Dank *[FEE-len dahnk]* thank you very much

danken *[DAHN-ken]* to thank

dann *[dahn]* then

Datum, n. *[DAA-tum]* date (calendar)

dauern *[DOW-ern]* to last; to take time

Dauerwelle, f. *[DOW-e(r)-vehl-leh]* permanent wave

Daumen, m. *[DOW-men]* thumb

das *[dahs]* the

daß *[dahs]* that (which)

DDR, f. *[day-day-ehr]* East Germany

Decke, f. *[DEH-keh]* blanket; ceiling

decken *[DEHK-en]* to cover

denken *[DEHN-ken]* to think

Denkmal, n. *[DEHNK-maal]* monument

der *[dehr]* the

desinfizieren *[dehs-in-fi-TSEE-ren]* to disinfect

deutsch *[doych]* German

Deutschland *[DOYCH-lahnt]* Germany

Dezember, m. *[deh-TSEHM-be(r)]* December

Dia, n. *[DEE-ah]* slide (photo)

Diabetiker, m. *[dee-ah-BAY-ti-ke(r)]* diabetic

Diät, f. *[dee-AYT]* diet

dick *[dik]* fat; thick

die *[dee]* the

Dieb m. *[deep]* thief

dienen *[DEE-nen]* to serve

Dienstag, m. *[DEENS-taak]* Tuesday

diese, -r, -s *[DEE-zeh, {-ze(r), -zehs}]* this, these

Dieselöl, n. *[DEE-zel-u(r)l]* diesel fuel

Ding, n. *[ding]* thing

direkt *[dee-REHKT]* direct

Dirigent, m. *[di-ri-GEHNT]* conductor (orchestra)

Dokument, n. *[do-koo-MEHNT]* document

Dollar, m. *[DOL-lahr]* dollar

Dom, m. *[dohm]* cathedral

Donner, m. *[DON-ne(r)]* thunder

Donnerstag, m. *[DON-nehrs-taak]* Thursday

Doppelbett, n. *[DOP-pehl-beht]* double bed

Doppelzimmer, n. *[DOP-pehl-tsim-me(r)]* double room

Dorf, n. *[dorf]* village

dort *[dort]* there

Dose, f. *[DOH-seh]* can (container)

Draht, m. *[draht]* wire

Drama, n. *[DRAA-mah]* drama

draußen *[DROWS-sen]* outdoors

drehen *[DREH-en]* to turn

drei *[drye]* three

dreißig *[DRYES-sikh]* thirty

dreizehn *[DRYE-tsayn]* thirteen

dringend *[DRING-ent]* urgent

drinnen *[DRIN-nen]* inside

dritte, -r, -s *[DRIT-teh, {-te(r), -tehs}]* third

Drogerie, f. *[dro-geh-REE]* drugstore

Druck, m. *[druk]* pressure

drucken *[DRUK-en]* to print

drücken *[DREWK-en]* to press; to push (a button)

du *[doo]* you

dunkel *[DUN-kel]* dark

dünn *[dewn]* thin

durch *[durkh]* across (movement); by; through

Durchfall, m. *[DURKH-fahl]* diarrhea

durchgebraten *[durkh-geh-BRAA-ten]* well-done (meat)

durchschnittlich *[DURKH-shnit-likh]* average

Durst haben *[durst HAA-ben]* to be thirsty

Dusche, f. *[DOO-sheh]* shower

Dutzend, n. *[DUT-sehnt]* dozen

E

Ebbe, f. *[EHB-eh]* low tide

Ebene, f. *[AY-beh-neh]* level

echt *[ehkht]* genuine; real

Ecke, f. *[EH-keh]* corner

Ehefrau, f. *[AY-eh-frow]* wife

Ehemann, m. *[AY-eh-mahn]* husband

Eier, pl. *[EYE-e(r)]* eggs

eigentlich *[EYE-gehnt-likh]* actually

eilen *[EYE-len]* to hurry

es eilig haben *[ehs EYE-likh HAA-ben]* to be in a hurry

ein(-e) *[ine, INE-eh]* a, an

Einbahnstraße, f. *[INE-baan-shtrahs-seh]* one-way street

eindrucksvoll *[INE-druks-fol]* impressive

Eingang, m. *[INE-gahng]* entrance

Eingangshalle, f. *[INE-gahngs-hahl-leh]* lobby

einheimisch *[INE-hye-mish]* native

einige *[INE-i-geh]* some; few

Einkäufe, pl. *[INE-koy-feh]* purchases

einkaufen gehen *[INE-kow-fen GAY-en]* to go shopping

Einkaufszentrum, n. *[INE-kowfs-tsehn-trum]* shopping center

einladen *[INE-laa-den]* to invite

einlaufen *[INE-low-fen]* shrink

einlösen *[INE-lu(r)-zen]* to cash

einmal *[INE-maal]* once

eins *[ines]* one

einschenken *[INE-shehn-ken]* to pour

per Einschreiben *[pehr INE-shrye-ben]* registered mail

einstellen *[INE-shtehl-len]* to adjust

Eintopf, m. *[INE-topf]* stew

sich eintragen *[zikh INE-traa-gen]* to register

Eintritt, m. *[INE-trit]* admission

Eintrittsgeld, n. *[INE-trits-gehlt]* admission fee; entrance fee

einverstanden, *[INE-fehr-shtahn-den]* agreed

einwickeln *[INE-vi-keln]* to wrap

Einzelzimmer, n. *[INE-tsel-tsim-me(r)]* single room

einzigartig *[INE-tsikh-ahr-tikh]* unique

Eis, n. *[ice]* ice; ice cream

Eisbahn, f. *[ICE-baan]* skating ring

Eisen, n. *[EYE-zen]* iron (metal)

Eisenbahn, f. *[EYE-zen-baan]* railroad

Eisenwarenhandlung, f. *[EYE-zen-vaa-ren-hahnt-lung]* hardware store

Eiswürfel, m. *[ICE-vewr-fel]* ice cube

elektrisch *[eh-LEHK-trish]* electric

elf *[ehlf]* eleven

Elfenbein, n. *[EHL-fen-bine]* ivory

Ellbogen, m. *[EHL-boh-gen]* elbow

empfangen *[ehmp-FAHNG-en]* to receive

Empfänger, m. *[ehmp-FEHNG-e(r)]* receiver (letter)

empfehlen *[ehmp-FAY-len]* to recommend

Ende, n. *[EHN-deh]* end

zu Ende *[tsoo EHN-deh]* over (finished)

eng *[ehng]* narrow

Engel, m. *[EHN-gel]* angel

England, n. *[EHNG-lahnt]* England

englisch *[EHNG-lish]* English

entdecken *[ehnt-DEHK-en]* to discover

Ente, f. *[EHN-teh]* duck

Entfernung, f. *[ehnt-FEHR-nung]* distance

entscheiden *[ehnt-SHYE-den]* to decide

sich entschuldigen *[zikh ehnt-SHOOL-di-gen]* to apologize; to excuse

Entschuldigung, f. *[ehnt-SHOOL-di-gung]* apology

enttäuscht *[ehnt-TOYSHT]* disappointed

entwickeln *[ehnt-VIK-eln]* to develop

er *[ehr]* he

sich erbrechen *[zikh ehr-BREHKH-en]* to vomit

Erbse, f. *[EHRP-seh]* pea

Erdbeere, f. *[EHRT-bay-reh]* strawberry

Erdgeschoß, n. *[EHRT-geh-shos]* ground floor

Erfahrung, f. *[ehr-FAA-rung]* experience

Erfolg, m. *[ehr-FOLK]* success

erfrischend *[ehr-FRISH-ent]* refreshing

Ergebnis, n. *[ehr-GAYP-nis]* result

erhalten *[ehr-HAHL-ten]* to receive

erhöhen *[ehr-HU(R)-en]* to increase

sich erholen *[zikh ehr-HOH-len]* to recover

sich erinnern *[zikh eh-RIN-ern]* to remember

erkältet *[ehr-KEHL-tet]* cold (sick)

erklären *[ehr-KLEHR-en]* to explain

erlauben *[ehr-LOW-ben]* to permit

erlaubt *[ehr-LOWPT]* allowed

erledigen *[ehr-LAY-di-gen]* to finish

Ermäßigung, f. *[ehr-MAYS-si-gung]* reduction (price)

ernst *[ehrnst]* serious

Ersatzreifen, m. *[ehr-ZAHTS-rife-en]* spare tire

Ersatzteile, pl. *[ehr-ZAHTS-tile-eh]* spare parts

erschöpft *[ehr-SHU(R)PFT]* exhausted

ersetzen *[ehr-ZEHT-sen]* to replace

erstaunlich *[ehr-SHTOWN-likh]* amazing

erste (-r, -s) *[EHR-steh {-ste(r), -stehs}]* first

Erwachsene, pl. *[ehr-VAHK-seh-neh]* adults

erwähnen *[ehr-VAY-nen]* to mention

erwarten *[ehr-VAAR-ten]* to expect

erzählen *[ehr-TSAY-len]* to tell

Erzählung, f. *[ehr-TSAY-lung]* story (tale)

es tut mir leid *[ehs toot meer lite]* I am sorry

Essen, n. *[EHS-sen]* food

essen *[EHS-sen]* to eat

Essig, m. *[EHS-sikh]* vinegar

Eßlöffel, m. *[EHS-lu(r)-fel]* tablespoon

Eßzimmer, n. *[EHS-tsim-me(r)]* dining room

Etage, f. *[eh-TAH-zheh]* story (floor)

Etikett, n. *[eh-ti-KEHT]* label

etwas *[EHT-vahs]* any; some; something

Europa, n. *[oy-ROH-pah]* Europe

evangelisch *[ay-fahn-GAY-lish]* Protestant

extra *[EHK-strah]* extra

F

Fabrik, f. *[fah-BREEK]* factory

Faden, m. *[FAA-den]* thread

Fähre, f. *[FEH-reh]* ferry

fahren *[FAA-ren]* to drive; to ride

Fahrer, m. *[FAA-re(r)]* driver

Fahrgast, m. *[FAAR-gahst]* passenger

einfache Fahrkarte, f. *[INE-fahkh-eh FAAR-kahr-teh]* one-way ticket

Fahrplan, m. *[FAAR-plaan]* timetable

Fahrpreis, m. *[FAAR-price]* fare (fee)

Fahrrad, n. *[FAAR-raat]* bicycle

Fahrt, f. *[faart]* journey; ride

fallen *[FAHL-len]* to fall

falsch *[fahlsh]* false; wrong

Familie, f. *[fah-MEEL-yeh]* family

fangen *[FAHN-gen]* to catch

Farbe, f. *[FAHR-beh]* color

Farbfilm, m. *[FAHRP-film]* color film

Farbstoff, m. *[FAHRP-shtof]* dye

fast *[fahst]* almost; nearly

Februar, m. *[FAY-broo-aar]* February

Feder, f. *[FAY-de(r)]* spring (mechanical)

Fehler, m. *[FAY-le(r)]* error

Feiertag, m. *[FYE-e(r)-taak]* holiday

Feige, f. *[FYE-geh]* fig

Feile, f. *[FYE-leh]* file

fein *[fine]* fine (quality)

Feinkostgeschäft, n. *[FINE-kost-geh-shehft]* delicatessen

Feinschmecker, m. *[FINE-shmehk-e(r)]* gourmet

Feld, n. *[fehlt]* field

Felsen, m. *[FEHL-zen]* cliff

Fenster, n. *[FEHN-ste(r)]* window

Fensterladen, m. *[FEHN-ste(r)-laa-den]* shutter

Ferien, pl. *[FEHR-yen]* holidays; vacation

Ferienort, m. *[FEHR-yen-ort]* resort (place)

Ferngespräch, n. *[FEHRN-geh-spraykh]* long-distance call

Fernglas, n. *[FEHRN-glaas]* binoculars

Fernseher, m. *[FEHRN-zay-e(r)]* television (set)

Ferse, f. *[FEHR-zeh]* heel (of shoe)

fertig sein *[FEHR-tikh]* to be ready

Fest, n. *[fehst]* festival

Festung, f. *[FEHS-tung]* fortress

Fett, n. *[feht]* fat

feucht *[foykht]* damp

Feuer, n. *[FOY-e(r)]* fire

Feuerwehr, f. *[FOY-e(r)-vehr]* fire department

Feuerzeug, n. [FOY-e(r)-tsoyk] (cigarette) lighter

Fieber, n. [FEE-be(r)] fever

Filet, n. [fee-LAY] fillet

Film, m. [film] film; movie

Filmrolle, f. [FILM-rol-leh] roll (film)

Filz, m. [filts] felt (cloth)

finden [FIN-den] to find

Finger, m. [FIN-ge(r)] finger

Fisch, m. [fish] fish

flach [flahkh] flat

Flasche, f. [FLAHSH-eh] bottle

Fleck, m. [flehk] stain

Fleisch, n. [flyshe] meat

Fleischer, m. [FLYE-she(r)] butcher

Fleischerei, f. [flye-sheh-RYE] butcher shop

flicken [FLIK-en] to mend

fließen [FLEES-sen] flow

fliegen [FLEE-gen] to fly

Flohmarkt, m. [FLOH-mahrkt] flea market

Flug, m. [flook] flight

Flügel, m. [FLEW-gel] wing

Fluggesellschaft, f. [FLOOK-geh-zehl-shahft] airline

Flughafen, m. [FLOOK-haa-fen] airport

Flugzeug, n. [FLOOK-tsoyk] airplane

Fluß, m. [floos] river

Flüssigkeit, f. [FLEWS-sikh-kite] fluid

Flut, f. [floot] high tide

folgen [FOL-gen] to follow

Forelle, f. [fo-REHL-leh] trout

Format, n. [for-MAAT] format

Formular, n. [for-moo-LAHR] form

fortsetzen [FORT-zeht-sen] to continue

Foto machen [FOH-toh MAHKH-en] to take a photo

Foto, n. [FOH-toh] photograph

Fotoapparat, m. [FOH-toh-ah-pah-raat] camera

fotographieren [fot-toh-grah-FEE-ren] to photograph

Fotokopie, f. [fot-toh-koh-PEE] photocopy

Frage, f. [FRAA-geh] question

fragen [FRAA-gen] to ask

Frankreich, n. [FRAHNK-ryekh] France

Frau, f. [frow] wife; woman; Mrs., Ms

Fräulein, n. [FROY-line] Miss

frei [frye] clear (not blocked); free; vacant

Freitag, m. [FRYE-taak] Friday

fremd [frehmt] foreign

Fremdenverkehrsbüro, n. [FREHM-den-fehr-kehrs-bew-roh] tourist office

Freude, f. [FROY-deh] joy

Freund, (-in), m., f. [FROYNT, FROYN-din] friend

freundlich [FROYNT-likh] friendly

Friedhof, m. [FREET-hohf] cemetery

frieren [FREE-ren] to freeze

frisch [frish] fresh

Friseur, m. [fri-ZUR] barber; hairdresser

Frisur, f. [fri-ZOOR] haircut

froh [froh] glad

fröhlich [FRU(R)-likh] merry

Frosch, m. [frohsh] frog

247

Frost, m. *[frost]* frost

früh *[frew]* early

Frühling, m. *[FREW-ling]* spring (season)

Frühstück, n. *[FREW-shtewk]* breakfast

Fuchs, m. *[fooks]* fox

sich fühlen *[zikh FEW-len]* to feel

führen *[FEW-ren]* to lead

Führerschein, m. *[FEWR-e(r)-shine]* driver's license

Führung, f. *[FEW-rung]* guided tour

Füllfederhalter, m. *[FEWL-fay-de(r)-hahl-te(r)]* fountain pen

Fundbüro, n. *[FUNT-bew-roh]* lost and found

fünf *[fewnf]* five

fünfzehn *[FEWNF-tsayn]* fifteen

fünfzig *[FEWNF-tsikh]* fifty

für *[fewr]* for

Fuß, m. *[foos]* foot

zu Fuß *[tsoo foos]* on foot

Fußball, m. *[FOOS-bahl]* soccer

Fußgänger, m. *[FOOS-gehng-e(r)]* pedestrian

Fußgängerzone, f. *[FOOS-gehng-e(r)-tsoh-neh]* pedestrian zone

Fußpuder, m. *[FOOS-poo-de(r)]* foot powder

Fußweg, m. *[FOOS-vehk]* footpath

G

Gabel, f. *[GAA-bel]* fork

Galerie, f. *[gah-leh-REE]* gallery

Gang, m. *[gahng]* course (meal); gear (car)

Gans, f. *[gahns]* goose

ganz *[gahnts]* whole

gar nicht *[gaar nikht]* not at all

Garage, f. *[gah-RAH-zheh]* garage

Garderobe, f. *[gar-deh-ROH-beh]* checkroom (theater)

Garnele, f. *[gahr-NAY-leh]* shrimp

Garten, m. *[GAAR-ten]* garden

Gas, n. *[gahs]* gas

Gaspedal, n. *[GAHS-peh-daal]* accelerator

Gastfreundschaft, f. *[GAHST-froynt-shahft]* hospitality

Gastgeber, m. *[GAHST-gay-be(r)]* host

Gasthaus, n. *[GAHST-hows]* inn

Gatte, m. *[GAHT-teh]* spouse

Gattin, f. *[GAHT-tin]* spouse

Gebäck, n. *[geh-BEHK]* pastry

gebacken *[geh-BAH-ken]* baked

Gebäude, n. *[geh-BOY-deh]* building

geben *[GAY-ben]* to give

Gebiet, n. *[geh-BEET]* area

Gebiß, n. *[geh-BIS]* denture

es gibt *[ehs gipt]* there are (is)

geboren *[geh-BOR-en]* born

gebraten *[geh-BRAA-ten]* fried; roasted

zu stark gebraten *[tsoo shtahrk geh-BRAA-ten]* overdone

gebraucht [geh-BROWKHT]
used

gebrochen [geh-BROKH-en]
broken

Gebühr, f. [geh-BEWR]
commission; charge; toll

Geburtstag, m. [geh-BURTS-taak] birthday

Gefahr, f. [geh-FAAR] danger

gefährlich [geh-FEHR-likh]
dangerous

Gefallen, m. [geh-FAHL-len]
favor

gefallen [geh-FAHL-len] to
like

Geflügel, n. [geh-FLEW-gel]
fowl

gefroren [geh-FROH-ren]
frozen

gegen [GAY-gen] against;
toward(s)

Gegend, f. [GAY-gehnt] area

Gegenstand, m. [GAY-gen-shtahnt] object

Gegenteil, n. [GAY-gen-tile]
opposite

gegenüber [gay-gen-EW-be(r)]
across; opposite (across
from)

gegrillt [geh-GRILT] grilled

gehen [GAY-en] to go; to
walk

Gehirn, n. [geh-HEERN] brain

gehören [geh-HU(R)-en] to
belong

Geist, m. [gyest] mind

gekocht [geh-KOKHT] boiled;
cooked

gelb [gehlp] yellow

Geld, n. [gehlt] money

Geldstrafe, f. [GEHLT-shtrah-feh] fine (penalty)

Gelegenheit, f. [geh-LAY-gen-hite] opportunity

Gelenk, n. [geh-LEHNK] joint

Gemälde, n. [geh-MEHL-deh]
painting

gemalt [geh-MAALT] painted

Gemüse, n. [geh-MEW-zeh]
vegetable

Genehmigung, f. [geh-NAY-mi-gung] permit (pass)

genießen [geh-NEES-sen]
enjoy

genug [geh-NOOK] enough

Gepäck, n. [geh-PEHK]
baggage; luggage

Gepäckaufbewahrung, f.
[geh-PEHK-owf-beh-vaa-rung]
baggage checkroom;
checkroom

Gepäckausgabe, f. [geh-PEHK-ows-gaa-beh] baggage claim

Gepäckkontrolle, f. [geh-PEHK-kon-trol-leh] baggage check

Gepäckträger, m. [geh-PEHK-tray-ge(r)] porter

Gepäckwagen, m. [geh-PEHK-vaa-gen] baggage car

gerade [geh-RAA-deh] straight

Gerät, n. [geh-RAYT]
appliance

geräuchert [geh-ROY-khert]
smoked

Gericht, n. [geh-RIKHT] court;
dish (food)

gern [gehrn] gladly

gern haben [gehrn HAA-ben]
to like

Geschäft, n. [geh-SHEHFT]
business; store

Geschäftsführer, m. *[geh-SHEHFTS-few-re(r)]* manager

Geschäftsreise, f. *[geh-SHEHFTS-rye-zeh]* business trip

Geschenk, n. *[geh-SHEHNK]* present (gift)

Geschichte, f. *[geh-SHIKH-teh]* history

geschieden *[geh-SHEE-den]* divorced

geschloßen *[geh-SHLOS-sen]* closed

Geschmack, n. *[geh-SHMAHK]* flavor

Geschwindigkeit, f. *[geh-SHVIN-dikh-kite]* speed

Geschwindigkeitsbegrenzung, f. *[geh-SHVIN-dikh-kites-beh-GREHN-tsung]* speed limit

Geschwür, n. *[geh-SHVEWR]* ulcer

Gesellschaft, f. *[geh-ZEHL-shahft]* company

Gesicht, n. *[ge-ZIKHT]* face

Gesichtscreme, f. *[geh-ZIKHTS-kraym]* face cream

gespannt *[geh-SHPAHNT]* tense

Gespräch, n. *[geh-SHPRAYKH]* conversation

Gespräch mit Voranmeldung *[geh-SHPRAYKH mit FOHR-ahn-mehl-dung]* person-to-person call

gestern *[GEHS-tern]* yesterday

Gesundheit, f. *[geh-ZUNT-hite]* health

Getränk, n. *[geh-TREHNK]* beverage; drink

Getriebe, n. *[geh-TREE-beh]* transmission

getrocknet *[geh-TROK-net]* dried

Gewicht, n. *[geh-VIKHT]* weight

gewinnen *[geh-VIN-nen]* to win

gewiß *[geh-VIS]* certain

Gewohnheit, f. *[geh-VOHN-hite]* habit

gewöhnlich *[geh-VU(R)N-likh]* ordinary; usual

Gewürz, n. *[geh-VEWRTS]* spice

Gift, n. *[gift]* poison

Gin, m. *[jin]* gin (drink)

Gipfel, m. *[GIP-fel]* peak

Glas, n. *[glaas]* glass; jar

glatt *[glaht]* smooth

glauben *[GLOW-ben]* to believe; to think (believe)

gleich *[glyekh]* equal; right away

gleiche *[GLYE-kheh]* same

Gleis, n. *[glice]* track (train)

Glück, n. *[glewk]* luck

viel Glück *[feel glewk]* good luck

glücklich *[GLEWK-likh]* happy

Glühbirne, f. *[GLEW-beer-neh]* electric bulb

Gold, n. *[golt]* gold

Golfplatz, m. *[GOLF-plahts]* golf course

Gott, m. *[got]* god

Gottesdienst, m. *[GOT-tehs-deenst]* religious service

Grab, n. *[grahp]* grave; tomb

Gramm, n. *[graam]* gram

Grammatik, f. *[grah-MAH-tik]* grammar

Gras, n. *[grahs]* grass

grau *[grow]* gray

Grenze, f. *[GREHN-tseh]* border

grillen *[GRIL-len]* to broil

Grippe, f. *[GRIP-peh]* flu

groß *[grohs]* big; great; large; tall

Größe, f. *[GRU(R)S-eh]* size

Großeltern, pl. *[GROHS-ehl-tern]* grandparents

großzügig, *[GROHS-tsew-gikh]* generous

grün *[grewn]* green

Grund, m. *[grunt]* reason

Grundstück, n. *[GRUNT-shtewk]* property

Gruß, m. *[groos]* greeting

Grüße, pl. *[GREWS-eh]* regards

mit freundlichen Grüßen *[mit FROYNT-likh-en GREWS-en]* sincerely (yours)

gültig *[GEWL-tikh]* valid

Gummi, m. *[GOOM-mee]* rubber

Gummiband, n. *[GOOM-mee-bahnt]* rubber band

Gurke, f. *[GOOR-keh]* cucumber

Gürtel, m. *[GEWR-tel]* belt

gut *[goot]* good; well

H

Haar, n. *[haar]* hair

Haarbürste, f. *[HAAR-bewr-steh]* hairbrush

Haarnadel, f. *[HAAR-naa-dehl]* hairpin

Haartrockner, m. *[HAAR-trok-ne(r)]* hair dryer

Haarwaschmittel, n. *[HAAR-vahsh-mit-tel]* shampoo

haben *[HAA-ben]* to have

Hafen, m. *[HAA-fen]* harbor; port

Hafenanlage, f. *[HAA-fen-ahn-laa-geh]* dock

halb *[hahlp]* half

Hälfte, f. *[HEHLF-teh]* half

Halle, f. *[HAHL-leh]* hall

Hallo! *[HAH-loh]* hello! (phone)

Hals, m. *[hahls]* neck; throat

Halskette, f. *[HAHLS-keh-teh]* necklace

Halsschmerzen, pl. *[HAHLS-shmehr-tsen]* sore throat

halten *[HAHL-ten]* to hold

Hammer, m. *[HAHM-me(r)]* hammer

Hand, f. *[hahnt]* hand

handgearbeitet *[HAHNT-geh-ahr-bite-et]* handmade

Handgelenk, n. *[HAHNT-geh-lehnk]* wrist

Handgepäck, n. *[HAHNT-geh-pehk]* carry-on luggage

Handschuh, m. *[HAHNT-shoo]* glove

Handtasche, f. *[HAHNT-tahsh-eh]* handbag; purse

Handtuch, n. *[HAHNT-tookh]* towel

hart, *[hahrt]* hard (tough)

Hase, m. *[HAA-zeh]* rabbit

häßlich *[HEHS-likh]* ugly

häufig *[HOY-fikh]* frequent

Hauptrolle, f. *[HOWPT-rol-leh]* lead (stage)

251

Hauptstadt, f. *[HOWPT-shtaht]* capital

Haus, *[hows]* home; house

nach Hause gehen *[nahkh HOW-zeh GAY-en]* to go home

zu Hause *[tsoo HOW-zeh]* (at) home

Hausschuhe, pl. *[HOWS-shoo-eh]* slippers

Haut, f. *[howt]* skin

heben *[HAY-ben]* to lift

Heftpflaster, n. *[HEHFT-pflahs-te(r)]* adhesive tape

heilig *[HYE-likh]* holy

Heilmittel, n. *[HILE-mit-tel]* remedy

Heim, n. *[hime]* home

Heimatadresse, f. *[HYE-maat-ah-drehs-seh]* home address

heiß *[hice]* hot

heißen *[HICE-sen]* to be named

heißlaufen *[HICE-low-fen]* to overheat (motor)

Heizgerät, n. *[HITES-geh-rayt]* heater

Heizkörper, m. *[HITES-ku(r)-pe(r)]* radiator

helfen *[HEHL-fen]* to help

hellbraun *[HEHL-brown]* tan

Hemd, n. *[hehmt]* shirt

Herbst, m. *[hehrpst]* autumn

Herr, m. *[hehr]* gentleman; Mr.

Herrentoilette, f. *[HEHR-ren-toy-leht-teh]* men's room

herum *[heh-RUM]* around

Herz, n. *[hehrts]* heart

Herzkrankheit, f. *[HEHRTS-krahnk-hite]* heart trouble

Heuschnupfen, m. *[HOY-shnup-fen]* hay fever

heute *[HOY-teh]* today

heute abend *[HOY-teh AA-behnt]* tonight

hier *[heer]* here

hiesig *[HEE-zikh]* local

Hilfe, f. *[HIL-feh]* help

Himbeere, f. *[HIM-bay-reh]* raspberry

Himmel, m. *[HIM-mel]* heaven; sky

hinauf *[hin-OWF]* up

sich hinlegen *[zikh HIN-lay-gen]* to lie (down)

hinten *[HIN-ten]* behind; rear

Hinterhof, m. *[HIN-te(r)-hohf]* courtyard

hinunter *[hin-UN-te(r)]* down

Hitze, f. *[HIT-seh]* heat

hoch *[hohkh]* high

Hochzeit, f. *[HOKH-tsite]* wedding

Hoffnung, f. *[HOF-nung]* hope

höflich *[HU(R)F-likh]* polite

Höhe, f. *[HU(R)-eh]* height

Höhle, f. *[HU(R)-leh]* cave

holen *[HOH-len]* to get (obtain)

Hölle, f. *[HU(R)-leh]* hell

Holz, n. *[holts]* wood (material)

Honig, m. *[HOH-nikh]* honey

hören *[HU(R)-en]* to hear; to listen

Hörer, m. *[HU(R)-e(r)]* receiver (phone)

Hose, f. *[HOH-zeh]* pants; trousers

Hotel, n. *[ho-TEL]*

Hoteljunge, m. *[ho-TEL-yun-geh]* bellboy

hübsch *[hewpsh]* pretty

Hüfte, f. *[HEWF-teh]* hip

Hügel, m. *[HEW-gel]* hill

Huhn, n. *[hoon]* chicken

Hühnerauge, n. *[HEW-ne(r)-ow-geh]* corn (foot)

Hummer, m. *[HUM-me(r)]* lobster

Hund, m. *[hunt]* dog

hundert *[HUN-dert]* hundred

Hunger haben *[HUN-ge(r) HAA-ben]* to be hungry

Hunger, m. *[HUN-ge(r)]* hunger

Hupe, f. *[HOO-peh]* horn (car)

Husten, m. *[HOOS-ten]* cough

husten *[HOOS-ten]* to cough

Hut, m. *[hoot]* hat

Hütte, f. *[HEW-teh]* hut

Ihr *[eer]* you

immer *[IM-me(r)]* always

in *[in]* in

inbegriffen *[IN-beh-grif-fen]* included

Infektion, f. *[in-fehk-TSYOHN]* infection

Inflation, f. *[in-flah-TSYOHN]* inflation

Ingwer, m. *[ING-vehr]* ginger

Inhalt, m. *[IN-hahlt]* contents

Insektenschutz, m. *[in-ZEHK-ten-shuts]* insect repellent

Insel, f. *[IN-zel]* island

interessant *[in-teh-reh-SAHNT]* interesting

Interesse, n. *[in-teh-REHS-seh]* interest

sich interessieren für *[zikh in-teh-rehs-SEE-ren fewr]* to be interested in

irgend etwas *[IR-gehnt EHT-vahs]* anything

irgend jemand *[IR-gehnt YAY-mahnt]* anybody, anyone

irgendwo *[IR-gehnt-voh]* somewhere

Irrtum, m. *[EER-toom]* mistake

J

ja *[yaa]* yes

Jacke, f. *[YAH-keh]* jacket

Jahr, n. *[yaar]* year

Jahreszeit, f. *[YAA-rehs-tsite]* season

Jahrhundert, n. *[YAAR-hun-dert]* century

Jahrzehnt, n. *[YAAR-tsehnt]* decade

Januar, m. *[YAH-noo-aar]* January

Japan, n. *[YAH-pahn]* Japan

jede (-r, -s) *[YAY-deh {-e(r), -ehs}]* each; every

jedenfalls *[YAY-den-fahls]* anyway

jemals *[YAY-maals]* ever

jemand *[YAY-mahnt]* someone

jene (-r, -s) *[YEH-neh, {-ne(r), -nehs}]* that

jenseits *[YEHN-zites]* beyond

jetzt *[yehtst]* now

Jod, n. *[yoht]* iodine

jüdisch *[YEW-dish]* Jewish

Jugendherberge, f. *[YOO-gehnt-hehr-behr-geh]* youth hostel

Juli, m. *[YOO-lee]* July

jung *[yung]* young

Junge, m. *[YUN-geh]* boy

Juni, m. *[YOO-nee]* June

Juwelier, m. *[yoo-veh-LEER]* jeweler

K

Kaffee, m. *[KAH-feh]* coffee

Kalbfleisch, n. *[KAHLP-flyshe]* veal

kalt *[kahlt]* cold

Kamm, m. *[kahm]* comb

Kaninchen, n. *[kah-NEEN-khen]* rabbit

kann *[kahn]* to be able; can (1st and 3rd person singular only)

Kapelle, f. *[kah-PEHL-leh]* chapel

Kappe, f. *[KAHP-peh]* cap

kaputt *[kah-PUT]* broken

Karotte, f. *[kah-ROT-teh]* carrot

Karte, f. *[KAHR-teh]* map; ticket

Kartoffel, f. *[kahr-TOF-Fel]* potato

Käse, m. *[KAY-zeh]* cheese

Kasse, f. *[KAHS-seh]* box office; cash desk

Kassierer, (-in) m., f. *[kah-SEE-re(r), {-reh-rin}]* teller (bank)

Kastanie, f. *[kah-STAHN-yeh]* chestnut

Kater, m. *[KAA-te(r)]* hangover

Kathedrale, f. *[kah-teh-DRAAL-eh]* cathedral

katholisch *[kah-TOH-lish]* Catholic

Katze, f. *[KAHT-seh]* cat

kaufen *[KOW-fen]* to buy

Kaufhaus, n. *[KOWF-hows]* department store

Kaugummi, m. *[KOW-goom-mee]* chewing gum

kein *[kine]* none

Kekse, pl. *[KAYK-seh]* cookies

Kellner, (-in) m., f. *[KEHL-ner, KEHL-neh-rin]* waiter, waitress

kennen *[KEHN-nen]* to know; to be familiar with

Keramik, f. *[keh-RAH-mik]* pottery

Kerze, f. *[KEHRT-seh]* candle

Kette, f. *[KEHT-teh]* chain

Kiefer, m. *[KEE-fe(r)]* jaw

Kilo(gramm), n. *[KEE-loh {GRAAM}]* kilogram

Kilometer, m. *[kee-loh-MAY-te(r)]* kilometer

Kind, n. *[kint]* child

Kinderarzt, m. *[KIN-de(r)-ahrtst]* pediatrician

Kinn, n. *[kin]* chin

Kino, n. *[KEE-noh]* cinema; movie theater

Kirche, f. *[KIR-kheh]* church

Kirsche, f. *[KIR-sheh]* cherry

Klappstuhl, m. *[KLAHP-sthool]* folding chair

klar *[klahr]* clear

Klasse, f. *[KLAHS-seh]* class

klassisch, *[KLAHS-sish]* classic

Klavier, n. *[klah-VEER]* piano

Kleid, n. *[klite]* dress

Kleider, pl. *[KLYE-de(r)]* clothes

Kleiderbügel, m. *[KLYE-de(r)-bew-gel]* hanger (clothes)

klein *[kline]* little; small

Kleingeld, n. *[KLINE-gehlt]* change (money)

Klimaanlage, f. *[KLEE-mah-ahn-laa-geh]* air conditioner

klimatisiert *[klee-mah-ti-ZEERT]* air-conditioned

Klinge, f. *[KLING-eh]* blade (razor)

Klingel, f. *[KLING-el]* bell (door)

klingeln *[KLING-eln]* to ring

klopfen *[KLOP-fen]* to knock

Kloster, n. *[KLOH-ste(r)]* convent; monastery

Klub, m. *[kloop]* club

Knie, n. *[knee]* knee

Knoblauch, m. *[KNOH-blowkh]* garlic

Knöchel, m. *[KNU(R)-khel]* ankle

Knochen, m. *[KNOKH-en]* bone

Knopf, m. *[knopf]* button, knob

knusprig *[KNOOS-prikh]* crisp

kochen *[KOKH-en]* to cook

koffeinfrei *[kof-feh-EEN-frye]* decaffinated

Koffer, m. *[KOF-fe(r)]* suitcase

Kofferraum, m. *[KOF-fe(r)-rowm]* trunk (car)

Kohl, m. *[kohl]* cabbage

Kolleg(e), (-in), m., f. *[kol-LAY-geh; -gin]* colleague

komisch *[KOH-mish]* funny

kommen *[KOM-men]* to come

Komödie, f. *[ko-MU(R)-dyeh]* comedy

Konditorei, f. *[kon-dee-to-RYE]* pastry shop

können, *[KU(R)-nen]* to be able; can

könnte *[KU(R)N-teh]* could (1st and 3rd person singular only)

Konsulat, n. *[kon-zu-LAHT]* consulate

Kontaktlinsen, pl. *[kon-TAHKT-lin-zen]* contact lens

Konto, n. *[KON-toh]* account

Konzert, n. *[kon-TSEHRT]* concert

Kopf, m. *[kopf]* head

Kopfkissen, n. *[KOPF-kis-sen]* pillow

Kopfkissenbezug, m. *[KOPF-kis-sen-beh-tsook]* pillowcase

Kopfsalat, m. *[KOPF-zah-laat]* lettuce

Kopfschmerzen, pl. *[KOPF-shmehr-tsen]* headache

Korb, m. *[korp]* basket

Kordsamt, m. *[KORT-zahmt]* corduroy

Korkenzieher, m. *[KOR-ken-tsee-e(r)]* corkscrew

Körper, m. *[KU(R)R-pe(r)]* body

koscher *[KOH-she(r)]* kosher

Kosten, pl. *[KOS-ten]* costs

kosten *[KOS-ten]* to cost

köstlich *[KU(R)ST-likh]* delicious

Kotelett, n. *[kot-LEHT]* cutlet; chop

Kotflügel, m. *[KOHT-flew-gel]* fender

kräftig *[KREHF-tikh]* powerful

Kragen, m. *[KRAA-gen]* collar

Krampf, m. *[krahmpf]* cramp

krank, *[krahnk]* ill

Krankenhaus, n. *[KRAHN-ken-hows]* hospital

Krankenkasse, f. *[KRAHN-ken-kahs-seh]* health insurance

Krankenschwester, f. *[KRAHN-ken-shvehs-te(r)]* nurse

Krankenwagen, m. *[KRAHN-ken-vaa-gen]* ambulance

Krankheit, f. *[KRAHNK-hite]* disease; sickness

Kräuter, pl. *[KROY-te(r)]* herbs

Krawatte, f. *[krah-VAHT-teh]* necktie; tie

Kreditkarte, f. *[kray-DEET-kahr-teh]* credit card

Kreuz, n. *[kroyts]* cross

Kreuzung, f. *[KROY-tsung]* crossroads; intersection

Krieg, m. *[kreek]* war

Krug, m. *[krook]* pitcher

Kruste, f. *[KROOS-teh]* crust

Küche, f. *[KEW-kheh]* cuisine; kitchen

Kuchen, m. *[KOO-khen]* cake

Kugelschreiber, m. *[KOO-gel-shrye-be(r)]* pen (ball point)

kühl *[kewl]* cool

kühlen *[KEW-len]* to chill

Kühler, m. *[KEW-le(r)]* radiator (car)

Kund(e), (-in), m., f. *[KUN-deh; KUN-din]* client; customer

Kunst, f. *[kunst]* art

Künstler, m. *[KEWNST-le(r)]* artist

künstlich *[KEWNST-likh]* artificial

Kupfer, n. *[KUP-fe(r)]* copper

Kupplung, f. *[KUP-lung]* clutch (car)

Kurort, m. *[KOOR-ort]* spa

Kurve, f. *[KOOR-veh]* curve; turn

kurz *[koorts]* short

kürzlich *[KEWRTS-likh]* recently

Kusine, f. *[koo-ZEE-neh]* cousin

Kuß, m. *[kus]* kiss

küssen *[KEWS-sen]* to kiss

Küste, f. *[KEWS-teh]* coast

L

lächeln *[LEHKH-eln]* to smile

lachen *[LAHKH-en]* to laugh

Laden, m. *[LAA-den]* shop

Lammfleisch, n. *[LAHM-flyshe]* lamb

Lampe, f. *[LAHM-peh]* lamp

Land, n. *[lahnt]* country; land

landen, *[LAHN-den]* to land

Landschaft, f. *[LAHNT-shahft]* countryside

landschaftlich schöne Straße *[LAHNT-shahft-likh SHU(R)-neh SHTRAHS-eh]* scenic route

Landstraße, f. *[LAHNT-shtrahs-seh]* highway

lang *[lahng]* long

Länge, f. *[LEHNG-eh]* length

langlaufskifahren *[LAHNG-lowf-shee-faa-ren]* cross-country skiing

langsam *[LAHNG-zahm]* slow(ly)

langsam fahren *[LAHNG-zahm FAA-ren]* to slow down

Lärm, m. *[lehrm]* noise

lassen *[LAHS-sen]* to leave (behind); to let

Lastwagen, m. *[LAHST-vaagen]* truck

laufen *[LOW-fen]* to run

laut *[lowt]* aloud; noisy

Lautsprecher, m. *[LOWT-sprehkh-e(r)]* speaker (stereo)

Leben, n. *[LAY-ben]* life

leben *[LAY-ben]* to live

Lebensmittelgeschäft, n. *[LAY-bens-mit-tel-geh-shehft]* grocery store

Leber, f. *[LAY-be(r)]* liver

lecken *[LEHK-en]* to leak

lecker *[LEHK-e(r)]* delicious

Leder, n. *[LAY-de(r)]* leather

ledig *[LAY-dikh]* single (unmarried)

leer *[lehr]* empty

lehren *[LEHR-en]* to teach

leicht *[lyekht]* easy; light (weight)

leider *[LYE-de(r)]* unfortunately

leihen *[LYE-en]* to lend

Leinen, n. *[LINE-en]* linen

Leiter, f. *[LYE-te(r)]* ladder

Lenkrad, n. *[LEHNK-raat]* steering wheel

lernen *[LEHR-nen]* to learn

lesen *[LAY-zen]* to read

letzte *[LEHTS-teh]* last

Leute, pl. *[LOY-teh]* people

Licht, n. *[likht]* light

lieb *[leep]* dear

Liebe, f. *[LEE-beh]* love

lieben *[LEE-ben]* to love

lieber *[LEE-be(r)]* rather

Lied, n. *[leet]* song

liefern *[LEE-fern]* to deliver

Lieferung, f. *[LEE-feh-rung]* delivery

Lift, m. *[lift]* elevator

Likör, m. *[li-KUR]* liqueur

Limonade, f. *[lee-moh-NAA-deh]* lemonade

Limone, f. *[li-MOH-neh]* lime

Lineal, n. *[lee-nay-AAL]* ruler

Linie, f. *[LEEN-yeh]* line

links *[links]* left

Lippe, f. *[LIP-eh]* lip

Lippenstift, m. *[LIP-pen-shtift]* lipstick

Liste, f. *[LIS-teh]* list

Liter, m. *[LEE-te(r)]* liter

Loch, n. *[lohkh]* hole

Locke, f. *[LOK-eh]* curl

Lockenwickler, m. *[LOK-en-vik-le(r)]* curler

Löffel, m. *[LU(R)F-el]* spoon

Lotion, f. *[loh-TSYOHN]* lotion

Luft, f. *[luft]* air

Luftmatraze, f. *[LUFT-mah-trah-tseh]* air mattress

Luftpost, f. *[LUFT-post]* airmail

Lunge, f. *[LUNG-eh]* lung

Luxus, m. *[LUKS-us]* luxury

M

machen *[MAHKH-en]* to make

macht nichts *[mahkht nikhts]* never mind

Mädchen, n. *[MAYT-khen]* girl

257

Magen, m. *[MAA-gen]* stomach

Magenschmerzen, pl. *[MAA-gen-shmehr-tsen]* stomach-ache

Magenverstimmung, f. *[MAA-gen-fehr-shtim-ung]* indigestion; upset stomach

Mahlzeit, f. *[MAAL-tsite]* meal

Mai, m. *[mye]* May

Mais, m. *[mice]* corn

Mal, n. *[maal]* time

Maler, m. *[MAA-le(r)]* painter

manchmal *[MAHNCH-maal]* sometimes

Mandarine, f. *[mahn-dah-REE-neh]* tangerine

Mandel, f. *[MAHN-del]* almond

Maniküre, f. *[mah-ni-KEW-reh]* manicure

Mann, m. *[mahn]* husband; man

Mannschaft, f. *[MAHN-shahft]* team

Mantel, m. *[MAHN-tel]* coat; overcoat

Markt, m. *[mahrkt]* market

Marmelade, f. *[mahr-meh-LAA-deh]* jam

März, m. *[mehrts]* March

Maschine, f. *[mah-SHEE-neh]* machine

Massage, f. *[mah-SAA-zheh]* massage

massiv *[mah-SEEF]* solid

Matraze, f. *[mah-TRAH-tseh]* mattress

Mauer, f. *[MOW-e(r)]* wall (exterior)

Mechaniker, m. *[meh-KHAH-ni-ke(r)]* mechanic

Medikament, n. *[meh-di-kah-MEHNT]* drug; medicine

Meer, n. *[mayr]* sea

Meeresfrüchte, pl. *[MAY-rehs-frewkh-teh]* seafood

Mehl, n. *[mayl]* flour

mehr *[mehr]* more

mehrere *[MEH-reh-reh]* several

Mehrwertsteuer, f. *[MEHR-vehrt-shtoy-e(r)]* value-added tax

Melone, f. *[meh-LOH-neh]* melon

Menge, f. *[MEHNG-eh]* quantity

eine Menge *[INE-eh MEHNG-eh]* a lot

Menstruationsbeschwerden, pl. *[mehn-stru-ah-TSYOHNZ-beh-shvehr-den]* menstrual pains

Messe, f. *[MEHS-seh]* mass (church)

messen *[MEHS-sen]* to measure

Messer, n. *[MEHS-se(r)]* knife

Meter, m. *[MAY-te(r)]* meter (length)

Metzger, m. *[MEHTS-ge(r)]* butcher

Metzgerei, f. *[mehts-geh-RYE]* butcher shop

Miete, f. *[MEE-teh]* rent

mieten *[MEE-ten]* to hire (rent)

Milch, f. *[milkh]* milk

mild *[milt]* mild

Milliarde, f. [mil-YAAR-deh] billion

Million, f. [mil-YOHN] million

mindestens [MIN-dehs-tens] at least

Mineralwasser, n. [mi-neh-RAAL-vahs-se(r)] mineral water

Minute, f. [mi-NOO-teh] minute

Minze, f. [MIN-tseh] mint

mit [mit] with

Mittag, m. [MIT-taak] noon

Mittagessen, n. [MIT-taak-ehs-en] lunch

Mitte, f. [MIT-teh] middle

Mittel, n. [MIT-tel] means

Mitternacht, f. [MIT-te(r)-nahkht] midnight

Mittwoch, m. [MIT-vokh] Wednesday

Möbel, pl. [MU(R)-bel] furniture

möchten [MU(R)KH-ten] would like

Mode, f. [MOH-deh] fashion

modern [mo-DEHRN] modern

mögen [MU(R)-gen] to like

möglich [MU(R)-glikh] possible

Molkerei, f. [mohl-keh-RYE] dairy

Monat, m. [MOH-naat] month

Mond, m. [mohnt] moon

Montag, m. [MOHN-taak] Monday

Morgen, m. [MOR-gen] morning

morgen, [MOR-gen] tomorrow

Morgenrock, m. [MOR-gen-rok] dressing gown

Moschee, f. [mo-SHAY] mosque

Motor, m. [moh-TOHR] engine; motor

Motorrad, n. [moh-TOHR-raat] motorcycle

müde [MEW-deh] tired

Mund, m. [munt] mouth

Mundwasser, n. [MUNT-vahs-se(r)] mouthwash

Münze, f. [MEWN-tseh] coin

Muscheln, pl. [MOO-shehln] mussels

Museum, n. [moo-ZAY-um] museum

Musik, f. [moo-ZEEK] music

Musikkapelle, f. [moo-ZEEK-kah-pehl-leh] band

Muskel, m. [MUS-kel] muscle

müssen [MEWS-sen] must

Mutter, f. [MUT-te(r)] mother

Mütze, f. [MEWT-seh] cap

N

naß [nahs] wet

nach [nahkh] after; to

Nachbar, m. [NAHKH-baar] neighbor

Nachbarschaft, f. [NAHKH-baar-shahft] neighborhood

nachher [NAHKH-hehr] afterward

Nachmittag, m. [NAHKH-mit-taak] afternoon

Nachricht, f. [NAKHK-rikht] message

nächst [naykhst] next

Nacht, f. [nahkht] night

Nachthemd, n. *[NAHKHT-hehmt]* nightgown

Nachtisch, m. *[NAHKH-tish]* dessert

Nachtlokal, n. *[NAHKHT-loh-kaal]* nightclub

nackt *[nahkt]* naked

Nadel, f. *[NAA-del]* needle

Nagel, m. *[NAA-gel]* nail (finger)

Nagellack, m. *[NAA-gel-lahk]* nail polish

nah *[naa]* near

nahe *[NAA-eh]* close (near)

in der Nähe *[in dehr NAY-eh]* nearby

nähen *[NAY-en]* to sew

Nahverkehrszug, m. *[NAA-fehr-kehrs-tsook]* local train

Name, m. *[NAA-meh]* name

Nase, f. *[NAA-zeh]* nose

Natur, f. *[nah-TOOR]* nature

natürlich *[nah-TEWR-likh]* of course

Nebel, m. *[NAY-bel]* fog

neben *[NAY-ben]* beside

nehmen *[NAY-men]* to take

nein *[nine]* no

Nerv, m. *[nehrf]* nerve

nett *[neht]* nice; kind

Netz, n. *[nehts]* net

neu *[noy]* new

Neujahr, n. *[NOY-yaar]* new year

neun *[noyn]* nine

neunte *[NOYN-teh]* ninth

neunzehn *[NOYN-tsayn]* nineteen

neunzig *[NOYN-tsikh]* ninety

nicht *[nikht]* not

Nichtraucher, m. *[NIKHT-row-khe(r)]* nonsmoker

nichts *[nikhts]* nothing

nie *[nee]* never

niedrig *[NEE-drikh]* low

niemand *[NEE-mahnt]* no one

Niere, f. *[NEE-reh]* kidney

noch *[nohkh]* still; yet

noch ein(-e) *[nohkh ine/INE-eh]* another

noch einmal *[nohkh INE-maal]* again

Norden, m. *[NOR-den]* north

nördlich *[NU(R)RT-likh]* north

normal *[nor-MAAL]* regular

Notausgang, m. *[NOHT-ows-gahng]* emergency exit

Notfall, m. *[NOHT-fahl]* emergency

nötig *[NU(R)-tikh]* necessary

Notizheft, n. *[no-TEETS-hehft]* notebook

November, m. *[no-VEHM-be(r)]* November

nüchtern *[NEWKH-tern]* sober

Nudeln, pl. *[NOO-deln]* noodles

null *[nul]* zero

Nummer, f. *[NUM-me(r)]* number

nur *[noor]* just (only); only

Nuß, f. *[noos]* nut

nützlich *[NEWTS-likh]* useful

O

ob *[op]* if

oben *[OH-ben]* above; up

obere *[OH-beh-reh]* upper

Oberkellner, m. *[OH-be(r)-kehl-ne(r)]* headwaiter

Oberschule, f. *[OH-be(r)-shoo-leh]* high school

Objektiv, n. *[op-yehk-TEEF]* camera lens

Obst, n. *[opst]* fruit

oder *[OH-de(r)]* or

Ofen m. *[OH-fen]* oven

offen *[OF-fen]* open

öffentlich *[U(R)F-ehnt-likh]* public

öffnen *[U(R)F-nen]* to open

oft *[oft]* often

ohne *[OH-neh]* without

Ohr, n. *[ohr]* ear

Ohrenschmerzen, pl. *[OH-ren-shmehr-tsen]* earache

Ohrring, m. *[OHR-ring]* earring

okay, *[o-kay]* okay

Oktober, m. *[ok-TOH-be(r)]* October

Öl, n. *[u(r)l]* oil

Olive, f. *[o-LEE-veh]* olive

Omelett, n. *[om-LEHT]* omelet

Onkel, m. *[OHN-kel]* uncle

Oper, f. *[OH-pe(r)]* opera

Operation, f. *[o-peh-rah-TSYOHN]* operation

Optiker, m. *[OP-tik-e(r)]* optician

Orange, f. *[oh-RAHN-zheh]* orange

Orangensaft, m. *[oh-RAHN-zhen-sahft]* orange juice

Orchester, n. *[or-KEHS-te(r)]* orchestra

Ordnung, f. *[ORT-nung]* order

Ort, m. *[ort]* place

Ortsgespräch, n. *[ORTS-geh-spraykh]* local phone call

Osten, m. *[OS-ten]* east

Ostern, pl. *[OS-tern]* Easter

Österreich, n. *[U(R)S-teh-ryekh]* Austria

Österreicher(-in), m. (f.) *[U(R)S-teh-ryekh-e(r)/eh-rin]* Austrian

österreichish *[U(R)S-teh-rye-khish]* Austrian

Ozean, m. *[OH-tsay-ahn]* ocean

P

Paar, n. *[paar]* pair

packen *[PAH-ken]* to pack

Paket, n. *[pah-KAYT]* package; parcel

Palast, m. *[pah-LAHST]* palace

Pampelmuse, f. *[pahm-pehl-MOO-zeh]* grapefruit

Panne, f. *[PAHN-neh]* breakdown

Papier, n. *[pah-PEER]* paper

Papiertuch, n. *[pah-PEER-tookh]* tissue

Parfüm, n. *[pahr-FEWM]* perfume

Park, m. *[pahrk]* park

Parken verboten *[PAHR-ken fehr-BOH-ten]* parking prohibited

parken *[PAHR-ken]* to park

Parkplatz, m. *[PAHRK-plahts]* parking lot

Parkscheibe, f. *[PAHRK-shye-beh]* parking disk

Parkuhr, f. *[PAHRK-oor]* parking meter

Party, f. *[PAHR-tee]* party (celebration)

261

Paß, m. *[pahs]* mountain pass

passen *[PAHS-sen]* to fit

Pelze, pl. *[PEHL-tseh]* furs

Pension, f. *[pehn-ZYOHN]* boardinghouse

perfekt *[pehr-FEHKT]* perfect

Periode, f. *[peh-ree-OH-deh]* period (menstrual)

Person, f. *[pehr-ZOHN]* person

persönlich *[pehr-ZU(R)N-likh]* personal

Petersilie, f. *[pay-te(r)-ZEEL-yeh]* parsley

Pfad, m. *[pfaat]* path

Pfannkuchen, m. *[PFAHN-koo-khen]* pancake

Pfarrer, m. *[PFAHR-e(r)]* minister (clergyman)

Pfeffer, m. *[PFEHF-fe(r)]* pepper

Pfeife, f. *[PFIFE-eh]* pipe

Pfeifentabak, m. *[PFIFE-en-tah-bahk]* pipe tobacco

Pferd, n. *[pfehrt]* horse

Pfirsich, m. *[PFIR-zikh]* peach

Pflaume, f. *[PFLOW-meh]* plum

Picknick, n. *[PIK-nik]* picnic

Pier, m. *[peer]* pier

Pille, f. *[PIL-eh]* pill

Pilot, m. *[pee-LOHT]* pilot

Pilz, m. *[pilts]* mushroom

Piste, f. *[PIS-teh]* runway (plane)

Plan, m. *[plaan]* map; plan

planen, *[PLAA-nen]* to plan

Planetarium, n. *[plah-neh-TAH-ree-oom]* planetarium

Plattenspieler, m. *[PLAHT-ten-shpee-le(r)]* record player

Platz, m. *[plahts]* place; seat; square (town)

Plombe, f. *[PLOM-beh]* filling (tooth)

plötzlich *[PLU(R)TS-likh]* suddenly

Polen, n. *[POH-len]* Poland

polieren *[po-LEE-ren]* to shine (shoes); to polish

Polizei, f. *[po-lee-TSYE]* police

Polizeiwache, f. *[po-lee-TSYE-vahkh-eh]* police station

Polizist, m. *[po-lee-TSIST]* policeman

Portier, m. *[por-TYAY]* doorman

Portion, f. *[por-TSYOHN]* portion

Porto, n. *[POR-toh]* postage

Post, f. *[post]* mail

Postamt, n. *[POST-ahmt]* post office

Postanweisung, f. *[POST-ahn-vye-zung]* money order

Postfach, n. *[POST-fahkh]* post office box

Postkarte, f. *[POST-kahr-teh]* postcard

postlagernd *[POST-laa-gehrnt]* general delivery

Postleitzahl, f. *[POST-lite-tsaal]* zip code

praktisch *[PRAHK-tish]* practical

Preis, m. *[price]* price

Preiselbeere, f. *[PRICE-ehl-bay-reh]* cranberry

Preisskala, f. *[PRICE-skah-lah]* price range

preiswert *[PRICE-vehrt]* inexpensive

Presse, f. *[PREHS-seh]* press (media)

Priester, m. *[PREES-te(r)]* priest

privat *[pri-VAAT]* private

Privatunterricht, m. *[pri-VAAT-un-teh-rikht]* private lessons

probieren *[pro-BEER-en]* to try

Programm, n. *[proh-GRAAM]* program

provisorisch *[pro-vee-ZOH-rish]* temporary

Puder, m. *[POO-de(r)]* powder

Pullover, m. *[pul-LOH-ve(r)]* sweater

Pulver, n. *[PUL-ve(r)]* powder

Pumpe, f. *[PUM-peh]* pump

pünktlich *[PEWNK-likh]* on time

Puppe, f. *[PUP-peh]* doll

putzen *[PUT-sen]* to shine

Pyjama, m. *[pi-JAA-maa]* pajamas

Q

Quadrat, n. *[kvah-DRAHT]* square (geometric)

Qualität, f. *[kvah-li-TAYT]* quality

Quelle, f. *[KVEHL-leh]* spring (of water)

Quetschung, f. *[KVEHT-khung]* bruise

Quiche, f. *[keesh]* quiche

Quittung, f. *[KVIT-tung]* receipt

R

R-Gespräch, n. *[EHR-geh-shpraykh]* collect call

Rabatt, m. *[raa-BAHT]* discount

Rabbiner, m. *[rah-BEE-ne(r)]* rabbi

Rad, n. *[raat]* wheel

Radfahren, n. *[RAAT-faa-ren]* cycling

Radiergummi, m. *[rah-DEER-goom-mee]* rubber eraser

Radieschen, n. *[raa-DEES-khen]* radish

Radio, n. *[RAA-dee-oh]* radio

Rahmen, m. *[RAA-men]* frame

Rasen, m. *[RAA-zen]* lawn

Rasierapparat, m. *[rah-ZEER-ah-pah-raat]* shaver

Rasiercreme, f. *[rah-ZEER-kraym]* shaving cream

rasieren *[rah-ZEE-ren]* to shave

Rasierklinge, f. *[rah-ZEER-kling-eh]* razor blade

Rasierwasser, n. *[rah-ZEER-vahs-se(r)]* after-shave lotion

Rathaus, n. *[RAAT-hows]* city hall; town hall

Raub, m. *[rowp]* robbery

rauchen *[ROWKH-en]* to smoke

Raucherabteil *[ROWKH-e(r)-ahp-tile]* smoking section

Rechnung, f. *[REHKH-nung]* bill (restaurant); check

Recht haben *[rehkht HAA-ben]* to be right

rechts *[rehkhts]* right (direction)

Rechtsanwalt, m. *[REHKHTS-ahn-vahlt]* attorney; lawyer

263

rechtshändig *[REHKHTS-hehn-dikh]* right-handed

reden *[RAY-den]* to talk

Reformhaus, n. *[reh-FORM-hows]* health food store

Regal, n. *[ray-GAAL]* shelf

Regel, f. *[RAY-gel]* rule

regelmäßig *[RAY-gel-mays-ikh]* regular

Regen, m. *[RAY-gen]* rain

Regenmantel, m. *[RAY-gen-mahn-tel]* raincoat

Regenschirm, m. *[RAY-gen-shirm]* umbrella

reich *[ryekh]* rich

Reifen, m. *[RYE-fen]* tire (car)

Reifenpanne, f. *[RYE-fen-pahn-neh]* flat tire; puncture

Reihe, f. *[RYE-eh]* row (theater)

reinigen *[RYE-ni-gen]* to clean

Reinigung, f. *[RYE-ni-gung]* dry cleaner's

Reis, m. *[rice]* rice

Reise, f. *[RYE-zeh]* trip

Reisebüro, n. *[RYE-zeh-bew-roh]* travel agency

Reiseführer, m. *[RYE-zeh-few-re(r)]* guidebook

Reisekrankheit, f. *[RYE-zeh-krahnk-hite]* motion sickness

reisen *[RYE-zen]* to travel

(Reise-)Paß, m. *[{RYE-zeh-}pahs]* passport

Reisescheck, m. *[RYE-zeh-shehk]* traveler's check

reißen *[RICE-sen]* to tear

Reißverschluß, m. *[RICE-fehr-shlus]* zipper

reiten *[RYE-ten]* to ride (a horse)

Reklamation, f. *[reh-klah-mah-TSIOHN]* complaint

Religion, f. *[ray-li-GYOHN]* religion

Rennbahn, f. *[REHN-baan]* race track

Reparatur, f. *[reh-pah-rah-TOOR]* repair

reparieren, *[reh-pah-REE-ren]* to fix; to repair

reservieren lassen *[reh-zehr-VEER-en LAHS-sen]* to book; to reserve

Reservierung, f. *[reh-zehr-VEE-rung]* reservation

Restaurant, n. *[rehs-to-RAHNT]* restaurant

retten *[REHT-ten]* to save (person)

Rettungsschwimmer, m. *[REH-tungs-shvim-me(r)]* lifeguard

Rezept, n. *[reh-TZEHPT]* prescription

richtig *[RIKH-tikh]* right (correct)

Richtung, f. *[RIKH-tung]* direction

Riemen, m. *[REE-men]* strap

Rindfleisch, n. *[RINT-flyshe]* beef

Ring, m. *[ring]* ring

Rippe, f. *[RIP-peh]* rib

Risiko, n. *[REE-zee-koh]* risk

Rock, m. *[rok]* skirt

Roggenbrot, n. *[ROG-gen-broht]* rye bread

roh *[roh]* raw

Rolle, f. *[ROL-leh]* roll (stage)

rollen *[ROL-len]* to roll

Rolltreppe, f. *[ROL-trehp-peh]* escalator

Roman, m. *[roh-MAAN]* novel

Röntgenaufname, f. *[RU(R)NT-gen-owf-naa-meh]* X ray

rosa *[ROH-zah]* pink

Rose, f. *[ROH-zeh]* rose

Rosé, m. *[roh-ZAY]* rosé wine

Rosinen, pl. *[roh-ZEE-nen]* raisins

rot *[roht]* red

Rouge, n. *[roozh]* rouge

Rücken, m. *[REWK-en]* back (body part)

Rückenschmerzen, pl. *[REWK-en-shmehr-tsen]* backache

Rückerstattung, f. *[REWK-ehr-shtah-tung]* refund

Rückfahrkarte, f. *[REWK-faar-kahr-teh]* round-trip ticket

Ruderboot, n. *[ROO-de(r)-boht]* rowboat

Ruhe, f. *[ROO-eh]* rest

Ruhestand, m. *[ROO-eh-shtahnt]* retirement

ruhig *[ROO-ikh]* calm; quiet

Rühreier, pl. *[REW-eye-e(r)]* scrambled eggs

Ruinen, pl. *[roo-EE-nen]* ruins

rund *[runt]* round

Rundfahrt, f. *[RUNT-faart]* (bus) tour

rutschig *[RUT-shikh]* slippery

S

Sache, f. *[ZAHKH-eh]* thing

Sackgasse, f. *[ZAHK-gaas-seh]* dead end

Saft, m. *[zahft]* juice

sagen *[ZAA-gen]* to say

Sahne, f. *[ZAA-neh]* cream

Salat, m. *[zah-LAAT]* salad

Salz, n. *[zahlts]* salt

salzig *[ZAHL-tsikh]* salty

sammeln *[ZAHM-eln]* to collect

Samstag, m. *[ZAHMS-taak]* Saturday

Samt, m. *[zahmt]* velvet

Sand, m. *[zahnt]* sand

Sandwich, n. *[SAHNT-vitch]* sandwich

Satz, m. *[zahts]* sentence (grammar)

sauber *[ZOW-be(r)]* clean

sauer *[ZOW-e(r)]* sour

Säuglingsnahrung, f. *[SOYK-lings-naa-rung]* baby food

Säure, f. *[ZOY-reh]* acid

Schachtel, f. *[SHAHKH-tel]* box

schade! *[SHAA-deh]* too bad!

wie Schade! *[vee SHAA-deh]* what a pity!

schädlich *[SHAYT-likh]* harmful

Schaf, n. *[shahf]* sheep

Schal, m. *[shahl]* scarf

Schale, f. *[SHAH-leh]* shell

Schallplatte, f. *[SHAHL-plaht-teh]* record (disc)

Schalter, m. *[SHAHL-te(r)]* switch

Schatten, m. *[SHAHT-ten]* shade, shadow

Schatz, m. *[shahts]* treasure

schätzen *[SHEHTS-en]* to estimate

Schaufenster, n. *[SHOW-fehn-ste(r)]* show window

Schaumwein, m. *[SHOWM-vine]* sparkling wine

Scheck, m. *[shehk]* check

Scheckbuch, n. *[SHEHK-bookh]* check book

Scheibe, f. *[SHYE-beh]* slice

Schein, m. *[shine]* banknote

scheinen *[SHINE-en]* to seem

Scheinwerfer, m. *[SHINE-vehr-fe(r)]* headlight

Schenkel, m. *[SHEHN-kel]* thigh

Schere, f. *[SHAY-reh]* scissors

scheußlich *[SHOYS-likh]* awful

schicken *[SHIK-en]* to send

schieben *[SHEE-ben]* to push (a car)

Schiff, n. *[shif]* ship

Schild, n. *[shilt]* sign

Schinken, m. *[SHIN-ken]* ham

schlafen *[SHLAH-fen]* to sleep

Schlafsack, m. *[SHLAHF-zahk]* sleeping bag

Schlafwagen, m. *[SHLAHF-vaa-gen]* sleeping car

Schlafzimmer, n. *[SHLAHF-tsim-me(r)]* bedroom

schlagen *[SHLAA-gen]* to hit

Schlange, f. *[SHLAHNG-eh]* line (of people); snake

Schlange stehen *[SHLAHNG-eh shtay-en]* to stand in line

schlecht *[shlehkht]* bad

schlechter *[SHLEHKH-te(r)]* worse

schließen *[SHLEES-sen]* to close; to shut

Schließfach, n. *[SHLEES-fahkh]* baggage locker

Schloß, n. *[shlos]* castle; palace

schlucken *[SHLUK-en]* swallow

Schlüpfer, m. *[SHLEWP-fer]* panties

Schlüssel, m. *[SHLEWS-sel]* key

schmackhaft *[SHMAHK-hahft]* tasty

schmecken *[SHMEHK-en]* to taste

Schmerz, m. *[shmehrts]* ache; pain

schmerzen *[SHMEHR-tsen]* to hurt

Schmuck, m. *[shmuk]* jewelry

schmutzig *[SHMUT-tsikh]* dirty

Schnalle, f. *[SHNAHL-leh]* buckle

Schnecke, f. *[SHNEH-keh]* snail

Schnee, m. *[shnay]* snow

schneiden *[SHNYE-den]* to cut

Schneider, m. *[SHNYE-de(r)]* tailor

schneien *[SHNYE-en]* to snow

schnell *[shnehl]* fast; quick(ly)

Schnellimbiss, m. *[SHNEHL-im-bis]* snack bar

Schnellzug, m. *[SHNEHL-tsook]* express train

Schnittwunde, f. *[SHNIT-vun-deh]* cut (wound)

Schnur, f. *[shnoor]* string

Schnurrbart, m. *[SHNOOR-bahrt]* mustache

Schnürsenkel, pl. *[SHNEWR-zehn-kel]* shoelaces

Schokolade, f. *[sho-ko-LAA-deh]* chocolate

schon *[shon]* already

schön *[shu(r)n]* attractive; beautiful

Schönheitssalon, m. *[SHU(R)N-hite-zah-lohng]* beauty salon

Schrank, m. *[shrahnk]* closet

Schraubenzieher, m. *[SHROW-ben-tsee-e(r)]* screwdriver

schrecklich *[SHREHK-likh]* awful

schreiben *[SHRYE-ben]* to write

Schreibmaschine, f. *[SHRIPE-mah-shee-neh]* typewriter

Schreibtisch, m. *[SHRIPE-tish]* desk

Schreibwaren, pl. *[SHRIPE-vaa-ren]* stationery

Schriftsteller, m. *[SHRIFT-shtehl-le(r)]* writer

Schublade, f. *[SHOOP-laa-deh]* drawer

Schuh, m. *[shoo]* shoe

Schuld, f. *[shoolt]* debt

schulden *[SHOOL-den]* to owe

Schule, f. *[SHOO-leh]* school

Schulter, f. *[SHOOL-te(r)]* shoulder

schwach *[shvahkh]* weak

Schwager, m. *[SHVAA-ge(r)]* brother-in-law

Schwägerin, f. *[SHVAY-geh-rin]* sister-in-law

Schwamm, m. *[shvahm]* sponge

schwanger *[SHVAHNG-e(r)]* pregnant

schwarz *[shvahrts]* black

Schwein, n. *[shvine]* pig

Schweinefleisch, n. *[SHVINE-eh-flyshe]* pork

Schweiz, f. *[dee shvites]* Switzerland

schweizerisch *[SHVYE-tseh-rish]* Swiss

schwer *[shvehr]* difficult; hard (difficult); heavy

Schwester, f. *[SHVEHS-te(r)]* sister

Schwiegermutter, f. *[SHVEE-ge(r)-MUT-te(r)]* mother-in-law

Schwiegervater, m. *[SHVEE-ge(r)-faa-te(r)]* father-in-law

Schwierigkeit, f. *[SHVEE-rikh-kite]* difficulty

Schwimmbad, n. *[SHVIM-baat]* swimming pool

schwimmen *[SHVIM-men]* to swim

schwindlig *[SHVINT-likh]* dizzy

sechs *[zehks]* six

sechzehn *[ZEHKH-tsayn]* sixteen

sechzig *[ZEHKH-tsikh]* sixty

See, m. *[zay]* lake

seekrank *[ZAY-krahnk]* seasick

sehen *[ZAY-en]* to see

Sehenswürdigkeit, f. *[ZAY-ens-vewr-dikh-kite]* attraction (sightseeing)

sehr *[zehr]* very

Seide, f. *[ZYE-deh]* silk

Seife, f. *[ZYE-feh]* soap

Seil, n. *[zile]* rope

sein *[zine]* to be

seit *[zite]* since

Seite, f. *[ZITE-eh]* side; page

Sekretär(in), m., f. *[zeh-kreh-TAYR {-in}]* secretary

Sekunde, f. *[zeh-KOON-deh]* second (time)

selbe *[ZEHL-beh]* same

selbst *[zehlpst]* even; myself

Sellerie, m. *[ZEHL-eh-ree]* celery

selten *[ZEHL-ten]* rare

seltsam *[ZEHLT-zahm]* strange

senden *[ZEHN-den]* to send

Senf, m. *[zehnf]* mustard

Seniorenpaß, m. *[zehn-YOR-en-pahs]* senior citizen's pass

senkrecht *[ZEHNK-rehkht]* vertical

September, m. *[zehp-TEHM-be(r)]* September

servieren *[zehr-VEE-ren]* to serve

Serviette, f. *[sehr-VYEHT-teh]* napkin

Sessel, m. *[ZEHS-sel]* armchair

sich setzen *[zikh ZEHT-sen]* to sit down

Shampoo, n. *[shahm-POO]* shampoo

sicher *[ZIKH-e(r)]* certain; certainly; safe; sure

Sicherheitsnadel, f. *[ZIKH-e(r)-hites-naa-del]* safety pin

Sicherheitsgurt, m. *[ZIKH-e(r)-hites-gurt]* seatbelt

Sie *[zee]* you

sie *[zee]* she; they

sieben *[ZEE-ben]* seven

siebte *[ZEEP-teh]* seventh

siebzehn *[ZEEP-tsayn]* seventeen

siebzig *[ZEEP-tsikh]* seventy

Silber, n. *[ZIL-be(r)]* silver

singen *[ZING-en]* to sing

Sirup, m. *[ZEE-rup]* syrup (cough)

Ski, m. *[shee]* ski

Skiausrüstung, f. *[SHEE-ows-rews-tung]* ski equipment

skifahren *[SHEE-faa-ren]* skiing

Skilift, m. *[SHEE-lift]* ski lift

Skulptur, f. *[skulp-TOOR]* sculpture

Smoking, m. *[SMOH-king]* tuxedo

Socken, pl. *[ZOK-en]* socks

Sofa, n. *[ZOH-fah]* sofa

sofort *[zoh-FORT]* at once; immediately

Sohle, f. *[ZOH-leh]* sole (shoe)

Sohn, m. *[zohn]* son

Sommer, m. *[ZOM-me(r)]* summer

Sonderangebot, n. *[ZON-de(r)-ahn-geh-boht]* bargain

Sonnabend, m. *[ZON-aa-behnt]* Saturday

Sonne, f. *[ZON-neh]* sun

Sonnenbrille, f. *[ZON-nen-bril-leh]* sunglasses

Sonnenöl, n. *[ZON-nen-u(r)l]* suntan lotion

sonnig *[ZON-ikh]* sunny

Sonntag, m. *[ZON-taak]* Sunday

sonst *[zonst]* otherwise

Sorge, f. *[ZOR-geh]* worry

sorgfältig *[ZORK-fehl-tikh]* careful

Sorte, f. *[ZOR-teh]* type (sort)

Soße, f. *[ZOH-zeh]* sauce

sparen *[SHPAA-ren]* to save (money)

Spargel, m. *[SHPAHR-gel]* asparagus

Spaβ haben *[shpahs HAA-ben]* to have fun

spät *[shpayt]* late

Spaziergang, m. *[shpah-TSEER-gahng]* walk

Speck, m. *[shpehk]* bacon

Speisekarte, f. *[SHPYE-zeh-kahr-teh]* menu

Speisesaal, m. *[SHPYE-zeh-zaal]* dining room

Speisewagen, m. *[SHPYE-zeh-vaa-gen]* dining car

Spesen, pl. *[SHPAY-zen]* expenses

Spezialität, f. *[shpeh-tsee-ah-lee-TAYT]* specialty

Spiegel, m. *[SHPEE-gel]* mirror

Spiel, n. *[shpeel]* game

spielen *[SHPEE-len]* to gamble; to play

Spielkarten, pl. *[SHPEEL-kahr-ten]* playing cards

Spielplatz, m. *[SHPEEL-plahts]* playground

Spielwarenladen, m. *[SHPEEL-vaa-ren-laa-den]* toy shop

Spielzeug, n. *[SHPEEL-tsoyk]* toy

Spinat, m. *[shpi-NAAT]* spinach

Spitze, f. *[SHPIT-seh]* lace; top

Sprache, f. *[SHPRAHKH-eh]* language

sprechen *[SHPREHKH-en]* to speak

Spritze, f. *[SHPRIT-seh]* injection

spülen *[SHPEW-len]* to rinse

Staat, m. *[shtaat]* state

Staatsangehörigkeit, f. *[SHTAATS-ahn-geh-hu(r)-rikh-kite]* nationality

Stadion, n. *[SHTAA-dyohn]* stadium

Stadt, f. *[shtaht]* city; town

Stahl, m. *[shtahl]* steel

stark *[shtahrk]* strong

Stärke, f. *[SHTEHR-keh]* starch (laundry)

statt *[shtaht]* instead of

Statue, f. *[SHTAH-too-eh]* statue

Stau, m. *[shtow]* traffic jam

Staub, m. *[shtowp]* dust

Steak, n. *[shtayk]* steak

Steckdose, f. *[SHTEHK-doh-zeh]* electrical outlet

Stecknadel, f. *[SHTEHK-naa-del]* pin

stehen *[SHTAY-en]* to stand

stehenbleiben *[SHTAY-en-blye-ben]* to stop

stehlen *[SHTEH-len]* to steal

steigen *[SHTYE-gen]* climb

Stein, m. *[shtine]* stone

Stelle, f. *[SHTEHL-leh]* job (employment); site

stellen *[SHTEHL-len]* to place; to put

Stern, m. *[shtehrn]* star

steuerfrei *[SHTOY-e(r)-frye]* tax-free

Stewardeβ, f. *[SHTOO-ahr-dehs]* stewardess

Stiefel, pl. *[SHTEE-fel]* boots

Stil, m. *[shteel]* style (fashion)

Stimme, f. *[SHTIM-meh]* voice

Stirn, f. *[shtirn]* forehead

269

Stock, m. *[shtok]* floor; stick (pole)

Stoff, m. *[shtof]* cloth; material

stören *[SHTU(R)-en]* to disturb

stoβen *[SHTOHS-en]* to bump

Stoβstange, f. *[SHTOHS-shtahng-eh]* bumper (car)

Stoβzeit, f. *[SHTOHS-tsite]* rush hour

Strand, m. *[shtrahnt]* beach

Straβe, f. *[SHTRAHS-seh]* street

Straβenbahn, f. *[SHTRAHS-sen-baan]* streetcar

Straβenkarte, f. *[SHTRAHS-sen-kahr-teh]* road map

Streichholz, n. *[SHTRYEKH-hohlts]* match

Streifen, m. *[SHTRIFE-en]* stripe

Stroh, n. *[shtroh]* straw

Stromspannung, f. *[SHTROHM-shpahn-nung]* voltage

Strumpf, m. *[shtrumpf]* stocking

Strumpfhose, f. *[SHTRUMPF-hoh-zeh]* panty hose; tights

Stück, n. *[shtewk]* piece; play (stage)

Student, m. *[shtoo-DEHNT]* student

studieren *[shtoo-DEE-ren]* to study

Stuhl, m. *[shtool]* chair

Stunde, f. *[SHTUN-deh]* hour

Sturm, m. *[shtoorm]* storm

suchen *[ZOO-khen]* to look for

Süden, m. *[ZEW-den]* south

Summe, f. *[ZOOM-meh]* sum

Supermarkt, m. *[ZOO-pe(r)-mahrkt]* supermarket

Suppe, f. *[ZOOP-peh]* soup

süβ *[zews]* sweet

Symptom, n. *[zewmp-TOHM]* symptom

Synagoge, f. *[zew-nah-GOH-geh]* synagogue

System, n. *[zews-TAYM]* system

T

Tabak, m. *[TAH-bahk]* tobacco

Tabakladen, m. *[tah-BAHK-laa-den]* tobacco shop

Tag, m. *[taak]* day

Tageszeitung, f. *[TAA-gehs-tsite-ung]* daily newspaper

täglich *[TAYG-likh]* daily

Tal, n. *[taal]* valley

Tankstelle, f. *[TAHNK-shteh-leh]* gas station

Tante, f. *[TAHN-teh]* aunt

Tanz, m. *[tahnts]* dance

tanzen *[TAHN-tsen]* to dance

Tarif, m. *[tah-REEF]* rate

Tasche, f. *[TAHSH-eh]* bag; pocket

Taschenlampe, f. *[TAHSH-en-lahm-peh]* flashlight

Taschenmesser, n. *[TAHSH-en-mehs-se(r)]* penknife

Taschentuch, n. *[TAHSH-en-took]* handkerchief

Tasse, f. *[TAHS-seh]* cup

taub *[towp]* deaf

Taube, f. *[TOW-beh]* pigeon

tausend *[TOW-zehnt]* thousand

Taxi, n. *[TAHK-see]* cab; taxi
Tee, m. *[toy]* tea
Teelöffel, m. *[TAY-lu(r)-fel]* teaspoon
Teich, m. *[tyekh]* pond
Teigwaren, pl. *[TIKE-vaa-ren]* pasta
Teil, m. *[tile]* part
teilen *[TILE-en]* to share
Telefon, n. *[tay-lay-FON]* telephone
Telefonbuch, n. *[tay-lay-FON-bookh]* telephone directory
Telefonzelle, f. *[tay-lay-FON-tsehl-leh]* telephone booth
Telegramm, n. *[tay-lay-GRAAM]* cable; telegram
Telex schicken *[TAY-lehks SHIK-en]* to telex
Teller, m. *[TEHL-le(r)]* plate
Tempel, m. *[TEHM-pel]* temple
Teppich, m. *[TEHP-pikh]* carpet; rug
teuer *[TOY-e(r)]* expensive
Teufel, m. *[TOY-fel]* devil
Theater, n. *[tay-AA-te(r)]* theater
Thermometer, n. *[tehr-mo-MAY-te(r)]* thermometer
tief *[teef]* deep
Tier, n. *[teer]* animal
Tierarzt, m. *[TEER-ahrtst]* veterinarian
Tierpark, m. *[TEER-pahrk]* zoo
Tinte, f. *[TIN-teh]* ink
Tisch, m. *[tish]* table
Tischdecke, f. *[TISH-deh-keh]* tablecloth
Toast, m. *[tohst]* toast

Tochter, f. *[TOKH-te(r)]* daughter
Tod, m. *[toht]* death
Toilette, f. *[toy-LEHT-teh]* restroom; toilet
Toilettenpapier, n. *[toy-LEHT-ten-pah-peer]* toilet paper
Tollwut, f. *[TOL-voot]* rabies
Tomate, f. *[toh-MAH-teh]* tomato
Tonbandgerät, n. *[TOHN-bahnt-geh-rayt]* tape recorder
Torte, f. *[TOR-teh]* pie
tot *[toht]* dead
Tourismus, m. *[too-RIS-moos]* tourism
Tourist, m. *[too-RIST]* tourist
tragen *[TRAA-gen]* to carry; to wear
traurig *[TROW-rikh]* sad
treffen *[TREHF-fen]* to meet
trennen *[TREHN-nen]* to part (separate)
Treppe, f. *[TREHP-peh]* stairs
Treppenhaus, n. *[TREHP-pen-hows]* staircase
trinken *[TRIN-ken]* to drink
Trinkgeld, n. *[TRINK-gehlt]* tip
Trinkwasser, n. *[TRINK-vahs-se(r)]* drinking water
trocken *[TROK-en]* dry
Tropfen, pl. *[TROP-fen]* drops
trotz *[trots]* despite
Truthahn, m. *[TROOT-haan]* turkey
Tschechoslowakei, f. *[cheh-kho-slo-vah-KYE]* Czechoslovakia
Tube, f. *[TOO-beh]* tube
Tuch, n. *[tookh]* shawl

271

tun *[toon]* to do

Tür, f. *[tewr]* door

Turm, m. *[toorm]* tower

Tüte, f. *[TEW-teh]* bag

typisch *[TEW-pish]* typical

U

U-bahnstation, f. *[OO-baan-shtah-tsyohn]* subway station

Übelkeit, f. *[EW-bel-kite]* nausea

üben *[EW-ben]* to practice

über *[EW-be(r)]* across (movement); over (above); via

überall *[EW-be(r)-ahl]* everywhere

Überdosis, f. *[EW-be(r)-doh-zis]* overdose

übergeben *[ew-be(r)-GAY-ben]* to present

überholen *[EW-be(r)-hoh-len]* to pass (car)

überlaufen *[ew-be(r)-LOW-fen]* overrun

übermorgen *[EW-be(r)-mor-gen]* day after tomorrow

übernachten *[EW-be(r)-nahkh-ten]* to stay (lodge)

Übernachtung mit Frühstück *[ew-be(r)-NAHKH-tung mit FREW-shtewk]* bed and breakfast

überprüfen *[EW-be(r)-PREW-fen]* to check

überqueren *[ew-be(r)-KVAY-ren]* to cross

übersetzen *[ew-be(r)-ZEHT-sen]* to translate

Überstunden, pl. *[EW-be(r)-shtun-den]* overtime

überweisen *[ew-be(r)-VYE-zen]* to transfer

überzeugen *[ew-be(r)-TSOY-gen]* to persuade

Uhr, f. *[oor]* clock; watch

Uhrmacher, m. *[OOR-mahkh-e(r)]* watchmaker

um *[um]* around

umgekehrt *[OOM-geh-kehrt]* vice versa

Umleitung, f. *[OOM-lite-ung]* detour (traffic)

Umschlag, m. *[OOM-shlahk]* envelope

umsteigen *[OOM-shtye-gen]* to change (bus, train)

Umwelt, f. *[OOM-vehlt]* environment

umziehen *[OOM-tsee-en]* move (to change residence)

unbedingt *[UN-beh-dinkt]* absolutely

unbequem *[UN-beh-kvaym]* uncomfortable

und *[unt]* and

Unfall, m. *[UN-fahl]* accident

Ungarn, n. *[UN-gahrn]* Hungary

ungefähr *[UN-geh-fayr]* about; approximately

ungerade *[UN-geh-raa-deh]* odd (number)

unglücklich *[UN-glewk-likh]* unhappy

Universität, f. *[oo-nee-vehr-zi-TAYT]* university

unmöglich *[un-MU(R)-glikh]* impossible

Unordnung, f. *[UN-ort-nung]* mess

unten *[UN-ten]* below

unter *[UN-te(r)]* among; under

Untergeschoβ, n. *[UN-te(r)-geh-shos]* basement

Untergrundbahn, f. *[UN-te(r)-grunt-baan]* subway

unterhalten *[un-te(r)-HAHL-ten]* to amuse

Unterhemd, n. *[UN-te(r)-hehmt]* undershirt

Unterhose, f. *[UN-te(r)-hoh-zeh]* underpants

Unterkunft, f. *[UN-te(r)-kunft]* accommodation

Unterrock, m. *[UN-te(r)-rok]* slip

unterschreiben *[un-te(r)-SHRYE-ben]* to sign

Untertasse, f. *[UN-te(r)-tahs-seh]* saucer

Unterwäsche, f. *[UN-te(r)-veh-sheh]* underwear

unzufrieden *[UN-tsoo-free-den]* dissatisfied

Urlaub, m. *[OOR-lowp]* vacation

V

Vater, m. *[FAA-te(r)]* father

vegetarisch *[veh-geh-TAH-rish]* vegetarian

Ventilator, m. *[vehn-ti-LAA-tor]* fan

Verabredung, f. *[fehr-AHP-ray-dung]* appointment

Verantwortung, f. *[fehr-AHNT-vor-tung]* responsibility

Verband, m. *[fehr-BAHNT]* bandage

Verbandkasten, m. *[fehr-BAHNT-kahs-ten]* first aid kit

verbieten *[fehr-BEE-ten]* to prohibit

verboten *[fehr-BOH-ten]* forbidden

Verbrechen, n. *[fehr-BREHKH-en]* crime

verbringen *[fehr-BRIN-gen]* to spend (time)

verdienen *[fehr-DEE-nen]* to earn

Vereinigte Königreich, n. *[fehr-EYE-nikh-teh KU(R)-nikh-ryekh]* United Kingdom

Vereinigten Staaten (von Amerika), f. *[fehr-EYE-nikh-ten SHTAA-ten {fon ah-MEH-ri-kah}]* United States

Vergangenheit, f. *[fehr-GAHNG-en-hite]* past

Vergaser, m. *[fehr-GAA-ze(r)]* carburetor

vergessen *[fehr-GEHS-sen]* to forget

vergleichen *[vehr-GLYE-khen]* to compare

Vergnügen, n. *[fehrk-NEW-gen]* pleasure

vergnügen *[fehrk-NEW-gen]* to amuse

Vergröβerung, f. *[fehr-GRU(R)S-eh-rung]* enlargement

verhaften *[fehr-HAHF-ten]* to arrest

verheiratet *[fehr-HYE-raa-tet]* married

Verkauf, m. *[fehr-KOWF]* sale

verkaufen *[fehr-KOW-fen]* to sell

Verkäufer, m. *[fehr-KOY-fe(r)]* salesman

Verkäuferin, f. *[fehr-KOY-feh-rin]* saleswoman

Verkehr, m. *[fehr-KEHR]* traffic

verkehrt herum *[vehr-KEHRT hehr-ROOM]* upside down

verlangen *[fehr-LAHNG-en]* to demand; to require

verletzen *[fehr-LEHT-sen]* to injure

sich verletzen *[zikh fehr-LEHT-sen]* to hurt oneself

verlieren *[fehr-LEER-en]* to lose

verlobt *[fehr-LOHPT]* engaged (betrothed)

verloren *[fehr-LOR-en]* lost

Verlust, m. *[fehr-LOOST]* loss

vermeiden *[fehr-MYE-den]* to avoid

vermieten *[fehr-MEE-ten]* to rent

Vermittlung, f. *[fehr-MIT-lung]* operator (phone)

Vermögen, n. *[fehr-MU(R)-gen]* fortune

vernünftig *[fehr-NEWNF-tikh]* reasonable

verrückt *[fehr-REWKT]* crazy

Versammlung, f. *[fehr-ZAHM-lung]* meeting

versäumen *[fehr-ZOY-men]* to miss

verschieden *[fehr-SHEE-den]* different

verschiffen *[fehr-SHIF-fen]* to ship

Verschluß, m. *[fehr-SHLUS]* shutter (camera)

verschwunden *[fehr-SHVUN-den]* to be missing

Versicherung, f. *[fehr-ZIKH-eh-rung]* insurance

Verspätung, f. *[fehr-SHPAY-tung]* delay

versprechen *[fehr-SHPREH-khen]* to promise

verstauchen *[fehr-SHTOW-khen]* to sprain

verstehen *[fehr-SHTAY-en]* to understand

versuchen *[fehr-ZOO-khen]* to try

vertraut sein mit *[fehr-TROWT zine mit]* to be familiar with

vertreten *[fehr-TRAY-ten]* to represent

Verwandte, m., f. *[fehr-VAHN-teh]* relative

Verwendung, f. *[fehr-VEHN-dung]* use (purpose)

verwirrt *[fehr-VIRT]* confused

Verzeihung, f. *[fehr-TSYE-ung]* pardon

verzollen *[fehr-TSOL-len]* to declare (custom)

Vetter, m. *[FEHT-te(r)]* cousin

viel *[feel]* much

viele *[FEE-leh]* many

vielleicht *[fee-LYEKHT]* maybe; perhaps

vier *[feer]* four

vierte (-r, -s) *[FEER-teh {-te(r), -tehs]* fourth

Viertel, n. *[FEER-tel]* quarter

vierzehn *[FEER-tsayn]* fourteen

vierzig *[FEER-tsikh]* forty

violett *[vee-oh-LEHT]* purple

Visum, n. *[VEE-zoom]* visa

Vogel, m. *[FOH-gel]* bird

Volksmusik, f. *[FOLKS-moo-zeek]* folk music

voll *[fol]* full

volltanken *[FOL-tahn-ken]* to fill up

von *[fon]* by; from; of

vor *[for]* ago; before

vorbereiten *[FOR-beh-rite-en]* to prepare

vorbestellt *[FOR-beh-shtehlt]* reserved

Vorfahrt gewähren *[FOR-faart geh-VAY-ren]* to yield (traffic)

vorgestern *[FOR-gehs-tern]* day before yesterday

Vorhang, m. *[FOR-hahng]* curtain

vormittags *[FOR-mit-tahks]* A.M.

vorne *[FOR-neh]* front

Vorort, m. *[FOR-ort]* suburb

Vorsicht, f. *[FOR-zikht]* caution

Vorsicht! *[FOR-zikht]* careful!

Vorspeise, f. *[FOR-shpye-zeh]* appetizer

vorstellen *[FOR-shtehl-len]* to introduce

Vorstellung, f. *[for-SHTEHL-lung]* performance

Vorwahlnummer, f. *[FOR-vaal-num-me(r)]* area code

vorwärts *[FOR-vehrts]* forward

vorziehen *[FOR-tsee-en]* to prefer

W

Wagen, m. *[VAA-gen]* car

Wagenheber, m. *[VAA-gen-hay-be(r)]* jack (car)

Wahl, f. *[vaal]* choice

wählen *[VAY-len]* to dial

wahr *[vaar]* true

während *[VAY-rehnt]* during

Währung, f. *[VAY-rung]* currency

Wald, m. *[vahlt]* forest

Wand, f. *[vahnt]* wall (interior)

Wanderung, f. *[VAHN-deh-rung]* hike

Wange, f. *[VAHN-geh]* cheek

wann *[vahn]* when

warm *[vahrm]* warm

warten *[VAAR-ten]* to wait

Wartesaal, m. *[VAAR-teh-zaal]* waiting room

warum *[vah-ROOM]* why

was *[vahs]* what

Waschbecken, n. *[VAHSH-beh-ken]* sink; washbasin

waschen *[VAHSH-en]* to wash

Wäscherei, f. *[veh-sheh-RYE]* laundry

Waschsalon, m. *[VAHSCH-zaa-long]* laundromat

Wasser, n. *[VAHS-se(r)]* water

fließendes Wasser, n. *[FLEES-en-dehs VAHS-se(r)]* running water

wasserdicht *[VAHS-se(r)-dikht]* waterproof

Wasserfall, m. *[VAHS-se(r)-fahl]* waterfall

Wasserhahn, m. *[VAHS-se(r)-haan]* faucet; tap

Watte, f. *[VAHT-teh]* cotton wool

Wechselkurs, m. *[VEHK-sel-koors]* exchange rate

wechseln *[VEHK-seln]* to change; to exchange

275

Wechselstube, f. *[VEHK-sehl-shtoo-beh]* currency exchange office

wecken *[VEHK-en]* to wake

Wecker, m. *[VEH-ke(r)]* alarm clock

Weg, m. *[vehk]* way

weg *[vehk]* away

weggehen *[VEHK-gay-en]* to go away

weh tun *[vay toon]* to hurt

weich *[vyekh]* soft

Weihnachten, pl. *[VYE-nahkh-ten]* Christmas

weil *[vile]* because

Wein, m. *[vine]* wine

Weinberg, m. *[VINE-behrk]* vineyard

weinen *[VINE-en]* to cry

Weinkarte, f. *[VINE-kahr-teh]* wine list

Weinladen, m. *[VINE-laa-den]* wine shop

Weintraube, f. *[VINE-trow-beh]* grape

weiβ *[vice]* white

weit *[vite]* far; wide

welche (-r, -s) *[VEHL-kheh, {-khe(r), -khehs]* which

Welle, f. *[VEHL-leh]* wave

Welt, f. *[vehlt]* world

wenige *[VEH-ni-geh]* few

weniger *[VAY-neh-ge(r)]* less

wenigstens *[VAY-nikh-stens]* at least

wenn *[vehn]* if; when

wer *[vehr]* who

Werbung, f. *[VEHR-bung]* advertising

Werkzeug, n. *[VEHRK-tsoyk]* tool

Wert, m. *[vehrt]* value

wertlos *[VEHRT-lohs]* worthless

wertvoll *[VEHRT-fol]* valuable

West(en), m. *[VEHST {-en}]* west

Weste, f. *[VEHS-teh]* vest

wetten *[VEHT-ten]* to bet

Wetter, n. *[VEH-te(r)]* weather

Wetterbericht, m. *[VEHT-te(r)-beh-rikht]* weather forecast

wichtig *[VIKH-tikh]* important

wie *[vee]* as; how; like (as)

wieder *[VEE-de(r)]* again

wiederholen *[vee-de(r)-HOH-len]* to repeat

auf Wiedersehen *[owf VEE-de(r)-zay-en]* good-bye

wiegen *[VEE-gen]* to weigh

Wien, n. *[veen]* Vienna

wieviel *[VEE-feel]* how much

wild *[vilt]* wild

Wildleder, n. *[VILT-lay-de(r)]* suede

Wind, m. *[vint]* wind

Windel, f. *[VIN-del]* diaper

Windschutzscheibe, f. *[WINT-shuts-shye-beh]* windshield

Winter, m. *[VIN-te(r)]* winter

wir *[veer]* we

wirklich *[VIRK-likh]* really

wissen *[VIS-sen]* to know

Witwe, f. *[VIT-veh]* widow

Witwer, m. *[VIT-ve(r)]* widower

Witz, m. *[vits]* joke

wo *[voh]* where

Woche, f. *[VOKH-eh]* week

Wochenende, n. *[VOKH-en-ehn-deh]* weekend

wohl *[vohl]* well

Wohnung, f. *[VOH-nung]* apartment

Wohnwagen, m. *[VOHN-vaa-gen]* trailer

Wohnzimmer, n. *[VOHN-tsim-me(r)]* living room

Wolke, f. *[VOL-keh]* cloud

Wolle, f. *[VOL-leh]* wool

wollen *[VOL-len]* to want

Wort, n. *[vort]* word

Wörterbuch, n. *[VU(R)-te(r)-bookh]* dictionary

Wunde, f. *[VUN-deh]* wound

wunderbar *[VUN-de(r)-baar]* wonderful

Wunsch, m. *[voonsh]* desire; wish

wünschen *[VEWN-shen]* to wish

würde *[VU(R)-deh]* would

Wurst, f. *[voorst]* sausage

Würze, pl. *[VEWR-tseh]* seasoning

Wurzel, f. *[VUR-tsel]* root

wütend *[VEW-tehnt]* angry

Z

zäh *[tsay]* tough

zählen *[TSAY-len]* to count

Zahn, m. *[tsaan]* tooth

Zahnarzt, m. *[TSAAN-ahrtst]* dentist

Zahnbürste, f. *[TSAAN-bewr-steh]* toothbrush

Zahnpasta, f. *[TSAAN-pahs-tah]* toothpaste

Zahnschmerzen, pl. *[TSAAN-shmehrt-sen]* toothache

Zange, f. *[TSAHNG-eh]* pliers

Zäpfchen, n. *[TSEHPF-khen]* suppository

zart *[tsahrt]* tender

Zebrastreifen, m. *[TSAY-brah-shtrife-en]* crosswalk

Zehe, f. *[TSEH-eh]* toe

zehn *[tsayn]* ten

zehnte *[TSAYN-teh]* tenth

Zeichenpapier, n. *[TSYE-khen-pah-peer]* drawing paper

zeigen *[TSYE-gen]* to show

Zeit, f. *[tsite]* time

Zeitschrift, f. *[TSITE-shrift]* magazine

Zeitung, f. *[TSYE-tung]* newspaper

Zeitungsstand, m. *[TSYE-tungs-shtahnt]* newspaper stand

Zeitverschwendung, f. *[TSITE-vehr-shvehn-dung]* waste of time

Zelle, f. *[TSEHL-leh]* cell

Zelt, n. *[tsehlt]* tent

zelten *[TSEHL-ten]* to camp

Zentrum, n. *[TSEHN-trum]* center; downtown

zerbrechen *[tsehr-BREH-khen]* to break

Zeugnis, n. *[TSOYK-nis]* certificate

ziehen *[TSEE-en]* to pull

ziemlich *[TSEEM-likh]* quite; rather (quite)

Zigarette, f. *[tsi-gaa-REHT-teh]* cigarette

Zigarre, f. *[tsi-GAA-reh]* cigar

Zimmer, n. *[TSIM-me(r)]* room

Zimmerbedienung, f. *[TSIM-me(r)-beh-dee-nung]* room service

Zimmermädchen, n. *[TSIM-me(r)-mayt-khen]* maid

277

Zitrone, f. *[tsi-TROH-neh]* lemon

Zoll, m. *[tsol]* customs; duty (customs)

zollfrei *[TSOL-frye]* duty-free

Zoo, m. *[tsoh]* zoo

zu *[tsoo]* to

Zucker, m. *[TSUK-e(r)]* sugar

Zuckerkrankheit, f. *[TSUK-e(r)-krahnk-hite]* diabetes

Zug, m. *[tsook]* train

zuhören *[TSOO-hur-en]* to listen

Zukunft, f. *[TSOO-kunft]* future

Zündkerze, f. *[TSEWNT-kehr-tseh]* spark plug

Zündung, f. *[TSEWN-dung]* ignition

zunehmen *[TSOO-nay-men]* to gain weight

Zunge, f. *[TSUN-geh]* tongue

zurück *[tsoo-REWK]* back (direction)

zurück sein *[tsoo-REWK zine]* to be back; to get back

zurückgeben *[tsoo-REWK-gay-ben]* to return (something)

zurückkommen *[tsoo-REWK-kom-men]* to return (come back)

zusammen *[tsoo-ZAHM-men]* together

zusätzlich *[TSOO-zehts-likh]* extra

Zutritt, m. *[TSOO-trit]* admission

zwanzig *[TSVAHN-tsikh]* twenty

zwei *[tsvye]* two

zweimal *[TSVYE-maal]* twice

zweite *[TSVYE-teh]* second

Zwiebel, f. *[TSVEE-bel]* onion

zwischen *[TSVISH-en]* among; between

zwölf *[tsvu(r)lf]* twelve